The Life of
ALEKSANDR BLOK

———

VOLUME I
The Distant Thunder
1880–1908

The Life of
ALEKSANDR BLOK

VOLUME I

The Distant Thunder
1880–1908

AVRIL PYMAN

OXFORD   LONDON   NEW YORK
OXFORD UNIVERSITY PRESS
1979

Oxford University Press, Walton Street, Oxford OX2 6DP

OXFORD LONDON GLASGOW
NEW YORK TORONTO MELBOURNE WELLINGTON
IBADAN NAIROBI DAR ES SALAAM CAPE TOWN
KUALA LUMPUR SINGAPORE JAKARTA HONG KONG TOKYO
DELHI BOMBAY CALCUTTA MADRAS KARACHI

British Library Cataloguing in Publication Data
Pyman, Avril
  Aleksandr Blok.
  Vol. 1: The distant thunder, 1880–1908.
  1. Blok, Aleksandr Aleksandrovich – Biography
  2. Poets, Russian – 20th century – Biography
  891.7'1'3   PG3453.B6Z/   78-40201

ISBN 0–19–211714–9

Printed in Great Britain by
Butler and Tanner Ltd, Frome and London

For Kirill

CONTENTS

LIST OF ILLUSTRATIONS

Plates

Illustrations in the text

PREFACE

Since I began to study Russian and heard *The Twelve* read (in French and Russian) at an elementary language class at the École des Langues Orientales in Paris in 1948, Aleksandr Blok has been important to me. We live, as he so clearly saw, at a time when one age of the world, the one in whose cultural and spiritual traditions we have been raised, is dying, and another, unknown, challenging, and often frightening, is coming into being. This is the central theme of our time. But since the span of our lives is not commensurate with such great historical shifts we have perhaps a heightened craving for the homely, the intimate, the momentary; all that gives colour and fragrance to the life of the individual. We need also to feel that the slow flowing of history cannot altogether overwhelm us, in so far as we are partakers of eternal life. History and the unrepeatable, fragile truth of the individual are the stuff of Blok's mature poetry. In his youth he tried to write also about salvation and eternity, but this he found was not the sphere of poetry; Plato, whom he loved, needed no poets in his ideal Republic and Blok spoke always of the 'hell of art'. He limited himself deliberately to the purely human 'in the hope that people might glimpse, through what I write, something more'.

Research for this biography was begun in 1959 when, having obtained a Ph.D. from Cambridge University for a thesis on *The Origins of Russian Decadence 1890–1905 with Special Reference to the Works of D. S. Merezhkovsky*, I was granted a British Council Scholarship to work on Aleksandr Blok in Leningrad. On my return to England in 1961 I prepared the introduction, notes, and bibliographies for my edition of Blok's *Selected Poems* (Pergamon Press, 1972). In 1963 I returned to Russia to marry the artist Kirill Sokolov and lived in Moscow from 1963 to 1974. In the Soviet Union I earned my living by translating, from Russian into English, and edited two more books—on Evgeniy Shvarts and Mikhail Bulgakov—for Pergamon's Russian series. In 1973 Oxford University Press commissioned the present life of Blok, so that I resumed my research and brought it up to date before leaving Moscow in August 1974.

It has always been a *life* of Blok that I have wanted to write. My first book was prepared in haste, before I had time to digest the evidence, and its main purpose was to make available to other scholars the yield of my research in Leningrad and Moscow, where I was given most generous access to archive material and met many people who had known Blok. What I would have liked to do then, and have now at last attempted, was to introduce this great poet to a wider public which does not know Russian.

To do this through the poetry itself is probably impossible in English. Certainly it is beyond my powers. In this book I have used my own translations of the poems rather than selecting the best from the work of others, for the sake of unity and, in part, convenience. Blok was a poet of mood and music. He said himself that there is no content without form, and the forms he elected to use ranged from sophisticated free verse to the street ballad and the sentimental refrain. My versions follow as closely as I have found compatible with acceptable English the rhyme-scheme and rhythms of the original. They are intended as illustrations to the book and bear no more likeness to the living Russian originals than do the faded landscapes and stiff family photographs also reproduced here. They do, however, bear some likeness to the form as well as the content of the poems, and that is their primary purpose. On the whole it seems to me that line-by-line prose renderings are useful only in conjunction with the original text or, in certain cases, where the excellencies of a poem are visual or cerebral. More often than not, I have avoided quoting whole poems, particularly the greatest, best-known, and most frequently translated (there are already more than twelve English versions of *The Twelve*), and have relied on free description, or have used passages from Blok's prose which echo the themes of his poetry.

The interrelationship between Blok's life and his poetry was constant. At one stage he actually spoke of having made his life into art and, when he repented of this, having come to the conclusion that the artist should remain, in life, an ordinary man, it was largely because he felt nothing worthwhile could be written without continuous, 'not bookish' contact with life itself. 'It is my habit', he wrote once, 'to compare facts from all spheres of life that happen to be within my field of vision at any given moment, and I am quite certain that, taken all together, they constitute a single musical pressure-head' (III. 297).[a]

In this biography I touch on certain aspects of Blok's private life

---

[a] References here and in the text to Blok's own writings are to the eight-volume Collected Works, *Sobraniye Sochineniy* (Moscow–Leningrad, 1960–3) (referred to by volume and page number only) or to the volume of his notebooks, *Zapisnye Knizhki* (Moscow, 1965), published as a pendant to that edition (referred to as 'Z.K.', with the page number and usually the date of the entry quoted).

which, though fully illuminated in the still unpublished memoirs of his wife Lyubov' Dmitriyevna Blok,[b] have hitherto been hinted at rather than discussed, perhaps because it was considered the time was not yet ripe, perhaps because of a mistaken care for the poet's posthumous reputation. The compassionate frankness of Lyubov' Dmitriyevna's 'most unconventional words', as she herself called them, is a far better safeguard of her husband's memory than the hints and evasions which have given birth to a plethora of theories, according to which Blok suffered variously from homosexual tendencies, impotence, insatiable and cynical lust, or even an incestuous passion for his own mother.... Blok himself destroyed everything in his perfectly ordered archives with which he did not desire the rest of the world to be acquainted and there is no need to cover up for him because he paid the price, in pain of body and mind, of the life he himself so ruthlessly described in his poetry and in his diaries.

My story begins with Blok's home, Shakhmatovo, of which, when I visited it in the spring of 1974, nothing remained but a rutted cart track and the green silence of the surrounding woods and fields. This silence, it appears, will soon be broken. In the newspaper *Pravda* (2 March 1977) the Ministry of Culture of the USSR announced its intention of reconstructing the house and outbuildings on the original site as they were in the poet's time. I do not know whether Blok would have been honoured or distressed. Probably both.

A.P.

East Lilburn, Northumberland
15 December 1977

---

[b] It is to be hoped that these memoirs (which have already provided material for a stage play of questionable taste), together with the wonderfully intelligent letters to Blok which show his wife in an altogether more sympathetic light, will be published *in full* in a forthcoming number of the Moscow publication *Literaturnoye Nasledstvo*.

ACKNOWLEDGEMENTS

These are complicated by the fact that research for this biography was undertaken in two quite separate sessions. I have already thanked those who helped me at Cambridge and in my 1959–61 research in Leningrad and Moscow in the preface to *Aleksandr Blok: Selected Poems* (Pergamon Press, 1972), and all I would add here is that my gratitude grows rather than diminishes with the years. In youth, one takes things for granted. In retrospect, I am quite astonished at the generosity with which busy people gave of their time, tired people their help and enthusiasm. This biography, indeed, is scarcely my own at all, but—to quote a very different Russian poet, the late Aleksandr Tvardovsky—'An insignificant down-payment/On a great debt to others owed.'

For my further session of research in 1973–4 I am indebted to Nikolay Pavlovich Il'in, who, though suffering from an acute heart condition, allowed me to work for many hours amongst his unique collection, to copy documents, to order photocopies, to ask questions, and to find many of the answers in his own exhaustive and masterly bibliographical compilation of Blok's publications and the articles about his work which appeared in the periodical press during his lifetime. Astonishingly, this *magnum opus*, an invaluable work of reference, still awaits a publisher. N. P. Il'in introduced me to V. P. Enisherlov, who kindly allowed me to join an expedition he was conducting to Shakhmatovo. There Vladimir Petrovich, a nephew of 'Ferol' Kublitsky-Piottukh, Blok's first cousin who shared so much of his boyhood, was able to show me many places about the grounds where the poet, as he wrote to a friend at the age of twenty-one, could have walked 'at night and blindfold'.

I should also like to thank Oxford University Press, the Great Britain–USSR Association, and Mikhail Pavlovich Alekseyev of the Institute of Russian Literature (Pushkin House), Leningrad, for their combined and effective assistance in helping me to obtain official permission to bring out of the Soviet Union in 1974 all the manuscript notes for this work.

This biography has been written in solitude over years of family ill-health and often difficult readjustment. I have to thank my husband, Kirill Konstantinovich Sokolov, for keeping me at it and giving constant priority to my writing. The other person to whom I owe more than I can say is the editor Catharine Carver, who has given unstintingly of her time, talent, and experience to help reduce the work from a meandering saga of almost half a million words to the much more readable and coherent form it now bears.

A.P.

CHAPTER I

Roots

(1880–1889, and before)

1

We were sitting—all the family—drinking tea under the limes at sunset.
Beyond the lilacs the mist was already rising from the gully.

The sound of scythes being sharpened came to us. It was the peasants from
the next estate who had come out to mow the merchant's meadow. They
were not shouting and swearing as they usually did. The scythes went swinging through the grass, about twenty of them; you could tell by the sound.

Suddenly one of the men started up a song. Effortlessly, the powerful
silvery tenor poured forth, immediately flooding gully, grove and garden.
What with the lilacs and the mist you could not see anything, but I could
tell by the voice that it was Grigory Khripunov singing; only I would never
have thought that weedy little Grigory from the factory had such a powerful voice.

The men took up the song. And we suddenly felt dreadfully awkward.

I don't know the tune, can't catch the words; but the song swells and
swells. Never have the neighbour's men sung like that before. I feel embarrassed to remain seated, have a tickle in my throat and want to cry. I jump
up and run off into a far corner of the garden.

It was after that that everything began to go to pieces. The men who
had been singing brought in syphilis from Moscow and spread it all through
the neighbouring villages. The merchant whose meadow was being mown
took to the bottle and once, when drunk, set fire to his own hay lofts. The
deacon began getting illegitimate children. The ceiling in Fyedot's *izba* fell
in completely and Fyedot did nothing about it. In our family the old people
began to die and the young people to grow old. My grandfather began
to say the most stupid things, quite unlike his old self. As for me, the next
morning I went and cut down the ancient lilac.

That lilac was centenarian, aristocratic, the flowers were pale bluish and
sparse, and the trunk so gnarled it almost defied the axe. I chopped it all
down and beyond it rose a grove of birches. I cut down the birches too,
and beyond them was the gully. From the bottom of the gully I could

now see nothing but my own house rising above my head. It stood open
to every wind and storm. If I were to dig underneath it, it would collapse
and bury me.... (VI. 169–70)

Aleksandr Blok rewrote these recollections of his twenty-first
summer at Shakhmatovo, his grandfather's country home, after the
1917 revolution and the sacking of the house by the local peasantry.
He first noted the incident ('The peasants sang on 23 July') when
it occurred, in the summer of 1902, returned to it in 1908–9, and
again in 1919. The final date the fragment bears in his Collected
Works—19 March 1921—places it among the last things he wrote.

The incident, like Blok's poetry, is symbolic, not allegorical. It
happened. The lime trees still stand, struggling for life among tall
young pines. The gully plunges steeply and the view is open where
the poet cut down the birches: a gentle valley along the bottom of
which meanders a small river; grey-roofed villages, presumably still
inhabited by the descendants of Fyedot; mixed forest, the dark outline of firs jagged against the lacy tenderness of silver birch and sturdy
growth of hazel and alder. Where the gully runs back into the woods,
a boggy patch drained by a trickling stream and a smiling rent of
blue in the forest roof show where the 'wild' part of the garden ended
in a man-made 'woodland pool'. Then, as now, the forest took over.

Still standing sentinel where Blok's grandmother's window once
looked out, a great silver poplar is slowly dying. Brown, unhappy
bamboos, cultivated by the poet's botanist grandfather, linger in dila-
pidated clumps by what was formerly the south front, but the site
of the house itself is marked only by a tangle of white-blossomed,
red-berried bushes. If you grope about for long enough in the tangle
you can still find a few bricks from the stove. Everything else has
gone: fences, benches, outhouses. Only the stillness remains, for there
is no road to Shakhmatovo—just a muddy cart track, as in the poet's
time, when guests were met with horses, many hushed and fragrant
miles away, at the nearest railway station.

A long way up the valley, but no further than the eye can see,
rises a round forest-clad hill. Here, in a fortress-laboratory, extra-
sturdily built against possible catastrophe from within, lived the great
chemist Dmitriy Ivanovich Mendeleyev, who looked like an Old
Testament prophet and had been known to take off from his lofty
rural stronghold on the wings of the wind—in an air balloon. Here,
shy and unattainable, lived the princess, the magician's daughter,
Lyubov' Dmitriyevna Mendeleyeva, whom Blok courted spasmodically throughout a dreamy youth.

Riding his white horse Malchik up the long open valley, the poet would pass through the village of Tarakanovo, where a baroque eighteenth-century chapel rose incongruously pink and elegant above the village pond. Here, in 1903, he and Lyubov' Dmitriyevna were married, and the villagers brought snow-white geese to the door. The geese—or their descendants—are still there, but rooks fly in and out of the raftered cupola. The village school is a Blok museum, containing only photographs and reproductions. What survived of the sack of Shakhmatovo, from window bolts to family icons, the peasants distributed amongst themselves, and exercise-books with rough and fair copies of Blok's poetry were 'used up' in this very building by the local schoolchildren.

Revertitur in terram suam unde erat; to return unto the earth from whence you came: this was Blok's prescription for all the ills of twentieth-century European culture, and it is the fate which overtook his own heritage, both material and spiritual.

2

Shakhmatovo belonged to the poet's maternal grandfather, Andrey Nikolayevich Beketov. Aleksandr Blok was his oldest grandson, the last scion of his line, though not of his name.

He was born on 16 November 1880 to Aleksandra, the third of Beketov's four daughters, in the residence of the Rector of the University of St. Petersburg, a position held by his grandfather from 1875 to 1883. Aleksandra Andreyevna did not return to her husband after her son's birth; he never lived in his father's house and only began to visit his paternal relatives in his first years at University. In a ten-page autobiography, written at the age of thirty-four, the poet was careful to stress that he had been brought up in his mother's family, which he described in affectionate detail.

The name Beketov is common enough in Russia and is said to derive from the Circassian Bey (or Bek). The history of this particular family can be traced back along a meandering and pleasant middle way between intellectual distinction and political obscurity until the line is lost in the mists of the troublous sixteenth century. By the late eighteenth century the family were wealthy, firmly rooted landed gentry, connected by marriage or friendship with many well-known figures of the Russian Enlightenment: the sentimental poet Dmitriyev, the Karamzins, Denis Davydov, Prince Vyazemsky, and the Decembrist Yakushkin are some of the names closely woven into their family history before Blok's grandfather and his two brothers appeared on the scene in the idealistic 1840s. The Beketov brothers were not, as Blok's father's family still were at that time, outsiders of foreign origin dependent on court favour. The whole structure of society upheld them, and the end of their wealth, which did not survive the emancipation of the serfs, was by no means the end of their position in that society.

Andrey Nikolayevich and his brothers, Aleksey and Nikolay, had in their youth been the centre of a circle of young people very close to the potentially revolutionary Petrashevsky group of Utopian socialists. A graduate of the Engineering Academy, where Aleksey Beketov, the elder brother, completed his studies, wrote of this circle:

In the course of my life I have seen a good many educated, agreeable, courteous people straining every nerve to start up a circle, but with no success: the Beketovs made no effort whatsoever, indeed the circle was rather a nuisance to them as it hindered their studies, but, nevertheless, it came into being. Everyone was attracted by the lovable personality of the elder brother, Aleksey Nikolayevich. He was the embodiment of kindness and integrity and, at the same time, was possessed of a cultivated mind and an ardent soul, easily moved to indignation by any injustice, quick to sympathize with every disinterested, honest aspiration.[1] [a]

In 1846, the misanthropic, sensitive Fyëdor Dostoyevsky, also a student at the Engineering Academy, wrote to his brother Mikhail of the two elder Beketovs: 'They are people of sense, clever, with excellent hearts, nobility of character, determination. They have healed me by their company.'[2]

In the following year, however, the Beketovs' father, then still a wealthy landlord in the province of Penza, undertook a journey to St. Petersburg accompanied—or so it is rumoured in family reminiscences—by three cooks and several head of live cattle so that he should not be deprived of his favourite cuts of veal on the journey. The purpose of the journey, however, was a serious one. He came to remove his all-too-conspicuous sons from the capital to the University of Kazan. That old Nikolay Beketov had his ear close to the ground is evident, for by the end of the year one member of his sons' circle had been sent down from the University, and shortly afterwards, Dostoyevsky and several other friends from the kindred but more overtly political Petrashevsky group were standing on the

[a] Superscript figures in the text refer to the Reference Notes at p. 333.

scaffold, numb and light-headed with shock, hearing their death sentences commuted to hard labour in Siberia.

After the completion of their studies in the safe backwater of Kazan the younger Beketov brothers had to look after themselves financially. The eldest, Aleksey, retired, after their father's death, to lead—on a very modest scale—the life of a country gentleman on the one estate remaining from the formerly very considerable family possessions, Urleyka in the province of Saratov, and worked hard as chairman of the governing board of the local *zemstvo*.[b] Nikolay Beketov, the youngest brother, attained academician's rank as a research chemist and acted as director of studies to the royal children.

Andrey, Blok's grandfather, combined a distinguished scientific career as a botanist with an active interest in current affairs. He was a vigorous and enlightened Rector of Petersburg University, pioneered the cause of higher education for women, and was accounted, in conservative circles, a positive 'Robespierre', more for the incorruptible independence of his radical opinions than for any violent revolutionary leanings.

Extremely scrupulous in money matters, the Beketovs never seem to have lamented their lost wealth. When first married, Andrey Beketov and his wife, Elizaveta Grigor'evna, were, considering their position in society, as poor as church mice. The very modest Shakhmatovo estate, for instance, acquired in 1875 on the advice of Beketov's great friend Dmitriy Mendeleyev, was not bought outright but paid for on a system of instalments over many years. It was a problem to scrape together the money to travel abroad or to take a first-class ticket on the train or a room in a good hotel.

Andrey Beketov's wife and daughters all contributed to family expenses by their writing and translations. On the other hand, to earn money was never the primary object of their work and, although careful to keep within their budget, it never occurred to any of them to trade in either their time or their integrity to augment it. Work they looked upon as service, the privilege and duty of cultivated minds. Words such as 'profit', 'career', and 'ambition' scarcely came into their vocabulary. Clannish and self-sufficient, it would never have occurred to them to cultivate influential or famous people. Nevertheless, life itself brought them constantly into contact with the influential and the famous. Indeed, Professor Beketov was, to use his own irreverent expression, 'an important snout' in his own right.

[b] Local government. Service on the *zemstva*, considered the nurseries of Russian parliamentarism, was elected and unpaid.

Beketov's development followed in the path of Francophile[c] radicalism and branched off sharply from that of his old acquaintance Dostoyevsky. The two finally clashed publicly in print when Dostoyevsky accused Beketov, who in his capacity as Rector had come down heavily in defence of some University students in a case of newspaper provocation, of trying to implement a second 'liberal' censorship over the Russian press.[3] Yet Beketov, although he disapproved of Dostoyevsky's politics and preferred the writing of Turgenev, Tolstoy, and Goethe, could never bring himself to condemn the great novelist as man and artist.

Not so his wife Elizaveta Grigor'evna. For her, Dostoyevsky was an odious figure, an obscurantist. Her father, Grigoriy Karelin, a lieutenant typical of the free-thinking, high-spirited officer caste of Pushkin's time, had once permitted himself an incautious jest at the expense of Alexander I's redoubtable war minister Arakcheyev. This led to his making a name for himself not as an artillery officer but, owing largely to an enforced change of residence, as an explorer of Central Asia and Siberia. His four daughters were therefore all born far from the metropolis in Orenburg. Later, the family was allowed to return to the Moscow province and settled on a small country estate, Trubitsyno, which was to serve as a holiday home for Andrey Beketov's and Elizaveta Grigor'evna's family until the purchase of Shakhmatovo.

At Trubitsyno, Aleksandra Nikolayevna, Karelin's wife, who had herself received an excellent education at the pension of a certain Mme Schroeder in Petersburg, under such remarkable lecturers as Pletnev and Grech, and whose heavy crown of braided hair had once inspired Pushkin to write her verses,[d] did her best to make up for the impossibility of affording regular tutors. Her daughters grew up fluent in German and French and well read in all the European classics and, when forced to take in the daughters of the wealthier nobility to eke out her inadequate means, Aleksandra Nikolayevna found Elizaveta, even at the age of fifteen, a great help in instructing other young ladies in history and geography.

Brought up to hard work, comparative poverty and self-discipline, Blok's grandmother inherited much of her father's adventurous brilliance and lucid Voltairean sense of fun. Her daughter Maria, Blok's youngest aunt and first biographer, ventures the

---

[c] The Beketov brothers, whose mother died when they were very young, were brought up by a Swiss French governess, a convinced republican, and spoke the language as well as their native Russian.

[d] 'Vokrug lileynogo chela ty kosu dvazhdy obvila'.

opinion that her parents' marriage was not ideally happy, but that their differences were well hidden from their children. Be that as it may, Beketov's expansive talents and enthusiastic, sometimes almost childlike spontaneity found an excellent foil in the steady, humorous competence of his wife. It was she—and later their eldest daughter Katya, on whom the Professor lavished the greatest devotion of his romantic heart—who managed the estate of Shakhmatovo; in so far, that is, as it was managed at all. The master of the house was only called upon when it was necessary to 'shout a little', as his daughter Maria puts it. On these occasions, 'having more or less ineffectually fulfilled his function', as Anna Ivanovna Mendeleyeva recalled, 'he would immediately reassume his usual good-natured expression and, with a self-satisfied smile, quite obviously overestimating his contribution, would hasten back to his books and herbarium'.[4]

Blok's own recollections of his grandmother are full of respect and lively gratitude:

She was extremely well-read and spoke several languages; her personal philosophy was astonishingly lively and original, her style vivid, her use of language—precise and bold. . . . The abstract and 'subtle' was less in my grandmother's line, her style was too clear-cut, there were always a great many everyday words and expressions. In her, an exceptionally definite character was united with a mind as clear as the country summer mornings when she would sit down to work before first light. Year after year I dimly remember, as I remember all my childhood, her voice, the embroidery frames on which woollen flowers blossomed with amazing speed, bright patchwork quilts sewn of carefully hoarded scraps that were of no use to anyone and—over all this—a kind of irretrievable health and merriment. . . .   (VII. 9–10)

Elizaveta Beketova's favourite contemporary author was Anton Chekhov—the stories rather than the plays, as one might expect—and she treasured a letter of thanks from that author written after the appearance of her translations of two of his stories into French in the *Revue des deux mondes*. Between them, she and her husband had some personal acquaintance with almost all the distinguished Russian writers of their day.[c] But Elizaveta Grigor'evna, though she

[c] Amongst others, with Gogol, Tyutchev (a neighbour at Trubitsyno), the Slavophile brothers Aksakov, Dostoyevsky, Tolstoy, Apollon Grigor'ev, Polonsky, Maykov, and the family of Vladimir Solov'ev, to whom the Karelins were related by marriage. Professor Beketov was an associate of Saltykov-Shchedrin, with whom he used to dine regularly at the Borelli restaurant in Petersburg, and was the chief speaker at Turgenev's Jubilee reception in 1878.

revered literature, did not suffer from an unduly pious attitude towards writers: her dislikes were as marked as her likes and included Tolstoy's moral tracts and her husband's favourite Part Two of *Faust*—written, she declared cheerfully, expressly 'to set all those deep-thinking Germans guessing'.

For all their simplicity and charm, the Beketovs had one major shortcoming: they were intellectually exclusive, knowing themselves to be 'exceptional people'. Unlike their grandson, they took this comfortable knowledge for granted, and imparted their fastidious and self-confident intellectualism, together with all their most excellent qualities, their 'fortitude of mind and body' and 'militant romanticism',[5] to their four daughters.

Of the four, Katya, the eldest, married late and died young. She was the only one to publish original works, one volume of stories and one of verse, printed posthumously. To judge by the photographs she was the prettiest of the four girls, and the shape of the fine, heavy-lidded eyes recalls Blok's own. She and Aleksandra, the poet's mother, were the most vivid and gifted sisters, Sofia and Maria the steadier. Katya and Maria were considered 'the clever ones'. Aleksandra, though the second youngest, was the first to wed. Shortly afterwards, Sofia, two years her senior, married Adam Kublitsky-Piottukh, a rather dandified young man, proud of his Polish origins, later to become a successful lawyer, and still later a moderately prosperous Soviet civil servant working on Gosplan.

The youngest daughter, Maria Beketova, the rather shadowy family chronicler, was everybody's confidante. Modestly, she writes of herself: 'having no admirers of my own I always did all I could to further the romances of others'.[6] Her diaries show her to have been made much more unhappy by her plainness (in photographs she appears painfully thin, large-mouthed, heavy cheek-boned, and gawky) than she ever allowed to appear in her published works; to have been jealous of her father's obvious and probably rather tactlessly expressed preference for Katya; to have indulged in passionate rows with her dearest sister Alya (Blok's mother, Aleksandra), to whom she remained a faithful friend all her life long; and to have suffered deeply from unrequited love. She had all her family's defenceless decency and uprightness, and was an effective servant of enlightenment, publishing translations from Polish, French, and German as well as popular books, among others, *The History of England*. After her nephew's death, Maria Beketova put in a great deal of painstaking and invaluable work on her detailed and lively biography and on helping to edit his letters and diaries.

It is primarily to Maria that we owe our extensive knowledge of Blok's mother, who was her senior by barely two years and so inseparable from her in girlhood that the two were known collectively as 'Mul'-Al' '^f^. According to her sister, Aleksandra was a flighty schoolgirl, the despair of her teachers and of several young men in whom, 'without in the least intending to', she sometimes 'inspired very deep feelings'. Graceful and kittenish rather than pretty, with her big mouth, tip-tilted nose, and softly curling hair, Aleksandra makes a very charming figure in her youthful photographs. Maria tells us they do not do her justice: 'No photograph can convey the tenderness and brilliance of her colouring, the charm of her smile and movements, yet the beauty of my sister was all in these things, faces like hers are not photogenic.'[7]

Yet Aleksandra was not only high-spirited but correspondingly highly strung, indeed, hypersensitive. Maria recounts a strange incident from their girlhood:

One fine August evening she was taken for a boat ride on the Neva with an aunt and us sisters. Past our boat came floating the body of a drowned man. The sight of his body, the soaked pink shirt and the plastered hair, produced a shattering impression on her: she could hardly walk home, and there such a weakness came over her that her legs literally gave way beneath her.... For almost three days she neither ate nor slept but stared before her with fixed eyes and said nothing. The whole world seemed to have taken on a peculiar colouring for her, nothing made sense any more, as though nothing existed. It was not a feeling of fear or pity but a kind of unconscious, mystic horror before the tragedy of life and the inevitability of fate. If, at that time, she had been able to exteriorize and formulate her feelings, she would have expressed them in the single question: 'If that is how things are, why go on living?'[8]

Here we have the first moment of clinical depression, the first upsurge of metaphysical rebellion in the family of the man whose company the young Dostoyevsky had found 'healing'. The note was struck again and again throughout Aleksandra's life; and it was to echo on through the life and poetry of her son, recurring again and again like a Wagnerian theme and rising, in his last illness, to an overpowering crescendo.

Like her mother, Aleksandra wielded a lively pen; her letters have a nervous sensibility, an analytic lucidity and a purely feminine, almost feline propensity to unsheathe politely velveted claws that make them entertaining as well as remarkably revealing reading. She

^f^ 'Mul' ' is a shortened version of 'Mulya', one of the innumerable Russian diminutives for Maria.

could turn very tolerable lyric verse but published only translations and children's poetry. She translated, more accurately but with less ease and verve than her mother, from the French. Above all things, Aleksandra loved nature, music and literature, in that order. Her tastes were in part formed by her parents, in part a reaction against their enlightened calm. She could not abide Turgenev, but loved Dostoyevsky, and was the first of her family to take an interest in European decadence, avidly reading and translating Baudelaire.

It was Aleksandra who introduced Aleksandr L'vovich Blok to the Beketov family. . . .

3

Aleksandr Blok hardly knew his father, was never influenced by him, but recognized a certain affinity and remembered him 'in his blood' (VII. 12).

The Blok family were in a sense the antithesis of the Beketovs. They represented a different branch of the nobility, not rooted in the land but serving the throne as specialists in various capacities at court and in the civil service. Like many families who have risen to eminence in a country not their own and consistently married above their original status, the Bloks had their own innocent myth about their origins, which later generations undoubtedly believed and which the poet himself repeats in his autobiography. This was that their ancestor, a member of the German nobility, had come to Russia to take up the post of personal physician to Tsar Aleksey Mikhailovich, the father of Peter the Great.

In fact, two Blok brothers first came to Russia somewhat later, in the middle of the eighteenth century. Their father was an army sawbones in the garrison of Duke Karl Leopold in Demütz and their mother—a baker's daughter. Younger sons in a modestly circumstanced family of six, Christian Ludwig and Johann Friedrich Blok set out to Russia to follow their luck and their father's profession shortly after his death in 1752.[8] By 1763 Christian Ludwig, the elder of the two, was demonstrating surgery and anatomy at the Admiralty hospital in Kronstadt while his brother worked as a naval surgeon on board ship. Christian Ludwig died a bachelor in 1766. Johann Friedrich married a woman of German origin and, twenty years later, in 1787, became personal physician to the Empress Cath-

[8] Russian records of a later date grant them medical degrees from Rostok and Berlin. The archives of the University of Rostok, it seems, do not confirm this.

erine the Great at Tsarkoye Selo, where he achieved bureaucratic rank as councillor to a government ministry.[h] Russian patents of nobility were finally granted to the Blok family under Paul I.[9]

Johann Friedrich had five children and the family continued to distinguish itself in the spheres of medicine, law, and government administration. The poet's grandfather, purely German by blood but already of the third generation in Russian service, a *Kammerjunker*, marshal of the nobility, and vice-director of Customs, was the first male Blok to marry a Russian. His bride, Ariadna Cherkasova, daughter of the governor of Novgorod, was a lady of considerable means and determined character. The Bloks were Lutherans, but Ariadna Blok insisted on her four children being brought up in the Orthodox faith.

Her favourite, the eldest, the poet's father Aleksandr, resembled her in face. Born in 1852 in Pskov, in the home of his maternal grandfather Governor Cherkasov, an aristocrat of refined appearance with a reputation for harshness, Aleksandr L'vovich received his schooling in the ancient provincial capital of Novgorod. Having matriculated with a gold medal in 1870 he entered the Faculty of Jurisprudence at Petersburg University where, four years later, after submitting a dissertation on civic administration in Russia, he remained to work under Professor A. D. Gradovsky, intending to pursue an academic career. This was a somewhat unusual occupation for one of his family, and was proof of a dour independence of character which had already led him to leave his father's home while still a student and to earn his living by giving tuition. Now, abandoning the highest sphere of the Petersburg bureaucracy which formed his parents' social milieu, Aleksandr L'vovich began to frequent Anna Pavlovna Filosofova's salon and other circles of the liberal intelligentsia.

When, in 1876, he passed his Master's examination and two years later accepted the offer of a chair at Warsaw University, Gradovsky wrote congratulating the Rector there on his new professor, praising the young man's knowledge, his talent for exposition, and general character: 'He may confidently be accounted among the most erudite, alive people with an excellent general background.'[10]

At that time, Aleksandr L'vovich was indeed an 'alive' person, and this he showed in his choice of friends. Anna Pavlovna Filosofova[i] presided over one of the most celebrated liberal salons of her day.

[h] In eighteenth-century Russia, one councillor or assessor in each Kollegiya or ministry had, by statute, to be a foreigner in Russian service.

[i] She figures in Blok's poem *Retribution* as Anna Vrevskaya.

An ardent feminist, she was also a beauty and an accomplished hostess who had the gift of bringing together and making welcome people from the most different spheres of society. At her home you could meet men of power and influence rubbing shoulders with liberals and revolutionaries, artists and writers.

Aleksandr L'vovich Blok's development, however, was warped by circumstance. His contemporaries were the Populists, committed but rather muddled and emotional philanthropists who preached a doctrine of enlightened egotism and 'small deeds'. These 'joyless organizers of human happiness', as Vasiliy Rozanov called them, unlike the energetic generation of the '60s, were too moderate and ineffectual to satisfy the teeming energies of contemporary Russia. They had their violent, romantic 'doubles' in the revolutionary terrorists who eventually, in 1882, succeeded in assassinating the Tsar-Liberator, Alexander II, and bringing down upon their country the long twilight of reaction which came to be identified with the name of Pobedonostsev, a statesman whose avowed aim was 'to halt Russia's development' in order, as he believed, to hold in check the uncontrollable forces ready to break forth at the first sign of economic or social change. Aleksandr L'vovich was neither populist nor revolutionary, for both groups lacked two qualities with which he himself was abundantly endowed: a harsh sense of the realities of political power and of the vulnerability of the cultivated individual at a time 'when the people are beginning to awake' (III. 463); and the capacity for artistic ecstasy. A morose individualist, his thought moved in convulsive zigzags of paradox and irony. Indeed, the man's whole character was a paradox. He combined an analytic, fiercely practical legal mind with a Dionysiac passion for beauty, particularly in music; a sadistic sexual temperament with an extremely rigorous, 'protestant' conscience; the psychology of a born administrator and member of the ruling classes with a questing spirit and iconoclastic nature. Apart from this, he had inherited a certain mental instability from his father, who ended his days in a home for nervous and psychic disorders. As his own son was later to recall, there was 'something convulsive and terrible about his whole personality' (VII. 12).

It is scarcely surprising that Beketov family tradition relates how Dostoyevsky, a fellow guest at Anna Filosofova's salon, noticed the young scholar and, intrigued by his demonic aura, thought of modelling a character on him. '*Si non e vero, e ben trovato*', was his son's comment on this particular legend.

Before Aleksandra Beketova's father was elected Rector of Petersburg University, she met Aleksandr L'vovich at the house of a school friend and, the next thing she knew, he had taken a box at the opera (to hear Rubinstein's *The Demon!*) and invited the friend's family on condition that Aleksandra would make one of the party. When, shortly after Aleksandra first introduced her new admirer to her parents, the Beketovs moved to the spacious Rector's house, they found that their position and their four unmarried daughters drew up to a hundred visitors every Saturday. These, for want of means to provide wine and supper, they entertained on tea, sandwiches, and home-made jam. Downstairs, the Rector and his more serious guests enjoyed quiet philosophical conversation, while upstairs the young people danced, made music and played *petits-jeux*. This is not quite the kind of society in which it is easiest to imagine Aleksandr L'vovich Blok—mixing with high-principled, liberal-minded students and University teachers. Here, things were a great deal less sophisticated than at Anna Filosofova's—indeed, the Beketovs' 'at homes' were essentially an extension of University society. Nevertheless, the family was so unpretentiously distinguished, the atmosphere so easy and open-hearted, Aleksandr L'vovich's own paradoxical witticisms and romantic performance at the grand piano so generously appreciated, that he cannot but have enjoyed the experience. The great reception room of the Rector's house, decorated with plants and flowers from the University Botanical Gardens, its windows full of snow-light from the frozen Neva or, in summer, of the sparkle from its stately-flowing waters, must in itself have been a pleasure to any man of taste.

Taste Aleksandr L'vovich certainly had, and he showed it not least when he so determinedly set himself to court Beketov's third daughter, perceiving behind her lively prettiness a passionate, intuitive mind whose quality had hitherto gone all unsuspected and which he believed he would cultivate and discipline to rare heights. Aleksandra, however, was only just seventeen and enjoying herself. She turned down his first proposal and he stopped coming to the receptions. But the family kept telling her she would never meet a more interesting or worthwhile suitor and one day, when he came to see her father on business, she waited for him in the hall and they made it up and became engaged. In January 1879, the couple were wedded amidst a plethora of stars and garters and official gold braid. Professor Blok bore off his eighteen-year-old bride to Warsaw that same day.

Here he took up his appointment at the University and embarked upon a controversial book on Lorentz Stein,[11] which Aleksandra had to copy out for him in long-hand day by day. This thoroughly radical book, condemned to be burnt by the censor, was saved only thanks to Professor Blok's influential connections, and he was eventually able to submit the published volume as his thesis for the degree of Master of State Law at Petersburg University. It was to defend this thesis at a viva voce examination that Aleksandr L'vovich next brought his wife to St. Petersburg, two years after their marriage.

Professor Beketov, a doting and rather fussy father, was distressed to see his lively teen-age daughter transformed into a pale, low-spirited woman obviously labouring under considerable nervous strain. To make matters worse Aleksandra was pregnant—for the second time, having given birth to one still-born child in Warsaw in the first year of marriage. One day, hearing her cry out in her room, the old man rushed upstairs to find his son-in-law in the act of striking her. With a muttered apology to the effect that he 'had thought nobody was at home', Aleksandr L'vovich stalked past the astonished Rector and slammed out of the house.

Andrey Nikolayevich was a gentle and civilized person, but he was also used to his own way and something of a patriarch. A model of old-fashioned chivalry in his own personal relations with the fair sex, he was noted in public life as an advocate of emancipation. He was not, in other words, the man to stand by while any woman of his blood was mistreated, never mind a young girl eight months pregnant. With the help of the family doctor he persuaded his daughter not to accompany Aleksandr L'vovich back to Warsaw until safely delivered of her child.

Yet there was a quality in this gently nurtured young woman which responded to Aleksandr L'vovich's harsh intellect and to that stormy, artistic temperament which had made the tastes and opinions of her own family appear almost insipid. Maria Beketova tells us that the couple had known moments of 'rare harmony' and that Aleksandr L'vovich had appreciated and known how to cultivate his wife's tastes and develop her mind as none of her subsequent admirers were to do. Nevertheless, it must be admitted that Professor Beketov had good reason for his interference. Aleksandr L'vovich's youngest brother, the gentle Ivan Blok, had tried to warn Aleksandra against accepting his brother's proposal, so the instability of the man's character must have been known to his family before the marriage. Although he did his wife no serious physical harm, Aleksandr L'vovich had constantly bullied and humiliated her, playing now the severe schoolmaster, now the jealous lover, now the miserly holder of the purse strings who questioned her every expenditure.

Unused to restraint of any kind, alone in a strange country, sometimes so frightened 'the hair literally stirred on her head', Aleksandra had never complained, and a sad little poem, written four years after their separation, showed how hard she found it to forget her first husband. He, in his turn, did all he could to induce her to return to him, and refused to grant her a divorce for almost eight years.

4

This was how it happened that Aleksandr Blok came into the world in the Rector's house. He was born very early one Sunday morning while the usual Saturday reception was still going on downstairs. Aleksandra was the first daughter to bear Andrey Beketov a grandson and, with a houseful of women on his hands, the old man was delighted. Never was a child more welcome. His great-grandmother Aleksandra Nikolayevna Karelina, his grandmother, a retired nanny who, in the best Russian tradition, was living in the house on pension, and youthful aunts all took turns to nurse him. His young mother, radiantly happy to have borne a live son, fed him at the breast.

Then, with the Christmas holidays, came the real father, Aleksandr L'vovich Blok, hot-foot from Warsaw. Eager to see the colour of his son's eyes (greyish-green, as it happened, like his own), he swept down on the sleeping infant and raised its lids, as though it were an inanimate object. Exasperated by Beketov baby-worship and probably conscious that family influence had alienated Aleksandra, he naturally took out his impatience on his wife, then, after a series of painful scenes, betook himself to his parents' house up the road, demanding that Aleksandra call on him daily—which she did.

The stress of his stormy presence brought on trouble with the young mother's milk, and both she and the baby ceased to do well. The doctor would not permit them to return to Warsaw after the New Year and after Blok's departure Professor Beketov, gradually and, for a man of his ardent temper, very gently and tactfully, persuaded his daughter not to return to her husband—for the sake of the boy. And so it was that Aleksandr Aleksandrovich Blok came to be brought up as 'Sasha Beketov'.[j]

As was to be expected, Aleksandr L'vovich did not take his wife's decision, communicated to him by letter in the spring of 1881, lying down. A shower of letters, reasoning, cajoling, and even threatening

---

[j] Not legally, of course. But to the Mendeleyevs at least, the grandson of Dmitriy Ivanovich's great friend Beketov and the heir to Shakhmatovo was naturally known by his grandfather's name.

to take her and her infant son by force, culminated in a telegram signed by the Rector of Warsaw University which read: 'Blok gravely ill. Wife's presence essential'. Professor Beketov, for all his unworldliness, proved more than a match for his demonic son-in-law; to a polite enquiry of his old friend the Warsaw Rector as to the progress of Professor Blok's illness, he received the incisive reply: 'Blok in perfect health'.

Aleksandra, who was after all only twenty, soon began to recover her youth and spirits. As to baby Sasha—he found himself heir-apparent to a most delightful pocket kingdom, poor enough in toys and luxuries but rich beyond all measure in people, beauty and loving attention.

With such devoted care, the baby's early delicacy was soon over-come and he became a physically robust, though always nervous and easily over-excited child. Summers at Shakhmatovo, where he lived in a separate annex with his mother, nanny, and great-grandmother, guaranteed his healthy development, though, like most perfectly contented children, he was in no hurry to walk or talk. In the winter months he lived on the top floor of the Rector's house in the room next to that of his great-grandmother, with whom in those very early years he spent much time. A relic of a sterner, less sentimental age, the old lady could still recite the superb odes of the eighteenth-century poet Derzhavin and was a devotee of the full-blooded romanti-cism of Schiller and Lamartine.

As a toddler, Sasha was carried into his Aunt Katya's bedroom each morning. Katya was a later riser and would play with the child and make much of him, so that when he learnt to walk he continued independently the tradition of running in to wake her. At noon every day he was solemnly conducted to his grandmother's room, the win-dows of which opened on to the Neva, to wait for the cannon to fire the midday salute. Here, in the spring, he would watch the boats passing up and down the great water-way. In the winter, 'in his grandfather's study, the windows of which also opened on to the Neva, he would sit for long at a time on the carpet looking at the pictures in the heavy volumes of Buffon and Brokgauz'.[12]

The city of Petersburg too, turned her fairest face to him. In winter his walks were along the granite pavements of the sunny University Embankment, the near side flanked by clean-lined, early eighteenth-century buildings, the opposite bank culminating in the golden spire of the Admiralty. In spring and autumn, Nanny Sonya led him through the University precincts to the Botanical Gardens, tucked away behind the white-columned Stock Exchange: gardens which

Andrey Nikolayevich Beketov,
Blok's grandfather.

Elizaveta Grigor'evna Beketova,
Blok's grandmother.

Lev and Ariadna Blok, the poet's paternal grandfather and grandmother.
(From the collection of N. P. Il'in)

Engagement photograph of Aleksandr L'vovich Blok and Aleksandra Andreyevna Beketova, the poet's father and mother (1879).

his own grandfather had founded back in the '60s. Sometimes the children of the University staff would be taken to promenade up and down the famous 'University Corridor'. Here, according to Blok's future mother-in-law, whose somewhat sugary recollections are not always strictly accurate but who can certainly be relied upon to remember what the children wore, he occasionally met her daughter Lyubov':

There goes a little man in enormous dark glasses, drowning in a long winter coat with a disproportionately large fur collar. It is 'Kot-Murlyka', Professor Nikolay Petrovich Wagner. In his pocket he always carried his favourite white rat, which enjoyed the utmost liberty, often climbing out for a breath of air and, to the great delight of the children, of whom there were always very many in the corridor, poking out its white muzzle and pink ears. Amongst the others stands out the neat figure of a blond boy in a blue coat with huge, light eyes and a bee-stung upper lip. Silently he examines the rat, then, just as silently and attentively, switches his gaze to a tiny blue-eyed, rosy-cheeked girl in a golden velveteen coat and hat from beneath which springs rebellious, thick, bright golden hair. The little girl, her arms sticking stiffly out from her sides like a doll's, her feet in the smallest imaginable white felt boots, is lost in ecstatic contemplation of the rat as it peers out from beneath the professor's collar. Both children are with their nannies who bid one another good-day and make the children do the same. The boy's warm white mitten goes out to meet the similar mitten of the small girl. They were little Sasha Blok and his future wife Lyuba Mendeleyeva.[13]

All this, however, was nothing compared with Shakhmatovo. Aunt Katya, writing to her sister, Sofia, gives us a glimpse of Blok's second summer, telling laughingly how the child pestered her when she settled down to sketch and how she fed him wild strawberries:

There's really nothing to write, but just imagine how lovely it is here. The windows are open, the lamps are shining brightly in the dining room; in the blue room (where I am writing), the lamps are lit too, everywhere there are posies of forget-me-not, jasmine and wild roses, under the windows the jasmine bushes make more posies. Manya[k] is playing Les Huguenots 'Per l'onor, per la fe'. Papa and Mama are sitting on the stairs of the veranda, Alya is wandering from one to the other ... Beeba[l] is an angel from heaven, a tiny precious bird, a bundle of mischief and a rowdy. I adore him, and so does everyone else.[14]

[k] A common diminutive for Maria.
[l] One of the family nicknames for Blok, who was also known by the usual abbreviations of his name: Sasha, Sashen'ka, Sashuryonok.

Given so idyllic a home, it is hardly surprising that Blok's third winter, spent with his mother, Aunt Maria, grandmother, and nanny in Trieste and Florence, left no trace on his conscious memory. In fact, he spent most of his time there walking and playing with his patient and gently imaginative Russian Nanny Sonya, who did not finally leave him until, when he was seven, his mother decided he no longer needed a nurse, and who was to visit him regularly on his name day all his life long.

One visible sign of the journey remained: an '*image sainte*' of the Blessed Virgin, presented to 'Alessandro' by the landlady's daughter, Sophia, which his mother had framed and hung above his bed. He kept it always.

5

The preceding winter in Petersburg had been marked by a change in the fortunes of the Beketov family. The rising tide of political reaction after the assassination of Alexander II in March 1882 had led to an exacerbation of the traditionally bad relationships between University students and the police. The civil authorities looked upon the universities as forcing-houses of revolution and the relations between police and students had reached a state of open enmity, of 'no holds barred'. Every December there was trouble between police and students which led to arrests and brawling on the University premises. Professor Beketov, who was convinced that these scenes were deliberately provoked by the police, went to the city governor and informed him that he would not stay on as Rector if the gendarmes were again allowed to enter the University precincts. At the same time, he gave an undertaking that he would be personally responsible for keeping order and thus obtained a pledge that the police would not intervene. Making the point that the liberal traditions of the University were in their hands, he harangued the students for hours on end, coming home hoarse with exhaustion, and obtained a number of individual promises to refrain from demonstrations or political meetings.

This had happened several times before, but always some incident had set inflammable student tempers ablaze, and the promises had been forgotten. So it was this time. Disorderly behaviour and meetings began again and the city governor, too, forgot his promise.

One day, my sister Aleksandra and I looked out of the window and saw black crowds of policemen flooding into the University courtyard like a swarm of locusts. With heavy hearts we contemplated this spectacle. My sister wept, we both felt deeply injured for our beloved University, which seemed to us to have been defiled, and felt the threat to its alumni. And, indeed, the students were taken into custody, registered with the police, and many of them expelled, after which our father handed in his resignation and ceased to be Rector.[15]

The inevitable corollary of this was the evacuation of the enchanting Rector's house and a considerable readjustment in the budget of the Professor's numerous dependants. Needless to say, however, Andrey Beketov enjoyed the unqualified support of his family, and Aleksandra, though by no means public-spirited at this time, retained the basic idea that a principle was something very much more important than a position—and passed it on to her son. The Beketovs removed to a flat near the Summer Gardens where Sasha Blok, like Evgeniy Onegin, was now taken out walking. Nanny Sonya was temporarily absent, and Sasha and his mother had to share a bedroom with a tiresome temporary who was always talking about her last post (with a general's family).

This first flat was followed by various others, one damp, one cramped, another too expensive for the Beketovs' now still further reduced means. But Sasha had the run of all of them, the same people surrounded him and, in later life, they merged into a vague memory of Christmas trees, spacious, high-ceilinged reception rooms, and being read to sleep, his eyes wandering dreamily from his rocking horse to the green *lampadka* burning before the icon in the corner of the room. The Beketovs, for all their free-thinking, observed national customs and religious feasts, of which Blok remained aware all his life, often dating his letters by the Church calendar 'Trinity Sunday', 'All Saints', etc.

Meanwhile, at Shakhmatovo, the world of nature was disclosing itself to him with limpid generosity. When the family returned from Italy they found a new room with a French window made for Sasha and his mother out of the old kitchen. In the nursery annexe were Aunt Sofia and her first-born, Feliks Adamovich, whom Sasha promptly nicknamed Ferol. In the summer of 1884, Professor Beketov began to take his eldest grandson, who had grown slim and wiry and very sturdy on his feet, for long walks in the vast, state-owned forest of Praslovo that stretched for many miles in both directions immediately behind their house. As Katya wrote to her mother:

... the most untiring of all is Sasha, and more and more often he and Dedisya[m] go off walking together, just the two of them, turning down all other

[m] Family distortion of *dedushka*, grandfather.

company. As the ground is still very boggy, they come home wet, and dirty into the bargain: Dedisya carries Sashurka in his arms and gets all muddied from his dirty little feet.[16]

Ferol in his brief memoir of their childhood recalls that his cousin would never join in general family expeditions but liked only to walk alone, with his grandfather or, many years later, with his wife.[17] To the small boy, these early expeditions were a delight and an education.

My own memories of my grandfather are very happy; he and I would wander for hours over the meadows and the marshes and through the track-less woods; sometimes we covered tens of versts, losing our way in the forest; we dug up grasses and herbs by the roots for his botanical collection; as we did so he named the plants and, defining them, would teach me the elements of botany, so that even now I remember many botanical names. I remember how delighted we were when we found a special early-flower-ing pear tree, a species unknown to the Moscow flora, and a very fine-fronded, low-growing kind of bracken; I still look for that bracken every year on the same hill, but I have never found it again—evidently it had seeded itself there by chance and then died out.

(VII. 8)

Blok's first letter to his grandfather begins, as a matter of course, 'I love you very much', and the second, after the same opening, con-tinues: '. . . Mama has told me you will come here in ten days' time. Then we will go walking again—far away. . . .' This was the summer of 1891 when Blok was ten. The following year, Katya's sudden death was to face the good old man with great sorrow, thoughts of age and death, and longings for a personal immortality in which he only half believed. And so, as Sasha Blok grew up and Andrey Beketov grew old, the pattern of their summers gradually changed. Blok spent more time playing with Ferol and Ferol's younger brother, Andryusha; later, he took to walking alone, fishing, and exploring on horseback. On 13 August 1894 Professor Beketov wrote to his daughter Sofia from Shakhmatovo:

I have begun to tire very easily, a real old crock. I get very weary and tired even after a comparatively short walk. And indeed there is no one for me to walk with. Our Sashuronechek now rides horseback; and anyway I would be ashamed to drag him along with me as nowadays I walk so slowly.[18]

Nevertheless, Maria Beketova tells us that it was during this summer that Sasha and his grandfather had particular fun with a home-made kite which they flew together from the wind-swept field up behind the house, and how, another time, they set off in the trap for the nearest town and, on the return journey, came across some rare wild flowers.

It is worth remembering that both Blok's grandparents were natural pedagogues. Apart from giving him a lifelong love of nature, Blok's happy relationship with his affectionate, spontaneous grand-father cannot but have led to his absorbing a great deal of the old man's way of thinking. The two qualities that particularly distinguished Andrey Beketov were an unaffected reverence for the natural world and a great sense of personal, individual freedom and of its corollary: personal, individual responsibility. Among the books from the poet's library now preserved in Pushkin House, there is a collection of popular scientific articles *On the Life of Nature and People* with the inscription 'To my dear Sashurenok from the Author, A.B.' which strikes the note for that theme of harmony which is so fundamental to Blok's poetry:

Man's love of nature is very understandable; he is himself a part of this nature and lives one life with it; with every single thing in nature he is in contact, in strict accord, in *harmony*. And *if* the artificial environment of town life sometimes decreases the awareness of this harmony, it is easily recovered as soon as man gets into the unconfined out-of-doors, as soon as he breathes in the fresh air of fields and woods. This harmonious contact between man and nature undoubtedly goes to show that the same contact must exist between all other natural phenomena. *The task of science consists precisely in this: to determine the laws of universal harmony, and in this respect all sciences go to make up one indivisible whole.*[19]

Aleksandr Blok's last great article, in which he formulated his artistic credo, was to define the poet's task as 'the release of harmony from the timeless womb of the elements'. Life, however, had by then taught him one lesson that his genial grandparent, in spite of all his material ups and downs, contrived to ignore: that 'to test hearts with harmony is not a peaceable occupation' (vi. 165).

Meanwhile, however, the boy was steeped in harmony, 'abund-ant, pressed down and running over'. By the age of seven he knew the surrounding woodland as well as any of the grown-ups: particu-larly, like any self-respecting Russian child, all the best places for lily-of-the-valley, wild strawberries, and various kinds of mush-rooms. For want of companionship of his own age in these earliest years he made friends with the Beketovs' agent, who also acted as government forester, 'a gentle old man with a sly sense of humour'[20] who would take him for whole days at a time to watch the felling of trees in some distant part of the woods. A source of particular pride to him was to be allowed to help in some task about the fields or woods, such as marking off the sown patches of ploughed land, and he would put heart and soul into doing it well. The more colourful among the peasants (to whom Grandfather Beketov gave French nicknames such as Jacob-Fidèle and Philippe-le-Bel) provided entertaining company, and it is easy to imagine the Professor's grandson, like a very junior Jim Hawkins hanging on the words of Long John Silver, sitting at the feet of 'the brigand Fyëdor Kuranov (known as Kuran), who, they said, had murder on his soul', who had a nose 'bluish-crimson from vodka' and who was eventually killed in 'a fist-fight'. Apart from family and tenants, little Sasha's greatest friends were animals: the thirty-year-old Seriy, a grey horse his grandfather actually allowed him to drive; dogs of all descriptions; cats and kittens; hedgehogs, hares; even frogs and insects.

Maria Beketova tells us how, sitting down to morning tea at the table beneath the limes, Aleksandra was revolted to find two singularly large caterpillars, one pink and one green, on the seat. Calling to Sasha to take them away, she remarked shuddering: 'What repulsive creatures!' Sasha lifted them up and carried them off, retorting placatingly as he did so: 'But *they* think they're very beautiful.'[21]

6

It was not only literature, but life itself that inundated the child 'with lyrical waves, scarcely connected as yet with any particular names'. Yet his apprenticeship to letters began even earlier than his first introduction to botany. His mother and grandmother used to make up stories and verses for him, verses with funny, round, well-chosen words and comically broken rhythms. One of the reasons everybody so disliked the temporary nanny who looked after Sasha in his third winter was her hopeless lack of literary taste: 'Sasha could abide neither her conversation nor her verses',[21] notes Aunt Maria with rare asperity. Nanny Sonya, on the other hand, read him tales and legends and Zhukovsky's ballads. Pushkin's *Poltava*, a stirring account in verse of Peter the Great's victory over the Swedes, provided him with a whole winter's game in which he careered round the current Beketov flat in cardboard armour and helmet, shooting left and right, brandishing a toy sword and transforming in his imagination all the other members of that busy household, each going about his own task, into friend or foe, alive or dead, as it suited his play. Aunt Maria, for instance, who spent long hours practising her scales at the grand piano, was known for years to come as 'the Swedish musician'.

It was his great-grandmother Aleksandra Karelina who taught Sasha his letters—in secret from his mother, so that the five-year-old boy had the pleasure of astonishing his adored and adoring parent with his 'suddenly' acquired ability to read. He preferred, however, to be read to—at first listening most readily to comic or robust children's books such as *Struwwelpeter*, then, at about six years of age, graduating to the 'heroic', 'fantastic', and 'lyrical'. Here he seems to have accepted pell-mell various classics of world literature of very different degrees of difficulty: Pushkin's verse tale *Tsar Saltan*, which delights Russians from the age of three onwards; Zhukovsky's stirring translation of *The Eve of St. John* and, again in Zhukovsky's translation, *Le Cid*, after listening to which he promptly nicknamed Nanny Sonya, who was extremely short-sighted, 'Don Njanjaio the noble, called the Blind'.

He knew no hesitation about reciting aloud either as a very small child or at any other age, but his pre-school repertoire was by no means precocious and was graded according to audience. Party-pieces, for instance, were usually infantile and comic, liberally interspersed with animal noises. His favourite ballads he would declaim only to Nanny Sonya and his mother. Lyric verse, especially of the intensely musical, romantic kind that appealed to some particularly deep-rooted need, he would recite 'at night, alone':

... and we heard from the next room how in a sleepy voice, still lisping a little, he began to recite Polonsky's 'Rocked in the Storm':

> Thunder, din: the ship is pitching,
> Dark the seething sea ...
> Wet wind whistles through the rigging
> Tattered sails blow free.

Of course, at that age he understood little enough of these verses, but there was something about them that pleased him.[22]

Maria Beketova suggests it was their 'lyricism': it is tempting to assume that what really delighted the boy was their form: the laconism and the music of the words, the rhythm and onomatopoeia. Of these formative first impressions, the poet wrote in his autobiography:

The dominant literary values and ideals in my family were of an old-fashioned kind. In vulgar parlance, as Verlaine would have put it, '*éloquence*' here occupied the place of honour; my mother alone was constantly filled with rebellious feeling and care for the new, and my aspirations to '*musique*' found support in her. However, no one in the family ever persecuted me, no one did otherwise than love and indulge me. And it is to that dear, old-fashioned '*éloquence*' that I shall be obliged till my dying day that, for me, literature did not begin with Verlaine, or with any form of decadence.

(VII. 12)

Sasha's first original poetic efforts were, predictably, about animals. They rhyme and scan—even those composed at the age of five—and show a humorously tender attitude to the vagaries of animal appetite, mood and digestion. Probably as a small child he made up a number of unrecorded 'funny' verses with Nanny Sonya, since he continued to do so, with much laughing and enjoyment, after her marriage, whenever she came to visit him.

The sunny atmosphere of mutual affection and rarefied harmony which pervaded the boy's childhood is shown even in his treatment of inanimate objects:

> On the sill
> In the still–
> ness the glass-holder
> Stands
> And behind,
> Just behind,
> The drinking-glass
> Lies
>
> And the glass
> Speaks out
> Why . . .
> Do you know
> I
> Love you?
>
> The glass-holder
> Replies
> Ah my neighbour
> My dear
> So do I
> Love
> You
> Too.

Words were his playthings. The composition of verse went hand in hand with the invention of charades, riddles, parodies, and games of *bouts-rimés*. From the age of eight or nine he began to produce 'magazines' for and with the help of his mother.[23] The titles of the very earliest efforts, painstakingly written out on double-lined exercise-books with all the wrong capital letters and atrocious spelling, are expressive in themselves. One of the more ambitious, covering two exercise-books, is called 'The Ship'. Born in a great port, Blok loved and drew ships all his life; in his private system of associations, they were at once harbingers of great joy and symbols of a hard-held course through life, of struggle and adventure in search of the promised land. Other titles of a more domestic kind were 'A Journal for Children', 'The Cat's Journal', 'Mamulya's Album', 'For My Little Tiny'."

These very early literary efforts are marked by the contrast between the boy's laconism and vigorous, easy-to-read folk-tale style—quite an achievement for a beginner—and the nursery content: toys and pets, Christmas trees and Easter eggs. Sasha's feeling for words had clearly been cultivated, effortlessly and playfully, far beyond his experience of life or even his technical literacy.

Occasionally, an entry betrays a more literary influence: a story about herd boys around a fire which immediately calls to mind Turgenev's 'Bezhin Meadow', or a splendid Robinson Crusoe tale entitled 'The Storm', beginning 'I was born in England'.

7

When Blok was almost nine years old, in the summer of 1889, his mother at last obtained a divorce from his father. Friends say that Professor Blok had long continued to hope for his wife's return, advertising his fidelity by always wearing his wedding ring. Now, however, he wanted to marry again: someone, he said himself, 'rather like Alya.'

Maria Timofeyevna Belayeva was of mixed Russian and Scottish parentage. Her parents had died young, leaving her to bring up a family of younger brothers, all of whom had followed in their father's footsteps to become professional soldiers. Not having a benevolent and possessive parent to command her return, she bore with Aleksandr L'vovich somewhat longer than her predecessor. Her first

" Blok's mother was very small and slender and the sturdily growing boy began early to call her his *Kroshka* ('crumb') and his *Kapelka* ('tiny drop'), affectionate diminutives best not rendered literally as they are less arch in the Russian—'Little Dorrit', for instance, always being translated as 'Kroshka Dorrit'.

child, a son, born dead, he had hoped to call Aleksandr, as though to efface and replace his elder son, now growing up in cheerful oblivion of his origins in the alien sunshine of the Beketov household. In 1892, Maria Timofeyevna bore him a daughter, Angelina. Four years later she too left her husband, because of his uncontrolled behaviour towards her in the presence of the child who, after an attempt to intervene in a violent scene, had begun to stammer. Returning to Petersburg, where she lived in the flat of one of her brothers, an officer in the Artillery, she did not marry again; neither did Aleksandr L'vovich.

Neither wife refused Professor Blok access to his children nor, although by no means generous with money, did he attempt to deny financial responsibility towards them. Yet on his rare visits to his son and daughter he had no idea how to establish a relationship, and remained a stranger to both. So the two children grew up in the same city, scarcely aware of one another's existence, and met for the first time over his death-bed in 1909, when Angelina was seventeen, Blok twenty-nine.

Aleksandra remarried less than a month after the divorce came through. It was her sister Sofia's brother-in-law, Lieutenant Frants Feliksovich Kublitsky-Piottukh of the Grenadier Guards, who became Sasha's stepfather. Both Aleksandra and old Professor Beketov had considered for some time that the sensitive, passionate child who, during the last year or so, had become increasingly self-willed and reserved, needed a man's influence. He had, they noticed, been growing more and more silent: a benevolent, attentive, thoughtful silence, but with a hint of stubbornness about it, of good-natured evasion, of guarded retreat. Perhaps this withdrawal was an inevitable corollary of his integrity. Aunt Maria tells us that:

He never lied and was totally devoid of cunning or slyness. These qualities were inborn, there was never any need to influence him in this respect. Apart from this, he was a very proud child. It was extremely difficult to persuade him to ask pardon; he did not like to wheedle or to indulge in cupboard love as many children do.... If anything revolted him, then he could never overcome his revulsion, if anything attracted him, the attraction was irresistible. So it was till the end and, when life itself began to bend him, he broke.[24]

As a child and all his life long, Blok's sole defences against life were humour, irony, and—silence. Characteristic in this respect is the sad story of his French lessons. When she considered Sasha old enough to do without a nanny, his mother followed the family tradition and engaged a French governess, for the first time when he was seven years old, and, as a second attempt, when he was nine. 'But he never learnt to converse in French for the simple reason that, even then, he hardly conversed at all even in Russian.'[25]

The boy accepted his stepfather unquestioningly—indeed with rather less resentment than he had accepted the occasional visit from his father, in whom as a small child he had evidently sensed some kind of threat.[°] Family relationships did not interest him. His mother attributed this to heredity:

... if you love him, do not expect sentiments of him ... That's the way he is. He has it from his father and his mother. I, too, am an unfeeling, or, as some people say, a 'soulless' person.... Sasha lives by passions and by the spirit. That has been so since his very earliest years. Sentiments have always been alien to him. Judge as you will, drop him from your acquaintance, but don't look to gather figs from a thornbush,[26]

she once wrote to her son's greatest friend. To many 'countries', as he later called them, of the spirit and the imagination, Sasha's mother had now become his most trusted guide, but these were countries into which Frants Feliksovich did not intrude. He also, of course, loved her most tenderly for herself, but love seems at that time to have been an all-embracing charitable radiance spread over his entire circle: his family, Nanny Sonya, the family doctor, dogs, cats, and horses, rather than an affair of possessive emotion or jealousy. His stepfather was, as the brother of Aunt Sofia's husband and the uncle of Ferol and Andryusha, already within the orbit of this general benevolence. True Frants Feliksovich did nothing to draw Sasha out or to introduce him to a more manly world: both Aleksandra and Andrey Beketov were disappointed in his lack of paternal instinct, but there is no evidence that Sasha himself gave the problem any thought at all.

His stepfather was a kind, honourable, conventional army officer who suffered from poor health (kidney trouble and weak lungs), and was passionately interested in the affairs of his regiment and in little else. The only taste he seems to have shared with his wife and stepson was a great love of animals. 'The puss-cats', Blok wrote his grandmother during his third winter in his stepfather's flat in the Grenadier Barracks, 'often stroll through all the rooms and eat lots, especially

---

[°] One of his earliest memories was of sticking a pin into Aleksandr L'vovich's arm as the latter sat talking to his mother. Since his father came to Petersburg no oftener than twice a year, the sense of menace soon faded, to be replaced by bored indifference.

the big one, who swallows a chicken-bone in one second whenever Frants and I give her one....'[27] These puss-cats, and the dogs Boy and Norka, the latter described as 'very hideous' and the former as having 'long ears, a sad face and yellow eyebrows',[28] form the background to a cosy, traditional way of life in which Frants figures benevolently.

If anybody was jealous, it was Frants; he was, however, quite prepared to tolerate Aleksandra's son, although, unlike the Beketovs, he was of the 'seen-and-not-heard' school and offended his wife by not allowing Sasha to pursue his many games and interests all over his apartment as the Beketovs had done. Sasha, somewhat puzzled but too proud to need telling twice and not unduly upset, 'began to keep to his own corner'.[29]

He now for the first time had a room of his own where he could, if he felt like it, entertain children of his own age, such as Visha Grek, another officer's son, and a little girl called Natasha Ivanova, or could simply get on with whatever happened to be absorbing his interest at the moment. Beyond providing batmen as baby-sitters when he took his wife out in the evenings, finding a soldier in his regiment to give Sasha lessons in book-binding, and being pleasant to the child at table, his stepfather made no attempt to enter into these interests.

Aleksandra, somewhat daunted, now found herself more fully responsible for her son than she had been in her father's family. Sasha, for his part, accepted Frants, superficially and unthinkingly, just as he later accepted Aunt Katya's death, neglecting even to mention her in the autobiographical poem *Retribution*, in which he grants Professor Beketov only three daughters, the oldest of whom is obviously Sofia, and gives his mother the fairy-tale position of 'youngest'. He had loved 'Katyulya' and she had given him much but, for him, she was simply an integral part of his delightful, hazy childhood.

His mother's marriage did not break the continuity of this childhood. Summers, as before, were spent at Shakhmatovo. There was, however, one very important change.

The boy's winter home was now the Grenadier Barracks, which stand to this day, flanked by the same ugly red-brick factory whose 'yellow windows' were to exercise such a baleful fascination over the young poet in later years. The Barracks were situated in a part of St. Petersburg very different from the original centre of government, the Vasilievsky Island, on which the Rector's house where Blok was born and his paternal grandparents' residence both stood, or from the elegant residential areas behind the Summer Gardens which the boy had previously known best. This new situation made a deep impression upon his poetry and, indeed, upon his whole outlook.

The Petrogradskaya Storona[p] is one of the large, low-lying islands in the Neva delta on which Petersburg was originally built, the island where the eighteenth-century city centre meets the industrial suburbs. On the shore of the Neva stands the Peter-Paul fortress, one of the oldest architectural complexes of the city. In the circling walls of the bastion are damp, ill-lit cells where political prisoners languished from the time of Peter the Great to the summer and autumn of 1917, when the poet Aleksandr Blok was to work there every day, editing materials from the depositions of Tsarist dignitaries for his report on *The Last Days of the Imperial Regime*. From within the fortress, above the eighteenth-century sepulchre-church containing the tombs of the House of Romanov, a needle-slender golden spire raises a prayerful golden angel high above the flat, grey waters and the granite banks of the city. This is the shore that looks towards the Winter Palace.

The Grenadier Barracks guard the rear approaches to the island. They look over the Bol'shaya Nevka, a busy industrial water-way, as wide or wider than the Thames at Vauxhall, on the far bank of which rise towering factory chimneys. The mists, writhing along rivers and canals, the frozen splinters of damp which appear to swarm about the yellow street-lamps, lend the whole quasi-industrial, quasi-imperial townscape a quality of vaporous illusion. Here, for the first time, Blok's world touched on that of the factory worker, the world of muck and money, of the *nouveaux riches* and the city poor. From the islands opposite the barracks, in 1905, the workers were to march out in procession, and from the barracks Frants, distressed but disciplined, was to lead a detachment of Grenadiers to hold the bridges against them. It was thanks to seventeen winters spent on the Petrogradskaya Storona that Blok grew to know his city in all its tragic division.

In the meantime, 'Frantsik' was included in the Beketov idyll and when, two or three years after Aleksandra's remarriage, her husband's ill-health kept them in Petersburg while Sasha was already revelling in the first strawberries at Shakhmatovo, her son could write with perfect sincerity:

I am missing the III Class, you, Frantsik, and many other things left behind in Petersburg including 'Sidetikon' and ordinary glue.
    When I finish this I'll go and sit with Granny in the dining room.
    Good-bye, my dearest tiny, the Lord be with you.

[p] At that time still called the Peterburgskaya Storona.

Kiss Frantsik, I miss him terribly. Mama my dearest, come as soon as you can—Your

SASHURA[30]

The winter after her marriage, Blok's mother engaged a student to coach Sasha and eighteen months later (September 1891) he entered the Vvedensky School for Boys, an undistinguished academy selected for its closeness to the Barracks on the same island. In winter, Petersburg bridges, long and wind-swept, are death-traps to the delicate and to this day students on the lowest government grants will take a tram for one stop to avoid walking across a bridge in really cold weather. In her anxiety for her son's health, however, Aleksandra Andreyevna had given insufficient thought to the school itself.

CHAPTER II

Éducation sentimentale

(1890–1898)

1

Mama took me to school; for the first time in my life, straight from a
homely and quiet family I found myself in a crowd of close-cropped, loudly
shouting little boys; I was inexpressibly terrified of something, I would
gladly have run away or hidden somewhere; but across the doors of the
classroom, although they stood open, I sensed an unseen line that might
not be overstepped.

I was put to sit at the front desk, right before the teacher's rostrum which
was set hard up against it and which was about to be occupied by the Latin
master. . . . The desk was only intended for two people and I was a third,
this first time, because there was no place for me in the class. Next to me,
looking me over suspiciously, sat completely strange boys. Beyond the
doors I was aware of the long corridor, then the big recreation room, then
some sort of a passage with pillars and a broad staircase with turns in it;
there, somewhere, already approaching and getting nearer every second,
came the terrible teacher; if I make a run for it he will be bound to catch
me somewhere out there and bring me back into the class, and that will
be still worse.

The main thing about this feeling was that I no longer belonged to
myself, that I had been given away to someone and something and that
this was now irrevocable. To give vent to my despair and horror, to express
it by words or movement or simply by tears was unthinkable. False shame
would not allow it.

Sitting absolutely still, I raised my eyes and looked straight ahead of
me. . . .

(VI. 39–40)

So, less than three months after the immense events of October
1917, Blok was to recall his first day at school.

'. . . Later on', Aunt Maria writes, 'he became accustomed to it,
able to cope, but his mother understood her mistake: she should not

have sent him to school direct from such an exceptional environment so young and unprepared."[1]

The school was a day school, not a boarding school, and there was no corporal punishment. Blok was physically strong and tall for his age, and the only time we hear of his being in a fight (in his third year) he seems to have enjoyed it. It would be wrong, therefore, to suppose that, having been reared in a hothouse atmosphere, he was suddenly thrust out into rough and brutal 'real life'.

The world in which Blok found himself was unpleasing rather than cruel. Up till now it had been natural to him to be truthful, chivalrous, brave, and courteous, because this was expected of him. His reading had led him to expect that he would have to venture out into the world and win his spurs. Dragons, dangers, hardships: all these would inevitably await him when he rode out beyond the borders of his domain, away from the beloved protection of his own people whose protector he was, in his turn, to become. He might, probably would, perish in search of 'the promised land', but his end would be tragic and glorious, his immortality—in the continuance of all that he stood for. Such is the symbolism that runs unbroken through his early poetry and through the dreams that he noted in his diary. The symbolism surrounding the persona of the heir and the theme of the quest flowed naturally from his life, more even than from his reading.

Now, however, a crop-headed new boy still quite uncritical of things and people, he had, instead of going on to the next step in this Rousseauesque upbringing by people worthy of respect and emulation, been 'given away' into a world of ugliness and boredom, mediocrity, cupidity, and false values. The result was not rebellion but rejection.

Later Blok became more conscious and critical of his own aliena-tion, but a certain aloof withdrawal, bordering on total disassociation from the vulgarities of early twentieth-century life, became part of his nature. This was, and remained, an outer crust; a stiff, dazzling armour. A successful joke, a flash of sincerity, a shadow of weariness even, and the vizor would be up to reveal a totally unguarded face, a child's merry, confiding smile, a child's uninhibited tenderness.

Meanwhile, for the next eight years, the boy attended the Vve-densky School, and the armour became—almost—a shell.

Two ex-pupils of the school, A. A. Shilov, who was a pupil there from 1891 to 1899, and S. M. Alyansky, who attended the school from 1902 to 1905, gave their recollections of the place to V. N. Knyazhnin, Blok's biographer:

The pupils were children of the lower civil servant class or of the wealthier *meschanstvo*[a] with an extremely low intellectual level. School was something to be got through as an unpleasant and inessential but obligatory chore. The dearest wish of the great majority was, of course, to obtain satisfactory marks without doing any work. Amongst my acquaintances[b] there were types who had managed to sit on the school benches for eleven years instead of eight.... There were others who left to become minor civil servants after only four years. Then there was a third lot who were swallowed whole by the school's near neighbour, the Pavlov Military School, and still others who, after leaving school, having hung about for a year or two on the fringes of the Faculty of Law at the University, volunteered for the armed forces. And these were the best of all possible destinies! For many of the boys simply dropped out of normal society, having begun from their second year or thereabouts to go in for 'street courtships' and, thanks to the nearness of the *café chantant*, ... for an early acquaintance with taverns and all aspects of love.... There was not only no interest in learning as such but virtually none even in reading for its own sake. Even politics which, for some, was a kind of saving revelation—insofar as they offered an albeit illusory semblance of self-education (schoolboy politics in those days always began with self-education) and certain higher spiritual aims—not even politics touched this school.[2]

Blok's own description of the pupils and teachers offers no brighter picture:

... they taught almost exclusively out of textbooks, making no attempt to infuse spirit into them, taught ferociously and pig-headedly, year in, year out, wasting innumerable hours.... The children quickly became debauched. Amongst us there were several sick, stupid and weak-minded. We learnt to smoke, our talk and drawings were full of indecencies. By the time they were halfway through school many boys were already having affairs.... The masters and teachers were all, I think, without exception, unhappy people: poor, overloaded with lessons, humiliated by the directors.

It was only the Latin teacher 'of whom everyone, including myself, was more frightened than any of the others', who awoke the boy's sympathy. 'I suspect he was always hungry, which helped to make him ultra-sensitive, as there were among us several wealthy boys with watch chains, sprouting moustaches and specially tailored jackets....' The poor Latin teacher, afflicted with chronic toothache and unsightly blackheads, abode in a state of 'permanent fury'. 'Yet', the poet added on the wondering note of compassion he always had

[a] Lower middle class.
[b] Knyazhnin does not make it clear whether he is here quoting Shilov or Alyansky.

for the sociologically, or physically, disadvantaged: 'he was, essentially, a very timid, shy, and morally clean person' (VI. 41–3).

Whether Blok's liking for the Latin master was due to his interest in Latin and the ease with which he soon came to construe the classics or the other way about, it is hard to say. Certainly Greek and Latin were his favourite subjects at school and later he bore the unmistakable marks of a 'classics man'. Especially he loved the strong dignity of 'the solemn Latin' (III. 99) and the epigraphs from the Roman poets to several of his books of verse and to individual poems were more than a scholarly conceit.

In other subjects Blok was a very average pupil. Frankly weak in mathematics, he did not shine at all in the junior school, even earning, in one of his reports, the patronizing comment that 'Blok needs help in Russian language'. His mother's letters to her mother during his fourth year at school are full of tolerant and rather amused complaints of the difficulty of making her son work.

Now that we are home again Sashura is supposed to be swotting history, i.e. on the sofa, yawning, Ilovaysky in hand, he is distracting me from writing this letter. Since yesterday we have sprouted small wings, very small as yet. The head told me that, if he has two 4's in the main subjects in his annual report, there is no need even to make a special request that he should be moved up without examination. They will move him up automatically. Now everything depends on Surovtsev, the Russian teacher. And so yesterday I went to see him and asked if there was any hope of Sashura getting a 4 in his subject in his annual report. To begin with he talked a lot of pious rubbish of an Orthodox character, complaining that Sashura had written a poor essay on 'The Significance of Cyril and Methodius in the History of Enlightenment' whereas the school chapel is dedicated to Cyril and Methodius. I felt like tearing him to pieces for this, but I was polite and sweet to the highest degree and, in the end, he said that Blok was not such a bad boy, quite bright, and that he presumed there would be no objection to his being moved up without an examination. Now on the morning of 16 May, they will announce the names of all the pupils who are to move up without an examination. Sashura, in the meantime, has no wish whatsoever to spend these last three days studying and, instead of revising Ilovaysky, has taken his Christmas tree rabbit from the window and is grooming it with his own brush and comb, assuring me that he, Sashura, that is, not the rabbit, has already lost weight from his efforts. All this boils down to the hope that we may be able to get away' next week, perhaps all three of us.[3]

In the next letter she is less sanguine:

' To Shakhmatovo.

It is still not clear how Sashura's affairs are going. .... He has been told to revise everything carefully, but he just gazes out of the windows at the steamers, sulks when we implore him to work and, when I tried revising with him from the book, it turned out that there really is a lot he doesn't know, yet still he sulks. All these troubles of ours should soon be over and then we shall breathe freely if only we don't have to hang about here until the beginning of June, trembling at the prospect of exams. .... But Sashurka worries me. From time to time he comes to me in his new felt slippers with his shaven head and mutters various comforting things, such as that the books he is expected to learn from are 'full of dreadfully stupid things and there's no understanding them'.—I don't argue and in my heart I admit that, if not exactly stupid, then *Russian Literature in its Most Ancient Monuments* is at best a cruel bore, but what is one to do when so much depends on it?[4]

This particular incident ended happily, when Blok, to his own exuberant and ill-deserved delight, was moved up without an exam, and the whole family was able to leave for Shakhmatovo as planned.

Yet even as the boy approached his final examinations three years later there was little change in the tone of his mother's letters:

I am sitting at home waiting for Sashura, who has gone out for a walk, to come home and take tea with me. We are both for an early bed tonight as tomorrow he has Divinity. Sashura has swotted quite a lot but, on his own admission, is very hazy about that same Divinity. I cannot tell whether he really knows it or not because, as you know, there is no getting any very precise answers out of him on such subjects.[5]

Then, a week later:

Yesterday he received a contemptible 3 for History. We intended to reproach him and make him feel ashamed of himself but all this broke up on an indifference and sang-froid worthy of a better object.[6]

The next letter announced with relief that the final examinations would be over by 29 May and that the family hoped to leave for Shakhmatovo on 1 June:

I must tell you that he is just managing to scrape through them and I long for him to get them over as soon as possible because he is quite pale and thin, not from revising or hard work, but from sheer terror.[7]

Blok, in other words, did not live up to his father's gold metal from the high school of Novgorod or to the formidable academic achievements of other members of his family.[d] He had the lowest

[d] His matriculation certificate from the Vvedensky School attests that 'Aleksandr Blok of the Orthodox Faith, son of a State Councillor, born 16 November 1880 in St. Petersburg, studied for seven years in the St. Petersburg Vvedensky School' where, 'on the basis of

opinion of his school, which he described as 'dreadfully plebeian' and quite alien to his own 'thoughts, manners and feelings'.[8] Indeed his one idea was to bag a seat by the wall and 'lie low'. In this he was obviously aided and abetted, albeit within the bounds of decorum, by his mother, whose main concern throughout term-time was clearly 'to get it over as soon as possible' and to escape to Shakhmatovo, where she felt her son to be living not only a happier but a truer and fuller life.

Whether a father's guidance could have combated the dreariness of the Vvedensky School is open to doubt. As it was, the Beketovs were indulgent, Frants Feliksovich uninterested. Aleksandr L'vovich provided 300 roubles a year for his son's maintenance, in return for which he required from Aleksandra a precise account of the spending of the money and of Sasha's progress, which she sent him punctiliously. This formal financial dependence, however, does not seem to have opened the doors to paternal influence. The dry, incisive pedantry, the sheer capacity for hard work, the masculine element of willpower that characterized Aleksandr L'vovich were never imposed from without upon his son. Very gradually, in a much softened form, they did emerge in the poet's own character, at first under the beneficial influence of the University, where in the course of the next six or seven years he was to prove himself a first-class scholar, and later in the strength of the demands made upon him by life itself and by his own sense of duty and vocation.

Meanwhile neither Blok nor the Beketovs cared two hoots for the dull school. His real education, 'the *éducation sentimentale* of a Russian gentleman', as he called it himself, went on at home: at Shakhmatovo and within the family circle in St. Petersburg.

2

A slender boy, with wavy fair hair, merry, mischievous, sociable in childhood; more and more reserved with the years, withdrawing himself from people and from the 'philistine' circumstances of daily life, at times downright dour—there is the portrait of Sasha Blok. His open, serene smile was replaced by a constant slightly melancholy and even ironic expression—turned to everything and to almost everyone in his environment. Sasha's character in youth was gentle and self-controlled, his flashes of acerbity were comparatively rare.[9]

observation throughout the time of his studies ... his conduct has on the whole been excellent and his written work satisfactory, his industriousness good and his love of learning very considerable in all subjects of the school course'. According to the detailed list of marks, the only subject in which he appears to have distinguished himself was the seemingly quite irrelevant one of Mathematical Geography.

So Blok was remembered by Sofia's elder son, his cousin Feliks (Ferol) Kublitsky-Piottukh. The half-Polish Ferol, who grew up to be a very cultivated European gentleman and never really forgave Blok for writing *The Twelve*, was three years his junior; his brother Andryusha was five years younger than Blok and a deaf-mute. 'At first', Maria Beketova tells us, 'the cousins made themselves understood by signs, then a teacher from the deaf and dumb institute taught Andryusha to speak and lip-read.' Here too Sasha fell naturally into the role of the heir, the future head of the clan. 'He never quarrelled with his cousins. He was fond of them: never wounded their pride, never showed off and, even in play, never knocked them about.'[10]

In the winter two other pairs of distant cousins, the Nedzvetskys, connections of the Beketovs, and the Lozinskys, who were relatives on the Kublitsky-Piottukh side, would meet up with Ferol, Andryusha, and Sasha Blok at week-ends and on holidays. A dancing master was engaged by Aunt Sofia and the young people were drilled in all the graces of the ballroom. In Petersburg as at Shakhmatovo Sasha was the undisputed leader, popular all round but hero-worshipped by the youngest members: the lively, affectionate Andryusha—of whom Blok himself always remained extremely fond—and Kolya Lozinsky who, having been brought up to speak better French than Russian, hailed Sasha ecstatically as '*Alexandre trois, notre roi*'. When Sasha's mother took him to visit Aunt Sofia on Saturdays, the children would have the whole house turned upside down in a few moments. While they were small they simply indulged in games of the imagination and pillow fights; as they grew up and began to be taken first to the ballet and then to the theatre, they staged 'plays' and charades. Several members of the family recall the irresistibly absurd impression of Sasha's long schoolboy legs dangling from the top of a solid mahogany wardrobe as he enacted the part of one of Bluebeard's shrinking wives, shrieking for help from the top of her tower.

Of the holidays at Shakhmatovo, Ferol recalls that the first of the clan to depart for the country would be Elizaveta Grigor'evna, who would prepare the household for the coming of the rest of the family. In the second half of May the schoolchildren and their parents would begin to arrive and all those already installed would come out on to the porch to greet each trap-load of new arrivals.

Andrey and Elizaveta Beketov, whose position obliged them to lead a highly social life in Petersburg, saw Shakhmatovo as a retreat where they could relax in the intimacy of their own family circle and intended to keep it so.

It was always emphasized that we live 'in the country' and not 'at a dacha'. The dacha way of life was a synonym for vulgarity. Grandmother Elizaveta Grigor'evna was particularly intolerant on the subject of keeping ourselves to ourselves, being possessed of an exacting and witty though not always impartial gift for summing up other people.... This was a manifestation of that Beketov exclusiveness ... which was to show itself so acutely in the character of Sasha Blok in his later years.[11]

Ferol, who seems to have been a bit of a snob himself, albeit of a very different kind, was here putting his own interpretation on the 'Beketov exclusiveness'. Maria Beketova expresses it differently: 'At that time,' she recalls apologetically, 'we were dreadfully given to ridicule and, being quick to see the funny side of people, often failed to notice their serious qualities.'[12] Blok himself, in his auto-biographical poem *Retribution*, recalls half affectionately, half in exasperation, how the family had 'its own catchwords, its own customs', and how they put 'inverted commas' on everything from the outside world (III. 314).

Like all children, the 'Beketov' boys had crazes, one of the most violent but short-lived being for croquet. Once, when taking a particularly hearty swipe at the ball, Sasha accidentally gave Andryusha a hard knock with his mallet and the small deaf boy insisted loyally through tears and blood: 'It wasn't Sashura's fault, Sashura didn't mean to....' Ferol also recalls that Blok enjoyed doing exercises on a trapeze and rings that were fixed up for the boys' use in the garden and that he loved physical work: digging, trimming, chopping and clearing out shrubbery, 'to the horror of our grandmother who disliked what she considered "excessive" tidiness in gardens and considered that everything was best left as it had been or as it grew naturally.'[13]

As the boys got older, they were allowed to ride out alone on horseback and would range about Shakhmatovo to a radius of ten to fifteen kilometres. Sasha loved exploring, 'always tried to get further away, to new places, along little-used forest roads, to discover new views and distances....' The boys would set out in the cool of the evening and would often return, Ferol remembered, with the darkness:

The red, full moon would be rising, the white mist lying like a shroud along the river and creeping up towards the house. On the way home we liked to have races which, of course, was not at all good for the tired horses. Sasha usually beat me and my brother on his larger gray mount, known as 'Malchik'. It was not a quiet horse: when young it had been kept for a long time in a dark stable and its sight was impaired so that it was nervous and often shied violently, but Sasha was accustomed to its tricks and managed it pretty well.[14]

3

It was with the assistance of Ferol and, to a lesser extent, of his second cousins in Petersburg, that Blok embarked upon his next 'journal', *The Messenger*, a serious undertaking which he kept up for more than two years, from 1894 to 1897. The word *Vestnik* (Messenger) and the month and year of each issue were cut out, presumably from the title-page of the journal *Vestnik Inostrannoy Literatury* where Blok's mother and aunts published their translations, and glued on to the cover. Everything was done to make the 'publication' look like a real magazine: there were lists of contents and illustrations, an explanation of the picture on the cover, even advertisements, mostly of a humorous character. The 'editor' of the journal was Aleksandr Blok, the 'censor' A. A. Kublitsky-Piottukh, the contributors Aleksandr Blok, his cousins, and the entire Beketov family. Sasha Blok may have been a lazy schoolboy, but he was a most painstaking editor, and the layout and calligraphy of *The Messenger* is a remarkable achievement for a teen-age boy with many other interesting things to do.

In the issue of *The Messenger* for March 1896, Blok 'published' his first 'scholarly' contribution to the journal, an essay on 'The Origins of Russian Literature' in which he dwelt reverently on the actual process of making and copying books. It obviously pleased him to recall the saintly scholars of times gone by: Euphrosinia, Princess of Polotsk, and Vladimir Vasilkovich, Prince of Volynia, as he applied himself to the monthly task of copying out the family manuscripts, placing titles, underlining, gluing pictures, finishing each separate contribution with a flourishing 'The End'. All his life Aleksandr Blok was to preserve this reverence for the written word. The letters he received were filed away under the name of the correspondent; his own works were catalogued, as was his library; photographs and picture postcards acquired travelling abroad were pasted into albums; he edited and re-edited his own poetry, rearranging, recopying, annotating; his diaries and notebooks, meticulously numbered and dated, he revised and censored before his death, leaving his archive in perfect order. *The Messenger* was Blok's apprenticeship to literature and, like the apprentices of medieval times, he began as a jack-of-all-trades and general dogsbody.

Blok's own literary contributions to his journal were light-hearted in the extreme. The earlier numbers contain some attempts at serious verse. These show a transition to grown-up style as painful and inevitable as the transition from the effortless brilliance of children's drawings to the adolescent's first attempts at perspective and purely visual representation. The child's verses had been delightful in themselves. These are 'promising'—but derivative. Later on, Blok's contributions were limited to translations, drawings, and parodies like the humorous poem in the metre of *Hiawatha* with its memorable opening lines:

> Full of strawberries and fury
> In the verdant kitchen garden
> Stood I midst the blowing woodbine
> On the dusty garden pathway....

Apart from comic verse and parody there were several serialized adventure stories geared to the taste of Andryusha and Kolya and featuring 'a yellow-necked hippopotamus in search of victims' in the South American jungle, or murder and sudden death in the fog-bound London docks. Every type of journalism was assayed, from art reviews to a pompous obituary for the Emperor Alexander III, 'now at rest in the Lord'. The journal provided gossip-column-style news of Shakhmatovo, chronicling such events as the birth of a litter of puppies to Blok's favourite setter bitch, Diana, the celebration of Andrey Beketov's seventieth birthday, and Aleksandr Blok's being thrown from his horse. It also published a play, 'A Journey to Italy', written and performed by the cousins, and reviews of their theatrical efforts.

Of the boys, Ferol, often under the pseudonym 'Parvus', was the most enthusiastic and conscientious contributor. In July 1896 a precocious eleven-year-old second cousin, a relation on the Karelin side of the family, Sergey Solov'ev, made his début with a story of how he spent the day at the home of a holy priest's wife deep in the forest. This warmly, romantically Slavophile piece was unusual for *The Messenger*, but Blok was always ready to indulge his younger cousins. When Sergey, who had a reputation for piety, had first been brought to Shakhmatovo at the age of eight, he had even thought to entertain this new relation by celebrating 'morning liturgy' in the garden. Sergey, who really did grow up to become a priest, was the nephew of the religious philosopher Vladimir Solov'ev and, over the next ten years, he and his family were to play an important part in the development of Blok's thought and poetry. In the meantime, he received for his contribution 'a box of chocolate sardines as a present' and an assurance that a more substantial honorarium would follow.[15] Andryusha Kublitsky-Piottukh also made his literary début that summer: a tragic 'Tale of Three Cocks', written with a supreme disregard for spelling and grammar. Professor Beketov's first and last contribution to *The Messenger* was to illustrate this story, and it is typical of the whole Beketov atmosphere that it should have been made in support of the naturally backward deaf-mute youngest grandson.

The number for December 1896 flaunts a multi-coloured page, the very calligraphy of which seems to shriek with relief, on which it is inscribed that 'The Editor of the journal *The Messenger* has the honour to announce that he does NOT intend to continue publication in 1897.' The letter of resignation which follows gives no explanation, but is complemented by a graceful note from Blok's mother:

With heartfelt sorrow I inform all the subscribers of the termination of the publication of the journal *The Messenger*. This journal has existed for three years and has gradually gone into decline at the wish of the editor himself. The causes of this decline are a mystery. The editor is in a state of despondency.

A. KUBLITSKY-PIOTTUKH. Censor
2 November 1896

The aunts and uncles, who had been greatly entertained by their offsprings' efforts, signed a formal request that *The Messenger* should not go into liquidation, which Blok duly stamped and acknowledged in red crayon 'Deeply touched. A. Blok'. Nevertheless, the journal did not run to more than one further number, memorable only for Blok's drawing, 'A Northern Winter', which anticipates to a remarkable degree many images of *The Twelve*.

Blok's contributions to *The Messenger* and its supplements give little clue to his development as an artist. Indeed, he did not yet think of himself as an artist. In his own eyes, as in his family's, he was rather a local princeling, growing up to excel gracefully at everything he enjoyed doing. Literature was important to him rather as the ability to play the harp and sing songs were important to the heroes of Tannhäuser, but it was not yet a vocation, and the Beketov mentality did not admit the concept of a 'career'. Several years after Blok had left school and entered University, he was still extremely vague about what he wanted to do in life and at the time he gave up *The Messenger*, in his mid-teens, he does not appear to have given the matter any practical consideration whatsoever. There was no spur of boyish

Blok's drawing of a Russian winter, 1897

ambition or competitive effort. At home, Sasha had no rivals. School
he despised. Although he was not insensitive to criticism and later
even said of himself that he was afflicted with 'monstrous pride'[c]
(*Z.K.* 130, entry for January 1909), it was not in Blok's nature to
impose himself on other people, to want to be a leader or to court
popularity.

In this, he was unlike many of his future colleagues: the ambitious
Valeriy Bryusov, for instance, who, at the age of sixteen, had already
determined that there was going to be a Symbolist movement in
Russian literature and that he would be its leader; or his exact contemporary Boris Bugayev (later to be known as Andrey Bely) who,
in Polivanov's excellent School for Boys in Moscow, was already
making a name for himself as a budding genius; unlike even his own
precocious young cousin Sergey Solov'ev, who would have thought
shame to write in anything but the 'new', impressionistic, 'decadent'
style. There had been nothing new or precocious about *The Messenger*. Its editor, luxuriating in a compelling imagination and an
appreciative audience of younger boys, had been indulging in a
purely private, family undertaking, and it petered out naturally
together with his childhood.

4

By the time Blok was sixteen, his day-dreams were veering away
from adventure and schoolboy pranks and jokes towards romance.
Love became the constant topic of his conversations with his
school friends, the son of a wealthy Jewish engineer, Foss, and Koka
Gunn, an artist's son who, like Blok himself, was part German.
Together with Blok's earliest friend from the Grenadier Barracks,
Visha Grek, now an officer cadet who tended to model himself on
Lermontov, these would-be sophisticates would stroll the streets
exchanging ideas and experiences, or forgather at one of their homes
to listen to Foss playing the violin or to Blok reciting. They also
had other rendezvous, singly or together, of a less innocent character,
and the themes that now occupied their minds were scarcely suitable
for a family journal.

Coupled with this new interest in 'love' and romance was Blok's
growing passion for the theatre. Having outgrown the craze for editing, he had gradually developed a new, still more absorbing craze
for declamation.

[c] The word Blok uses is *samolyubiye*, lit, 'self-love'. In Russian, however, it is used
where we would use 'pride' or 'self-regard'.

It had begun with the first time he saw a play, on 16 January 1894:

Today Mummy and I went, just the two of us, to the Aleksandrinsky Theatre and saw *The Fruits of Enlightenment*.... We sat in the stalls in the fifth row. The theatre was so empty that in all the rows in the front there were only eight people, so that we could see everything very well. Today was only the second time I have ever been to the theatre and I find that the ballet *The Sleeping Beauty* is a bore and altogether repulsive compared to it.[16]

By the summer of 1896 when he went with Ferol and Aunt Sofia to see the All-Russian Industrial Fair at Nizhniy-Novgorod, the fifteen-year-old Blok was able to impress his young cousin during the intervals of a provincial performance by talking easily of how this or that artist of the Aleksandrinsky Theatre would have interpreted this or that part.

'A Journey to Italy' and a Kozma Prutkov play staged at Shakhmatovo in this same summer marked the beginning of a positive orgy of private theatricals. Sasha and Ferol, clad in togas made of sheets and with wreaths of real oak leaves, leant picturesquely against white altars before a backdrop of the Acropolis painted 'on a huge piece of white cardboard propped up against a birch tree'. Everybody laughed and the witticisms and non sequiturs of Kozma Prutkov passed into the family vocabulary, particularly into Blok's own, for at this stage he was beginning to hide more and more from the cold curiosity of the outer world and the loving attention of his own people behind a quasi-sophisticated facade of jest. His humour, then as ever, was based on understatement, and he affected a phlegmatic air, talking little and 'through his nose'.

In company, he enjoyed 'taking off' his favourite actors and amused his elders greatly by very slightly exaggerated imitations of the matinée idol of the day, Dalmatov. He excelled, too, at making serious sob stuff, such as Nekrasov's 'The Hospital', sound extraordinarily funny by subtly overpedalling the pathos.

Sasha's gifts, however, were not confined to the comic. At sixteen he was already astonishingly handsome: well made, lean-faced, fair-haired, with a dreamy sweetness about the mouth and eyes and an erect, arrogant carriage. Aptukhtin's 'The Madman' and monologues from Pushkin's *Little Tragedies* formed a part of his repertoire, but it was Shakespeare's great romantic heroes who fascinated him at this time: Hamlet, Othello, Romeo. It seems likely that in these pre-eminently tragic 'declamations' the boy found an outlet for those deeper emotions and perplexities which it would have been quite unthinkable for him to express openly in his own words: for which, indeed, he had as yet no words of his own. Hamlet was his favourite part and the words 'Nymph, in thy orisons be all my sins remembered' he spoke, says Maria Beketova, 'with an indescribable intensity and magic'.[17]

CHAPTER III

Paradise Lost

(1896–1900)

The foundation of every artist's will and faith lies in the subconscious.

(v. 313)

1

Looking back to his youth when planning the poem *Retribution* in 1911, Blok wrote: 'There were no outward events in my hero's biography. He led a quiet life with his family in the Pobedonostsev period. From childhood he had been silent but, ever more insistently, an uneasy, ill-defined excitement was building up within him' (III. 460).

Blok was never in a hurry to grow up and no 'events' intervened to precipitate the process. He wandered in a lyrical haze, then, 'by mistake, one Sunday' he 'lost his soul' ... and found himself groping outcast in 'the lilac mists', the 'hell of art'. The memory, the 'anamnesis' as he himself often called it, using the word in its Platonic sense, of an idyllic childhood free of all constraint, remained with him as a touchstone. It was the first foundation, but the years overlaid it with a dark silt of pride, rebellious sensuality and tragedy, which Blok, like Vladimir Solov'ev before him, considered somehow essential to the growth of art.[a] The 'sense of excitement' of which he wrote was more than the singing of the blood in the veins of a growing boy. It was the beginning of an awareness of the world: neither the dull, ugly world of school and the street nor the enclosed world of family, but of that greater Whole by which the individual and all mankind must ever stand or fall.

Blok's poetry tells the story of his attempt to enter and to understand that greater world. It was not easy and, at seventeen, when

---

[a] In this connection, Blok himself would often quote Solov'ev's lines on 'light from darkness' and the divine roses which could not have grown to flower had they not been rooted in the dark womb of earth. (See VII. 51, III. 24, V. 192, etc.)

he first began to write serious verse, he was not yet prepared to face the fact that to achieve his object he must renounce, inwardly at least, all that he most loved: the homeliness, the serenity and harmony of his childhood, in order 'by way of catastrophes and falls' gradually to emancipate himself 'from the Russian gentleman's *éducation senti-mentale* by the same process as that which transforms coal into diamonds' (III. 298).

This came to him, as things did in those green, horse-drawn days, very slowly, over a period of more than ten years in fact, before, in the play *The Song of Fate*, written in 1908, he was ready to picture himself definitely setting forth from his 'quiet white house' to discover Russia and the world (IV. 104–7).

The 'catastrophes and falls', however, began much earlier. Biographically speaking, the whole process received its first impulse from those 'onsets of despair and irony' which accompanied his 'first thoughts of love at the age of fifteen' (VII. 13), feelings that undoubtedly lie behind his mother's reference to his 'state of despondency' at the beginning of November 1896.

November was always a bad month, for Aleksandr as for Aleksandra. Petersburg, the northern capital of a northern country, has the same latitudes as those Scandinavian lands whose folklore sees the end of the world as the triumph of the frost giants, the coming of eternal winter. For natives of Petersburg, the despair of oncoming winter is the natural symbol of all other despairs. So it was for Blok who, in his bleakest poem, 'A Voice from the Chorus', was to write of 'the cold and dark of days to come' in terms of apocalyptic foreboding, and to associate them first and foremost with a spring that fails and a sun that does not rise (III. 62–3).

As for Aleksandra, 'The winter months were particularly hard for her. She felt worst in November and, like her son, was very quick to feel the approach of spring, which always gave her new vigour.'[1]

The year 1896 was a particularly difficult one for Blok's mother. Up till then, in spite of her depressive temperament and the growing disillusionment with life that set in after her second marriage, she had contrived to put a brave, even a gay face on things. She had, however, sometimes felt doubtful whether she ought not to have reconciled herself to her destiny in the person of her first husband, and was beset by a mounting sense of guilt at having entered into a second marriage. Like many sensitive persons of depressive temperament, she was savage in self-judgement. After her sister's death, Maria Beketova recalled that 'In this case she condemned herself irreprievably and considered that, by entering into this marriage, she had not only deprived her son of all that our family had been able to give him but had made him suffer from the attitude of his step-father and from the milieu into which he had been projected by her caprice.'[2]

The only things that attracted Aleksandra Andreyevna herself in army life were the romantic traditions and ceremonies. Frants Felikso-vich, unimpressive in civilian life, had an excellent seat on a horse and made a fine figure leading out his battalion in full uniform. Watching him at such moments, she could imagine herself in love. But day-to-day routine at the Barracks, the philistine conversations and unsavoury intrigues, Frants's genuine absorption in his career and failure to perceive the dreariness of serving under an oppressive government in time of peace: all these alienated her and made her long for her own family. Frants, 'although definitely superior to the majority of his companions and not at all a vulgarian', shared neither her literary nor her spiritual interests and she felt she had 'no one to advise her about her son'.[3]

When Sasha was eleven years old and Aleksandra in her early thirties, she had expressed this concern in a pathetic little poem:

> Oh Lord, I pray thee, stoop to help
> This suffering soul of mine.
> Nor dreams, nor purpose, nor illusion,
> All, all, is understood, and all
> Now leaves me cold. Life is delusion
> And from life I have taken all.
> And joy was an hallucination.
> Deceit and dreams of untried youth.
> Now, in despair and desperation,
> I've understood this dreadful truth:
> There is no life ... and yet there is
> One dearest flower, my child, my dove—
> My rebel spirit finds in his
> Alone companionship and love....
>
> And when I think the day must come
> For him as well when faith will fly
> And heavy hatred on my son
> Will like a loathsome shadow lie ...
> That thought it is that racks my mind,
> Bends me to earth and leaves me blind
> And groping in a flood of pain

Aleksandra Andreyevna with Blok aged two (1883).

The Rector's house, where Blok was born, and the end of the long main building of St. Petersburg University: photographed in the 1890s.

The Grenadier Barracks, Blok's home from 1889 to 1906, photographed in the 1890s.

A drawing by Blok of the façade of the house at Shakhmatovo, 1898.

View from the front of the house at Shakhmatovo. (From the collection of N. P. Il'in)

Rising so fiercely through my brain
That from its rush my mind grows dark ...
Tortured and broken my poor heart ...
And with my heart's blood ebbs my love.

14 December 1892[4]

At that time Aleksandra was presumably able to keep these moods from her son, but four years later, in that same winter of 1896, she took a turn for the worse and

... began to suffer from epileptoid attacks which were accompanied by preceding periods of insight, began with a brief loss of consciousness and ended in an agonizing state of hopeless misery and a feeling of isolation from the rest of the world approaching insanity. Constant anxiety, a melancholia which at times reached the intensity of suicidal mania, and a growing tendency to take a tragic view of all aspects of life—there is the picture of her condition at that time. Acute pains in the region of the heart together with these violent attacks forced my sister to take medical advice. She was found to be suffering from a clear case of heart disease which was already in an advanced state (underdevelopment of both mitral valves), and carbonaceous mineral spring baths were prescribed.[5]

2

So it came about that, instead of packing up as usual for Shakhmatovo at the end of the summer term of 1897, Sasha Blok escorted his mother and Aunt Maria to the German health resort of Bad Nauheim. Here, the hitherto retiring sixteen-year-old astonished everybody, himself included, by seducing a high-ranking grass widow of Ukrainian origin whose years, though she admitted to a mere thirty-two, actually numbered considerably more than twice his own.

The country life of the Beketovs, their love of animals, their dislike of visitors, etc., all make them sound so 'English' that it comes as rather a shock to find not only the twice-wed and susceptible Aleksandra, but even the staid and virtuous Maria treating the whole affair in a thoroughly 'continental' fashion as a rather charming initiation into the art of love. True, Blok's mother did worry at first, but this Maria writes off as a symptom of her usual over-anxiety for her *detochka*, her 'little child', as she called him till the day of his death. True, also, Maria's unpublished diaries and other papers contain irritable reflections on Sasha's selfishness and complete forgetfulness of his duty to his relatives, on the 'heartlessness' of the lady and her 'unworthy' behaviour in leading him on. In retrospect, however, she presented the affair as a half-comic, half-poetic idyll.

A Russian friend . . . offered to introduce us to . . . Kseniya Mikhailovna Sadovskaya who was unwell, taking the waters and very bored, having no acquaintance in Nauheim. We agreed and were soon introduced to a strikingly handsome lady, obviously on the lookout for *divertissement*. She was a tall, dark-haired woman with an enchanting, delicate profile and . . . magnificent blue eyes. . . . The meeting took place in a pleasant corner of the park where they sold yoghurt. When the introduction had been made and we had sat down about the rustic table with our yoghurt, Kseniya Mikhailovna asked flirtatiously, 'And why has the young man nothing to say for himself?' But the young man in his school shirt was so confused and enchanted by this woman that he had lost all ability to say anything whatsoever. . . .[6]

How it came about Aunt Maria could not tell, but soon Sasha and Kseniya were meeting every day. 'Rising early, Sasha ran to buy her roses, took tickets for the baths for her',[7] after which they 'strolled together about the park, and boated on the lake, when she would sing, which pleased him greatly.'[8]

Aleksandra Andreyevna wrote to her parents in the same vein of tolerant amusement that she adopted towards her son's schoolwork: 'Our Sasha has been a-courting with great success and captured the heart of a *grande dame* of thirty-two, the mother of three children and the wife of an Acting State Counsellor.' 'He courts her most assiduously,' she informed them in another letter,

accompanies her absolutely everywhere. She flirts with him and is gracious. It is comical to see Sashura in this part. With a rose in his buttonhole, carefully dressed, he sets off in her train, carrying her rug or shawl, but his conversation is as often as not confined to nods. I do not know if anything will come of this courtship for Sashura in the sense of making him more grown up, more like a young man. Scarcely . . .[9]

It did and it did not. Maria Beketova's assumption that her nephew resisted Sadovskaya's advances in Bad Nauheim and only became her lover later in Petersburg is not necessarily accurate. Blok's childhood straightforwardness did not pass effortlessly into the 'merciless frankness' of his maturity. There was a period, beginning at about this time or a little earlier and lasting until the breakdown of his 'idyllic' relationship with his young wife and friends had taught him the appalling dangers of deception and self-deception, when he was wholly honest neither with himself nor with other people. It may well be that, questioned too closely by his mother as to his relationship with his 'grande dame', he gave her to understand that he was more seduced than seducing and that nothing had really happened. Certainly, after Nauheim he shrouded the whole affair in romantic secrecy: stolen rendezvous in closed carriages, letters to a Poste Restante address, etc. This may have had more to do with compulsory religious observance at school than with the desire to keep secrets from his family. In the spring of 1898, for instance, he wrote to Sadovskaya:

I cannot wait to see you again until Friday. If you possibly can, come on Thursday, I shall wait for you on the Second Line[b] opposite the house; I need only to see you and to know that you are with me; but on Friday I can't come because I've got to go to confession, and in the evening too. What a strange coincidence. (VIII. 8)

There was, however, not so much deliberate deception about all this as a very real loss of spiritual and emotional bearings. Sadovskaya enchanted him. She was his type: big, spontaneous, and talented rather than intellectual. He was tremendously grateful to her and, after his poor hole-and-corner schoolboy experiences of lust, this elegant, accomplished lady seemed a very goddess. His first serious poetry was written after their coming together and the memory of her returned again and again, culminating in a nostalgic cycle written and entitled 'Twelve Years Later'.

Yet the whole affair had arisen out of boredom and obviously had no future. Even so, it was not until August 1901 that Blok found the courage to make a definite break with the older woman, who had become fond of him and, at one stage, even insulted his youthful pride by offering to pay his fare to revisit Bad Nauheim with her. When he finally made the break, he wrote:

I must warn you that this time I am going to write a quite open and true letter, which is somehow something that has not always happened to me up to now. But still, even then I was not quite false towards you, because I was very doubtful and while I was writing letters I really did feel that emotion which at other times I did not feel any longer, scarcely at all.[10]

And this after he had been sighing for more than three years after the seemingly unattainable charms of Mendeleyev's daughter who all his life, though aware that it was not altogether true,[c] he was to think of as his 'first love'.

In his relationship with Sadovskaya, it was the idea of romance

[b] The streets on the Vasilievsky Ostrov were known as 'Lines' and numbered, not named.
[c] Cf. Z.K. 172–3, entry for September 1910.

(which enchanted him) rather than that of sex (which bothered him and was to bedevil his whole adult life) which Blok chose to dwell upon, and his emotions were, above all, raw material for his acting and poetry. He was rising seventeen and quite intoxicated with the intensity of his own feelings.

3

At Nauheim Blok, whiling away the time spent sipping the waters at 'rustic tables', had filled in a form of 'confession' in which he declared his favourite occupation to be 'the theatre', his ambition to become 'an actor of the Imperial Theatre' (while continuing to live, by the way, at Shakhmatovo); and the manner in which he wished to die: 'On the stage of a heart attack.' Naturally nothing would do for him now that he had really fallen in love but to play Romeo and that same summer of 1897, after the departure of Ferol and Andryusha from Shakhmatovo, he performed the monologue at the bier of Juliet for the edification of his aunt, his mother, and his grandfather. The latter had suffered a stroke while the family were at Nauheim and was now in his second childhood and confined to a wheelchair. He continued, however, to take a lively interest in all that concerned Sasha.

The next summer, school behind him at last, Blok decided to stage the balcony scene at Shakhmatovo. The only available Juliet was 'Auntie Lipa', a friend of Maria Beketova's, a jolly Petersburg schoolmarm in her late thirties whom Blok had always liked for her funniness and good nature, but whose only qualification for the stage was a gift for making people laugh. This, however, did not deter the aspiring Romeo, who rigged up a 'balcony' out of his old apparatus of trapeze and horizontal bars and persuaded his grandmother to sew him a costume. Everyone was delighted with the costume, contrived from an old school uniform and an abundance of pale blue braid, not least Grandmother herself who, in spite of age and infirmity, set out to find (and found) a falcon's feather in the fields behind the house to stick in her beloved grandson's handsome blue bonnet.

All that remained was to begin the play, but this they could not do for some time because the moon hid stubbornly behind the clouds and would not light the scene. The chairs for the ladies had long since been set out along the garden path. It was quite late but Grandfather flatly refused to be put to bed and kept asking when the play was to begin. All of us, with exasperation and hope, watched the moon. At last it emerged from behind the clouds. Then Juliet clambered on to her balcony and assumed a dreamy pose. The audience was summoned and the play began. Romeo spoke with *élan* and tenderness. He was very poetic and totally engrossed in Shakespeare's romantic story, quite oblivious of the down-to-earth intonations of his Juliet. Everything was going smoothly when suddenly something dreadful occurred: on the path leading down to the lawn where Romeo was standing appeared the clumsy form of our huge, shaggy watchdog Arapka who had slipped into the garden from the yard through a wicket gate carelessly left open. His tongue hanging out and breathing heavily as usual in his impenetrable coat, he advanced slowly upon Sasha, innocently wagging his tail, counting on his usual benevolent reception. This interruption absolutely ruined the play. The mood was broken, my sister and I were struggling with uncontrollable giggles and poor Romeo was deeply offended. Naturally he broke off the dialogue and with a distraught and angry face set about driving off Arapka. Of course the dog fled and the wicket gate was carefully latched, but too late. Sasha got into the most dreadful mood, flatly refused to go on with the play and made no further efforts to renew his attempts.[11]

This fiasco was compensated for by visits to Professor Beketov's old friend Dmitriy Ivanovich Mendeleyev whose numerous family, as it turned out, were as keen on theatricals as Sasha Blok. The Beketovs had occasionally visited the Mendeleyevs and the other way round throughout Blok's childhood, but the distance was too great to allow for any intimacy between the children. Indeed, the Mendeleyevs' governess recalls that, on the only occasion that she can remember Grandfather Beketov bringing Blok to call, at the age of fourteen, he was 'too elegant' for his future wife Lyuba and her brother Vanya, and they ran away and hid, leaving the well-brought-up young stranger to the mercy of the governess and the younger children.[12]

A counter-story provided by the sister of Blok's tutor, Maria Gribovskaya, recounts an earlier visit by Mendeleyev to Professor Beketov. This time it was Mendeleyev who brought his nine-year-old daughter Lyubov' to Shakhmatovo, but Sasha Blok had been too busy building Roman aqueducts down by the pond to do much about 'receiving' the little girl, while the two great men, as was their habit, had settled down to talk the world to rights in a haze of pipe smoke.[13]

Now, however, things were very different. Lyubov' Dmitryevna was just sixteen and Blok, in his own eyes at least, an experienced lady-killer. Lyubov', with ambitions to become an actress, could find nothing to interest her in the brothers, cousins and friends who filled the large Mendeleyev household: rather better off and, thanks to the energetic châtelaine Anna Ivanovna, a great deal more sociable than the Beketovs'. Now, in the person of 'Sasha Beketov', who had ridden over to call on them wearing high soft boots and mounted on his spirited white horse, she was presented with the ideal *jeune premier*. He was quite unlike anyone she knew—a sophisticated dandy, he seemed to her, with cold eyes. Yet from the very first moment she was intrigued and solemn. At the same time, she was not prepared to sit back and watch the livelier girls in the house party engaging all the visitor's attention and very soon began with all the 'inward fluids' of her being to seek to attract this attention to herself. 'Outwardly', she wrote not long before her death in 1939,

I was apparently extremely self-contained and cold—Blok always told me and wrote me so afterwards. But this inner activity of mine was not wasted and very soon I began to notice with something like fright that Blok had, yes, he quite definitely had, transferred his attention to me, and that now it was he who was encircling me with attention. Still, as all this was not only unspoken but reserved, repressed, invisible, hidden, it was still always possible to doubt, yes or no? Is it really or does it only seem?[14]

As for Blok, he acquired not only an exquisite leading lady, a whole year and a bit younger than himself, but a full cast of enthusiastic amateurs, a barn which made a very adequate theatre and a large mixed audience which had not known him ever since he was in short coats.

Then there was Lyubov', with her heavy, arched brows, merry button nose and child's eyes, sly and twinkling blue under the severely lowered lids; Lyubov' in a decorous pink blouse, with one thick golden braid hanging down her back in traditional Russian style. When he first saw her coming to meet him through the early summer garden down a sunny avenue of sapling limes, he knew that this was where his experience of love should have begun. . . .

Dazzled, as though before an overwhelming revelation of life as it should have been, he averted his eyes from the too-happy vision, and flung himself into make-believe, into changing the direction of the Boblovo theatricals.

Rather like Blok and his cousins in previous years, the Mendeleyevs had hitherto been content with home-made funny plays. Blok introduced the classics: *Hamlet*, Griboyedov's *Woe from Wit*, and the scene at the fountain from Pushkin's *Boris Godunov*. In all three he played the hero's part. Lyubov' Dmitriyevna acted Ophelia and

Sophia in *Woe From Wit*, but ceded the role of the haughty Polish princess Marina in *Boris Godunov* to an older cousin.

As Ophelia Lyubov' wore a white dress with a square *décolleté* and pale lilac in the slashed sleeves and at the hem. At her belt hung a pearl-embroidered *'aumônière'*. In the mad scene her loose, wavy hair was entwined with wildflowers and cloaked her whole figure to below the knees. In her hands Ophelia held a sheaf of pink hollyhock, convolvulus and wild hops mixed with other wildflowers. The hops had been gathered for the occasion by Hamlet and Ophelia themselves in the forest round Boblovo.[15]

Blok made a stately Hamlet, 'a true Prince of Denmark', according to Lyubov' Dmitriyevna's elder half-sister, who played the Queen. She, too, was impressed with his rendering of 'Nymph, in thy orisons ...': 'He spoke it slowly, slowly, distinctly and prayerfully: a kind of connection with her to whom Hamlet was addressing these words filled them to overflowing with thought and feeling.'[16]

The young people played to an audience of about two hundred made up of friends, relatives, and local peasants. The peasants, accustomed only to clowning at local fairs, thought it their duty to laugh. The greater the pathos of the moment, the harder the actors tried, the louder grew the laughter. This disturbed the audience but does not seem to have broken the enchantment for the performers. Lyubov' and Aleksandr were wholly taken up with some curious shared experience in which the tragedy they were playing foreshadowed the tragedy of their lives.

Lyubov', looking back to the awkwardness and the enchantment of that evening, left this account from behind the scenes:

The first and only bolder step I took towards Blok in those years was the evening we played *Hamlet*. We were already in our costumes as Hamlet and Ophelia. I felt more confident.... We were sitting in the wings half-hidden from the others as the stage was being set. We sat at the edge of the platform. Blok sat on the platform as on a bench, at my feet, because my stool was on the platform itself. We talked about something more personal than usual and the most important thing, the uncanny thing was that I did not avoid him, I looked into his eyes, we were together, we were closer than the words of the conversation. This conversation, lasting about ten minutes, was all our 'romance' in those first years, beyond the experience of the 'actor',beyond the experience of the well-brought-up young lady, in a land of black cloaks, swords and berets, in a land where crazy Ophelia bends above the stream in which she is fated to perish. This conversation remained a real tie between me and Blok when we met later in

town, already totally on the plane of the 'young lady' and 'the student'.
When, still later, we began to drift apart, when I became estranged from
Blok, experiencing my feeling for this 'cold dandy' as a humiliation, I still
said to myself: 'But it did happen.'

There was that one conversation and our return home after it. The way
from the 'theatre'—a hay barn—to the house led through some very young
birch trees, hardly a man's height. The August nights are black in the
Moscow province and 'the stars were unusually large'. Somehow it happened that, still in our costumes (we changed in the house), Blok and I escaped
from all the fuss after the play and, Ophelia and Hamlet still, alone together
we walked off into that uncanny night. We were still in the world of that
same conversation and it was not frightening when straight before us, right
across the wide vault of the sky, a huge, blue-gleaming meteor slowly
traced a long arc. 'Then suddenly, a midnight star was falling'. . . .

Before nature, before the life of nature and its participation in life (or
Fate), Blok and I, as we found out afterwards, breathed in unison. This
blue 'midnight star' had said everything there was to say. It did not matter
that 'the answer was withheld'.—The child Ophelia would not have been
able to put into words anything of that which had just shone forth for a
moment before our eyes and in our hearts.

Our hands did not meet, even, and we looked straight ahead. And we
were sixteen and seventeen years old.[17]

The next night, on 2 August 1898, Blok wrote these verses, which
Lyubov' quotes in full in her memoir:

> I walked in darkness on to cares and laughter,
> Above—the unseen world of spirits shone
> And close behind my thought poured rippling after
> In trill on vibrant trill the feathered nightbirds' song.
> 'Why, why art thou a child?' my thoughts repeated.
> 'Why, why a child?' the nightbird echoed clear
> When in the silent, gloomy, darkened theatre
> The shade of my Ophelia appeared,
> And I, poor Hamlet, like a man enchanted,
> Awaited the reply, the longed-for: yes.
> The answer was withheld, and 'Are you honest?!?!'
> I asked Ophelia in my soul's distress.
> Then suddenly, a midnight star was falling
> And once again the serpent stung my mind . . .
> I walked in darkness, only echo calling:
> 'Why, why, art thou a child, dear love divine?'

> (I. 382,649)

This is the first poem about Lyubov', and the first of the Hamlet
and Ophelia cycle. In spite of the beginner's lapses—the 'feathered

nightbirds' and the double exclamation and interrogation marks—
Blok was beginning to find his voice. The power of music had
entered his poetry and already he was learning to ride the element
and to control it.[d]

4

Lyubov', however, was still a child indeed. Blok saw little of her
over the next few years, and these years, though outwardly uneventful,
were not happy ones.

Aleksandra Andreyevna had been young enough to profit from
the treatment at Bad Nauheim. Her heart condition was alleviated
and her nerves, for the time being, soothed. Nevertheless, this first
serious onset of depression can scarcely have been kept from her son
at the time and must, together with the collapse of his grandfather's
health, have cast a gloom over his home life throughout his eighteenth
year. Conversely, it may well have been worry about her son
that contributed to the rapid degeneration in Aleksandra's condition.
If the affair with Sadovskaya had been disturbing, much more so
was the fact of Sasha's acquaintanceship with the Petersburg brothels
and the consequent threat to his health.

Looking back to his first attempts at serious poetry, which he
began to write in the autumn of 1897 after their return from Bad
Nauheim and at first showed only to his mother, Blok recalled that
'illness' was one of his earliest themes (VII. 339). It is thus a reasonable
assumption—since Blok was singularly healthy in every other respect—that
he was first infected with some form of venereal disease
while still a schoolboy.[e] Whatever the exact chronology of the boy's
recurrent infection, there can be no doubt that its psychological effect
on him was very great. For one thing, in those days treatment was
painful and embarrassing and there was no sure or quick cure.
Although it was not until 1912 that Blok began seriously to suspect
syphilis, he was, as a very young man, under the impression that

[d] He did not publish the poem until 1911 (*Collected Poems*, vol. I). Then he cut out the
eight middle lines, thus almost eliminating the biographical content, but maintained the
connection with *Hamlet* by substituting 'Ophelia mine' in the last line for the original '*divnaya
moya*' (rendered here as 'dear love divine'). What is left is a distilled, highly esoteric
symbolist lyric. Blok's early verse, however, did not improve with cutting. It became too
abstract. Blok himself discovered this only towards the end of his life when he tried to
slash the *Verses about the Most Beautiful Lady* in an effort to reduce them to the austere
laconism of his later work. Then he stopped in time and restored almost all the cuts.

[e] The first definite mention Blok himself makes of venereal disease is in the autumn of
1899.

it would be dangerous and wrong for him to have children and doubtful about his right to marry.

Worse than this, early experience determined his feeling that to have physical intercourse with a woman was necessarily to humiliate her and was essentially the expression of a drive to self-destruction. By association, these elements of 'demonic' self-assertion and despair became a kind of pre-condition to passion. What could the sordid excitements of the brothels have to do with women like Auntie Katya, laughing amidst her laces and flowers and clean linen when he had run in to wake her as a small boy? With his delicate, fanatically cleanly little mother? With the innocent Lyubov' Mendeleyeva?

Lyubov' herself wrote in her reminiscences:

Undoubtedly there had been a physical trauma here. It was no adored mistress who had introduced him to life, but a chance-met, impersonal woman bought for (a night) a few minutes. And the humiliating, tormenting pains ... Aphrodite-Urania^f and Aphrodite of the streets are set apart from one another by a whole abyss. ... Even K.M.S.^{g} did not play the part she should have played, even she was more 'Urania' than was needed for a first meeting to help the youth's love to become love in all its fullness. But for Blok that is how it remained—a dualism which cleft his whole life.[18]

Indeed, looking back at his affair with Sadovskaya when he revisited Bad Nauheim twelve years later, Blok wrote:

My first infatuation, if I am not mistaken, was accompanied by a sweet feeling of repulsion for the sexual act (it is impossible to unite oneself with a very beautiful woman, for that one should choose only those who are plain of face). Perhaps, though, this was so with me before.

(Z.K. 149, undated entry between 20 and 25 June 1909)

So it came about that his relationship with Lyubov' Mendeleyeva fitted so readily into the given archetypal pattern of Hamlet's relationship with Ophelia:

... I did love you once. ... You should not have believed me. For virtue cannot so inoculate our old stock but we shall relish of it. I loved you not. ... Get thee to a Nunnerie. Why wouldst thou be a breeder of sinners? I am myself indifferent honest, but yet I could accuse me of such things, that it were better my mother had not borne me. ... Go to, I'll no more on't, it hath made me mad. I say, we will have no more marriages. ...[19]

^{f} Urania, surname for Aphrodite as she personifies the purest aspect of physical love, was hymned by the German Romantics but does not figure in the pantheon of Blok's poetry. Trying to define the Eternal Feminine in his adolescent diary, he says: 'In Her is all that is pure in Astarte and Aphrodite' (VII. 36).

^{g} i.e. Sadovskaya.

It was this 'physical trauma', never fully realized or understood, rather than any conventional sense of sin (this came much later, was sociological in character and bound up with the theme of retribution and with the refusal of a higher calling), that made such a devastating impression on the mind and physiological reactions of the proud, sensitive boy. Mentally and spiritually, he was totally unequipped to sort out this kind of trouble. In Russia in the 1890s even the Church itself, into whose hands the schools committed the moral upbringing of their charges, had no definite teaching about sex. Prurient rather than puritan, the Orthodox clergy of the day preserved so massive a silence on the subject that a country priest was quoted as complaining that married couples did not know 'whether to spit or make the sign of the Cross before having intercourse'.[20] In theory, if not in practice, secular society tended towards an emancipated hedonism and, as a schoolboy, Blok absorbed the hazy idea that Christian asceticism was unhealthy and tended to gloss over his youthful passions as 'the sunshine of Hellas in me' ... a sunshine which, in his maturity, he was savagely to admit 'never *was* in me' (VII. 342. Entry for 17 (30) August 1918). He was not as ashamed of visiting brothels as an English Protestant boy might have been, nor did he go in fear of hell fire as an Italian Catholic might have done. Indeed, for a young man brought up between the Grenadier Barracks and the Vvedensky School for Boys, the way he took to satisfy the desires of youth was by no means exceptional. Thus it was not so much guilt which haunted Blok's youth, still less fear of exposure, as the sheer ugliness of his experiences and the complete divorce between what he himself called the 'countries' of physical passion and all that had been good and joyful in his life so far.

'I shall never desert you', he wrote hopefully to Sadovskaya in the spring after their first meeting; 'that would be to bury all my best aspirations, to resign all my life to that really dull life, all my youth to that dull, unsightly youth that lies in store for me!'[21] He seems at this time to have accepted this unsightliness as inevitable. Life at school had not equipped him to combat ugliness. Yet life at home had led him to expect beauty. In the 'enlightened' minds of the elder Beketovs there was no place for such concepts as the Fall. To Blok's grandfather, the idea of paradise had remained a reality, not paradise lost but paradise-just-around-the-next-corner, a realm of harmony to be discovered and established by hard-working men of good will and good sense. Although observing the outward conventions of the Orthodox Christianity he nominally professed, he had, like many of his generation, drifted into easy habits of double-think on religious matters—or, as Blok was to put it in *Retribution*, of 'double-belief'. It was no effort to him to regard life with real veneration. The harmony behind the workings of nature: this could be called God. 'So-to-speak Perfection', was the term Andrey Bely said the Moscow professoriate applied to the Deity in converse with their children.

In Beketov's eyes, however, a great mind like Goethe or a courageous revolutionary martyr were a great deal closer to perfection than, say, the village priest at Shakhmatovo with his gross appearance, manners, and appetites. Still further from the ideal of Perfection were the wordly congregations in the great cathedrals of St. Petersburg, which he had frequently been obliged to attend in his official capacity as Rector, and where, as his grandson later wrote, it was hard to tell which was shining brightest: the icons or the soldiers' helmets (VIII. 275).

Blok's mother, the person closest to him throughout his adolescence, had inherited many of her parents' attitudes: their anti-clericalism, their faith in mankind, their apparently unassuming but actually formidable pride. In her case, though, these values were asserted with a touch of Nietzschean pathos: 'We can do everything . . . ,' she once wrote to a friend; 'there is nothing impossible for man. . . . What would be the point of all our ardent strivings if this were not so? Man should set no limits to his desires, or to his efforts to attain them.'[22] Yet her sister tells us that she had a low opinion of humanity in general, 'considering that endless ages would have to pass before man became man indeed and that, for the present, low instincts had the upper hand'.[23]

Given such a view, it was natural that Aleksandra should have been on the look-out for a faith that would help her to span the gulf of scepticism, help mankind to win across the 'endless ages'. Morality in the sense of individual virtue was no lodestar to one of her generation, whose criteria were essentially aesthetic rather than ethical. 'She found it easy to forgive real vices and large-scale shortcomings', but reacted 'with hypersensitive intolerance to all kinds of philistinism, vulgarity, self-satisfaction, satiety and lying'.[24] At family gatherings and on social occasions, Aleksandra showed an increasing tendency to shock people by her unconventional, often paradoxical opinions. She would wittily and ferociously debunk such conventional objects of veneration as the Old Testament, while in the same breath preaching passionately that 'life should be religious', that 'everything, even art itself, should arise out of religion'.[25] It was typical of the Russian Nineties that her search for religious truth was concerned with fullness of being rather than with moral codes; it is equally typical that she was constantly brought up short by an inbred conviction of the transcendental quality of God.

Undoubtedly, Aleksandra talked to and before Blok of her religious quest. She stimulated him to ponder the questions which tormented her and to consider his own problems in the light of these questions, but she had few positive moral values to offer him, for her own were in disarray and she was no authoritarian hypocrite to seek to impose a code in which she did not herself believe.

Blok always avoided talking about religion, but the poems he dedicated to his mother over this period are a kind of dialogue on the very themes of which he was so reluctant to speak. With remarkably protective tenderness, the boy seeks to recall his 'little one' from those desolations where her spirit so often wandered to the 'life and the fire of the heart'. It is Kant's 'starry heaven above', where the stars are 'out of reach' and the moonlight is 'pale, soulless, and empty', that symbolize his mother's religious quest, doomed to failure by the unknowability of God.

Yet it is typical of Blok's poetry that even such 'philosophical' lyrics were suggested by some apprehensible sensual impression: in the case of the poem just quoted, by the warm night sky of Shakhmatovo. The poem immediately preceding 'To My Mother' (1. 7) bears the same date, July 1898, and simply describes the full moon, 'an immutable, wondrous circle', shining silently over the pale meadow before the house and making an apparent desolation of the seething, seeding grasses (1. 6).

Although the models for his early poetry were romantic and neoclassical, Blok's sensibility was already symbolist and the verses are vibrant with unacknowledged awareness of mysterious 'correspondences'. It was these links, intuitively perceived, that were to lead him, over the next few years, to the very threshold of the contemplative life. For the moment, however, nothing could have been further from his thoughts. He was imbued with the Beketov attitudes: hope in man; faith in ultimate perfection; anti-clericalism; modest pride. The universe, he believed, was ultimately harmonious and man fit to rule therein.

Yet there were built-in discrepancies which he now began to discover 'in his blood', for Blok inherited not only his mother's melancholic humour but also the dark legacy of his father's demonic temperament, a legacy that was not consonant with the humane and chivalrous Beketov ethic. The contrast between these deeply personal,

inbred traits and the expectations of early childhood amounted to
an exceptionally conscious experience of paradise lost.

This experience, too, he shared with his mother:

> How will you ever tell what ails us here?
> And, dearest friend, in what will you seek healing?
> Nor you, nor I, when winter fogs are wreathing,
> Can see what gives dominion to despair.

(I. 31)

The Christian concept of a 'second Adam' sent to redeem a fallen
world was something Blok's pride always found it hard to accept;
the individual, he felt, should be the agent of his own salvation, yet
how was this possible if he were also the agent of his own Fall?

This problem of paradise lost and redemption is at the root of all
Blok's preoccupation with Christianity, as it is at the root of his lifelong demonism, of resentment against the Author of perfection who
had permitted him to be deprived of wholeness. In his adolescent
poetry, as later throughout his life, he was unwilling to acknowledge
man's responsibility for the fallen state of the individual, or of
humanity at large.

> And should our minds believe that, on some long-past showing,
> Another's sin robbed rest of all content
> And to the earth our burdened souls has bent
> With toil beyond our strength and loss beyond our knowing?

(I. 31)

Yet no Russian poet, with the possible exception of Lermontov, ever
felt more acutely that sense of loss; and this feeling is strongest in
the early poetry, 'Before the Light'.

5

Inwardly, the years from eighteen to twenty-one were years of great
perplexity, intense spiritual growth and painful concentration. Outwardly, however, they form a rather absurd stretch of sheer dol-
drums in the life of a young man too well-bred, too good-looking,
too physically vigorous and emotionally dreamy to be consistently
miserable. The mask of flippancy had become almost a second skin,
and Blok's contemporaries give us glimpses of a rather affected,
dandified youth trying his wings in grown-up society and posing
self-consciously over the process. 'How picturesquely Sasha smokes,'
one relative whispered to another at a formal family gathering at
the home of his uncle Pyëtr Blok,[26] and his cousin Sergey Solov'ev

remembered him with 'an aureole of golden curls, a rose in his buttonhole and a swagger cane ... on the look-out for fun'.[27]

To have finished school was a genuine emancipation and, since life presented him with no immediate challenge, 'fun' was naturally the order of the day. Shakhmatovo, after all, was not a kingdom that required a dedicated ruler but a summer country house, still quite competently managed by his grandmother. It was the city that claimed Blok's future—and that future looked grey and unattractive.

The next step was obviously the University and Blok elected, as other boys from his school tended to do, to enter the Faculty of Law 'because it was easiest (if one wanted it to be, that is)' (VII. 25). Blok's father, who was only informed of this deplorable reason for opting to follow in his footsteps after his son had decided, three years later, to switch to the Philological Faculty, agreed to finance him through University. In the first of a series of letters giving an account of his academic progress, the boy wrote: 'For the moment I am not thinking about the future and indeed it's early days, I suppose, for me to think about the future' (VIII. 7).

During his first two years as a student, Blok drifted into the social life of his father's family. He made his peace with his grandmother, Ariadna Blok, who had steadfastly refused to have any dealings with her favourite son's undutiful first wife, and made the acquaintance of his cousins, the Kachalovs, who shared his taste for the theatre. Somewhat later he began to visit regularly at the rather starchy home of his uncle Pyëtr, a man with considerable connections in government circles, whose practical function in his nephew's life was to pass on the allowance from Aleksandr L'vovich. Neither these meetings nor his involvement with jurisprudence, however, brought Blok any closer to his father, whom he continued to see only on the latter's Christmas or Easter visits to Petersburg. On these occasions, after his mother's death early in 1900, the Professor stayed with his brother Pyëtr L'vovich and met his son formally, at large family gatherings. Pyëtr L'vovich's son Georgiy, known in the family as Georges, afterwards remembered being rather disappointed in this 'demonic' uncle, who, so it was whispered, had terrorized two wives into fleeing his home. In the family album there had been a photograph of Aleksandr L'vovich in his youth: a melancholy profile with gloomily sunken chin and 'cruel', hooded eyes. But

When he came to stay with us for the first time,[h] I remember his appearance

---

[h] Before 1900, Aleksandr L'vovich had stayed with his mother who was living with the Kachalovs.

was not nearly so impressively infernal as I had imagined. He was not very tall: narrow-shouldered, stooping, with thin hair and a thin beard. He stammered and, most surprisingly of all, he was shy, just like Granny. He would sit in some dark corner, disliked meeting new people, at table was usually silent and, if he did put a word in, would immediately begin to laugh ... an embarrassed, unnatural, sardonic laugh.[28]

Aleksandr L'vovich's son, still unsure of himself in every respect, did not know how to begin to improve his acquaintance with this unprepossessing stranger and had no particular wish to do so. Later, however, he remembered how once or twice he had surprised his father's eyes upon him: ingratiating, benevolent, shy—and quick to look away.

Professor Blok, ironically disapproving of his handsome, aimless offspring, gave him much gratuitous and rather cynical advice, naturally unpalatable. From Warsaw, he sent copies of a course of his own lectures, which his graceless son did not even bother to read. This was a mistake. Cousin Georges, who later also took up the study of law, was quite astonished at the transformation that occurred in Sasha's father when he spoke on his own subject: 'I was dazzled by the extraordinary breadth of learning and the provocative acerbity of his opinions. He spoke with peculiar enthusiasm of Byzantium. It was as though a dark, hidden flame had suddenly blazed up before my eyes.'[29] This 'hidden flame' Blok never saw until it was too late. For the moment, his father merely seemed alien—and dull.

Blok was more interested in the theatre than in his studies or his family. Acting, however, soon disillusioned him. In his first year at University, he joined an amateur dramatic society run, he discovered later, by a notorious police informer. Here, under the pseudonym of Borsky, he played small parts and made his first acquaintance with backstage intrigue. Here also, as he later recalled, 'lustful feelings for the young actresses vented in quite other places ended in illness', a fact which served to emphasize the 'impossibility' of his love for Lyubov' Mendeleyeva and to deepen the awareness of his own outcast condition.

During the summer of 1899, still recovering from a course of treatment, he was forbidden to ride, which necessitated his making undignified visits to Boblovo in a cart. Naturally, his visits became less frequent and Lyubov', suspecting that he had lost interest in her, assumed indifference. Depressed by her severity, he would jolt home through the darkness of the summer night, the bushes on either side of the rutted lane aglint with glow-worms, and through the clip-

clop of his horse's plodding hooves a line came to him which might
serve as the epigraph to all his poetry:

> My only friend—on through the mists of night—
> The road ahead . . .[i]

Only the 'mounting sense of excitement' gave some coherence to
this aimless existence. This excitement found expression in a poetry
which, from the beginning, was confessional in character, not intended for publication: simply an outpouring of perplexity and
vexed, rebellious thoughts. This early poetry, which Blok later
published as a kind of prelude to the *First Volume* under the title
Ante Lucem, has its own theme: the theme of paradise lost, a state
of outcast loneliness grimly endured, which preceded the theme
of salvation of which the Lady is an image. Though often sad and
grey, it is rung through with virile notes of non-acceptance,
resentment and rebellion, whether demonic or angelic it is hard to
tell. On the one hand, the poet is 'in love with destruction' (1. 51).
Yet, as in Lermontov's poetry, the rebellion is that of a proud and
pure spirit which resents incarnation in a tainted world, imprisonment
in a spoilt body. From 1899 onwards, presentiments of a saving
revelation begin to make themselves felt, occasional at first and fleeting, then with ever-increasing power and conviction.

Inextricably bound up with the themes of paradise and the quest
for salvation is the theme of love: love tender, guilty, and sometimes
boyishly cruel—for Sadovskaya; love worshipful and chivalrous—
for Lyubov'; love philosophical and tragic—for Lyubov'-Ophelia.
The Hellenic songs of passion have as yet more of the classical trap-
pings than of the body of lust about them. Many of them, indeed,
are patently 'literary', harking back as far as the first decade of the
nineteenth century, to 'luxurious Batyushkov', the poet of Bacchic
revels. Very occasionally, the demonic note which dominates Blok's
mature poetry of passion is struck with an uncertain beginner's
hand. As in his later poetry, there are echoes of the sentimental
ballads which he always loved, and which Sadovskaya had sung to
him on the lake at Bad Nauheim.

It is, however, not romantic love but the search for God, for salvation or a way to salvation, that lends movement and purpose to this

---

[i] These two lines from the poem 'I am old in heart' (1. 22) have in fact been used by
D. E. Maksimov as the epigraph to his excellent study on 'The Idea of the Road in the
Poetical Consciousness of Al. Blok'. Here, beginning from the *Ante Lucem* verses, Maksimov points out the significance of this idea, expressed not only by repetition of synonyms
such as 'way', 'road', 'path', etc., but also by the frequent use of 'verbs of purposeful movement': 'I go'; 'the soul flies'; 'flies away'; 'sails'; 'seek'; 'aspire'.

early work. To begin with, the prevalent mood is one of anger at
the unattainability of the Deity:

> Life, like a riddle, is dark,
> Life, like a desert, is barren.
> Come then, at passion we'll play
> Some ease there is here from our torment
> Enough, fools, of troubling the sky
> The heavens are utterly silent.
> For you, to discover God here
> To your earthly minds is not given.
> In an empty, unsign-posted sphere
> You will blunder for ever and ever.
>
> .   .   .   .
>
> Come then, at passion we'll play,
> And abandon ourselves to its waves.
> Eternity is not for you.
> And silent is life—as the grave.

(I. 375)

Gradually, however, the 'cold thirst for redemption' grows
stronger and the poetry becomes more like prayer, but still with
angry undertones and back-slidings: 'I do not understand the joy
of heaven'; 'The Lord has not answered my prayer' (I. 65); 'My
cloister, where I languish godlessly'. The poet pictures himself running from this cloister where, 'beneath the molten granite vaults of
reason' there is no air for him to breath. He will plunge into another
kind of burning, the familiar heart of the earth where, though his
brain dissolve in madness, at least it will not simply melt away in
sepulchral darkness:

> And on the earth—my vulgar, healthy planet,
> I shall find all I seek, when I go mad!

(I. 67)

Yet persistently he returns, again and again: 'a smoky torch' 'burning
on the threshold of the ideal' (I. 21); banishing 'inspiration' (I. 64);
'seeking salvation' (I. 68); 'slowly, with heavy tread, and faithful'
(I. 69); tending fires in the mountains (I. 50, 68); swinging censers;
girding himself with a sword (I. 70).

The last symbol—the sword—is significant. It first appears on 6
December 1900 (I. 70) and it marks the passing of the *Ante Lucem*
poetry into the religious poetry of *The Most Beautiful Lady*.

CHAPTER IV

The Covenant

(Autumn 1900–Autumn 1901)

> In our first youth we were given a true covenant. Of the
> soul of the people and of ours, together with theirs reduced
> to ashes, we must say in simple courageous accents: 'May
> they rise again.' Perhaps we ourselves will perish, but the
> dawn of that *first* love will remain.
>
> (v. 435)

1

The mystical explosion which took place in Blok's inner world when
he was on the threshold of manhood had an absolute significance
for him which was more than biographical. Profoundly personal,
a direct result of self-imposed retreat and recollection, it yet represented a breakthrough into the objective and eternal or, as Blok put
it more simply, into 'that which is above and beyond myself' (v.
432).

   Essentially, it was a mystical experience of divine harmony, bound
up with the concept of the Eternal Feminine, Hagia Sophia, the Wisdom of God which is the Old Testament prototype of the Mother
of God, whom 'the Lord possessed in the beginning of His way,
before His works of old—set up from everlasting, from the beginning, ere ever the earth was' (Prov. 8: 22, 23). Yet it was also an
experience of something within the temporal process: the creation's
response to the Creator, the yearning of a spoilt world to be made
whole. For the concept of the Eternal Feminine is that of a *link*
between the human and the divine. The revelation, momentarily
granted, was one of nature as it should be, humanity as it should
be, the cosmos potentially redeemed and restored; the 'world soul'
within all these things growing gently and inevitably, as the corn
in the ear, the child in the womb, towards a new life.

   The other constant inspiration of Blok's poetry, which he called 'demonism', 'eternal masculinity', the impatient demand for 'a miracle before the time was ripe' (v. 435), was at once the antipode and corollary of this passive feminine principle. Somewhere, in the balance of a hair's breadth between the two, it was possible to achieve an art that bordered on religion. The Symbolist ideal was 'myth-making' and Blok noted at the time he was writing of the Most Beautiful Lady that myths 'are flowers of the earth. They retain their scent only to the border of religion. Higher than this, the myth has no place' (VII. 49, entry for 26 June 1902).

> I feel You[a] coming close. The years are passing by me.
> True always to one form, I know that You must come.
> All the horizon flames. The light will surely blind me.
> In longing and in love I watch. And I am dumb.
> All the horizon flames, so close the revelation,
> And yet I fear that You will come in *other* form.
>
> (I. 94)

The final incarnation, possible, perhaps, in life, in its own time, could not be forced in art.

The idea of the world soul romantically revealed as a beautiful, albeit transcendental, Feminine Being came to Blok not direct from the theology in which it was rooted but through his 'worldly' read-ing—particularly of Plato and the poetry of Vladimir Solov'ev. In the summer and autumn of 1900, Blok was reading and rereading the Socratic dialogues in Solov'ev's translation, and he speaks of 'a period of submission to God and Plato' (VII. 324) beginning at about this time. From the dialogues, which he found 'very misty and obscure' (VIII. 13–14, letter of 1 December 1900 to A. L. Blok), he appears to have absorbed a cognitive method suited to his own maxi-malist intellectual requirements and, at the same time, to the free continuation of that *éducation sentimentale* which had influenced him so much more deeply than all his formal studies at school and uni-versity. This was based on two concepts: the concept of ideas as *objec-tive essences*, independent of subjective, empirical experience, which provide at once the basis of true knowledge and the final (ontologi-cal) aspect of experience; and the Socratic concept of the inborn wisdom of the little child which needs to be 'recalled' to the grown man rather than implanted anew. The image of the child, always 'a child of goodness and light', heir by right rather than redemption to the Kingdom of Heaven, innocent of pretension and scoffing

---

[a] Blok always gives the pronouns referring to the Beautiful Lady a capital letter. See note p. 75.

at sophistry, is never far from Blok's thought. The spontaneous re-action of this child within himself is, for him, the touchstone of truth.

The Solov'ev influence was less direct than the Platonic. The idea of the Eternal Feminine was very much in the air at the time. Blok was prepared to receive it by the circumstances of his life, by his new-found idealism, by his reading of the Russian and German Romantics. In 1900, however, he still had only the slightest acquaint-ance with contemporary literature, and it was not so much through reading as through the family connection that he first came into the orbit of Solov'ev's thought.[1]

Nevertheless, it was with his mother's gift of a book of Solov'ev's collected poems, at Easter 1901, that he felt the somewhat hazy con-cept of a supreme feminine principle which was beginning to take shape in his poetry had received the seal of objective confirmation. The older poet's cult of Hagia Sophia, lyrical and worshipful, was yet laced with a romantic irony and desolate self-doubt which brought it right into the orbit of Blok's own experience. At the same time, the philosophic basis was powerfully reasoned in the author's preface to the poems and suspect erotic moments explained away as the necessary subsoil of mystical perception. True, Blok found Solov'ev's theory confusing. He considered for many years that to speak explicitly of the principle of the Eternal Feminine was to lose it, yet to some extent the philosopher's rationalization did help to lend form to his own intuitions. Also, he felt very strongly the 'sweetness and joy' of Solov'ev's ascetic vision and a sense of his own discipleship: 'it was not from scantiness but from abundance that his most rich cup ran over when he died (and a drop fell upon me amongst others)' (VIII. 128).

2

Vladimir Solov'ev was a connection of the Karelin family through his brother Mikhail's wife Olga. Olga (née Kovalenskaya) was the same age as Blok's mother, a professional artist and translator, an ardent disciple of Ruskin and admirer of the British Pre-Raphaelites. Her nervous, depressive temperament had found a precarious equi-librium in a late marriage to the historian Mikhail Solov'ev. Their only child, the precocious, devout Sergey who had once earned a box of chocolate sardines for his contribution to Blok's Messenger, hero-worshipped his cousin. Their mothers, too, were good friends. Aleksandra had a natural sympathy for Olga's temperamental difficulties and they shared a lively, typically 'Karelin' sense of the ridiculous. Aleksandra, moreover, had great faith in Olga's aesthetic judgement and it was to her, when Sasha Blok was still a schoolboy, that Aleksandra confided her growing love of Baudelaire and her interest in 'decadent' Russian literature, particularly in Zinaida Hippius and Dmitriy Merezhkovsky, the literary couple who, in the course of the 1890s, had become acknowledged leaders of aesthetic taste and of the 'new religious consciousness'[b] in St. Petersburg. Olga, loyal to her brother-in-law who rather disapproved of Merezhkovsky's neo-pagan ideas on religion, and herself devoted to classical health and clarity, replied that poetry should be 'harmonious' and 'sacred', whereas Zinaida Hippius, for all her talent, was 'morbid, somehow, and twisted'.[2]

Yet, in spite of her dislike of decadence, Olga's home was destined to become the nursery of the second generation of Russian Symbolism. In the autumn of 1897, she informed Aleksandra who was evidently still insisting on her affinity with Symbolism:

We read a lot of all that kind of thing here in the family; our rising generation, Sergey and his friend Borya Bugayev,[c] who, by the way, is already seventeen years old, are up to their eyes in the poets. It's rather early for Sergey, but what can one do? He is extremely fond of Borya and Borya is directly involved with it all. What a pity Sasha is not here, then we would have an actor too. On top of everything else there are constant rehearsals going on. Bless them, they might as well amuse themselves.[3]

Olga's wish to see Blok amongst her summer guests had been fulfilled in the following year. In the summer of 1898 he had finally torn himself away from Shakhmatovo to make the short but wearisome journey, twenty-eight versts in horse-drawn vehicles over bumpy cart tracks, to Dedovo, the home of Aleksandra Grigor'evna Kovalenskaya, Olga's mother and his own great-aunt. Here, Olga, Mikhail, and Sergey Solov'ev spent their summers as part of a large family gathering but living, as Blok wrote home to his mother, 'retired in their own annexe'.[4] Such loose-knit country-house summers were very much in the style set by Blok's own grandmother at Shakhmatovo, so that the poet's first impressions of the people

[b] The Merezhkovskys' 'new religious consciousness' was essentially an attempt to include the whole natural world, including human history, culture, and the exact sciences, in the sphere of religion. During the '90s they evolved from the idea of a 'synthesis' of classic paganism with Christianity to a new interpretation of Christianity itself.
[c] Boris Nikolayevich Bugayev, later to achieve a reputation equal to Blok's own under the pen name Andrey Bely.

who were to mean so much to him over the next four years were relaxed and domestic.

Indeed, to judge from Blok's letters home and his later recollections of the visit, he spent most of his time on that visit to Dedovo deliberately turning the head of a schoolgirl cousin with whom he had arrived, very smart and carefree, in a governess cart. 'Twice in the evening we have been out walking together rather too long for propriety—which she enjoyed very much because we walked arm-in-arm so that she felt herself to be quite the grown-up young lady....'[5] However, coming so soon after his conquest of Sadovskaya at Bad Nauheim and the thrilling ambiguity of the Hamlet–Ophelia relationship with Lyubov' Mendeleyeva, this insipid flirtation soon palled. Dedovo amateur theatricals also seemed rather tame after the Boblovo performances, although the aspiring *jeune premier* was not above relishing the impression he produced on a new audience.

Amidst the gaiety and bustle of his brief stay, Blok did not find time to accord the elder Solov'evs more than a passing approbation. Eventually, he found their reserve and quiet integrity very attractive—but this was not until the eve of his departure. So he returned to Shakhmatovo bearing with him a ruefully amused letter from Olga to his mother:

I expect you're wondering why I don't write more about Sasha. I haven't really got to know him from the inside, but from the outside I find him extremely handsome. I do so love that type, just like a Van Dyck portrait.... I couldn't get to know him because he's always on the go and very much in demand and it would be such a bore for him. Sergey is in ecstasies over him and in his eyes Sasha has become *the* authority on every conceivable question.[6]

Emboldened by her cousin's interest, Aleksandra sent her some of Blok's verses. Olga responded warmly but, true to her predilection for classical sobriety, at once sounded a warning: 'It seems to me that one should not step into a magic circle deliberately; the essence of the magic is that one suddenly finds oneself in the circle without realizing or understanding how it came about.'[7]

After this, Aleksandra continued to consult Olga about Sasha's fluctuating artistic ambitions. In spite of the apparent frivolity of their first meeting, contact with Vladimir Solov'ev's relatives gradually introduced a new and important influence into the boy's whole way of thinking. Even thanks to this frivolity, perhaps, the influence, though basically serious, was altogether summery, informal, joyous.

The last years of the philosopher's life were full of mystery, premonitions, and poetry and it was this aspect of Solov'ev that Blok discovered and came to love through Olga, Mikhail, and Sergey. He saw him not, as did many other writers of the time, as a dry, ascetic figure, but rather as a harbinger of abundant eschatological fulfilment. The philosopher's famous laugh—'generous, not corrosive, which he seemed to have absorbed into himself *par excellence* from all the other Solov'evs—Blok saw as 'one of the most essential elements' (VIII. 127) of his vision, and later, after unsuccessful attempts to wade through Solov'ev's theoretical works, he was to find a partial explanation for their lack of appeal in the idea that, while writing them, the venerable philosopher had 'suppressed the laughter in himself and turned away for a moment from childish games' (VIII. 129).

Once, Blok caught a brief glimpse of the man himself—at a relative's funeral in February 1900:

His body towering so high above the crowd that it took a whole moment for my eyes to travel upwards before they were brought up short by his own. Probably my soul was in my face, because Solov'ev returned my stare with a long, blue-grey look. I shall never forget it—the air was that colour too.

Afterwards I followed the coffin, walking behind Solov'ev, and saw the shabby old yellow fur on the disgraceful coat and the steely mane of hair. There were light snowflakes dancing—but he walked bare-headed.

(VIII. 128)

Years later, Blok still recalled with distaste how his uncle, the dapper Adam Kublitsky-Piottukh, beside whom he happened to be walking in the wake of the gangling philosopher, had muttered contemptuously: '*Ekaya oryasina!*' ('Great blockhead!') (VI. 446, 685; VIII. 128).

A few months after that encounter, in July 1900, Vladimir Solov'ev died. That summer, Blok again went to stay with Mikhail and Olga. At nineteen, he was already a very different person. The thrill of finding himself free at last from his long indenture at school had worn off. Disillusionment with the grown-up world—the stage, the University, the social life of Petersburg—had already set in. His romance with Lyubov' was in abeyance. For a large part of that summer, she was away from Boblovo, staying with relatives. The boy's quieter mood and philosophical reading opened the way to a closer relationship. After his visit Olga wrote to Aleksandra: 'We got on very well with your Sasha. We Solov'evs consider that he now belongs not only to you but, in part at least, to us.'[8]

It was in the autumn of 1900 that, on a wave of returning health, both physical and mental, the first devotional notes began to sound through Blok's *Ante Lucem* verses. Olga Solov'ev's next letter, dated 3 September 1900, recorded a momentous incident in the history of Russian Symbolism:

I want to begin by telling you some very agreeable news. Sasha's verses have produced an extraordinary, almost incomprehensible, startling, immense impression on Borya Bugayev, whose opinion we value very much and whom I consider to have the best understanding of all our acquaintance. Borya showed the verses to his friend Petrovsky,[d] a very strange, mystical and fantastic young man, and they had the same effect on him. What Borya actually said about the verses is better not passed on because it sounds too exaggerated, but it gave me pleasure and I think would have pleased you too. More than before, even, I would advise Sasha to send them to *Mir Iskusstva* or to Bryusov.[e9]

With this letter she enclosed three poems by Borya, characteristically entitled 'Though it be misty at daybreak', 'Tender is the paling east', and 'Know you the night is now failing?'.

So it came about that, at the turn of the century, the future Symbolists began to recognize one another, and the sign under which they met was the sign of change and renewal, of the imminent end of a long night and of approaching dawn. It was also the sign of Vladimir Solov'ev. To his admirers and disciples,[f] Solov'ev stood not only for eschatological mysticism and the cult of the Eternal Feminine. He stood also for clear thinking, religious moderation, and the desire, at least, for spiritual health and harmony. From its inception, the Solov'ev group adopted Olga's mistrust of the 'formless decadence' of St. Petersburg: of the aesthetic set which had formed around *Mir Iskusstva* and of the Merezhkovskys' new religious consciousness—even though they admitted a closer relationship to these than to any other contemporary trends and were prepared to enter into temporary tactical alliances with them. The hallmark of the Solov'evites was, from the outset, their profound conviction that their 'symbols' were not mere literary devices but stood for a noumenal reality. This conviction accounts for the 'startling', 'immense', 'exaggerated' impression produced on Bely by Blok's verse. For

[d] A. S. Petrovsky (1881–1959), a life-long friend of Andrey Bely, was at the time studying to become a priest in the Theological Seminary at Zagorsk. Later, like Bely, he took to anthroposophy.

[e] In 1900, Diaghilev's journal *Mir Iskusstva* (The World of Art) in Petersburg and Bryusov's newly formed publishing house Skorpion in Moscow were the only outlets for Symbolist work, which had not yet acquired literary respectability.

[f] Aleksandr Blok, Borya Bugayev, Sergey Solov'ev, and a small group of Bugayev's Moscow friends who later called themselves the Argonauts.

them both, this moment of recognition was the first intimation of 'the objective significancc' of 'thc noumenal quality of that power which had made our despondency bloom into hope' (VII. 346).

At the time, however, this was a purely private moment: it had nothing to do with 'literature' in Verlaine's sense of the word. Valeriy Bryusov, although he also had begun to visit at the Solov'evs', was for Sasha Blok in the autumn of 1900 an illustrious figure on the periphery of his acquaintance to whose notice he could not yet aspire. Instead, having no knowledge of the literary world and emboldened by his aunt's approval, Blok took two poems—one of them the terrible and prophetic 'Hamayun—bird of ill omen' inspired by a picture by the *Mir Iskusstva* artist Viktor Vasnetsov—to show to his grandfather's old friend V. P. Ostrogorsky, editor of the liberal journal *Mir Bozhiy*. So innocent was he in the ways of the world, that he simply walked into the editorial office without introduction and, too shy to announce himself as Andrey Beketov's grandson, slapped down the verses on Ostrogorsky's desk. The old man looked them over, heaved himself from his chair, and escorted the strange student to the door, telling him 'with benevolent ferocity' that he ought to be ashamed of himself to be writing such stuff when undergraduate politics were in a state of ferment and 'God knows what' was going on at the University (VII. 14). Outside in the cold autumn rain, Blok decided not to risk any more such humiliating experiences, and made no further attempt to publish for a full year.

Instead, he retired still deeper into his 'submission to God and Plato' and continued to live and to write poetry far from the hurly-burly of literary politics.

3

The year 1901, the first of the new century, was a key year for the whole of Blok's life, and not for his alone but for that of the whole Symbolist movement in Russia. Looking back from beyond the watershed of revolution, Blok was to maintain objectively that 'January 1901 already stood under quite a different sign from December 1900, ... the very beginning of the century was filled with essentially new auguries and presentiments' (VI. 154–5).

Subjectively, it was during the summer of 1901—which he called his 'mystic summer'—that Blok's discovery of his great theme of the Most Beautiful Lady led him to think of poetry as a kind of service and of himself as an artist, a status he was later to define as that of 'a man in bondage' (v. 403). The year also marked the irrevocable confirmation of his love for Lyubov' Mendeleyeva and, in so far as she became closely identified with the transcendent heroine of his poetry, predetermined the tortured course of their relationship.

To all appearances, however, January 1901 began ordinarily enough with the usual whirl of Christmas and New Year visits. It was not until things had calmed down somewhat that, on the 25th of the month, the first poem of the *Verses about the Most Beautiful Lady* came to Blok on 'an evening stroll down Monetnaya Street in a quite *extraordinary* state of mind' (VII. 243):

> I went out. Slowly there descended
> The winter twilight on the earth
> The young happenings of days gone by
> Came trustfully out of the dark.
> Came and stood behind my shoulders,
> And sang with the wind of spring ...
> And I walked with quiet steps,
> Perceiving eternity in the depths.
>
> (I. 75)

This moment of recollection heralded the approach of revelation, as yet unidentified. Only in the last verse of the next poem, which continues the theme of the singing winds of spring, is the voice on the wind that of a person (the intimate singular 'thy songs' [*pesny tvoi*] replaces the formal plural 'your'). The person is unspecified and is not here given a capital letter,[g] but it is noteworthy that the singing already awakes a lyrical rather than a contemplative response. The poet pictures himself as a stringed instrument, usually associated in Blok's poetry with yearning, sensuous love, weeping 'timidly, darkly and deeply' at the sound of the resonant singing. By the beginning of February, the singing voice, now linked with Paschal presentiments of Resurrection, is sounding a disturbing summons amongst the cold blue snows of the regimental churchyard: already 'She appears distinctly' (VII. 243).

Right from the beginning, however, there is a feeling of intense spiritual vigilance. The poet is straining every nerve to catch at something real but elusive. From the outset, he was later to remember, he had instinctively felt that She was 'flying away' (VII. 243) to some

---

[g] Blok's use of capital letters for the Lady led his first editor (P. P. Pertsov of *Novyy Put'*) to resort to a trick to avoid being banned for blasphemy. Alterations after preliminary censorship were forbidden, except for the correction of printers' errors, so Pertsov deliberately had the censor's copy set with lower-case pronouns and only raised the initial letters after the poetry was passed for publication.

greater task than that of revealing Herself to individuals, moving towards 'the manifestation of Herself in history'. This was a torment to him, as is evident from the verse: the poet feels that his very devotion bars Her way: *Her* desires are 'not of this world'; She is always retreating, lost somewhere in heights of 'sounding silence'; Her steps are 'distant'. Now and again, though, She comes very close and seems to bless him. The youth feels himself to be Her prophet, the wielder of the golden sword, the guardian of some immense and solemn mystery. At other times, the ardour of his prayer is such that the poetry itself becomes almost formless:

> God! God!
> O believe my prayer,
> In it my soul is burning!
> Deliver thine exhausted servant
> From the unequal battle.

(I. 79)

The struggle for concentration, for religious perception, is here so strenuous that he has no energy left to find aesthetically convincing form. It is earthly dreams that inspire poetry, but it is only when the poet renounces these and ventures into 'cold, dumb countries where there is neither love nor spring', where even 'a mother will not recognize her son', that, on the threshold of despair, he catches the longed-for echo of the Lady's distant steps and glimpses something of Her lofty purposes (I. 87).

His mother's gift of Solov'ev's poems, the coming of spring and the Easter season coincided to confirm Blok in his mystical intuitions. Struggling with uncongenial revision for examinations in law, he wrote to a new friend, Aleksandr Hippius,[h] quoting from Solov'ev's verses, 'neither about Easter nor the spring but, to my mind, well-suited to both', and joking with unwontedly Orthodox religious feeling: 'most likely you too are bogged down in your impressions of Ecclesiastical Law and so hardly in a state to profit from the "Light" of this coming Easter which really does seem to me to be "full of light"'.[10]

That year, Blok managed to pass his examinations with rather more distinction than usual, obtaining only one 3, in the History of Russian Law; a 4 (to his own astonishment) in Statistics; a 4 in Criminal Law; and a 5 in Roman Law. In one sphere of student life, however, his alienation persisted. Intense political unrest amongst the

---

[h] A fellow student who became a lifelong friend; he later occupied a modest place in literature under the pseudonym Al. Nadezhdin (d. 1942).

students, which came to a head that spring in demonstrations, boy-
cotts, and arrests, left him totally unmoved. Now and throughout
his University career he considered such goings-on thoroughly
absurd: an abuse of privilege rather than a genuine struggle against
injustice.

As spring slipped into summer, and particularly after Blok finally
escaped from the troublesome examinations and social distractions
of Petersburg to Shakhmatovo,[i] a new fullness and confidence began
to inform his poetry. There was a perhaps deceptive easing of
the struggle for religious inspiration. His diction took on a richer
solemnity. Slavonicisms became more frequent, as always in Russian
poetry when it aspires to religious heights, and the Beautiful Lady
herself is felt not so much as a wraith-like presence above the 'blue
snows' of the Petersburg graves, as embodied in the Russian landscape, in the fate and history of Russia, and in Lyubov', who was,
for Blok, herself an embodiment of that countryside they had both
known and loved since childhood.

> And then I seemed to see the Russian Venus,
> Draped in a pleated tunic's heavy folds,
> Impassive chastity and sorrow beyond measure
> In the calm dreaming of her features' mould.
>
> (I. 91)

This was the first poem of the mystic summer.

The 'aimless and beautiful existence' (VIII. 138) which Blok was
leading at Shakhmatovo seems to have led to a blossoming of effortless perceptions and insights. At one with nature, as throughout his
boyhood, he was no longer troubled by the dualistic nature of his
inspiration, although it was still implicit in all he wrote. Working
in the garden, riding far afield on his white horse, playing with Diana
and the other dogs, his senses alert yet relaxed, he no longer needed
to strain after 'pure' contemplation. For a brief while, he did
recapture the wisdom of the little child, perceiving eternity in the
present, paradise in momentary glimpses of the natural world, and—
above all—in his idyllic courtship of Lyubov'.

4

Since the summer of 1898 when, as Hamlet and Ophelia, Aleksandr
and Lyubov' had established their first tenuous relationship, they had

---

[i] Blok left for Shakhmatovo after his last examination on 22 May 1901.

continued to meet from time to time on a purely social basis. Lyubov'
had left school and, more to assert her independence than from any
serious desire to study, had enrolled in the Bestuzhev Courses[j] which
at that time offered Russian women an opportunity for further
education still denied them by the universities. There she subscribed
wholeheartedly to the exuberantly emancipated attitudes current
among young lady students of the time. Blok's impeccable appearance no longer found favour with her. His student's uniform with
its striking but unfashionable light blue collar was made to measure
by Frants Feliksovich's military tailor. His reddish-gold hair, which
had been close-clipped at school, now clustered round the disdainful
Teutonic face in luxuriant loose curls like a Greek god's, too long
for a man of action, too tidy for a real intellectual. His eyes, brooding
and grey-green under light, fine-drawn brows, she found positively
repellent, for she was accustomed to the heavy dark brows and
bright, animated gaze of her own family. Blok's manners, moreover,
were of a piece with his appearance. Lyubov' thought him over-
sophisticated, did not know how to answer his puns and paradoxes,
never quite knew when he intended irony, when he was serious. One
way and another, she had made up her mind that she must have
been mistaken in imagining this abominably cold and frivolous
young man, this typical Petersburg stuffed-shirt-in-the making, to
have been in love with her. Aggrieved and piqued in spite of herself,
she began to affect a disdainful indifference which had the unexpected
effect of placing her on the loftiest pinnacle of Blok's private esteem.
Together with his own probably unacknowledged shames and
doubts, it had been more than sufficient to keep him at arm's length
over the intervening two years.

Since these two years had also been a time of intense self-absorption and uncertainty for Blok himself, a time when he was gradually
shedding his old, uncritical schoolboy attitudes and acquiring a new
sense of direction and purpose, it had probably suited him very well
to adore Lyubov' at a safe distance. The relationship made no
demands on his time or thought, but was still able to stir him to
occasional poetry and to serve as a convenient emotional counterbalance to his waning passion for Sadovskaya. Lyubov' occupied a
secluded corner of his soul, a kind of 'secret garden' into which he
ventured at will and without obligation. This was precious to him,
but for all she knew he might never have spared her a thought.

Nevertheless, being very much a woman and a creature of instinct,

---

[j] Founded by Blok's grandfather, Andrey Beketov, but called after his colleague Bestuzhev, whose reputation was more acceptable.

Lyubov' had, of course, *felt* some unusual quality in Blok's attitude towards her. This troubled and vexed her more than she cared to admit, even to herself, but for some time she had been successful in putting it out of her mind.

It was not until she was almost nineteen years old that she became fully aware of herself as a woman. At this time she took to standing (draped and undraped) before a long mirror, admiring the purity of her skin, the voluptuous, virginal curves of her statuesque body, the magnificent cloak of golden hair and the vivid colouring of her face. This was the time when Isadora Duncan was propagating her aesthetic ideal of the free human body, when literature throughout Europe was celebrating a kind of neo-pagan emancipation of the flesh. Young ladies were casting off their corsets and dress designers, after decades of whalebone and padding, were going in for flowing, natural lines. Lyubov' was modern, wished to be fashionable, and believed herself to be emancipated. The daughter of 'enlightened' parents, she had friends in the world of art and was ambitious to become an actress. At the same time, she was in fact a remarkably sheltered, innocent girl just waking up to the possibilities of physical love.

In the summer of 1900 Anna Ivanovna had taken her daughter on a trip to Paris where, for the first time, she experienced the delight of new clothes the cut and colour of which really did something for her own highly individual style of beauty. Her self-confidence soared.

That winter, Blok had happened to run into mother and daughter at the theatre. Lyubov', glowing with a new bloom very different from the gauche enchantment she had exercised as Ophelia, wearing a blue-grey Parisian jacket which set off her marvellous colouring, was sufficiently in love with herself not to be thrown into confusion by Blok's apparent reserve. She sensed a change in him, too. He was simpler, more serious. The affected dandyism had vanished. In its place was a gentle concentration, an impression of profound reserve beneath the ever correct, well-mannered surface: not of deliberate withdrawal, but simply of depths. She liked him and had no hesitation in inviting him to call at her parents' home. When he did so, she liked him still more. They became natural together and discovered a number of common interests. As was *de rigueur* at that time, Lyubov's mother was present throughout the visit and Blok spoke more to her than to the daughter. But Lyubov' felt that all he said was for her benefit and *what* he said, particularly about the new trends in literature and art, interested her very much. Diffident and eager to learn, Lyubov' was at her best in the role of sympathetic listener. Blok left the Mendeleyev apartment more in love than ever before.

From the beginning of the summer of 1901 he began again to ride regularly to Boblovo—the pretext, as in 1898, being amateur theatricals. This summer, however, they were indeed nothing but a pretext. It was a year of extraordinary sunsets and sunrises. Alone in her room, Lyubov' would kneel at the window, watching the breathtaking permutations of light, awed and prayerful. To Blok, the splendours of the sky came as signs and portents; their rose and gold glows through all the poetry of the 'mystic summer'.

Certainly they were in love. Lyubov' always instinctively knew when Blok would come and took care to be sitting alone on the veranda. When, having stabled his horse, he came running lightly up the stairs to seek her out, she would be sitting there as if by chance, turning a sprig of verbena in her calm white hands, and they would stroll out into the garden or further afield into the woods and meadows. He quoted poetry to her and one day she said with certainty: 'But you wrote that yourself, didn't you?' After that he brought her everything he wrote. By the autumn she told him she believed him to be a great poet—as great as Fet,[k] a sacred name for them both—and, 'as at that time everything we said to one another was in absolute earnest and completely honest', it was, for her, a solemn declaration and, for him, the final confirmation of his calling. For the poet, Lyubov' was the perfect foil, the ideal companion of his 'mystic summer'; but she was to remember ruefully many years after his death how he 'never asked me for my verbena, nor did we once lose our way amongst the flowering shrubs'.

Yet there were compensations. Her pride found solace in the knowledge that theirs was no commonplace romance. Most of the verses Blok showed her she knew to be her own, inspired by her, unthinkable, even, without her. This lent a breathless excitement to their talk of poetry, to the walks and conversations which were almost immediately re-echoed and transformed in his verse. In a few poems, however, she did not recognize herself[l] and, from the outset, a new anguish entered her life which was to become a constant part of her being: 'that resentful jealousy that women feel towards art'.

Meanwhile, Blok's magnetism, that very power of suggestion

[k] Pseudonym for Afanasiy Shenshin (1820–92), one of Russia's greatest lyric poets, whose particular gift was to express moments of intense empathy between man and nature.
[l] The first of these, 'Quietly the evening shadows' (1. 77), definitely foreshadows the cold, snowy imagery of 'The Stranger' and Faina. The other poem, 'A new radiance floods the sky' (1. 456), is more conventionally religious.

which as a child had always assured him the leading role in games
of the imagination, was so compelling that, for the time being, it
overcame all her doubts.

Little by little I was drawn into this world where I already had my place,
or perhaps not I, but where everything was singing, everything half-
expressed, where these verses in some way or another all had their origin
in me. By these roundabout ways, half-statements and hints, Blok was giving me to understand something and I surrendered myself to the strange
enchantment of our relationship. Something resembling love but in fact
nothing but literary conversations, a retirement from life into another life,
into a shimmer of ideas, of singing images. Often I found words that he
had actually said to me in the poems. But still there were times when, with
a disappointed little smile, I would throw away that scarlet verbena of mine,
which had faded and lost its subtle aroma as unheeded as ... as that blessed
summer's day.''

These warm, idle, blessed days were probably the happiest of the
poet's life. He was as sublimely unconcerned with future problems
as with past wretchedness. The present was enough. He was in love,
he had found his vocation, the whole world around him was tense
with expectation, vibrant with hope. In the evening, God walked
in the garden. Aleksandr and Lyubov' knew that this was so, even
if they did not actually speak with Him. And so the year 1901 became
and remained 'of primary significance' for all Blok's work: ' "that
magic crystal" through which I first beheld, albeit "indistinctly" all
the "distance of a free romance" ' (I. 560).

Blok's letters throughout the spring and summer clearly show his
state of mind. 'The spring has felt its strength and is affecting my
own mood to the highest degree', he wrote his father in May (VIII.
16); and, a month later, to A. V. Hippius:

Lately I too have been no stranger to truly splendid moods, which up to
now used to visit me but seldom. I have been particularly struck by the
countryside all of which, at first glance, appears transformed. Everything,
however, is as it was, except for a few cuttings made through the surrounding forests which, by the way, have opened up some magnificent views.
When I realized that nothing had changed I was delighted all over again
for that very reason. One way and another there is a great deal to tell that
is good. ... I lead a largely contemplative existence. Yesterday I rode over
for the first time to the Mendeleyevs' when there was talk of a play on 29
June (St. Peter's Day) with a liberal message (for the people). But even
this no longer gets on my nerves. There will be a lot of drunks, I suppose,
and only a fraction of the play will actually be staged. I returned late at

night under a steady fall of rain. Even that I enjoyed, because all the time
on the horizon you could see a pale strip of sunset, a promise of good
weather to come.

(VIII. 16)

On 25 June he was already writing of three plays in which he was
to take part at Boblovo. Discreetly, he said nothing of his leading
lady....

Besides the riding hither and thither and the rehearsing ('all
of which I thoroughly enjoy') he was reading Flaubert and
Merezhkovsky's *Eternal Companions*, a book which provided him
with an excellent transition from the appreciation of familiar classics
to the acceptance of the basic tenets of Merezhkovsky's thought and
aesthetics. For his own amusement he was translating Renan's *Herod
the Great* and idly dipping into Pushkin and Vladimir Solov'ev.
Bryusov's first almanac, *Severnye Tsvety I*, opened his eyes on the
existence of a Russian school of Symbolist poetry.[m] Mystical insights,
'beyond the compass of the mind', visited him frequently; 'often I
feel a great lift of spirit which gives me intense happiness' (VIII. 17–
18).

A letter of 28 July tells cheerfully of a series of unrealized projects
for acting scenes from Shakespeare at neighbouring houses and of
a month's heat and drought: it breathes a summery timelessness, a
profoundly contented *far niente* which is at the same time 'very
joyous and very tense'. Blok refused Hippius's invitation to join him
at the seaside

because there is no money and, mainly, because I am attached to this part
of the world. There are only four of us[n] here at Shakhmatovo and for me
to leave would create too noticeable a gap. But that could be overcome.
The thing is that at the moment I am held here by a mystic magnet; to
go against this now would, I think, be a great sin against my own nature,
for it draws me more powerfully than ever before; and in this I feel a drastic
sense of impending change. You, of course, have the same inclination as
I have to idealize your own wishes (if it is acceptable to use the word 'idealize') and so you will understand....

(VIII. 20)

Two weeks later Blok was telling his friend of his 'discovery' of
Gogol and of a visit to the Solov'evs where he had found out much

---

[m] From 1901 onwards, Bryusov's publishing house Skorpion began to bring out its own
yearly almanac of new writing, borrowing Pushkin's title *Severnye Tsvety* (Northern
Flowers).

[n] Blok, his mother, and his grandparents.

Severnye Tsvety: cover of the 1903 issue in which Blok's first cycle for this almanac was published

that was new to him about the 'sovereign of his thoughts' and had
been deeply impressed by some verses written shortly before the philosopher's death and not yet published.

It was not until the summer was almost over and life beginning
to make specific demands on him again that this unforgettable, unrepeatable serenity began to cloud over: 'there is no longer the same
clarity and freedom from doubt. Neither is this evident in the facts
of my life . . .' (VIII. 23–4). He began purposely to drive out thought
by physical work (digging in the garden), and was beginning to feel
the time had come to return to Petersburg. References in his letters
to Hippius to the 'struggle against the flesh' show that this was a
familiar theme to the two young men and one on which they
thought much alike, encouraging one another to overcome temptation almost like a couple of postulant monks. Blok's last letter to
his friend before rejoining him for the autumn term in St. Petersburg
ends with the exclamation, 'But there must be darkness, too' (VIII.
241) and a quotation from Vladimir Solov'ev:

> Light from darkness. Up from the black earth
> The faces of thy roses
> Could not spring,
> If their dark roots were not embedded deep
> To draw their nourishment
> From that dim womb.[12]

In Lyubov's eyes, he had perceived a 'fatal flame' from which, re-
specting the taboo he himself had set between them, he steadfastly
concealed the 'kindred blaze' (I. 123) in his own. For a postulant,
this was playing with fire indeed. . . .

Rather pathetically, Lyubov' made a last attempt to impress him
before they both returned to town. 'I remember the goodbyes,' Blok
wrote in 1918. 'Lyubov' Dmitriyevna came down to take farewell
of me in the drawing room (a cold, bright autumn) with powder
on her face' (VII. 345).

5

Though the 'mystic summer' drew to a close, in Blok's poetry it
lives on as the nucleus of the *Verses about the Most Beautiful Lady*:
'The village of Shakhmatovo. Summer and autumn 1901.' This
poetry lacks the technical excitements of Blok's *Second Volume*, the
power and deceptively simple perfection of the *Third Volume*. Blok

himself was conscious of this and later[o] made a number of alterations 'more felicitous from the literary point of view', but finally restored the original readings[p] because he found the revision 'detrimental to the basic meaning' (I. 561).

The poetry of the 'mystic summer' has a beauty of its own. It is entirely unforced, 'given', convincing. It reads like one continuous meditation; melodious and visually evocative. The verses invoke landscapes and skyscapes which are spacious, horizontal, unconfined. There are echoes from other poets, but they are the echoes of voices heard and assimilated in some early dream: a cadence from a lullaby, a war song or folksong borne faintly on the breeze past the ears of a small boy absorbed in his own affairs—long since forgotten, never analysed but ever present in a lyrical subconscious haze on which the poet is here drawing for the first time. Not derivative, as much of Blok's earlier poetry had been, and—unlike much of his later work—totally inimitable, these verses are intensely personal: the poetry of a very young man on the threshold of life, of a passive listener full of latent power and tense expectations, of one who awaits a summons.

The settings are real, as in almost all Blok's poetry. They relate to his riding to and from Boblovo: the darkness before the dawn, the guiding stars, the curling white ground mists, sunset and sunrise. The core of the poetry is light: spiritual, transcendental and natural, imminent light. Even the sadness—not all the poems are joyful—is luminous. Later, the white mists will condense and turn into the Petersburg fogs, the hard, merciless rain, the blizzards and driving snows of his later poetry. The fall, the call, the departure from home and from Lyubov' herself are all foreshadowed in these verses, already inevitable. The 'distant thunder' on the poet's road will grow to the deafening roar of 'the collapse of the old world', which he was to hear when writing *The Twelve* in 1918. The theme of sorcery, the awareness of a hostile familiar or double, the 'mystic' idea of an alliance 'with nature against people'[q]—all are adumbrated in this enchanted poetic landscape through which, at a rocking canter, passes the eager figure of a real young man on a real white horse. Yet these are present only as dim shadows in misty sunlight, and the general impression remains one of intense radiance.

[o] In the second, much fuller edition of the poems published in January 1911.

[p] When preparing a third edition in 1918.

[q] Blok's definition of mysticism, as opposed to religion, made in his notebooks in 1906 (*Z.K.* 72–4). Cf. particularly two poems written in May 1901, 'All being and existence in accord' (I. 88) and 'They sound aloud and they rejoice' (I. 92).

The only other persona in this poetic country is Lyubov'. She has her real habitation on the high hill behind the jagged forests. She 'blooms alone', she is 'strong in azure', she looks out over a limitless landscape 'of sea and field and hill and forest' where birds 'cry to one another in the free heights, the mist rises and the skies glow red'. She is half identified with the mysterious Lady whose elusive singing and circling and flower-strewn procession to some distant goal place her infinitely beyond the poet's reach. Yet she is at the same time what she was indeed, a young girl just awakening to love who stood hand in hand with him upon some kind of threshold to contemplate the mystery and terror of life, a being all too full of drowsy joy, destined to lead another life and to seek after other ways than the 'hopeless road' of her lover. The signs and portents of the time, emanating, as Blok believed, from the stirrings of the World Soul, the Most Beautiful Lady, are above and beyond them both. Before Her immensity their figures dwindle to those of two beautiful, awe-struck children, 'servants of an impossible freedom', standing silent and reverent before 'an infinite mystery'.

The poet, however, remained solitary in his acute awareness of the fragility of this moment, doomed to pass 'into something other than itself' and to leave nothing behind but poetry. Yet this poetry he always looked upon as the record of his 'true covenant'. In the year of his death he said to his mother: 'I wrote only the *First Volume* ...'[13] and, to Nadezhda Pavlovich: 'These are the only poems I still love.'[14]

CHAPTER V

The Muster of Russian Symbolism

(Autumn 1901–Autumn 1902)

You are in sole possession of a treasure, but somewhere near by there are others who know about this treasure (or perhaps it only seems to you that they know, but that for the moment is immaterial to you). Hence the concept of us–we: a few initiates, Symbolists.

From the moment that these principles are seen to have taken root in the souls of several people Symbolism is born, a school arises. This is early youth, the childhood freshness of the first discoveries. Here, for the time being, no one is yet sure what world the other is occupying, he does not even know this for certain of himself; there is merely a general exchange of 'significant glances', agreeing only on the fact that a schism exists between this world and 'other worlds'; united forces marshal to the defense of these 'other' worlds, as yet unexplored. . . .

It was as though we had all been led up into a high mountain, from which we were shown all the kingdoms of the earth, bathed in the unexampled radiance of the lilac sunset; we surrendered ourselves to the sunset, lovely as queens but not beautiful as kings, and fled the ascetic challenge [podvig].[a] That was why it was so easy for the uninitiated to plunge down in our wake; that *is why Symbolism has become suspect*. . . .

(v. 426–7, 435)

1

That autumn Blok and his mother returned to St. Petersburg together on 10 September. On the train, they shared a carriage with

[a] The Russian word *podvig* cannot be translated by any one English word, as its meaning may be positive or negative according to context: i.e. it can mean either a heroic deed or an act of renunciation. Either way it involves asceticism: the subjection and training of self. I have interpreted it as I have understood it, according to context.

Mikhail Solov'ev who spoke of Borya Bugayev and his interest in Blok's verses. Probably they told him of the decision Blok had taken that August to transfer from the Faculty of Law to the Philological Faculty. Aleksandra Andreyevna approved heartily, but Aleksandr L'vovich had still to be informed. Evidently the son thought it more politic to confront his father with a *fait accompli*. The formalities took some time and it was not until 29 September, over a fortnight after his arrival in town, that Blok wrote his absent parent:

Now, in Petersburg, I have finally made up my mind to this most important step and have already handed in my request for a transfer to the Rector, of which I hasten to inform you as of an important change in my life.... My late laziness and irresponsibility have now passed off and instead I feel very definitely drawn towards philological studies for which, by the way, I now have a very tolerable grounding thanks to having worked through the first two years[b] of the Law Faculty's syllabus. The feeling that my studies were really necessary has hitherto been lacking and I could not envisage any (practical) aims in the future because I was terribly alienated from all that should in fact have been in complete harmony with my natural inclinations. Mama upholds me very much in my decision. I would like to know what you think about it. I have already begun to attend lectures. Regular studies begin as from Tuesday.

(VIII. 24–25)

Fortunately, Aleksandr L'vovich did not object to his son's sudden change of course. Blok's next letter (dated 16 October) gives an unusually uninhibited account of his lectures and the pleasure he takes in the harmony now reigning between his private interests and his studies (philosophy, Euripides, Greek poetry), and ends: 'I am so glad that you have reacted so sympathetically to my transfer.' For the first time, he offers his father a sample of his poetry: 'one of my latest poems' (VIII. 25–7).[c]

This willingness to risk his caustic father's judgement shows a considerable gain in self-confidence. Sure now of his vocation, Blok was suddenly anxious to learn. The letters describing his changed attitude to his studies were not designed to curry parental favour: they told no more than the truth. Throughout the ensuing year he attended lectures regularly, taking tidy, systematic notes even on the dullest and least frequented courses. Quiet, conspicuously neat and clean,

---

[b] Blok had taken three years to do this: from autumn 1898 to autumn 1901.

[c] The poem Blok included was 'Early morning. Unseen in the way' (I. 128), written on 4 October 1901 and later selected by B. V. Nikol'sky for publication in a collection of Petersburg University students' work (see p. 89). Nikol'sky insisted on the removal of the last stanza of the poem.

he moved among his fellow students with a gentle aloofness, still very much absorbed in his own inner world.

The only attempt he made to integrate with University social life was to join a circle of undergraduate poets who forgathered at the home of a University lecturer, B. V. Nikol'sky, an ambitious man of ultra-conservative opinions who had hit on poetry as a method of achieving popularity among the students. Here Blok made the acquaintance of Sergey Gorodetsky, a young poet who drew much on Russian folklore, and of Leonid Semyënov, an ardent monarchist who became a fairly frequent visitor to the Barracks. From the other aspiring poets, however, he remained aloof, though when the circle decided to publish its own collection of verse edited by Nikol'sky, he submitted several poems. A month or two later Nikol'sky had got around to selecting three contributions from 'that pathetic semi-decadent Blok'[1] and summoned him to discuss certain alterations on Sunday evening, 17 February 1902. He found Blok a likeable young man hopelessly led astray by the seductions of decadence and noted in his diary:

I sought to sober him up with all the vehement persuasiveness I have at my command in cases of this kind. There is, of course, no convincing such people, I know that very well myself; as well try to talk a syphilitic into getting well! But at least it is possible to persuade them to take treatment. And something of this sort I have achieved. When all's said and done it is a great bore for me. My God, what a bore! You waste energy, talent, time—and to what purpose? To knock some sense into foolish young boys of whom either nothing at all will come or very little.[2]

In the end, this grudging pedagogue lost the distinction of becoming Blok's first publisher, producing two or three poems, somewhat mauled and curtailed, in his *Literary-Artistic Collection by Students of St. Petersburg University*, which did not come out until the spring of 1903, after Blok had made his début in the professional 'decadent' press with cycles of poetry in the Merezhkovskys' *Novyy Put'* (The New Way)[d] and Bryusov's *Severnye Tsvety*.

As before, Blok continued to live an intense inner life. From the autumn of 1901 he again began to keep regular notebooks and diaries. These are full of thoughts about the modernist or decadent movement in literature, of which, influenced by his summer reading of *Severnye Tsvety* and Merezhkovsky's *Eternal Companions*, he was beginning to feel himself a part. His first note on the subject records

---

[d] The journal founded by the Merezhkovskys and D. Filosofov to disseminate their 'new religious consciousness'; it was published from 1903 to 1904.

the opinion, far from universally accepted at the time, that in Russia 'the new poetry' (he first called it 'decadence' then crossed this out) stemmed not from Western Europe but from Fet, Tyutchev, Solov'ev, and 'ideas', and 'was called into being by our historical and other requirements'. From the outset, Blok set himself the task of 'distinguishing the general trend of the new poetry from the individual particularities of decadence'. Under the date 30 October 1901 there is a conspectus of a lecture by Ivanov-Razumnik in which the latter makes much the same point, defining decadence as limited, subjective individualism and foretelling the inevitable collapse of true decadence—as opposed to 'innovation'.

Blok's reading lists for the winter of 1901–2 include, besides University set books and the Russian classics, all the fashionable names in the new Russian poetry (Bal'mont, Merezhkovsky, Fofanov, Minsky, Sologub, Bryusov, Zinaida Hippius, and others) and show that he was reading everything on which he could lay hands in the periodical press concerning contemporary literature. In the diary, begun in December 1901, this new interest found expression in an attempted analysis of the literary situation (VII. 21–37). Here, too, Blok set out to prove that the new poetry was neither more nor less than a return to the religious wellspring of all true culture. Modern poetry, he wrote, had three great themes: the Eternal Feminine, which Blok here saw as the *link* between the earthly and the divine; the suffering Christ; and the Devil. From this it is clear how profoundly he must at this time have been under the influence of the Merezhkovskys' writing and how startlingly unprepared to cope with this influence he had been left by all the compulsory religion at school. Like Zinaida Hippius in the story *The Mirrors*, which had been the first 'decadent' work to come his way,[e] and like Dmitriy Merezhkovsky in the works he had been reading over the summer and autumn of 1901, Blok actually equated the Devil with God: the two abysses which reflect one another: equally eternal, equally divine. Again and again, throughout this stumbling analysis, he made the point that extremes meet, that any mysticism is better than none, that joy and sorrow, passion and pure love, denial and affirmation are all one if carried to their extreme metaphysical limits. The artist, from classical antiquity to his own times, had invoked the return of the Golden Age. In the light of Merezhkovsky's teachings, the precursors of this Golden Age would be both Christ and Antichrist, and whichever the artist invoked he would be working the will of God.

[e] He read it in the summer of 1900.

These doctrines, falling as they did in the fruitful soil of a suppressed passion, had considerable influence on the content of Blok's
poetry. The innocent lucidity of the summer had gone. In the bust-
ling world of the city—the Barracks, the University, friends, relatives, money, and all the impressions and temptations of the street—
everything at once became more difficult. Blok continued to meet
Lyubov' regularly. He would wait for her outside the Bestuzhev
Courses and escort her home to her father's flat near the Sennaya
Ploshchad'. Instinctively, they sought to re-establish something of
the warm Russian simplicity of their country summer and began to
take refuge in the only oases of serenity amid the shifting complexi-
ties of the cold European capital: the churches.

It was Lyubov' who started it. Like many intellectuals of the
period, she considered herself above official religion and the ignorant,
often superstitious observance of the people. Her pride, moreover,
would not accept the idea of an intermediary between herself and
the Almighty, so she eschewed Confession and the normal day-to-
day practise of Orthodoxy. For the last year or more, she had been
seeking an outlet for her adolescent need to worship in the ecstatic
contemplation of nature (at Boblovo) and, in Petersburg, in a private
cult of certain icons of the Holy Virgin in quiet corners of the great
cathedrals. These she would visit at times when there were few people
and no service in progress.[3]

That autumn she introduced Blok to 'her cathedrals', notably, on
17 October, to the Kazan Cathedral, the colonnaded Petersburg imi-
tation of St. Peter's in Rome, which, together with the unwieldy
and ornate St. Isaac's, served them as meeting places for some time
to come. After his initiation to these special places, Blok would on
occasion visit them by himself and sometimes, unobserved or believing himself unobserved, he would follow Lyubov' in from the street
and watch her at her devotions. The hushed semi-darkness, with
the gleam of porphyry, lapis lazuli, and malachite pillars and the
pools of wavering light before the icons made by clusters of white
wax candles, provided a rich setting for poetry. Yet, as we read in
the lives of the saints, demons cluster thickly about holy places, and
already the artist in Blok was yielding to these demons, who, like
Faust's Mephistopheles, brought him wondrous gifts and were ready
to fulfil every whim of his imagination:

> To worship in the Lord's high dwelling
> With heart abased is my delight.
> Where sacred canticles are swelling,
> In shadowy throngs I merge from sight.

I fear my two-faced soul's dual aspect
And keep the visored helm of Grace
Most carefully closed upon my savage
And diabolic second face.

(1. 187)[f]

In addition to her studies at the Bestuzhev Courses, Lyubov' had reverted to her passion for acting and was attending Madame Chitau's drama classes and generally leading a full, busy student's life. This banal existence did not appeal to Blok. Only occasionally did he call at her home or accompany her to visit some mutual acquaintance such as the family of the artist M. P. Botkin, whose collection of French and Italian paintings was an attraction to both of them. He refused invitations to parties, preferring to wait for her outside, gazing up at the lighted windows behind which moved the silhouettes of dancing figures, keeping romantic vigil in the dark, cold street.

He would also wait for her outside Madame Chitau's. Sometimes he would see her home, sometimes merely watch her pass, sometimes follow her, dreaming dreams and evolving verses in his head as he did so.[g]

I would wait for one hour, two, three. Sometimes You[h] were not there at all. But, oh God, if You were. Then that rotten, vulgar, shabby front door I loved so much would creak and knock and bang. The light would gush out from the dim yellow lamp. Your figure would appear—Your every line so long familiar in each detail, studied, lovingly observed. I think You usually wore a semi-fashionable winter coat with black fur, not very new: a little hat and beneath it the huge, heavy golden knot of hair lay on the collar, drowning in the fur. The rosy glowing cheeks were set off by that same fur. You held up your dress with a little hand, the wrist long and curved in a black gauntlet glove, woollen or kid. In the other hand You held your muff and swung it a little as You walked. You walked quickly, swaying slightly ... looking straight in front of You, sometimes with a smile on Your lips.... So tall, 'stately', frosty. Sometimes, in the hardest frosts, Your hair would be covered by a white woollen head scarf.

---

[f] The poem of which these are the first two stanzas was written on 8 April 1902 and first published in Blok's *Collected Poems*, vol. I (1911). Lunacharsky, in his article on Blok, calls it 'a shrilly discordant poem which somehow got slipped into his first book of verse'.[4] In fact, it is the culminating expression of a growing duality within a whole cycle of 'cathedral' poems (1. 133, 156, 157, 159, 160, 161, 171, 180, 183, 187, 494, 505).

[g] Cf. the poems 'I waited long—you came out late' (1. 143), 'High up the wall dissolves in dark' (1. 158), and 'There in the street there stood a kind of house' (1. 192).

[h] Contrary to Russian usage, Blok consistently used a capital letter for the second person singular in his letters to Lyubov'—and later to Andrey Bely.

When I caught You up You would turn round with an extraordinarily familiar movement of the neck and shoulders and always to begin with Your eyes were unfriendly, withdrawn, cool. Your hand barely touched mine (and in general Your hand was always in a hurry to jerk away). If I happened to be coming towards You, You approached me stiffly. Sometimes this stiffness lasted all the time we were together. I got all tied up, said dreadfully stupid things (probably banal too) and lost courage; my soul would suddenly be overwhelmed by a kind of smothering wave.... And then all of a sudden, terribly seldom—but it *did* happen that way too!—a subtle word, a light whisper, a tiny movement, a momentary trembling—or perhaps it would be better for me to think that that was just my imagination....

(VII. 55)

So Blok recalled that curious winter in an unsent letter at the end of the following summer. Lyubov' was as bewildered as he. Was he in love with her? or was it her imagination? She was certainly not going to be the first to put her cards on the table. Socially, they were still on terms of the utmost formality, addressing one another by name and patronymic. But what, in the country, had been a natural enough hesitancy about growing up, an enjoyable, more or less mutual retreat into childhood and innocence, here in the more sophisticated atmosphere of the town became increasingly artificial.

Almost immediately, it began to seem to the poet as though his Lady's power was dwindling, the enchantment seeping away from their relationship. The last poem of the 'mystic summer', written at Shakhmatovo, is dated 2 September. Less than a week later, Blok left for St. Petersburg and wrote no more poetry until, on the 20th, he addressed some rather minatory verses to his inadequate beloved: he (the lyrical hero of the poems) is retreating into shadow; she must expect no more 'inspired words' and, although her image remains unclouded and radiant, this is 'only in immortality—not in this earthly life' (I. 125). The poems which follow seem to contain an undercurrent of reproach. It is as though, in his poetry, Blok was already aware of something which he long refused to admit in his conscious mind: that Lyubov' had no intention of remaining meekly in the place allotted to her by his Muse as the pure companion, the soul sister of his earthly days and his own private and exclusive incarnation of the Eternal Feminine.

On 6 October, he wrote an untitled poem (called 'Despair' in the manuscript) which records something akin to an Assumption: choirs of angels will greet Her as She withdraws from this world and gently divest Her of the symbolic garment of earthly sorrow, the hair shirt.

Her poet, mortal and fallible, stands desolate upon the 'frontier', unable to follow. The frontier he describes elsewhere as the 'frontier of the Knowability of God' and here the poet is brought up short not by 'the splendour of light' but by 'black smoke and inevitable gloom' (I. 129). The aestheticization of religion and the half-hearted asceticism of the last year were brewing up into an explosive, dangerous compound. It is, however, a measure of the reality of the light which had been so generously poured out upon Blok over this time that he was, even at this confused period of his life, instinctively aware of the darkness now gathering within him.

Throughout October and early November his verses reflect the wavering tensions of his stubborn struggle to maintain religious concentration and his fluctuating relationship with Lyubov'. Some are even written in the first person feminine, recording things she had said to him almost word for word.

Then his control broke. 'In November', Blok recalled when endeavouring to write a commentary on the Beautiful Lady verses, 'began my open sorcery. I invoked doubles' (VII. 345). This invocation of doubles must have sounded the dominant note of that winter, for the extremely self-conscious diary which Blok began to keep from 27 December opens with the words 'I have become dual' (VII. 19).

The reason for this schizophrenic development in Blok's poetry was clearly the struggle going on within him between the aspiring religious visionary and the demonic spirit who 'seeks perdition'; between ascetic vigilance and dark, destructive passion (transparently symbolized in his poetry as murder by stabbing). The would-be monk is doomed from the outset because, from the first, he permits himself a luxurious nostalgia for 'the one who commits the act and for the act itself ...' (VII. 19).

Inevitably, Blok was relinquishing his second experience of Eden, following tragically but voluntarily in the footsteps of the first man through accepted temptation to the toil and sorrow of a fallen world. Beyond the Fall the poet was already reaching out towards that incarnation, that 'becoming man' (*vochelovecheniye*) which was to be the true content of his later art.

The idea that some violent deed (involving sacrifice or self-sacrifice) was needed to effect this incarnation was suggested by his reading. In the spring of 1901 he had been deeply impressed by Zinaida Hippius's drama *Sacred Blood*, which put forward the idea of the murder (or ritual sacrifice) of a dearly loved and venerated fellow being as a way to salvation. The connection between an act of transgression, bound up with the idea of blood-letting or blood sacrifice, and salvation originated from Merezhkovsky's and Rozanov's thoughts on Dostoyevsky's heroes Raskolnikov and Kirillov. The idea of deliberately committing a crime to achieve emancipation from the moral law, as an act of will intended to bring the perpetrator close to the Nietszchean ideal of the Superman (Merezhkovsky, following Dostoyevsky, called it the idea of 'Mangodhood'), was exciting many minds.

Quite apart from literary associations, however, Blok's experience of duality was a very real one. So much so, indeed, that had he not been able to exteriorize the dilemma through his art, the doubles must either have taken possession of him in all earnest and destroyed his mental balance or have forced him to find some way of reconciling the two parts of his nature in a real-life compromise. As it was, he continued to run errands for his mother, attend lectures, take copious notes, and write the long-suffering object of his devotion polite letters beginning 'Deeply-respected Lyubov' Dmitriyevna' and ending 'profoundly devoted . . .'. As an artist, he was even rather pleased with the doubles: 'Although it didn't come off, it *is* a good thought for a poem: the murderer-double commits the act and fades out of the picture, whereas the contemplative who took no part in the murder receives the whole reward. A mad thought, but then the reward is madness . . .' (VII. 19).

As Dr. Jekyll was led on in his experiments by scientific fervour, so Blok was led on in his 'conjuring' by sheer artistic curiosity. To match his own 'diabolic second face' he began to call up another double, this time of the Beautiful Lady herself, one whom he named, for the time being, Izida: a cold snow maiden, 'singing among the steppes', whose 'aura was stormy and dark at the centre', insubstantial as were his own doubles, an almost malevolent succuba, over whom he could allow his sensuous fancy to play in a manner unthinkable in connection with the radiant majesty of the Most Beautiful Lady. The colouring, light, and atmosphere of the poetry all begin to change. Frosty smoke and fog, bonfires in the night, red city dawns—only occasionally now is there a glimpse of gold, a memory of blue, a light shining behind a distant window.

By the end of January 1902, Lyubov' could bear it no longer. On 18 January they had walked all day:

First we went into the Kazan Cathedral (we had been there before), and then to St. Isaac's. The wind was strong and cold, it was frosty, the sun was bright, cold. We walked all round the outside of the cathedral, then went in. Some nuns were whispering quietly to one another at the doors (they always are—they collect money there) and fell silent. The cathedral was almost empty. You were struck by the height, the vastness, the solemnity, the dimness. You even lowered Your voice. We went further in, stood at the feet of the pillars, looking upwards to the thin threads of hand rail on the stairs. The staircase led up into the dome. It looked enough to make anybody giddy. You began to speak of suicide, of how hard it would be to force oneself to jump down, that it would be easier to take poison: there is a poison that works quickly. Then we walked along the diagonals. The sun fell in slanting rays. Why did You want to stay in the dim, avoiding the filtered light from the windows? It spoilt the cathedral, spoilt your thoughts, but what more? ... Then we sat on an oak bench at the other end from the altar, nearer the General Post Office. And before that we had been walking *all day*. It grew late, we came out again, the nuns were still whispering. We went along Novy and Demidov Lanes and came out on the Sennaya. It seemed such a short way to me. You showed me the tavern where Svidrigaylov[i] had sat. We came out by the Obukhov Bridge and went on to the Hall[j] itself. From the bridge we took a last look at the sunset, but by then you did not want to stop. That was *the last time*.

(VII. 56)

So Blok recalled six months later in his Shakhmatovo diary for 29 August. Lyubov', her patience finally exhausted after this last cold, interminable walk, went home and dashed off a frank, passionate letter:

I can no longer remain in the same friendly relationship with you as before; up till now I was completely sincere in it, I give you my word. But now, if I were to keep it up any longer, I should have to begin pretending. Suddenly, quite unexpectedly and for absolutely no particular reason on your side or mine, it became quite clear to me to what extent we are alien to one another, how little you understand me. You look on me as though I were some kind of abstract idea; you have imagined all kinds of wonderful things about me and behind that fantastic fiction which existed only in your imagination you have failed to notice *me*, a live human being with a living soul.... I am a live human being and that is what I want to be, even with all my faults.

On his 'lofty heights', she concludes, she is 'cold, frightened and ... bored'.[5]

On 29 January, at their next 'chance' meeting, she informed him coldly that she wanted no more to do with him. At the last moment, however, pride prevented her from handing over the letter. It would,

---

[i] The character in Dostoyevsky's *Crime and Punishment*.
[j] The Hall of Weights and Measures. Lyubov's father had a government-owned flat in the building.

she thought, almost amount to a declaration. She was *not* going to be the one to speak first.

She was right. He had been cooling off. An unsent letter of 17 January speaks of 'the last thought of love' being 'still alive in the incorruptibility of memory'. Now, goaded by the sudden break, for which she offered no explanation whatsoever, he made a no doubt very satisfactory scene in the street and went home to write a salvo of letters. Lyubov' saw none of them, even as he remained in ignorance of hers to him.[6] Misunderstanding became almost total.

Yet the poet, as if drawn by a magnet, continued to seek her out. She, supposing he could not have taken in the fact that she had broken with him, considered it beneath her dignity to cut him dead or actually to run away from him in the street. As from 7 February, she tolerated his company and simply hardened her heart towards him inwardly. So they carried on through the spring of that year. There was even one point of real friction. Both the University and the Bestuzhev Courses were in a state of extreme political unrest and 'right-minded' students were boycotting examinations. Blok, who had enjoyed his first year in the Philological Faculty, particularly the return to Latin and Greek literature and A. I. Vvedensky's lectures in logic and philosophy, decided to sit his examinations in spite of popular disapproval. The fact that he had to face a good deal of disapprobation, even insults from his fellow students, rather confirmed him in this attitude. Lyubov', more conformist, disapproved of such civic spinelessness and told him so in no uncertain terms. By the autumn of 1902 she considered that she had freed herself of all feeling for him.

2

It is scarcely surprising that, confronted with the necessity of finding a poetic form for emotions and experiences of a completely different substance from those 'waves of lyricism' which had washed over him throughout his childhood and on which he had drawn so effortlessly in writing of his 'mystic summer', Blok had, throughout that winter, begun to look more and more towards the new literature for technical guidance. He was not formed by the new poetry, for he was more mature as a poet than as a person and had already developed a powerful individual voice on the basis of his Romantic and classical background. But now he approached modern poetry with much the same intention as a mining engineer would approach a hitherto un-explored geological field: to analyse its strata and to take from it what he needed.

The terminology of the new poetry—the abyss and the mirrors, the whispers and rustles, the demons and doubles and all the elements of Grand Guignol—had already been elaborated in Merezhkovsky's critical prose and in the poetry and short stories of Zinaida Hippius and Fyëdor Sologub. Konstantin Bal'mont provided multitudinous examples of the suggestive power of *'musique'*. Bryusov, both in his translations from Verhaeren and other European poets and in his own poetry, had begun to introduce the rhythms of the city and the tramping echoes of crowded streets. Inevitably, now that he had become fully aware of it, Blok was drawn into this world of modern art and letters of which he had until recently preserved an almost pristine ignorance.

Yet the most remarkable thing about this transitional period, dur-ing which the unique individual, the private person Aleksandr Alek-sandrovich Blok who happened to write rather good verses grew up to become a great twentieth-century poet, is the degree to which he retained his artistic independence. Echoes from contemporary literature did occur from time to time, but usually only as and when the poet needed them. Their cumulative effect was gradually to pull the *Verses about the Most Beautiful Lady* into the orbit of contemporary 'decadent' poetry, but, because Blok invariably wrote from within his own temperament and experience, borrowings were limited to single words, poetic phrases, and technical tricks.

In such phrases as 'going forth to meet the heralds of the End with wedding gifts' (1. 164) or 'thoughts haunted by white, vanished birds' (1. 185), it is easy to detect echoes of Merezhkovsky or Sologub, but he learnt most from the macabre urbanism of Valeriy Bryusov. Even this, however, Blok assimilated and made his own. This is parti-cularly to be felt in a truly Bryusovian piece written after a New Year visit to the Mendeleyevs. The guests had played the usual Rus-sian New Year fortune-telling games and, excited by some of the predictions and the presence of Lyubov', Blok had walked home alone over the long wooden bridge from the Vasilievsky Island and across the whole breadth of the Petrogradskaya Storona. On this frosty, lonely walk he had been caught up in an ecstatic awareness of his own separateness. He felt himself to be walking on ahead, a pillar of fire going on before him, and, behind him, a grey, wailing crowd of nameless people. Happy, free and elect, he strides forward, full of prophetic ecstacy, while the lifeless people, hand in nerveless

hand, murmur and shuffle behind him, their energy scarcely sufficient to breath the night air (I. 155).

This was the contemporary vision of the poet. Blok found his own
poetic experience coinciding with what others were writing. Bryusov, from whose poetic utterances on the subject Blok was to quote
nine years later in 'On the Present State of Russian Symbolism',
formulated it in a theoretical article: '... it was enough that the
thought that *all the world is within me* penetrated deeply into the
mind—and already the modern conception of art had arisen, our
conception. To express his *own* experiences, which is the only reality
accessible to the conscious mind, this is the task of the artist.'[7]

Yet, from the beginning, it was felt that, through this *self*-expres-
sion, the artist would eventually attain to the underlying, ideal truth
and from this win back into a more profound communion with
his fellows.[8]

As though from some outside source, this idea sprang up simul-
taneously in the minds of the most various writers. As Andrey Bely
was to write in his very first letter to Blok, at the end of 1902:

In the abyss of the individual there appeared something at once objective
and 'intimately' personal. The personal proved not to be individual. At
a time when everyone thought that he was advancing alone in the dark,
without hope, with a presentiment of disaster, it became apparent that
others were travelling the same road.[9]

The years 1901–2 saw the meeting of many minds which had 'been
travelling the same road', and the brief, exciting time, between 1901
and 1905, when the Russian Symbolist movement was in full spate
was aptly called, by a poet who witnessed the tail-end of it, the period
of 'collective creation'.[10] The architects of this period, arrant indivi-
dualists to a man, had gradually been drawn together by a common
unease which was changed almost overnight to a breathless sense of
expectation.

The first symptoms of this sudden influx of hope and energy had
become apparent in 1899, the year in which the decadents at last
established their own journal in St. Petersburg, *Mir Iskusstva*.[k] In this
year, Merezhkovsky had begun to turn away from paganism to seek

[k] This was made possible by the *brio* and organizing ability of the young Sergey Diaghilev, who obtained first the support of two wealthy patrons of the arts and then a royal
subsidy for the journal he edited from 1898 to 1904. Diaghilev was the nephew of the
Anna Pavlovna Filosofova whose at homes Blok's father had frequented in the '70s. Her
son, Dmitriy Filosofov, was literary editor of *Mir Iskusstva*. He became a close friend of
the Merezhkovskys and *Mir Iskusstva* published philosophic and aesthetic studies by D.
S. Merezhkovsky, V. Rozanov, N. Minsky, and Lev Shestov.

the 'whole fullness of truth' in Christianity alone; Aleksandr Dobrolyubov, one of the better-known Petersburg decadents, had stopped
advocating suicide in a room draped with black velvet, repented of
'unimaginable' sins, and retired to a monastery in the wilds where
he intended to meditate for a year and then either to write of his
spiritual experiences or become a village schoolmaster.

The practical necessity of founding journals and publishing houses
to handle their work also went far to cure decadent isolation. Bryusov, in Moscow, went one better than his Petersburg rivals and, with
the distinguished Lithuanian poet Yuris Baltrushaytis and Sergey
Aleksandrovich Polyakov, a poet and mathematician with a considerable acquaintance among the wealthy merchant families of
Moscow such as the Morozovs and Filipovs, founded the first
decadent publishing house: Skorpion.

Andrey Bely gives a picture of Bryusov at this time,

going about Moscow with his notebook and stub of pencil, organizing
young poets into a literary party, going dryly about the work of enlisting
contributors and editors for his journal, laying down the law and scolding,
encouraging, playing the fool and shedding, as a tree sheds its leaves, flurries
of curious quotations from obscure poets: French, Belgian, English, Czech,
Greek, Latvian, Polish, German—forging his battering ram with plodding
ox-like patience.[11]

In the following year, 1900, Bryusov made common cause with
the Merezhkovskys:

As potential customers, we[1] were received most amiably.... Merezhkovsky
preached about the time of unity having come. That all those who were
seeking new ways ought to unite. The most important thing, however,
was religion. Any mere novelty alien to religion was not worth preserving.[12]

Bryusov, in spite of his natural cynicism, was impressed by the
Merezhkovskys' sincerity, while privately retaining his interest in
'mere novelties'. He made an admirable job of his publishing house,
issuing in 1900 his own best collection to date, *Tertia Vigilia*, and
the Collected Works of Dobrolyubov with a preface by another
Petersburg decadent, Ivan Konevskoy, as well as the almanac *Severnye Tsvety* which brought Petersburg and Moscow authors together
within one cover.

By the first year of the new century, 1901, this preliminary work
had taken effect and decadent isolation was at an end. In the autumn,

[1] Polyakov and Bryusov. Zinaida Hippius was, according to Bryusov, particularly
impressed by Skorpion's ability to *pay* for manuscripts.

moreover, the Merezhkovskys, in alliance with their close friend Dmitriy Filosofov, Vasiliy Rozanov, and V. Ternavtsev,[m] obtained permission from Pobedonostsev, as Ober-Procurator of the Holy Synod, and Antonin, Metropolitan of St. Petersburg, to organize meetings between representatives of the Orthodox Church and the intelligentsia. In a country where there was neither right of assembly nor freedom of speech, these discussions between the cultural élite of the capital and the cowled, black-robed guardians of historical Christianity were something entirely new, a meeting of two worlds, of two separate cultures. While the two sides were still groping for a common language, sensational expectations died down and eventually the debate, which ranged from historical Christianity's attitude to secular culture and physical love to questions of freedom of conscience and the desirability of holding an Ecumenical Council to redefine basic dogma in view of the imminence of Armageddon, was overtaken by events. Nevertheless, when the first 'Religious-Philosophical Meeting' was held on the premises of the Geographical Society of St. Petersburg on 29 November 1901, it seemed to many as though the world were about to change, and this attempt to reconcile faith and enlightenment was a portentous symptom.

The Merezhkovskys decided to found their own journal, *Novyy Put'*, which they planned together with Filosofov and P. P. Pertsov, to disseminate the ideas discussed at the Religious-Philosophical meetings. They needed an efficient secretary, which explains their attempt to convert Bryusov.[n] In the meantime, their Christian initiative and alliance with Bryusov brought them into the orbit of Olga and Mikhail Solov'ev. In December 1901, when Merezhkovsky and Hippius were visiting Moscow, Bryusov took them to call on the Solov'evs. Here they also made the acquaintance of Borya Bugayev, who had just begun to publish under the pen name of Andrey Bely, suggested for him by Mikhail Solov'ev when he had placed his 'First Symphony' with Bryusov's Skorpion that same autumn.[o]

---

[m] An Orthodox Christian with intense sympathy for the intelligentsia's dream of the establishment of the Kingdom of God on Earth: he was an employee of the Holy Synod.

[n] Bryusov, though now a figure of some weight in literary circles, still lacked a periodical in which to publish his own poetry and propagate his aesthetic theories. For a while, he toyed with the idea of taking on *Novyy Put'*, but this would have meant moving to Petersburg and eventually he founded his own, more conventionally literary monthly, *Vesy* (The Balance), which began publication in 1904.

[o] It is symptomatic of the violent prejudice against decadents in academic circles that Bugayev could not contemplate compromising his distinguished parent by writing under his own name. When Blok began to publish his poetry, his father expressly asked him not to sign Al. Blok to avoid confusion with himself which, as he had no scruples in informing his son, he would have found most embarrassing.

Bugayev-Bely, impressed by rumours of the first meetings of the Religious Philosophical Society then buzzing round Moscow, went to the Solov'evs expecting to meet a Russian Luther. At first, however, he did not even notice Merezhkovsky. It was Hippius with her thin, heavily made-up face, top-heavy red hair-do, wasp-like figure, flamboyant jet cross,[p] and glittering monocle who riveted his attention.

She reminded him of a *charmeuse* by Aubrey Beardsley. Bryusov, on the other hand, as he bent attentively over the back of Hippius's chair, was more like a black devil by Felicien Rops. Merezhkovsky himself, brown-haired, brown-clad, very small and thin, lost in a large armchair, looked, thought Bely, like a cross between a deacon and a minor bureaucrat. His immediate reaction was to feel desperately sorry for Olga Solov'eva, who was obviously struggling with shattered illusions. The Merezhkovskys themselves were ill at ease, uncertain of their welcome in the Solov'ev household (Vladimir Solov'ev had criticized Merezhkovsky in *Mir Iskusstva*). Bryusov was defending pure aestheticism, 'glorifying God and the Devil'. It was painfully obvious that everybody, with the exception of the host and hostess, was out to make an impression.

Bely was repelled by the Merezhkovskys' aura, reminiscent of the green mists, the smoke and frost of Petersburg. This aura, whether or not it was suggested by the smoke from Hippius's scented cigarettes, troubled both him and Blok in their dealings with the Merezhkovskys over the next few years, but it did not prevent either from succumbing to their influence. Both, in fact, were at least partially subjugated from the moment this odd, lonely, intense couple came to turn on them the full force of their proselytizing zeal.

On this occasion Bely, recommended by Bryusov as 'the most interesting man in Moscow', immediately impressed the Merezhkovskys as a most desirable ally and at once became involved in one of his perennial platonic adulteries, desperately loyal to the Solov'evs yet irresistibly fascinated by the acquisitive charm of their Petersburg rivals. For him, as for Blok, this year 1901 was the definitive year for his whole future: 'It was a year of concord between life and philosophy of life, of new friendships, of first love, of my recognition by M. S. Solov'ev, Bryusov, the Merezhkovskys, the beginning of the biography of Andrey Bely.'[13]

---

[p] The Orthodox Christian, unless in holy orders, wears his cross on a long chain next to the skin, not as a necklace. Hippius, a born *poseuse*, had a flair for spiritual immodesty. For instance, for many years whe wore her hair in one braid, like an unmarried peasant girl, flaunting (or so people assumed) the unconsummated nature of her marriage.

3

It was not until March 1902 that Blok met the Merezhkovskys. He called on them to ask for a ticket to attend one of Dmitry Sergeyevich's lectures. Zinaida Hippius opened the door to him. She had heard of Blok from both Olga Solov'eva and Bely. They had shown her some of his verses which she had thought (and pronounced in a letter to Olga) outmoded: misty imitations of Fet and Polonsky.[q] Nevertheless, Bely's obvious enthusiasm for Blok's poetry could not be altogether disregarded and there was a quality about the deferential young man which immediately arrested her attention:

I did not think him handsome. Above the high, narrow forehead (everything in his face and in himself seemed high and narrow, although he was of medium height) was a thick cap of brown hair. The face was straight, immobile, as calm as though it were of wood or stone. A very interesting face. He made few movements and his voice matched this immobility: to me it, too, seemed 'narrow' yet at the same time it was deep and so hollow it seemed to come from the bottom of a well. Every word Blok enunciated slowly and with an effort, as though tearing himself away from some profound meditation.

At the same time

There was something endearing about the whole personality of this student. Yes, endearing, child-like—'not frightening' ... presumably because, in spite of the immobility, the seriousness, the woodenness, even, there was nothing 'grown-up' about him, none of that hopeless aspect of 'grown-upness' which makes people 'frightening'.[14]

Hippius gave Blok his ticket, introduced him to her husband, and showed him a letter from Bely in which the younger poet set out his mystical differences with Merezhkovsky in the esoteric language of early Symbolism which owed so much to Vladimir Solov'ev. This letter, to which Bely had not dared to set his name, signing it merely 'from a natural-science student', had impressed the Merezhkovskys so much that they showed it to all their acquaintances and then persuaded the author, whom they had had no difficulty in identifying as the young man they had met at the Solov'evs, to allow them to publish it in their journal.

Blok took the letter home and, that very evening, copied parts of it into his own diary:

'For two years now I have been undergoing a quite incomparable experience—I was waiting to see who would speak first.... And now *it has begun*.

[q] Ya. P. Polonsky (1819–98), a neo-classic poet much loved by Blok and his family.

The trumpet has sounded.... Vl. Solov'ev has delivered his lecture "On the End of World History". D. S. Merezhkovsky has spoken of *those who awoke too soon*.... Nature and people are no longer the same. "The end of the world is approaching." "He is knocking at the door." Is this so? Or does it just seem to be so?...

'We are silent, but events do not pass us by. "Either we, or no one" (the words are Merezhkovsky's). Perhaps we are only precursors of those who have received the "mark", in whose lifetime "it" will happen. Either way, we are participants (albeit indirectly) in the mystery that is unfolding.... as to "knowledge", then, in my—possibly quite mistaken—opinion, Merezhkovsky either knows *nothing at all*, or else he knows *too much*, but does not say all he knows.... and, indeed, why should he wake us if it is still too early, for after all "woe to those who waken too soon!"'

'There is nothing in this letter of mine but the agonized prayer to be more open, to give a *clear sign*, or to say nothing at all of *what is* hidden if *it* does indeed exist.'

To Blok, it was as though some more articulate *alter ego* had formulated his own thoughts and questions. He commented excitedly:

My criticism: does this not show a certain doubt of 'its' existence on Bugayev's part? If this is so, that would be terrible, as this would mean not God 'rejected', but God 'denied'!? 'The yearning of the spirit' is the abyss of death, and will be revealed here, if it has not already been so revealed, as the obverse of 'spiritual joy'.

Bugayev's letter ends with ten theses which everyone who has touched upon the *principal* must take into account. Here are some of them:

'(4) The sacred yearning is becoming intolerable.
'(5) In this stockpiling of horror one recognizes the approach of Antichrist.
'(6) In the air is the "Eternal Feminine" (the Woman Clothed with the Sun, destined to bear a male child, who is to pasture the peoples with a rod of iron).
'(7) But the Great Whore, also, sleeps not.
'(8) Christianity must pass from pink into white; the Christianity of St. John ("They made white their garments in the Blood of the Lamb."...)'
'(10) We must prepare for the unexpected, lest it take us unawares, because the storm is near and the waves roar and something dimly glimpsed is rising from the water'.

(VII. 42–3)

' Here Blok goes on to quote an occult list of white symbols, from the white horseman of the Apocalypse to white as the unification of number seven, from the seven churches to the seven seals.

On the 2nd of April, Blok noted respectfully that 'Mme Merezh-kovskaya' (Bryusov, in *his* diary, refers to her as 'Zinochka') had given him other letters from Bugayev to read and that, while the primary task before him was to *study* the long letter, these also were worthy of attention, because of their 'weight and chaos, youth and age, light and darkness'.

So Blok, as deeply impressed by Bely's passionate but questioning welcome of the Merezhkovskys' apocalyptic Christianity as Bely had been by *his* verses, recognized a spiritual brother. So awed was he by the similarity of their intuitions that he even hesitated to strike up a correspondence in case this should herald 'some sort of end'.

The impression produced by the Merezhkovskys was of another kind. There was no awe in Blok's feeling for them, but he was keenly interested, perhaps a little dazzled. Hippius, eleven years his senior, was friendly and sisterly. Blok, with his old-fashioned formality, felt honoured. Merezhkovsky laid down the law about art and religion, Eros and mystical love, history and the Coming of the End: subjects which had been central to Blok's thought and experience over the last two years. Overwhelmed by the older man's vehemence and erudition, as well as by Hippius's flattering attention to his own views, Blok fell under their spell as completely as his naturally with-drawn and self-sufficient nature would permit. In his autobiography, he acknowledged the importance the Merezhkovskys had in his de-velopment alongside that of the Solov'evs and Andrey Bely. He became altogether engrossed in the effort to understand their theories and kept up a 'mystical correspondence' with Hippius all through the summer of 1902. She, however, was acutely aware that Blok, her 'lunar friend' as she called him in her reminiscences, was not and never would be entirely 'theirs': 'It would be wrong to say that he was out of touch with real life; still less that he was "not clever". Yet at the same time everything we call philosophy, logic, meta-physics, simply bounced off him; it was not applicable to him.'[15] Merezhkovsky, less charitably, referred to Blok's avoidance of abstract speculation and tongue-tied retreat into spheres of mystical experience as 'Khlystovstvo!'[5]

Yet even in these most 'mystic' years Blok, while less articulate, was basically more rooted in the earth, more sober-minded than his

---

[5] The Khlysty were a sect who worked themselves up into a state of religious—and fre-quently erotic—ecstasy by dancing under the direction of men or women they believed to be reincarnations of Christ or the Madonna. The label stuck to Blok. His poetry had the mesmeric rhythms of such dancing and the 'antithesis' of the Most Beautiful Lady (the Stranger, the Snow Maiden, Faina) sometimes takes on the form of a sectarian madonna.

apparently rational mentors. He was not, as the Merezhkovskys were, looking for an experience which they had concluded logically they ought to be having: the experience of faith. Blok's point of departure *was* experience. He had felt something over the last two years which had completely altered his attitude to life and he wanted to know why; who else had been through anything similar; what it was all about.

Nor was Blok, like Andrey Bely, a prey to extreme nervous sensibility and frantic, uncontrollable complexes. He had his complexes, but he held them at a certain distance. He was not thick-skinned, but he was surrounded by the protective aura of the sufficiently loved. Bely's search for his own way in life and art was complicated by an emotional need to find substitute parents, by passionate, guilt-ridden personal relationships, whereas Blok was coolly uninhibited (he remained personally attached to the Merezhkovskys long after they ceased to influence him), and was thus free to concentrate—deliberately and at first, indeed, somewhat ponderously—on those points in the 'new religious consciousness' which were most immediately important to him.

'Can it be', Blok wrote in his diary shortly after this first meeting with the Merezhkovskys in the spring of 1902, 'that I too am coming to deny the autonomy of art and to accept its inevitable transformation into religion? I have felt an inclination that way (only I could not formulate it, whereas Bugayev, D. Merezhkovsky and Z. Hippius have opened it up)' (VII. 44). A line from his beloved Polonsky to the effect that church bells will always out-ring the poet's lyre was much in his thoughts.

Yet something held him back. His dilemma went too deep. He did not yet know the source of his own inspiration. Did his art come from this world, or from religion? He had felt from the beginning that the demands of religion were too absolute to admit of the kind of poetry he was now writing and that poetry itself was of the earth. 'I shall dissolve in God, then ...', he wrote resignedly in his diary (VII. 45).

Aleksandr Dobrolyubov had, according to his own lights, 'dissolved in God' when he disappeared from literature into the vast anonymity of Holy Russia.¹ Ivan Konevskoy, in his own way, had

¹ Dobrolyubov published two more books of poetry (in 1900 and 1905) and occasionally revisited his old friends such as Oreus (Konevskoy) and Bryusov before finally disappearing amongst the Russian people as leader of a religious sect. He is believed to have perished in 1944, having suffered many hardships, including imprisonment for militant pacifism.

'dissolved' also. He had been drowned while swimming, a fate ecstatically foreseen in his poetry, in the summer of 1901. To Blok, taking stock of the situation in a letter to his friend Aleksandr Hippius in the summer of 1902, these 'casualties among our advance guard' seemed to indicate that 'we have reached a frontier' (VIII. 37). To remain *with* God *and in* literature, as Bely and the Merezhkovskys tried to do, was, he felt from the beginning, to create a false situation. As Bryusov (of all people) later stated in a letter to Bely, they had not sufficient courage or willpower for 'an act of renunciation [*pod-vig*]'.[16] For Blok at that time the dilemma of whether or not to make such an 'act of renunciation' was immediate and existential. He was exhausted by the long struggle between his bodily needs and his ascetic aspirations, as well as by standing sentry to contain the mystical riot which threatened to engulf his poetry. The Merezhkovskys' reconciliation of opposites seemed, for a while, to offer a possible solution.

During the summer of 1902 he was reading Merezkhovsky's *Tolstoy and Dostoyevsky* and finding it 'extremely talented'. In this study Merezkhovsky presents Tolstoy as one who perceives the secrets of the flesh while Dostoyevsky plumbs the hidden depths of the human spirit. The theory of the 'equal sanctity of the flesh' naturally interested Blok intensely at that moment. His notebooks and diaries are scattered with extracts, abstracts, and stray thoughts from the prose and poetry of his new mentors. Merezhkovsky's critical work sent him back to the originals, and he reread Tolstoy's *Confession* and *The Cossacks* and Dostoyevsky's *The Diary of a Writer* and *Notes from Underground*, a seminal book for the whole of modernist literature.

The book of Dostoyevsky's that impressed him most, however, was *A Raw Youth*. In letters written over the summer of 1902 he quoted this uncomfortable novel several times and it was here he found a formula for the direction he felt his own poetry ought to be taking: 'All this is so vulgar and prosaic that it almost borders upon the fantastic.' In a letter to his father written 5 August 1902 Blok, probably conscious of the professorial eye of his distant parent, puts the idea in a more 'literary' form:

Abandoning the exaggeratedly fairy-tale quality of my recent mysticism, I still dream of a sharp (unexpected?) twist in the road, which is to lead us out of the 'darkness' (albeit 'universal') into God's good day.... In general one might say that my realism borders, and will evidently continue to border, on the fantastic (Dostoyevsky, *A Raw Youth*).

(VIII. 40)

Andrey Bely lecturing: silhouette by E. Kruglikova, 1914

..Но даю я душу смѣлую
Мое страданье Сотворившему.
Сказалъ Господь: Одежду бѣлую
Я посылаю - побѣдившему.

З. Гиппіусъ.

Zinaida Hippius deploring the decadence of decadence: caricature by Mitrich, August 1907

More and more firmly, even before he had 'entered literature' as
a published poet, Blok was becoming convinced that though his way
to God might lie through art, his art was not *of* God, but altogether
of the fallen world. In the conclusion of a concentrated meditation
on mythology he wrote:

It clearly follows that the true (heavenly) and not the false (mythological)
light can shine out *only* from darkness.... In this way, true liberation from
our earthly condition can occur only by way of complete παφος [suffering]
in earthly form (the theme of Dostoyevsky which pervades his whole view
of life).

(VII. 51)

Throughout the 1902 summer vacation he corresponded regularly
with Zinaida Hippius, and in his letters wrote not only of his difficulties in accepting the Merezkhovskys' rational 'synthesis' (VIII. 38–
9) but also of his fear of 'tempting God' (VIII. 32) by overmuch mystical rationalization. The synthesis he looked forward to, he wrote,
was 'final', 'apocalyptic', and universal: 'that very one of which it
was written: and there shall be no more curse'. Meanwhile life had
to be lived and it was not for the artist, 'deliberately to push away
the "sounds" of life in case they should drown out the "great rushing
sound"' (VIII. 29–31).

He was prepared, again like Dostoyevsky's raw youth, to suffer
the pains and torments of *three* earthly lives, but always (in his diary
as in his letters) he insisted that he would bear in his heart the image
of his first 'unopened flower of the covenant', the hope (and
memory) of salvation.

So, before Blok began to publish his poetry, his course was already
set. The Merezhkovskys were the last people to exercise a lasting
and profound influence. They prepared his mind for a new awareness
of literature and religion and subtly changed his attitude to his own
vocation. When Blok himself came to sum up their importance for
him, he said that the main thing they did for him was to wean him
from philistine attitudes '*otucheniye ot poshlosti*'' (VIII. 94).

It was under the direct influence of the Merezhkovskys that he
now, at the age of twenty-one, began to read and reread the classics
of Russian literature, to rethink the problems of his generation, to
reread the New Testament and collect his thoughts about religion.
Ever increasingly, he came to see himself as they, for all their faults
and manifest human foibles, saw *themselves*: not as 'consumers', but
as servants of life. This view of the writer's calling, allied to Blok's
inbred protective instinct instilled in him by the Beketov tradition,

combined to produce that rare sense of responsibility to his country and identification with his own mission as a poet which, more and more as time went by, set him apart from, and in some ways, perhaps, above so many of his literary contemporaries.

4

The Merezhkovskys' domination of Blok's thoughts throughout that summer of 1902 was made possible by a relaxation of the emotional and 'mystic' tension he had undergone over the last eighteen months. At the beginning of the holidays, Aunt Sofia came to stay at Shakhmatovo with Ferol and Andryusha—they had temporarily removed to Siberia—and Blok, back in the atmosphere of his adolescence, felt that 'something very precious had gone into abeyance for a while' and that he was 'beginning to run to fat' (VIII. 31).

The glorious weather of the 'mystic summer' was a distant memory. 'We have been having heavy rains', he wrote to a friend; 'the sun peeps out sometimes, everything is terribly green, secluded and wild, "as on the first day of creation"' (VIII. 32).

On 26 June 1902, the rain brought uneasy forebodings.

Today a light rain has been falling almost all day long. The night is terribly dark. . . . Grandfather is very bad. It seems to me that the end is near, today especially. The whispering of the rain was uncanny. There was a queer creaking under the floorboards. The dog is on edge. There is something wrong, something wrong.

(VII. 47)

Andrey Beketov died on 1 July. The end, after years of helpless senility, was what used to be called 'a merciful release' and none of the Beketovs were hypocritical enough to pretend otherwise. With their usual dislike of pomp they made light of the funeral, a semi-official occasion in Petersburg which Blok did not even attend. The village priest, protesting grumpily that he was not certain to which confession the Professor belonged since he had never been to the local church, was persuaded to come to the house and conduct the usual service over the 'newly presented'" before the body was dispatched to the capital for burial. Blok helped officiate, lighting the candles and joining in the responses. Afterwards, Aunt Maria remembered with satisfaction, they entertained the priest so well that he left reconciled to the family and in excellent spirits.

" The Orthodox description of one who has just died.

Blok always had a friendly feeling for death. He never looked on it as an end but rather as the supreme catharsis from which the individual emerges restored and renewed. A small cycle of poems commemorate his grandfather's departure. The first, written on the day he died, was entirely subjective, a jubilant tribute to the Eternal Feminine, the spirit of renewal and resurrection, who now, at this solemn moment, revisited him in all Her former splendour:

> She broke forth like a loud-singing fountain
> Disappeared in the depths of the sky
> Through the soundless blue silences mounting
> As a dream of great storms far away.
> In a hard country, all undiscerning,
> We lived exiled and strangers to tears.
> We were blind to the sweet roses burning,
> But we prayed on stark cliffs, full of fears.
> To our grim north She came like a whirlwind.
> Stood revealed, beyond precedent fair.
> Named Herself: Thought of Death. She was wearing
> The Sun, Moon, and Stars in Her hair.

(I. 201)

The second poem, actually entitled 'On the death of Grandfather' (I. 202) was, one feels, written in part at least to comfort his mother, aunt, and grandmother. It savours more than a little of a sentimental deathbed scene in some uplifting Victorian children's story, and is not at all in Blok's usual style, the 'mystic' moments being much too traditional and exterior to the poet's own sensibility. The poem tells how the attention of the watchers gathered about the deathbed is distracted by the draught from a suddenly opened window which 'rustles the pages of the sacred book'. Looking up they see an old man pass by the window, his hair white as the moon, walking with firm familiar steps and merry eyes. He waves at them affectionately as he strides away and suddenly they realize who it was and, lowering their eyes again to the sick man, see only the empty shell of his body, the eyes closed in death.

The other two poems, 'Fear not to perish in the way' (I. 203) and 'A youth, I light and tend the candles' (I. 204), were written within the week under the influence of the solemn and beautiful Orthodox prayers for the dead. The poet here sees death as a joyous reunion with 'the Bride'. To die seemed to him no more than to cross a 'border of fear' and, even as he rejoiced for his grandfather, it dawned on him that death represented a desirable way out from the stalemate of his present existence. It is a measure of Blok's confusion that he

Blok and his cousins in St. Petersburg. From left to right: Andryusha Kublitsky-Piottukh, Blok, Ferol Kublitsky-Piottukh.

Kseniya Mikhailovna Sadovskaya,
photographed in the 1890s.

Lyubov' Dmitriyevna Mendeleyeva as Ophelia,
1898.

Blok as Hamlet, 1898.

was, in the poems, actually seeking courage for suicide in the words of the church service (I. 203).

This growing preoccupation with death did not mean Blok was ready to acknowledge spiritual bankruptcy. It was rather a positive thing, another aspect of his winter preoccupation with the idea of transgression. He looked upon suicide as an act of will (in the style of Dostoyevsky's Kirillov) which would restore him for ever to the lost state of Grace. The other 'way'—also suggested by Dostoyevsky—'through complete $\pi\alpha\phi o\varsigma$ in earthly form' (VII. 51), appeared very daunting. Now, the alternative to death or to a sceptical acceptance of life with all its limitations quite clearly emerged as religious renunciation, excluding the very possibility of art. The first poem he had written at Shakhmatovo that summer illustrated his growing conviction that this was beyond his strength and contrary to his nature.

> I wander behind cloistered walls
> A joyless and a sombre monk.
> I watch the shuddering snowflakes fall,
> The pale dawn where the moon has sunk.
>
> Ah, night is long and dawn is pale
> In these grim northern lands of ours.
> And at the snow-blocked windowpane
> I sit in stubborn thought for hours.
>
> Immaculate eternal shrouds
> Are white: this snow is whiter still,
> And ever pale the candle wax,
> And washed with white the window sill.
>
> Strange is the cold of these still walls
> And alien this life's poverty.
> The brethren all are pale as death
> I fear this calm captivity.
>
> The dawn is pale, the night is long,
> As Matins ends the Mass must start.
> Ah, I myself am pale as snow,
> In stubborn thought—so poor in heart.

(I. 193)[v]

[v] Written in the village of Shakhmatovo, 11 June 1902. A note against the manuscript of the poem designates it as 'the first half of a diptych (cf. 1 August)'. In the second half, the monk is depicted as obeying a call to take heaven by storm which comes to him as he makes his way across the yellowing harvest fields (it is very rare for Blok to write of a season or landscape not immediately before him as here, in the winter scene of the June poem). In the second part, the suicide theme is clearly associated with rebellion.

His troubles, moreover, were not only theoretical. He could still see no way out of his dilemma with regard to Lyubov'. When, on 21 July, she returned from a protracted stay with relations and Blok rode over to Boblovo to greet her, she would hardly speak to him.

What to do now—I don't yet know. It may very well be that there will be another flare-up.... What precisely should I do?

I do *not* want embraces: because embraces (sudden consent)—are nothing but a momentary shock. Further there is just '*habit*'—a stinking monstrosity.

I do *not* want words. There have always been words and there always *will be*; words are infinitely fluctuating and there is no end to them in the foreseeable future. Everything that you say remains in the sphere of theory....

Is it true that I am prepared to give up EVERYTHING (i.e. the mystic content of life and contemplation) for one thing? *It is true*. Of course, one will win through to the 'synthesis' afterwards: The main thing is to get control of 'reality' and to 'operate' on reality. *Corpus ibi agere non potest, ubi non est!*[w]

I want more than words and more than embraces. I WANT THAT WHICH WILL HAPPEN. Everything that happens will be what I want. That is terrible, but true. It will happen and then it doesn't matter, it doesn't matter at all what. *I want that which will happen.* Because that which *should* happen and will happen—is what I want. Many poor wretches think that they are disillusioned because they wanted something different from what happened: they wanted nothing. If anybody wants something, then it happens. That is how it will be. That which I want will happen but I do not know what I want, and why should I expect to know it *yet*!

(VII. 52–3)

Obviously, Blok's philosophical studies and contemporary reading were weighing upon him almost as heavily as his perplexing love affair. The Nietzschean *amor fati* and the parallel cult of will so emphatically affirmed in this otherwise confused soliloquy were to remain basic to his understanding of life. Again and again, pondering the events of his life and death, one has the feeling that he *made* things happen 'because that which *should* and will happen is what I want'. What he wanted, however, was never personal gratification, but always, with rare consistency, ever since that 'mystic summer' when he had first felt himself to be a poet, the fulfilment of his tragic destiny as an artist.

As for day-to-day life, his deliberate renunciation of immediate aims, a settled policy of non-resistance to the evil of the day left him at the mercy of mood. At this time the condition was so acute that it

---
[w] 'The body can take no action where it is not.'

was only made bearable because the thought of death remained with him as a possible and perfectly viable way out. On 14 August he wrote in his diary:

My scepticism is the essence of my life. But will the essence of my death be the same? No. The time will come when I shall *know for certain* that my death is necessary for a certain moment.... This will be distinguished from other moments because it will contain a peculiarly intense accumulation of firm purpose and of the necessity of making an end. At the same time, not from despair ('Despair and die') but RATHER from a great indwelling *strength*, a potential energy that desires to become kinetic ecstasy (εχδταδις).... A man can put an end to himself. That is his supreme potential (power), his (*suprema potestas*).... Man's highest aim is to advance in the swiftest possible fashion (by the greatest possible strides). It is obvious (clear) that the expression of the most intense endeavour must be the greatest conceivable stride (*summus passus*). This is a leap from one preponderant condition into another. The preponderant condition is undoubtedly the condition of being alive. Man is first and foremost alive and only after that is he good, evil, happy, unhappy, loving, beloved, etc. It follows that the *summus passus* must be a stride out of this condition, that is out of life: and there is nowhere else to go from life except death (neither does man need anywhere else).... By putting an end to himself (in the moment that happens to suit him best, naturally) man asserts his *suprema potestas* through the medium of the *summus passus*.

(VII. 53–4)

He was held back, for the time being, by the eagerness of his creative temperament, already stirring responsively at the prospect of more full-blooded themes. Writing to his friend Aleksandr Hippius (VIII. 36–7), he formulated his growing conviction that religious renunciation must be absolute and exclude, as a pre-communion hymn of the Orthodox Church puts it, 'all the cares of this Earth'. While retaining the hope of eventual release from these cares, the artist is doomed to 'real-life drama', and he writes with regret and desire of the 'black day' into which he is preparing to cast himself from the clifftops of 'mystical contemplation'.[x]

In life, too, everything seemed to be moving either towards an end or towards a new beginning. After the death of Andrey Beketov, his daughters talked of selling Shakhmatovo, but eventually decided to take out a mortgage on the estate and to install an agent, a Latvian,

---

[x] The source of the term 'black day' which Blok gives in inverted commas is unknown, but it is surely relevant that Blok, after publishing his last collection of poems under the title *Grey Morning* (*Sedoye Utro*), said that were he to compile another he would call it *Black Day* (*Chernyy den'*).

Martyn, in the hopes that, if properly managed, it might pay its
way.

'This summer has been a kind of transitional one', Blok wrote to
Zinaida Hippius on 16 August, when the fate of the estate was still
under discussion:

Perhaps I may soon have to leave behind me everything to do with this
place and I am terribly attached to it, because from year to year I have
always spent the same summer months here. . . . I have people who are close
to me (I feel this closeness, of course, in different ways—in one way with
one, in another with another, except for Mama, with whom I feel it in
everything), and the view from the window is splendid, a green, quiet
garden, roses, mountain ash, lime trees, pines. But there is no place where
I could not walk without hesitation at night and blindfold. So sometimes
I wish for a change. Then we have been surrounded by sick people all summer; not to mention the recent death. All that doesn't exactly make for
animation. All life is slow, it offers very, very little counterbalance to
extreme mysticism. . . .

(VIII. 42–3)

As at the end of the preceding summer, he tried to tire out his
overactive mind by physical exercise, riding as far as forty versts in
a day, seeking restlessly for new places and courting a weariness that
would not come.

In a sense, he was undergoing an intense foretaste of all the loss
and loneliness of the next twenty years, something to which his very
youth and inexperience now left him almost unendurably vulnerable, and, by the time he returned to Petersburg, his personality was
beginning to disintegrate.

5

The poetry and diaries of the late summer and autumn of 1902 provide further proof of how unbearable Blok had become to himself.
He began to project the 'doubles' on to archetypal figures: Pierrot
and Harlequin (first on 6 August); the rich man and Lazarus (2 September); the Blessed Virgin and Antichrist (6 September). Strange
and pestilential little demons that bang and rustle in the darkness in-
vaded his verses (18 September). He became jealous even of himself.[y]
The confusion of sacred memory and presentiment of betrayal was
exteriorized in a strange poem: a description, as it were, of a most

---

[y] 'She stands so tall and slender' (I. 221); 'In yellow lamplight they made merry' (I. 224);
'He came to join the formal ball' (I. 227).

uncanonic icon depicting the crowd about Mary and the Christ-child at Epiphany and, amongst the crowd—Judas Iscariot, on horseback, smiling omnisciently behind a 'cold mask' (I. 227). For the first time, Lyubov' was cast as Columbine (7 October 1902). The image of himself as an old man returned persistently (I. 223). The incipient schizophrenia began even to affect his behaviour. He developed a strange predilection for tearing down posters in the street where Lyubov' continued to attend her drama classes. *'Quem Deus vult perdere—prius dementat'* (VII. 58), he quoted with some astonishment the first time he caught himself out in this mildly antisocial act.

He wrote Lyubov' desperate, ironic, confused letters (16 September and 31 October) which, needless to say, remained unsent. His diary dwells on thoughts of death and though, afraid that it might fall into the wrong hands, he refrains from mentioning Lyubov's name, there is a reference to a 'will' composed the previous December in which he lays down that his verses should be buried with him except any required by '——' (VII. 18–20). A September memorandum records that the price of a large military revolver was 26 roubles and puts forward the idea of buying a smaller one '(how much?)' and hiding it with his verses, Lyubov's letters (two formal notes!), and her photographs. Typically, the simple expedient of 'borrowing' some lethal weapon from his soldier stepfather never seems to have entered his absurdly honest, Beketov-trained head. Apparently to commit suicide with somebody else's pistol was just one of those things 'a gentleman does not do'. His diaries and notebooks for this autumn record in fascinated detail the whys and wherefores of several student suicides. Death had come very close.

On 1 October, Elizaveta Grigor'evna died and Blok laid her, too, in her coffin, as he had laid his grandfather exactly three months earlier. Less than two weeks later the theme of suicide began to take over his poetry ('He has gone out and vanished in the night', I. 229). Throughout the second half of October the leitmotiv of the Beautiful Lady—almost totally identified now with Death—was working up to a new crescendo.

By 7 November Blok was so broken in spirit that he actually decided to attend a students' dance at the Dvoryanskoye Sobraniye (Assembly Rooms) where he knew that he would meet Lyubov', with intent to force an explanation. He went armed with the following note:

My address: Peterburgskaya Storona. The Barracks of the Guards' Regiment of Grenadiers, the flat of Colonel Kublitsky, No. 13. 7 November 1902. Petersburg.

I beg that no one should be blamed for my death. Its causes are entirely abstract and have nothing to do with 'human' relationships. I believe in the One holy Catholic and Apostolic Church. I look for the Resurrection of the dead, and the life of the world to come. Amen.

ALEKSANDR BLOK, poet[17]

The letter, however, was not needed.

Lyubov' found herself leaving the Assembly Rooms with Blok and listening to the long-awaited declaration as one in a dream. Somewhat to her own surprise, she consented to become his wife. With conscious artificiality, she put up her face to be kissed. Numb and nervous, but rather proud of herself for all that, she informed her current confidante that she had ended the evening—'no, you'll *never* guess'—being kissed by Blok!

Blok went home and solemnly wrote in his diary:

> 7 November 1902
> The City of Petersburg.
> Dance given by the Bestuzhev Courses in the
> Assembly Rooms for the Nobility.
> Those of little faith shall see God.
> Mother of Light! I magnify Thee!
>
> ALEKSANDR BLOK, poet

(7–8 November)

> Today on 7 November 1902
> that was fulfilled, which has never been
> before and which I have been waiting for for years.
> I end this exercise book
> and also the exercise book with my poems
> this 7 November (on the night of the 7th–8th).
> With this I put the ticket, the letter, written
> before the party,[z] and so end
> both books this night.
> Today is Thursday.
> Saturday at 2 o'clock in the afternoon at the Kazan Cathedral.
> I am the first who in the merry
> Russian tongue the virtues of Felicia
> proclaimed.

The City of Petersburg
7–8 November 1902.

AL. BLOK
(VII. 65–6)

[z] The letter referred to is evidently the suicide note quoted above (see note 17) and the ticket is the invitation which gained Blok admittance to the ball.

CHAPTER VI

The Crossroads

(Autumn 1902–January 1904)

Yes, when I bore the great flame of love in my heart, made
up of the usual simple elements, yet invested with a new
content and a new meaning because the bearers of that love
were Lyubov' Dmitriyevna and I—'exceptional people'—
when I was full of that love which people will read about
in my books after I am dead, I used to take pleasure in setting
my beautiful horse prancing through the poverty-stricken
village. Just to show off, I enjoyed asking the way, which
I knew perfectly well beforehand, of some poor peasant or
of some comely peasant woman, just in order to exchange
flashing smiles with her and to make my heart jump a little
for no better reason than that I was young, the mist damp,
her eyes dark and my belt tight. All this had absolutely no
effect on my great love (or had it? what if all my future
falls and disintegration had their origin in this?) but, on the
contrary, set the flames of my youth, just my youth, leaping
and, together with my youth, that *other*, greater flame....
 The poor people were aware of all this. More aware of
it than I was, more consciously so. They knew that the
master was young, his horse stately, his smile attractive, that
his fiancée was lovely and that both were—gentlefolk. And
wait and see now—we'll show the gentry something,
pleasant or not.
 And they showed us.
 And they are showing us.... *And—I have not the right to
judge*.

(VII. 353–4)

1

A day or two after the banal proposal, they met in the Kazan Cathedral. Sitting on a bench by the wall in the half-darkness Blok took
Lyubov' in his arms—and they fell in love all over again. For a while
they kept their engagement a secret. They found a room where they

could meet and kiss. Almost, they came together, happily and naturally, but Lyubov' records that a momentary shrinking, the natural
fear of a conventionally brought-up and innocent girl of anticipating
the wedding night, was enough to bring back all Blok's complexes.
He began again to 'make up theories' why, even in marriage, their
relationship was so special that certain taboos should still be observed.
On a transparent excuse, he got rid of the room. Passion, he
explained, had nothing to do with love. It came and went. Inevitably,
he would be unfaithful to her in this respect—so why begin at all?
'And I?' asked Lyubov' desolately. 'And you, too,' replied her
worldly-wise suitor firmly. Lyubov' went home and cried as she was
no longer able to cry when everything happened just as he said it
would.[1]

Blok took to his bed. A chill? A recurrence of his horribly prosaic
sickness contracted in the Petersburg stews? Either way, it was a
retreat:

Something has happened to me which does not submit to my magic.
Before, I drew much from within myself, having the power to send certain
monsters to sleep and to prod others into wakefulness. Now I see that above
this power to draw things up from within stands Your, more perfect power
from without.... I recognized all the words from these legends which
spoke of how You were not and never would be with me. And I grew
accustomed to them and felt at home with them. I know separation, tormenting and infinite. To meet You face to face—that is something I do
not know.[2]

To this letter Lyubov' replied: 'I can only love, I understand nothing,
I want nothing, I love You.... to understand, to reason, to want—
is your *duty*.... I give my love into your hands without fear or
doubt.'[3]

Blok had made the proposal and had been accepted. Now he was
back—almost—where he had begun. There was, however, one vital
difference. He was no longer alone. He had bound himself to Lyubov', a living being of his own age, and there could be no more
thought of suicide. Sex was the devil and only time would show
what they were to do about it. Blok had too great a reverence for
life to force the issue either way.

Meanwhile there were letters to be written, trysts kept and missed,
relatives first to be deceived and then informed, rites to be observed
(the official blessing of the couple's engagement, before which both
went to Confession and took Holy Communion, took place in May
1903), photographs to be taken, a wedding to be planned and saved

for. The annexe at Shakhmatovo, too, had to be made ready and flowers and shrubs planted all about it; mock orange, hollyhock, tobacco, verbena, bird cherry, lilac, rose de Provence, a birch tree and a silver poplar (*Z.K.* 52). A new princess was coming to bring new hope and vitality to the quiet, heavily mortgaged little kingdom which Blok now shared with two nervous middle-aged women: his mother and his Aunt Maria. A young princess with a quiet conscience, plump and golden and full of fun.

The Romantic theory of the Eternal Feminine holds that, for each individual, the beloved serves as a link between the abstract questing masculine spirit and the rest of the world: humanity and nature. 'A poet', as John Keats told Fanny Brawne, 'is the most unpoetical of anything in existence, because he has no identity.' Blok felt that Lyubov' was helping him to establish a real identity beyond and apart from the creations of his own imagination, and tried to tell her so:

You are all my *youth*, my *living* hope, my *earthly* being....[4] If You should go, I shall completely disappear from the face of the earth, 'shall dissolve' in the creation and creating. When You are not there, I am so unthinkable that I suspect that, finally, some people are beginning to notice that I don't act of my own volition, that something inspires me from without.[5]

In a rare mood of fatigue, after their examinations in the spring, he wrote to her:

I grow weary of the ordinary and don't always want the absolutely out-of-the-ordinary. This is how I feel just now. And that is why at this moment I feel that I particularly need (apart from the absolutely extraordinary that is uniquely Yours) something else which You alone of all the world can give me: a woman's love, a *woman's*. It is our private life and our future that I am thinking about: to share the same walls, the same room, furniture, thoughts, feelings, to be one soul, full of 'compassion'—and all that is given only on one condition—marriage.[6]

Now that his face was firmly turned towards life again, the perennial longing to 'take on flesh' which was always to sweep over him as a kind of reaction against times of excessive abstraction, welled up with joyous insistence. In January 1903 he wrote to Aleksandr Hippius, who was about to depart for Siberia as tutor to Aunt Sofia's deaf son Andrey:

There is nothing more wonderful than birth, marriage, death—precisely because these are not replacements, not a break in the order of things, but a correction, a warning (sometimes), for those who have missed their way,

and always they touch with splendour, beauty, and some other quite inexpressible quality those who come into contact with them and who have
neither wept nor laughed from the heart for a long time.[7]

Meanwhile, Blok entered the world of the aesthetes of *Mir
Iskusstva* and the philosophers of the Religious-Philosophical Meetings like a man apart, who hearkens always to some inner voice. On
29 November 1902, he wrote to his father:

My verses[a] will not appear in the first number of *Novyy Put'*, but later they
have given me a firm undertaking. The editor (Pertsov) has written me
a too (exaggeratedly) flattering letter about my 'God-given' talent. . . .
Bryusov's Skorpion, which is not yet acquainted with me, has some
intentions towards me. In general opinions from Moscow are favourable.
Mir Iskusstva invite me to their *jours-fixes*, but I have only attended one,
where I found a number of celebrities—artists and writers—and a 'socializ-
ing' atmosphere which was quite alien to my inner, 'spiritual' state. . . .

(VIII. 47–8)

'The devil alone knows what is going on in the literary world',
he wrote Lyubov' a fortnight later:

We shall observe it from the sidelines and soon we shall hear and see
astonishing things. All this now touches me so closely that I cannot but
be interested in it. They all shout, and I am silent to the point of indecency
and through it all, immeasurably high and resonant, the songs about you
are singing themselves: words and phrases, sometimes just melodies without sounds, sometimes set to chance words which just happen to be running
through my head as freely and passively as the sound of the trees when
the wind is rocking them. It sings, it sings—and everything is forgotten,
all is light and vivid, solemn and mysterious. . . .[8]

The poems of the book Blok called *The Crossroads*, a subsection
still of the *Verses about the Most Beautiful Lady* written between his
engagement in November 1902 and mid-summer 1904, at first show
a triumphant recrudescence of the Beautiful Lady theme, more glad
and sunlit than ever before. The theme of the end of the world,
sometimes connected with the Lady and at others with scary apocalyptic urbanism and Antichrist, is strongly in evidence.

In this, as in all else after his betrothal, Blok was beginning to trust
to his own intuition and to shake off the tutelage of Solov'ev and,

---

[a] The cycle of ten poems about the Most Beautiful Lady, later included in the book
of that title, which were to be Blok's first published poems. They appeared in *Novyy Put'*,
no. 3, 1903.

more particularly, of Merezhkovsky, whom he had already set at a great distance from his own inner world:[b]

Here, perhaps, is the most basic and important refutation of Merezhkovsky's theory. His theory is fundamentally irreproachable (with the exception of a few details, perhaps). But ... it is boring. ... Boring, because it is *not* the end of the *world*, but only the end of world *history*....[c] He is like a signalling torch. He offers a *rational* way out, says: 'Come, come, oh Lord!' in the same tone of voice as 'Zina, haven't we any milk?' The torch has flashed its signal and gone out—until the next flash. The mouth laughs, the eyes are silent (always). The boredom of the repeated flashing. We no longer notice his signalling. We have grown 'accustomed'—a dreadful word for him; unbearable, most probably. We have grown accustomed to his world and he has lived through, forgotten, and been left behind by our convulsions.

(VII. 67–8)

Nevertheless, Lyubov' was jealous of Zinaida. For her Blok composed the charming poem 'The Tsaritsa gazed at the pictures' (I. 249), in which Hippius, the Queen (the Tsaritsa), is pictured as pondering ancient illuminated scripts, seeking truth in meditation and study, while Lyubov', the Princess (the Tsarevna), scatters corn for the white doves of the Spirit which come cooing down to her from the blue skies. Innocent and meek as the doves themselves, the Princess will 'pray away' the occult calculations of the Queen.

Gently, no longer forcing himself, Blok was beginning to look for harmony in the very sorrows of life: 'I have written some good verses ... they are of quite a different type—out of Dostoyevsky, and so Christian, that I could only have written them under your influence ...',[10] he wrote to his fiancée on Christmas Day and, two days later, he sent her the new poem, already somewhat nervous as to her reaction:

What do you say about that? There's decadence for you—isn't it? There formlessness.[d] It is simple and does happen in life on those borderlines where

---

[b] Cf. S. V. Panchenko's letter of 31 December 1902 in which he quotes Blok as having written to him, 'I too believe no one any more, neither Solov'ev nor Merezhkovsky.'[9]

[c] Blok's view of world history was, as befitted a sensitive artist of his generation, essentially Schopenhauerian: being a product of man's finite life on earth, history could have no ultimate meaning, for nothing '*essentially* better can ever come through either constitutions, or legal codes, or steam engines, or telegraphs'. Blok loved and hated history, as he loved and hated life on earth, but to neither did he attribute 'absolute' significance.

[d] The 'formlessness' was in fact a remarkably successful experiment in approximate rhyme and tonic (or accentual) verse, the casual, colloquial tone being achieved by unusually long (in some cases pentasyllabic) interspaces between the stressed feet. Other modernists (Bryusov, Dobrolyubov) had tried their hands at tonic verse (which in Old Russia had

Stavrogins go biting generals' ears. But it is 'Skorpionism' and will have
to go to Bryusov. They won't like it here. But perhaps it's nonsense? Write
me about it, the most important thing is what *you* think....[12]

These verses at last fulfil the promise in Blok's summer letter to
his father about 'a realism that borders on the fantastic'. Though Blok
declares them to be 'from Dostoyevsky', the strange sense of *déjà
vu* one has in reading them comes equally from Pushkin: Tatyana's
dream in *Evgeniy Onegin*. Certainly there is a smell of sulphur, a
dancing demonic chaos about the whole thing. This is no setting for
Nietzschean supermen. No one but Christ—who came, it must
always be remembered in the context of Russian literature, to call
sinners not the righteous—would venture into such a hornets' nest
as Blok here describes: no one but Christ would introduce His
immaculate Bride into such low company. The Christ of Dostoyevsky—and Blok's Christ too, from here until *The Twelve*—is
the Christ of sinners, the Christ who not only became man and died
for our salvation but who, before He rose again on the third day,
descended into hell.

> At the round tables all was shouting and noise,
> Restless shiftings from side to side,
> The liquor fumes had made everything dingy and close.
> Then suddenly someone came in—and a voice
> Rang through the hubbub: 'Here is my bride.'
>
> Nobody heard anything at all
> They were all squealing and grunting, like wild boars,
> But one, not knowing himself what for,
> Rocked on his feet and laughed, pointing out to them all
> The man and the girl who were coming in through the doors.
>
> She let her kerchief slip to the floor
> And all of them there, in anger and lust,
> As though some ill-auguring omen lay there before
> Them, fell on it with mindless squeals and tore
> It to shreds, then fouled each shred with blood and dust.

---

been the usual metre of the heroic saga [*bylina*] and of much folk poetry), and Hippius
in particular had made herself mistress of the genre and is said to have influenced Blok
in this respect. Yet it is typical that Blok should have used the tonic as he used every other
metre from classical iambs to the distinctive rhythmic beat of the factory *chastushka* not
for conscious formal experiment, but as they came to him, as they 'sang themselves'. His
mastery of music and rhythm is unsurpassed, yet the great bulk of his verse is written
in conventional metres and he appears to have given virtually no thought to formalistic
experiment as such. As here, he simply noted the achieved result with detached interest
as though the poem, once written, were no longer his.[11]

And when they had tired of it again
And crowded round the tables, side by side,
He pointed to where the girl was sitting quietly in
The dark corner, and cried in a clear voice above their din.
'Gentlemen! There is my bride.'

And suddenly, the one who had rocked on his feet and laughed
With hands outstretched in mindless greeting,
Fell to trembling, let his head sink in his arms—
And those who had yelled out in crazed alarm,
Suddenly heard the sound of weeping.

25 December 1902   (I. 252)

Lyubov's insistence on earthly values was desirable and necessary to Blok and to his poetry but, at the same time, he defended the validity of his own 'way', explaining it very patiently in terms that he knew she would understand:

This 'mysticism' (which you understand as something unearthly, beyond our sphere, 'theoretical') is the *very best* that I have ever had in me.... Mysticism is not 'theory', it is the *constant* sensation and constatation in oneself and in all around of mysterious, *living*, indestructible links, one thing with another and, through this, with the unknown. It is a religious awareness and not a misty clouding-up of the mind.... Your father accomplished a *mystic* action when, in the great concentration of his creative work, he discovered a *biological* law (a law of life), and these *biological* laws themselves are *mystical*, for they tell us of *causality*, that is of '*determinism*' (of dependence from). When the living sap rises through the stem, what is happening is a mystic process.... That is what mysticism is. It accepts me whole, I am in it and it is in me. It is my nature....
    From it I write poetry.
    Through it I came to love you. God alone knows, how that happened. That is why I always say that my love for you is *not ordinary.* I love all the time, as I pray. I know that it is *not ordinary love—not the same as between people who neither know nor believe. I know* many things *more than other people.* God grant that I may come to know still more.... It is more sad than I can say when you try to exorcise me from myself, as though I were possessed.... When you say 'without mysticism, please' it is as though you were pronouncing sentence of death—even over my verses.[13]

'I believed in Blok more than I believed in myself', Lyubov' wrote in her angry memoirs. More supple and generous to him then than to herself later, she yielded, as she had to do, and accepted to the end this difficult love which was so unlike 'ordinary love between people who neither know nor believe'.

2

Blok, serene in this new-found companionship, continued to observe the literary scene with a kind of detached wonder.

There in the world, in Russia and amongst us now, strange things are going on: in Moscow and in Petersburg. Pale people, old and young, are running hither and thither with presentiments of upheaval . . . and dragging people's minds after them, mine as well. But the heart, the heart which forgets nothing and sees everything, is anchored in the knowledge of You. . . . There— I am split up beyond count. Here—I am with You, whole and single.[14]

From Moscow, Olga Solov'eva, whose letters to Blok's mother about the personalities of the day 'running hither and thither with presentiments of upheaval' are a delight to read, surpassed herself with an account of a day which she called 'a cure for overweight':

At crack of dawn, when Misha [Mikhail Solov'ev] was not even out of bed, Borya [Andrey Bely] turned up and waited impatiently for Misha to come down so that he could read us the latest version of his Antichrist; it was necessary to resort to main force to give Misha the chance to have his first cup of coffee and his first cigarette without Antichrist. Antichrist, I think, is quite excellent (only don't tell anybody that it was Borya who wrote it, he is most insistent about that). But still, at the very start of the day in one's morning mood of common sense and thoughts about the house-keeping. . . ! What an enormous jump! Still, we both made it with great success and both got thoroughly worked up, I before Misha, perhaps, because I was thinking all the time that it wasn't just what the doctor had ordered for him (he had a slight temperature yesterday evening). Well, no sooner had Borya gone than along came Rachinsky[e] in a mood outside time and space and in a dreadful hurry to tell all as quickly as possible. Oh, you don't know who Rachinsky is, do you? He's a wonder, no less, 'A whirl-wind full of visions'. Only sometimes very exhausting; I always enjoy him but even my nerves begin to droop after two hours or so of him and Misha grows visibly thinner within half an hour and Seryëzha [Sergey Solov'ev, her son] quietly slips away when the atmosphere becomes really charged. First I sat with Rachinsky alone—Misha had to write a letter to Bryusov about Sasha's poetry—and all the time I was vaguely aware, through Christ, Nietzsche, the Cross and the Sword—Hosannah, Hosannah and Hosannah, that I was in a semi-indecent white negligée, terribly tight and dreadfully clinging, not fit for company of any sort, and I had sat through the whole of Antichrist in it and the hosannahs! The only comfort being that I dare say neither Borya nor Rachinsky would have noticed had I been stark

---

[e] Grigoriy Alekseyevich Rachinsky (1853–1939), translator, man of letters, and great friend of the Solov'ev family.

naked. That was the sort of day we had today; and now I come to think of it, they come like that quite frequently.[15]

Bryusov, Olga informed Aleksandra, had been to St. Petersburg again and had quite succumbed to the Merezhkovskys: 'He's sitting at home reading the Gospel! I think that Zina brought it off with her ankle, but Misha says her knee.'[16f] On 22 December, she told her cousin that Bely wanted to write to Blok. Her last letter, written on 31 December 1902, again spoke of Bely's wish to write and said: 'I loved Sasha's letter to Misha. All my fears that he would fall spiritually sick in the yallery-greenery mists are obviously quite unfounded.'[17]

Blok had written to M. S. Solov'ev, on 23 December 1902, about the placing of his verses with Skorpion:

Thank you again for all that. For me personally, apart from all other considerations, it is especially important that my verses be placed in a *Moscow* collection—because your Moscow is pure, white, and ancient, and I feel that more now with every new eccentricity of the Merezhkovskys and after every number of that cold, eclectic *Mir Iskusstva*. Its last number has finally, clearly and cynically, shown how ceremoniously our Diaghilevs and Benoises et al. click their heels while, from the other side, from yours, with what a shuddering strangeness 'flowers the heart' of Andrey Bely....

(VIII. 48–9)

On 3 January 1903 Blok wrote to Bely about the latter's article 'Forms of Art', which had so interested him in *Mir Iskusstva*. He stated the situation in his own poetry in the Solov'evian jargon which was by now second nature to both him and Bely: 'I am destined only to "live in white", but not "to create white"; it may be my lot to test the Whore of Babylon' (VIII. 54). Like his mentor, Vladimir Solov'ev, Blok occasionally took fright at the highfalutin nature of such statements and descended with a bump into sophisticated irony or sheer everyday, practical matters. This gave his style a choppy, masculine resilience which surprised Bely. He had not connected the author of *Verses about the Most Beautiful Lady* with either intellect or humour. Bely was a man at once enormously sensitive to others and inclined, as soon as their backs were turned, to fit them into his own essentially self-centred, hyperbolic schemae. So people

---

[f] Bryusov, when asked straight out by the Merezhkovskys whether or not he believed in Christ, replied: no, he did not. Their ideas of an apocalyptic Christianity, which looked towards the Christ who was to come in power and glory rather than towards the historical Man of Sorrows, fascinated and excited him, but he remained an uncommitted spiritual eclectic—hence the Solov'evs' ribald scepticism at his apparent conversion.

(even his own father who, when he eventually found out that the notorious decadent poet Andrey Bely was none other than his son Borya Bugayev, turned out to be really rather proud of the fact) were always taking him by surprise. Blok, perhaps more than anybody else, was a continual source of amazement to him, even posthumously.

On 4 January, Bely wrote to Blok—a pleasant introductory letter in an altogether more formal vein than Blok's to him. The letters crossed in the post. This touched off an extraordinarily esoteric, questioning correspondence.[18] To begin with, the impression is rather that of a meeting between any two healthy young male animals: they are walking round one another on stiff legs, intensely interested but bristling with formality and abstraction.

Then the frail Mikhail Solov'ev caught pneumonia. Olga had made Bely promise never to desert Seryëzha if ... On the night of 15–16 January 1903 Bely's father woke him, a candle dancing in his shaking hand, saying: 'You must go to the Solov'evs.'

Bely flung on his clothes and dashed round to find the doctor and Olga's sister at the Solov'evs' flat, Mikhail dead and Olga in a puddle of blood,

stretched out where she had hidden herself when the agony began, holding the door handle:
'Well—is it over?'—'No: he's still breathing!' 'He's alive!' 'It's over!' A shot!

It was 3.30 in the morning. Nothing might be touched until the police came. Seryëzha, who was at his aunt's house, must be told. Somehow the couple must be buried together, but suicide ... Christian burial ... !

Bely made his way through the frosty fog to Rachinsky. Rachinsky must have had high connections indeed, for he promised to arrange for Olga and Mikhail to be buried side by side near the grave of their illustrious brother in the grounds of the Novo-Devichiy Monastery. Then Bely went panting on—on foot, not a cab to be found at this unearthly morning hour—to Seryëzha.

Seryëzha was standing by the bed, his jacket pulled on all anyhow; his shoulders were hunched: he was frowning:
'Papa?'
'!'
'Mama?'
'!!'
'She too?'

I did not answer. . . .
'Herself?'
With dry dignity, like a man over the counter of a bank:
'I knew that!'
Pause.
'Borya'—he flung out an arm towards me as though he, not I, had
brought the news—'leave me for five minutes.' He showed me to the door
as though he were the older. 'I give you my word!'
Five minutes later he came out calm and severe: we knew what this self-
control must have cost him; if only he had cried out, wept. . . .
'Well!'[19]

Seryëzha, who was sixteen years old, was packed off for a while
to stay with relatives in Kharkov and Kiev, then returned to live
in Moscow with Rachinsky. His grandmother, Aleksandra Grig-
or'evna Kovalenskaya, 'almost lived there', and his great-aunt Sofia
Karelina also did what she could to help the orphan.

Blok had the news at once in a letter from Zinaida Hippius, who
happened to be in Moscow at the time. He broke it to his mother,
going down on his knees in front of her, taking her in his arms and
soothing and petting her—something not at all in the family style.
Bely had written Blok on 15 January:

Most respected Aleksandr Aleksandrovich,
I did not answer your letter. I was rather upset. At first by my father's
health. Then by the severe illness of M. S. Solov'ev. I am sure that you
will not be surprised at what I write, don't laugh. Mikhail Sergeyevich's
condition is very serious. It is necessary to pray. I believe in prayer.
  Pray.
  That is all I shall write you this time. About your letter—separately.
  I remain always at your service and sincerely devoted.
                                                  BORIS BUGAYEV[20]

Blok answered, shaken right out of his usual cool formality:

Dear, good Boris Nikolayevich,
Today, I received your letter. With the same post I heard about all that
has happened. I embrace you. I kiss you. It had to be like that, of course.
If you can write just a few words—how is Seryëzha? My dear, beloved—
I am with you. I love you.
                                            Your deeply devoted,
                                                  AL. BLOK[21]

Bely answered in exalted tones, repeating like a liturgy 'All is for
the best' and ending: 'Joyfully I kiss you.'[22]

Concern for the orphaned Seryëzha, a shared attitude to death as a joyful beginning, the natural closing of ranks about a fallen leader, the consciousness of their own youth and inexperience and the seemingly miraculous fact of their having begun to correspond literally in the nick of time: all these factors combined to make of the early stages of the profound love–hate relationship that was to develop between these two professor's sons something in the nature of a holy alliance.

Blok accepted Bely, as he never accepted Bryusov or the Merezhkovskys, into his heart and his family circle. Bely, who seems never to have had a private life in the way Blok did, had no such sanctum into which to admit his new 'brother'. Instead, he accorded Blok a probing, vulnerable devotion, a love so highly strung and 'ideal' that its transformation into hatred was almost inevitable. At times, Blok came to hate him too, yet they remained 'brothers', born of that great hope and expectation which had come to them both before they met.

Throughout the year 1903 they kept up an exchange of long, eager letters in which they explored one another's minds and beliefs, picked their way cautiously through contemporary literature, and weighed the merits of Petersburg and Moscow, the Merezhkovskys and Bryusov. Bely drew Blok out to tell him more clearly about his Cult of the Eternal Feminine.[g] Blok's painstaking answers show his mind to have been less quick and nimble than Bely's. He seldom pursued for long the will-o'-the-wisps of abstract thought but insisted on measuring everything against experience and on waiting for things to come clear 'of themselves'. There was in Blok's mysticism a deliberate and powerful passivity. He checked intuition by logic, but intuition was always his guiding star—this was his 'system'.... Though he often deferred to Bely's brilliant mind, encyclopedic learning, and to what, in his own modesty, he took to be his friend's more advanced spiritual state, the letters show Blok as the more mature of the two men. He seems always the older—though indeed the very intensity of the effort to put their souls on to paper over this first year shows how very young they both were.

---

[g] For this reason, and because of much that happened later, the correspondence is sometimes conceived of, quite wrongly, as an attempt on Bely's part to force Blok into theorizing, as a kind of intellectual rape perpetrated upon a confused but virginal contemplative soul. Any careful reading of Blok's diaries and letters over the preceding years must serve totally to disprove this idea. Blok had been absorbed in theory ever since the autumn of 1901.

3

The spring of 1903 brought Blok another friend: a man of no fame and no ambition who, while not a poet himself, lived in an intensely lyrical world with, as it were, an open border on to Blok's own, and thus came to influence his poetry, in his own unpretentious way, at least as deeply as did Andrey Bely.

Zhenya Ivanov was a law student. Red-haired, pale-faced, awkward, he was an ardent admirer of Merezhkovsky and Rozanov and a contributor to *Novyy Put'*. The younger son of a widowed mother (his father, of Old Believer,[h] merchant stock, had been a 'life nobleman'[i] and held an important post in a bank), Zhenya's interests were all wrapped up in religious, moral, and philosophical problems. His elder brother Aleksandr Pavlovich was an art critic and had written a book about an artist who, at this time, had already begun to interest Blok intensely: Mikhail Vrubel, a *Mir Iskusstva* painter obsessed by Lermontov's Demon and possessed of a rare, rhythmic gift for evoking the atmosphere and creatures of myth. Zhenya himself wrote little: children's stories, a copious diary, and occasional articles. When faced with the necessity of contributing to the family budget, he took on any unexacting clerkly job that was going. Yet he thought and felt like a true Symbolist, sharing the ideal of chivalrous love, the ability to see meanings behind everyday events and objects, the premonitions of change and catastrophe.

In one thing he differed. He was an Orthodox, practising, praying Christian with a tender conscience, almost unbearably refined by spiritual discipline. Zhenya lived his religion unobtrusively, making absolute demands on himself and virtually none on his fellows. This,

[h] In the seventeenth century reforms were instituted to bring the ritual of the Russian Orthodox Church, which had changed gradually during the isolation brought about by the Tartar occupation of South Russia and the virtual severance of communication with Constantinople, back into line with Greek Orthodox practice. A large section of the Russian Church, less adaptable than the Celtic Church in Britain when somewhat similar problems had arisen after a period of separation from Rome a thousand years before, refused to conform, resisting persuasion, persecution, and intense civic pressure. Enduringly independent, austere communities came into existence in the forests east of the Volga and achieved great prosperity as traders and farmers, preserving a strict patriarchal way of life and an indigenous conservative culture which only began to be eroded and reabsorbed into the mainstream of the nation's development in the second half of the nineteenth century (cf. for instance the novels of Melnikov-Pechersky). The Ivanov family were very much citizens of Petersburg and Orthodox in practice, but retained certain Old Believer attitudes, above all a hospitality which went hand in hand with awareness of their home and family as a stronghold of living faith.

[i] To be made a life nobleman was a personal honour comparable to a knighthood.

probably, was the source of his power, not so much to influence or to comfort as to help people find the truth in themselves:

From my adolescence I carried the Gospel everywhere I went, having no clear idea why. It lay in the side pocket over my heart and was never taken out or read when anyone was there to see. I even hid it. But it is with the Gospel as with the Cross; it has a mysterious presence. Not in me myself but in that which I carried with me, Aleksandr sensed Him in spirit, even if he did not recognize Him. And when he spoke seriously, or read his verses to me, he did not read them to me alone, but to Him whom I dared to carry on my person. It was not clearly expressed, either for him or for me, but it was still there in the secret of the spirit; without that constant turning in secret of Aleksandr to Christ with the question: 'But what would He say?' we cannot expect to understand the profundity of Al. Blok's works....[23]

This friend of Blok's, it has been said, had a gift for entering into other people's lives comparable to that of Dostoyevsky's heroes Prince Myshkin and Alyësha Karamazov.[24] Endowed with an artist's capacity for total empathy, Zhenya was quite free of the essential egotism of the creative personality. The result was that, once taken to the heart of the Blok family, he became everybody's friend and confidant. Blok and his family considered him 'the very best person' they knew.[j] He himself likened his friendship with Blok to Dante's and Virgil's pilgrimage through hell, a journey in which Blok played the part of the wise pagan guide.

The first meeting of these celestial pilgrims, however, came about in the most mundane circumstances:

On 6 March the first editorial 'evening' of *Novyy Put'* was held.... The organizers of the party were the Merezhkovskys. Zinaida Nikolayevna (Hippius-Merezhkovskaya) played hostess. The party was held in the empty editorial flat which was temporarily situated somewhere on the Nevsky Prospect. I went in: Bright lights ... a long table, a white tablecloth ... Flowers, wine, a fork supper, tea ... Gracious living: you'd hardly recognize your own friends, although they were all people who knew one another well, from *Novyy Put'* and *Mir Iskusstva*, and amongst them all 'he' ... Aleksandr Blok: not quite 'one of us', 'different'; that is why I noticed him straight away. I had not yet read his poetry, but my first impression was of a newly consecrated knight. Blok was tall and good-looking: an impression as of a mail shirt beneath the student jacket, an 'austere

[j] Ivanov outlived his friend by 21 years, eventually dying of starvation during the siege of Leningrad. The twentieth century has shown us only too often what starvation can do to ordinary people. It is a measure of Ivanov's quality that he is said to have shared and given things away till the end and that his family survived him.

cross' in his face, somewhere between the eyes, brows, and lips. About the face, smooth as an adolescent's, there was a frame of ash-blond hair with red-gold lights, curling down round the nape of the neck. We greeted one another as people do who have heard of one another beforehand. He smiled, checking the smile a little with his lips, not quite sure yet: 'how?' I sat next to him by Z. N. Hippius who poured out the tea, leaving the guests to help themselves to food. For some time we sat next to one another, neither saying a word. I stole a glance at him and noticed 'a waxen immobility of feature' about his face, as though he had put on a waxen mask. ...[k] This was particularly noticeable about the slightly parted lips. This peculiarity of his face many took for dead pride: many people (V. V. Rozanov, for instance) were extremely irritated by it. ... And so we sat and said nothing. ... I ... decided to make a simple opening move—as at a children's tea-party. I reached out for a plate of cheese sandwiches and, trying one, handed them to Al. Blok, implying that they were very good. Immediately Aleksandr Aleksandrovich came to life. A childishly open, rather mischievous smile lit up his whole face.[25]

Ivanov always insisted on the child in Blok; the slow, shy sense of fun, the riotous clowning, the utterly defenceless smile—'a demon with the smile of a Tamara', Anna Akhmatova later called him.[l] Ivanov, however, qualified this insistence in his own way:

But if he was a child, he was the kind of child we see on the icon of Our Lady of the Passion, where the Child has suddenly turned away from his Mother's breast, having seen the instruments of His passion, of His execution, held out towards Him by hovering angels.[26]

Blok and Ivanov met again at a second *Novyy Put'* reception, much less grand than the first owing to the extreme poverty of the journal. By this time Zhenya had read Blok's first cycle of poems in *Novyy Put'* and somehow the poet sensed through the strange young student's awkwardly expressed enthusiasm that here was a man who understood what he was writing about. Gradually the friendship ripened and, after Blok's marriage, the two men began to visit at each other's homes.

4

In the meantime, arrangements went forward for the wedding. Blok's mother had been ill again and had to go back to Bad Nauheim.

[k] The expressions 'waxen mask, 'austere cross', and 'dreadfully immobile features' are all suggested by Blok's poetry.

[l] In her *Poem without a Hero*. In Lermontov's poem, Tamara is the innocent Georgian maiden seduced by the Demon.

He planned to accompany her. The journey and the wedding had
to be carefully budgeted. Blok's father, who had been told about
the forthcoming marriage only on his regular Easter visit to St.
Petersburg, helped by increasing his son's allowance to an annual
1,000 roubles.

Seryëzha Solov'ev was informed, in great secrecy, of the forthcoming 'most important event' in Blok's life (VIII. 55–6). Rather
rashly, Blok also told Zinaida Hippius. She, like Queen Elizabeth,
resented young men at her court getting married, and put forth
all her sophisticated charm to recall him to the service of poetry and
ideal love. Zhenya Ivanov remembered how once,

... in May before the Merezhkovskys were due to leave for the country,
I called and found Aleksandr Aleksandrovich Blok with Zinaida Nikolayevna in her boudoir. They were both standing, absorbed in a conversation about poetry. And I was astonished at how differently Zinaida Nikolayevna Hippius conducted herself towards Blok than towards us ordinary
students. They were both standing in such striking poses in front of the
fireplace. Blok told me afterwards that Zinaida Nikolayevna had somehow
been particularly provocative that evening and that afterwards they had
gone walking until three o'clock in the morning.[27]

Blok afterwards told Andrey Bely how 'Madame Merezhkovskaya'
had spun out a long and difficult theory about marriage all through
a long spring night and how he had loved the night more than the
theory and could not really recall what she had been trying to tell
him.[28]

Hippius, having failed to recall Blok to the Merezhkovsky fold,
dryly informed their Petersburg acquaintances that he was in love
and spent his time walking in the suburbs 'to meet the spring and
gather snowdrops', which was why he was so seldom present at the
editorial gatherings of Novyy Put'. It seemed to her then, as later,
that Blok was anti-social.

Certainly, he had no feeling for the community of action which
she and Merezhkovsky were struggling to organize; yet it was in
this spring that he wrote:

> A dream of bright thoughts came upon me
> I dreamt that I was not alone.

On the banks of the Neva, as the ice broke and the water began to
flow freely again, he had seen people busy building bonfires and tar-
ring boats. They had looked happy and again he had thought of the
Lady 'manifesting Herself in history', surrounded by 'other warriors
and different heroes' (I. 91):

A thought of the spring is within me
I know that You are not alone.

(I. 271)

It was not that he deliberately evaded Hippius and her demands. Rather was it that the spring made the sense of expectation which had been growing in him all winter almost intolerable. He could not talk about this, but in his poetry the unanswered questions, indefinite pronouns, adjectives (often verbal adjectives) in place of nouns, the sighing sibilants and assonances, convey the essence of his mood:

> In the quiet air, never-showing, all-knowing,
> Someone is laughing, someone carefully hidden.
> Who is laughing there? Is it I, softly sobbing?
> Is it my heart there joyfully thudding?
> Is it spring come to the window—rosily, sleepily?
> Is it just my heart, in love and dreaming?
> My lucent Lady softly smiling in at me?
> Shall I know all? Or is it only seeming?

(I. 272)

Nevertheless, goaded by the curiosity of Hippius and others like her, Blok did make one clear statement in poetry about his Lyuba: 'the girl I serve', 'a rosy girl standing upon the threshold who told me that I was tall and handsome'. 'That is all my story, good people,' he wrote firmly. 'I never dreamt of a miracle—and you calm down, and forget about it too' (I. 279).

The course of the engagement ran ordinarily enough. There was a flare-up of early and acutely painful jealousy on Blok's mother's part (quickly smoothed over). Lyubov' quarrelled with her own mother over some practical arrangement and received her first severe curtain lecture from her fiancé: 'I am older than you and a man, yet I have managed to live all my life without concerning myself with such trifles ... they are not only of no significance; they do not even give anybody the least pleasure.'[29]

The Beketov way of life did not admit of family quarrels and nastinesses over practical arrangements, and Blok was frequently shocked by Lyubov's capacity for intrigue and occasional pettiness although, like other, more ordinary husbands, he was persistently to ascribe everything of which he disapproved in his wife to the influence of his 'in-laws'.

The Mendeleyevs, on their part, had to be persuaded that Blok, with three more years as an undergraduate ahead of him, poor financial prospects and tainted health, was a suitable partner for their daughter. Here, of course, Mendeleyev's friendship with Andrey Beketov played an important part. The old man, whose favourite light reading was *The Three Musketeers*, had no time for 'decadents' and 'mystics', but he respected Blok's personal uprightness and his own daughter's wishes. His consent to an early marriage was obtained and thereafter the consent of the University authorities, and the wedding was fixed to take place in the church at Tarakanovo, halfway between the two estates, on 17 August 1903.

On 27 May Aleksandr and his mother left for Germany. From Bad Nauheim, Blok complained to his father with the perennial irritation of the patriotic Russian who has to leave his own country in order to read his own best authors:

Here abroad you feel extremely cut off from all worlds. Your eye is caught by forbidden publications (in Russian) in the shop windows, of which I would have bought several had there not been the customs to think about. There are a great many of Tolstoy's books and *Osvobozhdeniye*[m] is to be seen sticking out of several people's pockets.[30]

Otherwise, there was little to do but write letters and take the waters. It was from Bad Nauheim that Blok wrote perhaps his most important letter to Andrey Bely, in which he tried hard to define, at his friend's request, exactly *what* he felt about the Most Beautiful Lady.[n]

One expedition he made while at Bad Nauheim, to the castle of the neighbouring town of Friedberg, the seat of Alice of Hessen-Nassau before her ill-fated marriage to Nicholas II, impressed him profoundly. Through a wicket gate in the wall, overgrown with climbing roses, Blok entered the enclosed world of a medieval walled garden and, looking out from the battlements across the prosaic, prosperous plains, came to the conclusion that the spirit of Europe was alive only in the past. In the prose piece 'The Maiden of the Rosy Gate and the King of the Ants' (v. 83–94, November 1906)[o] he

---

[m] *Liberation*, an illegal Russian newspaper.

[n] The letter[31] mentions the Stranger (the term, which did not appear until later in his poetry, seems to have had its origin in this correspondence), or 'Izida the Triple-Crowned' with whom the Lady was so fatally associated but from whom She differed essentially, as the sun differs from the moon, by virtue of Her lucent immutability, and seeks to define the relationship of the cult of the Most Beautiful Lady to Christianity and, more particularly, Her relationship to Christ.

[o] See also Blok's letter to Lyubov' Dmitriyevna of 24 June (N.S.) 1903, from Bad Nauheim (VIII. 58–61), which gives a detailed account of his first impressions of the walled garden at Friedberg, the poem 'In Love' (3 June 1905, II. 61), and Blok's notebook for 19 July 1903 (*Z.K.* 48–50).

recorded both his initial enchantment with the secluded garden and that bitter rebellion against Romanticism of all sorts which was to reach its apogee a few years later in his cruel harlequinade, the play *The Puppet Booth*.

During this dull stay at Bad Nauheim even his correspondence with Lyubov' took on an obligatory daily character. His poetry is painful and disillusioned. Once, in 'The day was grey and tender, grey as dull despond', the image of Sadovskaya returned to haunt him with languid shame (1. 284). It seemed again as though he were an old man, and the very thought that he was a poet called forth a dry cackle of self-mockery: 'I am weary of trusting to the books of rosy idiots like myself! To hell with dreams!' (1. 281).

After six weeks, Blok and his mother returned via Petersburg to a full-scale family gathering at Shakhmatovo. It must have been a trying time. At twenty-two Blok found himself master of the house and positively snowed under by practical arrangements, from hanging curtains to making sure there would be 'a stool for the little boy who carries the icon' at the church. Photographs of himself and Lyubov', his notebook records, were to be sent to 'Bugayev, Seryëzha, and Father', the latter being conspicuous by his absence, having done his duty to his son by providing the annual allowance and a great deal of unpalatable advice. Like the fairy who was *not* invited to the christening, however, he had bestowed a gift that was to cast a gloom over all the ensuing years: that cruel sensuality which Blok could never reconcile with his love for his 'little girl', Lyuba, and which he had no desire to pass on to a child.

Indeed, the poet's attitude to his father's family comes out curiously at this time. On 16 July, shortly after returning to Shakhmatovo and a month before his wedding, Blok noted in his diary:

Of the Blok family the following may yet intend to reproduce their species.
   1) Nikolay (suddenly in October?!)[p] and Georgiy Petrovich Blok.
   2) Olga and Sofia Kachalova.
   3) Ivan's daughters.
   The *first* would be the worst.
   Olga is already married. There would be an admixture of Shteyn blood in her child (I think that's her married name).
   If I have a child it will be worse than the verses. Just such another ...
I am a degenerate from the Blok family.... Tender. Romantic. But every bit as affected.

[p] The information in brackets inserted later.

And, in the midst of all these unhappy thoughts:

Lyuba, Lyubochka, Lyubushka.
   If Lyuba at last comes to understand what it's all about then nothing
will happen. I don't think Lyubochka will understand.

Then, a day or two later:

Lyuba does understand. I underestimated her. She understands better than
I do. (19 July. The Feast of St. Seraphim of Sarov.)

(*Z.K.* 50–1)

   His poetry—and he was writing freely again over the month at
Shakhmatovo before his wedding—shows that the despondency of
Bad Nauheim was left behind him. Excited by responsibility, the
poet sees himself again as the wielder of a great sword, the master
of 'Her' fate, vowed to keep a superhuman vigil until the coming
of the dawn (I. 286); yet the doubles are still crowding round him
and again he casts Lyubov' as Columbine (I. 287–8).
   The wedding is best described by Aunt Maria, the family
chronicler *par excellence*, and by Seryëzha Solov'ev, a very grown-
up and self-assured seventeen, who was acting as the groom's *schaffer.*[q] Maria Beketova records:

Frants Feliksovich came down from Petersburg for the wedding and Aunt
Sonya from Trubitsyno. She was devoted to Sasha and for all her seventy-
eight years was in complete possession of her faculties and interested in
everything that concerned him, including his poetry some of which she
appreciated....' The wedding was fixed for eleven o'clock in the morning.
It was a rainy day, only brightening up towards evening. All of us got
up early and dressed in our best. The bouquet that had been ordered from
Moscow for the bride failed to come in time. Sasha and his mother picked
large pink asters from the herbaceous border. The *schaffer*, Seryëzha Solo-
v'ev, solemnly bore the bouquet to Boblovo in a troika with horses hired
from Klin all ready for the bride and groom. The horses were handsome,

---

[q] According to Russian custom the bride and groom are each attended by a man, a
schaffer, so the function is not quite identical with that of best man. Blok asked Andrey
Bely to be *schaffer* to the bride, but he finally declined a few weeks before the wedding
and was replaced by a Polish friend, Count Razvadovsky, who made a great impression
on Seryëzha and shortly afterwards became a Roman Catholic monk. Blok described his
brief friendship with Razvadovsky as 'something big and blueish which afterwards lost
itself in the "azure vault beyond the world"' (VIII. 65). He was glad when Razvadovsky
took his vows although this happened when he himself was further than ever before from
the Church (VIII. 119).
   ' Andrey Bely maintained that Blok's early verses were instantly appreciated by old
people reared on the early nineteenth-century Romantic poet Vasiliy Zhukovsky, whereas
they left the intermediate generation—who found them quite incomprehensible—cold or
even indignant.

hefty, light grey, the high yoke over the middle horse was all decorated with ribbons. The driver a smart young fellow dressed to kill.

Mother and stepfather blessed Sasha with an icon of the Saviour. And Aunt Sonya blessed him too.[32]

Seryëzha takes up the tale:

... I came to take the bride to the church, bringing a pink bouquet. 'I'm ready,' said Lyubov' Dmitriyevna, and stood up. I waited at the door. The ceremony of the blessing began. Old Mendeleyev rapidly made the sign of the Cross over his daughter with a senile, trembling hand and just kept repeating: 'Christ be with you! Christ be with you.'[33]

Then Aunt Maria again:

The wedding took place in the old church in the village of Tarakanovo. It was not one of those modern parish churches but an old private chapel built by the landlord of those parts in the reign of Catherine the Great. ... We arrived early at the church and had rather a long wait for the bride. Sasha in his student's jacket was serious, concentrated, solemn.

For that day we had managed to get hold of a really very decent choir from the large village of Rogachevo. The rain let up for a while and we could see the guests arriving through the windows of the church. They were all relatives of the Mendeleyevs who lived in the neighbourhood. The horses were fresh and strong. The yokes decorated with sprays of oak. The church was soon packed. Then at last the troika appeared with the bride, her father, her sister Maria Dmitriyevna and a little boy to bear the icon. She entered the church on the arm of Dmitriy Ivanovich, who had put on all his medals for the occasion. He was extremely moved. The choir struck up: 'Come, turtle-dove.'

And in very truth—a dove ...

She was wed not in traditional silks, which would not have been suitable in this country setting: she wore a dress of snow-white batiste, effectively cut and with a very long train, flowers, a veil. It was impossible to look at the handsome young couple without emotion. Reverential, solemn, beautiful—how they prayed then! And indeed a great sacrament was being celebrated—the sacrament of the union of two souls, created one for the other. Even the old priest, a coarse man prejudiced against our family, was obviously touched and looked at bride and groom with a smile.[34]

Sergey Solov'ev says that the priest barked: 'Be so good as to cross yourself!' when Blok tried to take the wedding crown in his hands instead of kissing it, and Lyubov' Dmitriyevna remembers that, by mistake, she drank all the wine from the cup, and that there was an awkward moment when Blok asked her to kneel and she misunderstood and did not. Later, it seemed to her a bad omen that they forgot to kiss. Blok himself, however, and the whole Beketov clan, were obviously overwhelmingly relieved that everything passed off as well as it did. Dmitriy Ivanovich and Aleksandra Andreyevna were so moved that they wept throughout.

When the ceremony was over, the young couple continued for some time in prayer before the icons.

When they came out of the church they were met by peasants with bread and salt and white geese. Then they drove to Boblovo in their gaily decorated troika. We all followed them. As they entered the house the old nanny sprinkled them with hops. The mother of the bride, according to Russian custom, should not be present in church and Anna Ivanovna had observed the custom. In the spacious top-floor living room the table was laid. We were treated to a regular wedding feast. And out in the courtyard a crowd of peasant women in holiday costume forgathered and sang the praises of the bridegroom, the bride, and the guests. Refreshments were sent out to them, and money. When the champagne was poured out, Sergey Mikhailovich Solov'ev proposed the health of the newly-weds. But they did not remain with us till the end. They were hurrying to catch their train and left for Petersburg, where rooms had been prepared for them in Blok's stepfather's flat. A servant was waiting there to look after them.[35]

5

'The Bloks' rooms', continues Aunt Maria,

... were almost like a separate flat; they led off to one side and could only be reached through the hall. A big bedroom with windows on to the embankment and a little study with a window on to the light barracks corridor. The lower panes of the window had waxed paper glued over them with pictures of a knight and his lady in colour. The impression was one of bright stained glass. The furniture in the study was old, all Beketov stuff. The writing table was Blok's grandmother's, he used it all the rest of his life. Then there was his grandfather's settle, comfortable armchairs and chairs, and a bookcase. There was an Oriental rug on the floor.[36]

So began Blok's domestic life.

For a year, the couple succeeded in maintaining a 'white marriage'. Lyubov' wrote of their life together:

The fine-strung tenderness of our relationship could not be trimmed to fit the usual human 'brother and sister, father and daughter'. ... No! ... It was more painful, more tender, more impossible. ... And right from the beginning, from the first year of our life together, a kind of play-acting

sprang up between us, we found 'masks' for our feelings, surrounded ourselves with imaginary beings which had a life of their own as far as we
were concerned, and our language became quite esoteric. It is impossible
to tell about it in 'concrete' terms. It is quite inaccessible to a third party;
a kind of distant reflection of the world of his verses—and all those little
creatures of the forest, and all our childhood, and the crabs, and the donkey
in 'The Nightingale Garden'. And for this reason, whatever happened to
us, however much life tormented us, we always had a way out into this
world where we were securely inseparable, true and chaste. There, we
always felt safe and at ease, even if, at times, we wept over our earthly
misfortunes.[37]

It was not a comfortable situation: Lyubov' found it, on occasion,
downright humiliating, especially when Blok's mother, hoping she
might be with child, asked her whether this were so, touching off
one of those ugly scenes between the two women which, in spite
of their generous recognition of one another's individual stature and
importance in Blok's life, were eventually to make it impossible for
them to go on sharing a home.

Meanwhile, there were compensations. Lyubov' and Aleksandr
understood one another, they had agreed to let things take their
course, to decide nothing irrevocably. Full of admiration for her
understanding, he had persuaded her of the dignity of her role. She
moved in the reflected glory of his verse. Immediately after the marriage, though, he wrote little (three poems for September 1903, six
for October, seven for November). Peace and propinquity left him
temporarily without the desire to write. It was obviously impossible,
too, to continue in the old vein. His present Muse, he declared, was
no longer a sword but more like a peaceful scythe, fit only to cut
'the sleepy head of some small flower' (1. 536). By November, however, the familiar little demons were knocking at the walls and windows again: and the poetry immediately improved. They were
frightened of Lyubov', 'rosier than the spring, more severe than
the evening shadows' (1. 298), but still they knocked and in the
poet's heart was a wild whirling dance, past days like dead leaves
dancing, 'and in every circle of the dance I see the flame of sin ...'
(1. 299).

'All that has happened', he wrote at this time to Seryëzha Solov'ev,
'has cut off the way back to the childhood of life. And this is splendid
and all for the best.'[38]

Daily life, however, showed few signs of this growing maturity.
Living as children, Blok and his wife were naturally treated as children by the elders of the household. In the morning, they set out 'to

town' together, he for the University, she for the Bestuzhev Courses. Blok kept accounts of the allowance they received from Professors Blok and Mendeleyev. For October 1903 he recorded:

Money left over on 1 October, 54 roubles 80 copecks
Account for October

1 Oct Cemetery 3.70. Theatre 4.50.
2 ,, Self 4.60.
3 ,,
4 ,, Galoshes for little Rabbit [Zaychik] 3.50+.50.
5 ,,
6 ,, Dressmaker 25 roubles.
7 ,, Season ticket for Zaychik—6.50.
8 ,, Zaychik's bootees—2; further to the same 3.
9 ,, A muff—47.
10 ,, Self 1r.
11–14 ,,
15 ,, Zaychik 1r.
16 ,, Delo[5] 4.75.
Self 1r. 15c.
17 ,,
18 ,, Shlyapkin's lectures 1.10.
19–20
21 ,, Self 1r.
22 ,,
23 ,, Zaychik (for dressmaker) 1r.
24 ,,
25 ,, Self 1.50   Zaychik 1r.
26 ,,
27 ,, Self 2r. 25.
28 ,, Watch 2r.
Cigarettes 4.25.
29 ,, Concert at the Courses 2.50.
30 ,,
31 ,, Self 1r. Zaychik 1r.[39]

The November accounts begin with 75 roubles received making a credit balance of 35. Nowhere is there any mention of housekeeping—fruit, sweets, and a bucket seem to have been their only domestic purchases, and the couple apparently entertained their visitors (S. A. Sokolov, the editor of a new decadent publishing house, Grif, came to see them on 16 November, and Seryëzha Solov'ev stayed from the 12th to the 16th) at the expense of the Kublitskys. Blok was working hard, writing reviews for *Novyy Put'* and for

[5] A play by Sukhovo-Kobylin.

Bryusov's new monthly *Vesy*.[1] He was now publishing poetry regularly in the various decadent almanacs: Skorpion's *Severnye Tsvety* and Sokolov's *Almanakh Grif*. Over Grif there had been a good deal of trouble, stirred up, according to Andrey Bely who had originally encouraged Blok to publish with them, by the Merezhkovskys. Bryusov had thought of Grif as a kind of decadent second eleven to Skorpion, and was very upset to find that it could not get along without help from authors he had come to consider his own property—such as Bely. He tried to issue an ultimatum that no one should publish with both Grif and Skorpion, but this had the opposite effect. Bely refused to be dictated to and Blok followed his lead—an act of defiance which both subsequently regretted. Zinaida Hippius, always ready to add fuel to the flames, composed a parody in which Bryusov is depicted, inconstancy incarnate, surrounded by fawning mythical monsters, 'caressing the Griffon but loving the Scorpion'.

That winter, too, Blok actually began to make a little money from his writing by placing poems and reviews with the widely popular *Zhurnal dlya vsekh*.

Sometimes Lyuba would leave Blok at his studies to attend a concert (he always said he had no ear for music). Together, they watched the Maeterlinck plays brought to Petersburg and Moscow by the playwright's own troupe. On 30 November they attended a concert of songs, German *Lieder* and Russian songs, by the singer Olenina-d'Al'geym whose performance, particularly her rendering of Mussorgsky's 'Nursery', moved Blok so deeply that he dedicated a poem to her (I. 301).[2] On Christmas Eve, like the good children they were, Lyubov' and Aleksandr had a Christmas tree with gilded nuts at the Barracks and, on Christmas Day, they visited the Mendeleyevs. They saw the New Year in together, at church.

This, except for receiving and occasionally visiting friends, was the sum total of their social life for the first few months of their marriage. One of the first of their visitors had been Zhenya Ivanov.

After the summer gap in their acquaintance Ivanov had been rather shy of meeting Blok again for, like others of the poet's early admirers, he had difficulty in envisaging the knight of the Most Beautiful Lady as a married man. When he did finally run into Blok it was by chance on one of the windswept Petersburg bridges as the two swung along

[1] *Vesy* did not begin publication until January 1904, but material was already being collected for it.

[2] This poem, with its reminiscences of Nanny Sonya and one of the later Beketov flats, was probably the basis for the later and more successful 'Time to sleep, but I don't want to' (III. 266), most felicitously translated by Robin Kemball in the *Russian Review*, October 1959, 3091.

in opposite directions, concentrating on keeping their footing on the
slippery wooden pavements, treacherous with sludgy snow and wet
leaves. Blok had disarmed and astonished the absent-minded Zhenya
by hailing him by his (correctly remembered) name and patronymic.
As they exchanged addresses, Blok

never ceased hearkening and gazing into the ringing and whistling on the
bridge, and beyond the bridge, and somewhere further on still, like a warrior who feels the unseen presence of the enemy before a battle.... The
profoundly disturbed look on his face, as of one who sees into the future,
struck me deeply. We said good-bye. He strode away towards the Peterburgskaya Storona, over the bridge, and disappeared into a flurry of wet
snow driving in from the sea.[40]

On 15 December Zhenya had paid his promised visit. Typically,
he lost the way and turned up for lunch in the early dusk, having
blundered all round the Petrogradskaya Storona and then all round
the soldiers' quarters of the Barracks. Eventually, the regimental
clerk had directed him through an alley out on to the embankment
'to the white wing with columns' where the officers had their
apartments.

The sentry on duty sent him on to Flat No. 13 and the next
moment the exhausted Zhenya was being admitted by a smart batman. 'This way, sir. You are expected.'

I entered. The hall was white, light, an officer's coat and high fur hat on
the hall stand. A mirror in a mahogany frame.... Opposite: a door into
the half-dark drawing room. Out of the door, a bow-legged little dog came
skidding over the slippery painted floor-boards, glittering with polish; he
did not actually bark but seemed at a loss what to make of the new guest.
    A door opened from the left and Aleksandr Blok came out to meet me.
    The knight in his own home: welcoming, hospitable and lovable, his
armour laid aside, dressed in his working, 'Shakespeare' shirt.
    We greeted one another. He led me off to the left into a long room with
a tremendously high ceiling and tall window opposite which a low door
led into their bedroom, and another into the hall.
    In this room 'Lyuba' rose to greet me, Lyubov' Dmitriyevna.
    Lyuba, Aleksandr Aleksandrovich's wife, was like a little girl at that time,
only so very, very big—the daughter of a giant (the daughter of that vast
patriarchal figure, Mendeleyev).... She exuded simplicity and calm: the
depths of Russian waters with their hidden potential of storm shining under
the summer lightnings.... Soon we were called into the dining-room....
Aleksandr Aleksandrovich's 'Mama', Aleksandra Andreyevna, stood at the
table, waiting for us. She had the figure of a young girl and the face and
the eyes of a child that has often been struck across the face but has put
up with it all and forgotten: only the pain was left in the eyes and a kind

Aunt Maria and Blok's mother strolling in the garden at Shakhmatovo. In the background is Blok's apparatus, later to serve as the balcony for 'Juliet'. (From the collection of N. P. Il'in)

A road near Shakhmatovo.

Lyubov' Dmitriyevna in 1898.

Aleksandr Blok in student's uniform, 1903.

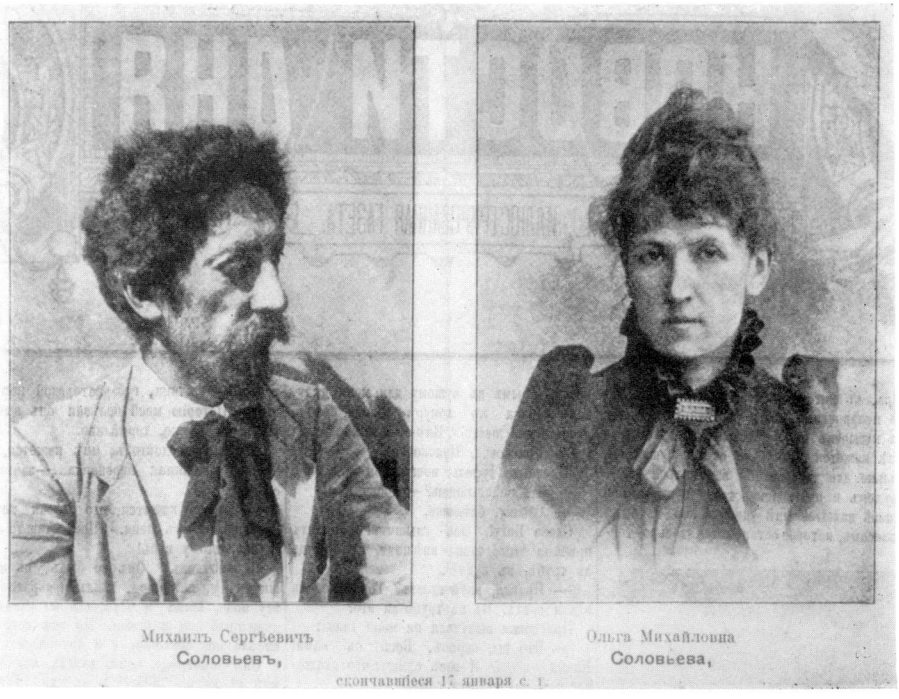

Михаилъ Сергѣевичъ
Соловьевъ,

Ольга Михайловна
Соловьева,

скончавшіеся 17 января с. г.

Mikhail and Olga Solov'ev: a newspaper photograph published with the report of his
death and her suicide. (From the Literary Museum, Moscow)

of knowledge. From the other side of the table rose Blok's stepfather, Frants Feliksovich, and introduced himself.

In him there was a curious contradiction between outward form and inner content. The uniform jacket on the extraordinarily unmilitary figure, round-shouldered and hollow-chested, the sharp pointed features of the face and the sharp pointed moustache and beard—and the soft soul, the eyes full of chesty grief (like a person with some illness of the chest), a soul devoted to the death to his duty and his wife.

The other guest was Visha Grek, a black-browed thick-bearded officer of the Grenadier Guards, the same age as Aleksandr Aleksandrovich and a childhood playmate....[41]

After lunch, the Bloks had taken Zhenya back to their room, where, from sheer shyness, he talked non-stop—'not letting anybody else get a word in'—then suddenly and precipitously took his leave, announcing that 'they'd be anxious about him at home'.

Blok must have seen through this awkward début, for at the Feast of the Baptism in the very heart of the Russian winter he sought Zhenya out in his own home, told him a quicker way to the Grenadier Barracks, and took the trouble to reassure his mother that no ill could befall his friend in his home and she was not to worry if he stayed late in future. Blok understood about families.

6

More and more, however, he was haunted by premonitions of the impossibility of continuing his own family existence: pleasant as it was, happy as it was.

The Blok Zhenya had met on the bridge was already in evidence in his poetry in the persona of a sleepless, homeless wanderer (I. 305), who tirelessly walks the streets of the capital, observing the shady night life; the processions of sewage carts; the comfortless wastes of the city outskirts; recording cruel incidents, typical *faits-du-jour* from the daily paper. Blok was not compassionate by nature; rather the opposite. His cult of the Beautiful Lady had expressly excluded philanthropic sociology and the 'kindness' of Christ.[42] Yet his present reaction to a spoilt world was different from the crushed acceptance he had experienced '*ante Lucem*', before the Light. The years of steadfast gazing into 'the cloud of unknowing', and now the sturdy companionship of his Zaychik—possibly even the unhappiness of their situation—had confirmed, not shattered his faith. Belief in paradise is quite different from belief in the possibility of human happiness.

It is belief in an absolute, in perfection: and it was against this belief that Blok was now beginning to measure poverty, the enslavement of man to machines, vice, hypocrisy. There is a note of detached horror in his poetry as he writes of these things:

> The house next door has yellow windows
> And every night—and every night:
> The pensive bolts grind in their sockets
> As people gather at the gate.
>
> The bolts are shot, the gate is locked.
> But on the wall, but on the wall,
> Someone immobile, someone black
> In the still evening counts them all.
>
> I hear it all: my room is lofty.
> His brassy voice that bids them go
> And bend their backs for other's profit
> Those people gathered there below.
>
> They will go in: and off they'll blunder
> Each to the load appointed him.
> And men will laugh behind the windows
> To see these paupers taken in.

(1. 302)

His poetry to the Most Beautiful Lady had been inextricably mixed up with that 'fairy-tale mysticism' which had flowed so naturally from the circumstances of the 'beautiful, aimless existence' of the past few years. Now that he had rejected contemplation and rejected the *summus passus* of death for life in the world, he had to adapt his poetry accordingly.

As always, Blok's motives were dual. The call 'to test the Whore of Babylon' of which he had written in his first letter to Bely, was not only a call to experience in his own life the sorrows and degradations of humanity, to 'take on flesh' in the higher sense of the words. The dark, self-destructive side of his nature demanded some outlet and he 'secretly longed for perdition', longed 'to toss his cap in the air' and did 'NOT WANT the torments of the Cross'.[43] Sometimes the two themes, the pull of the suffering world and his own demonic pride and sensuality (bound up with the old Romantic Rousseau-esque concept of freedom), were curiously united in a genre similar to that of the cruel romance:

> Along the riverside there stumbled a sick man.
> Beside him crawled a line of painted carts and caravans.

They were bringing a fun fair into the smoky town,
Beautiful gypsy women and their drunken men.

They were cracking jokes and squealing in the caravans,
And alongside them with his bundle limped the laden man.

He groaned and begged for a lift to his home.
A gypsy woman stretched out a brown hand and bade him come.

He ran up to her, hobbling, putting on a desperate spurt,
And threw his heavy burden up on to the cart.

But foam frothed on his lips, the run had done for him.
The gypsy woman leant from her cart and hauled the body in.

She sat him down beside her upon the driver's seat.
And the corpse lurched beside her, then tumbled to her feet.

And with a song of freedom she brought him back home
Where the wife was waiting for her dead husband to come.

(I. 311)

The most important influences of this winter were the painter
Vrubel, who seemed to Blok to have found the supreme expression
of his own presentiments in the cold violets, mother-of-pearl, and
crimsons of his palette, and Bryusov. 'I began writing you at night,
beside myself from reading *Urbi et Orbi*,'[v] Blok wrote to Seryëzha
Solov'ev on 6 December (VIII. 73), and to Bryusov himself some ten
days earlier:

... I read *Urbi et Orbi* every evening. Just now I have performed this evening
rite and in spite of all my natural *reserve* I simply cannot keep silent.

What will you do after *this*? Nothing, or—? I have heaps of verses in
my head, but *such* verses as you have written I would *never* have *supposed*
possible.... I can never hope to be on *a level* with you....   (VIII. 72)

Blok was looking for a new technique: one that would work by
shock rather than by the gentle, lyrical means he had used up till now.
To Seryëzha he wrote:

... the most difficult thing of all these days is to initiate others into your
own fairest dream.... To understand it, they must first come to love it,

---

[v] Bryusov's fourth collection, including verses written between 1901 and 1904. As
always, Bryusov here experimented with many genres (among them, not altogether suc-
cessfully, the 'factory song', the introduction of which into high poetry is often attributed
to Blok). In *Urbi et Orbi*, however, there is a genuine and courageous acceptance of spiritual
dereliction and a grim determination to continue in the service of art notwithstanding—
as in the famous poem in which he compares the sacred Symbolist concept of Dream
to a tired ox which he lashes on to draw the iron plough of his verse. In a poem addressed
directly to Blok and Bely, 'To my juniors' (*Mladshim*), the poet pictures himself as a sullen,
resentful figure, shut out from the lights and rejoicing of their mystical wedding feast by
heavily barred doors. Yet in all this, there is a glad and savage premonition of change
which cannot but have chimed with certain aspects of Blok's mood.

and as everybody is busy with their own affairs it is more contemporarily effective (whether more ETERNAL I do not know) to go to work with a dagger like Bryusov, like Vrubel.

(VIII. 79)

7

It was in this mood that Blok took Lyuba to Moscow to meet the Moscow Symbolists, Andrey Bely and his friends the 'Argonauts'. These admirers of Vladimir Solov'ev knew Blok's *Verses about the Most Beautiful Lady* not only from the published cycles but from handwritten copies circulated by Andrey Bely and the Solov'evs over the past two years. And so the Argonauts, young men from many walks of life united by a common interest in the occult and a common presentiment of impending change, were now awaiting, with a curiosity which perhaps exceeded the purely literary, the advent of the Beautiful Lady and her poet—heralded, of course, by a voluble Sergey Solov'ev who was seriously considering the possibility of an imminent millennium in which he himself was to embody the priestly principle represented by St. Peter, Bely the intellectual virtuosity of St. Paul, and Blok the pure, prophetic vision of the beloved disciple, St. John.

The Bloks arrived in Moscow by the night train on the morning of 10 January. Blok, apprehensive at the idea of having to stay with Lyubov's Mendeleyev relatives, had asked his cousin to put him up separately, but a happier solution had been found. The flat beneath Seryëzha's, belonging to a relative, the recently widowed Aleksandra Markonet, was temporarily vacant because 'Aunt Sasha' was in hospital with a nervous breakdown and, at Seryëzha's request, it was put at the disposal of the Bloks. So Blok and Lyuba came straight from the station, except for paying a brief courtesy call on Vladimir Fyëdorovich Markonet, Aunt Sasha's brother-in-law who lived across the courtyard from her flat, to breakfast with Seryëzha. According to Seryëzha and Blok himself, it was on this occasion that they first met Andrey Bely.[1'] Bely, whose recollection it was that this first meeting took place when they came to call on him, records the meeting at Seryëzha's flat as having happened later and as being

---

[1'] Blok sent his mother a day-to-day account of his visit to Moscow (cf. letters of 14–15 January 1904 and 19 January 1904, VIII. 81–8) from which it would appear that Bely and his friend Petrovsky were waiting for them at Sergey Solov'ev's flat on the day they arrived and that their first formal call on Bely at his home was at three o'clock on the following day. The same sequence of events is recorded in Blok's notebook (*Z.K.* 59).

gayer and more relaxed, and it was undoubtedly when he first received Blok in his own home that he sustained the full impact of the other's unfamiliar and unexpected personality:

... the bell rang and when I reached the hall it was to find a young man in a student's jacket, of very stately build, tall, broad-shouldered, slender-waisted, struggling out of his overcoat. It was A. A. Blok with Lyubov' Dmitriyevna. I was taken aback by A.A. (that was the first impression): his faultless manners, his 'sophistication' (in the best sense), what is known as *bon ton*. Everything about A.A. was *bon ton*, beginning with the jacket. ... He was dressed for making calls. A certain formality, an aura of polite society, more evident even than in A.A., immediately struck me in L.D. Together, they made a handsome pair, ideally suited, both in holiday spirits, well-dressed, elegant, fragrant with scent. The second thing that struck me about A.A. was the healthy colour of his face, the strength and straightness of the whole figure: there was something military about him, perhaps even something of the *dobriy molodets*.[x] The springiness and control of all his movements contrasted with the shyly smiling face, slightly inclined towards me, and the beautiful grey-blue eyes....

Bely had imagined Blok as he had described himself in his verses—'a dark and joyless monk': 'Short with a sickly, chalky-pale, big, heavy face, a long body, short thick legs, dressed in an ill-fitting jacket, very silent and unsmiling with tightly compressed lips and piercing, small blue eyes.'[44] Faced with the real Blok, Bely found him something of a disappointment, neither monkish nor romantic, 'nothing medieval, not a trace of Dante—more like Faust'. Earth and fire, he felt, were this man's elements. Not air, as he had supposed. Nothing ethereal about him whatsoever.

The confusion was mutual. Bely observed Blok with 'a mixture of delight, shyness, a certain feeling of reserve and at the same time of curiosity about his whole personality, right down to the quirk at the corners of his smiling mouth, to the wrinkles round the laughing eyes, to the face flushed now from frost and slightly weathered by wind', while Blok made polite and rather stilted conversation to him and his mother and Lyubov' Dmitriyevna preserved that easy, benevolent silence which was her forte in all her dealings with her husband's vociferous friends.

What struck one about her was the total absence of any *style moderne*. Her Titian and ancient Russian beauty was further set off by an elegant taste in clothes: white suited her best but she looked very well in black, too, and in bright red. Bely gave her roses and I—lilies.[45]

[x] The 'fine young man': the usual description of the dashing heroes of folk tales.

So Sergey Solov'ev. Bely, however, was, for the moment, more interested in Blok himself.

Sitting in the olive-green armchairs of the Bugayev drawing room, where a small Boren'ka Bugayev had once perched on the knees of a silver-haired professor from Leningrad, his father's old acquaintance and colleague Andrey Beketov, it was extraordinarily difficult to think of anything to say: Bely had felt himself and Blok to be plotters,

... underground agents of the future who had exchanged verses as though they had been projects of some future action we were destined to undertake together. But we could not now emerge from our 'underground'. Each of us had grown a mask firmly fixed by our social milieu as an essential defensive shield.

Their outward styles of behaviour were very different. Bely, in a typical brilliant, highly involved metaphor, compared those styles with the prevailing metres of their poetry. Blok masked himself behind a faultless façade of classic iambs or the controlled cavalry canter of his anapaests; Bely, on the other hand, was as impulsive and unstable in his company manners as were the fragile amphibrachae which, at that time, he found most suited to self-expression.

Anyone to have known me at that time would have said: here is a Muscovite, an intellectual, an optimist, an idealist, a bit of a Repetilov. ...[y] Rather comical, rather tactless, giving no thought to *bon ton*. Anyone setting eyes on Blok, on the other hand, would have said: there is a Peterbourgeois, not an intellectual at all, more of an 'aristocrat' ... yet beneath A.A.'s aristocratic sophistication was a maximalist: the officer Lermontov, perhaps, or Pestel.[z]

Blok did in fact have Decembrist blood (Yakushkin, not Pestel) and the fact that Bely here compared him to two serving officers, both stormily disaffected and critical of the regime they served, is not without significance. He would undoubtedly have felt more at home in an earlier age when the arts were compatible with a more active way of life.

[y] A character in Griboyedov's play *Woe from Wit*, a chatterbox and something of a sensation-monger.

[z] P. I. Pestel (1793–1826), an army officer of great promise said by his contemporaries to resemble Napoleon; a talented musician; best known for his authorship of *Russkaya Pravda*, a theory of government embodying those ruthlessly republican ideals for which, as head of the Southern Society of the Decembrists, he was eventually executed. Though a man of action, Pestel was described by Pushkin as 'one of the most original minds I know'.

So this 'Pestel' and this 'Repetilov' sat opposite one another and found they had nothing to talk about: 'the weather did not seem a fit subject and the Beautiful Lady was quite out of the question.'

Afterwards, Bely's flair for the grotesque suggested a startling but sufficiently apt description of the couple to which he promptly treated his fellow Argonauts: 'Blok, you know, is just like a carrot, and his wife is a turnip.' Looking at Blok's caricatures of himself (long and thin with a luxuriant curly top) and of his Lyuba, munificently plump with a small tuft as from a double crown shooting up from the top of her severe centre parting, you can see exactly what Bely meant.

It was Seryëzha's buffooning that eventually broke the ice and somehow made it possible to discuss the most solemn subjects. Like his uncle and father, Seryëzha Solov'ev made a shield and a weapon of roaring laughter and grotesque jokes. Back at the Markonets' flat, this somewhat rough-and-ready method effectively obliterated the initial awkwardness. Blok, said Bely, played up to his cousin:

... solemnly and with a perfectly straight face ... his great pale blue eyes gazing fixedly before him, he would say something that touched lightly on the borders of the absurd, setting his audience laughing uncontrollably by some elusive gesture or ... by the timbre of his voice.[46]

Lyuba and Sasha, playing host and hostess on their own for the first time in their borrowed flat, put aside all formality. It was impossible to feel shy of Lyuba ladling out steaming beetroot soup or of Blok 'running down to the shop at the corner to buy another tin of sardines'.[47]

Sensing 'Borya's' uncertainty, Blok fell easily into his customary role of elder brother: patient, attentive, kind. Bely, eager for just this sort of quiet tenderness and understanding, formed an ardent and possessive attachment. Sitting together in the still, actively listening presence of Lyubov' Dmitriyevna, the three young men soon found themselves speaking quietly and without exaggeration of Russia and of coming change, of the possibility of withdrawing from the contemporary world to some retreat of pastoral simplicity where, in mutual love and peaceful contemplation, they might await the End. Once more the dream of the monastic life touched Blok's heart: not the white, lonely monastery he had envisaged before his marriage, but a rosy community of wise and loving friends, something in the nature of Pushkin's 'cloistered retreat of work and guiltless ease'.

His confidence in Bely was not even shaken by the extravagant behaviour of the Argonauts. As always he was protected by good manners:

His every gesture was redolent of inborn courtesy and respect for the person he was talking to: if this person happened to be talking to him standing up, A.A. automatically rose from his chair and listened to him standing, his head slightly inclined, or gazing fixedly down at his toes, patiently waiting until his interlocutor should think of sitting down too. By this politeness he exercised a natural restraint on the outbursts of the Moscow Argonauts, a very fiery lot, given to wild gesticulation and liable to lose all sense of time and place at the most unsuitable moments.[48]

Bely describes one horrendous evening when everyone talked at the top of his voice about the Last Things, mixing the end of the world with fashionable mysticism of the table-turning variety. Blok 'went all dark and stony' and began to exude an atmosphere of utter hopelessness, an atmosphere of which Bely—not without reason—was much afraid. Looking at his new friend he felt 'as though all light had perished out of the world without trace'. Lyubov', watchful for Blok, already acutely aware of his vulnerability, smouldered with silent indignation. Bely was in despair.

Suddenly, Blok noticed his distress and, overcoming his own black mood, devoted the rest of the evening to comforting him. As they walked home through the softly falling snow,

L.D. was still angry but A.A. with his elusively tender words, brief phrases and humorously melancholic smile literally put me back on my feet. In that attention to my world which was alien to him in so many ways there was so much goodness, warmth, and understanding.[49]

Although Blok had reservations about some of Bely's friends (particularly the fierily scholastic Ellis-Kobylinsky, who had a nervous twitch and spat when he talked), the visit to Moscow was an immense success at the time and it was only in retrospect that the foolish blasphemies of that evening came back to him and suggested the strange, marionette-like figures of the mystics in his play The Puppet Booth.

Now, however, he and Lyuba were enjoying their emancipation from the 'grown-ups' and the regular hours of study which dominated their lives in Petersburg. True, they paid duty calls on Mendeleyev and Beketov relatives, who seemed terribly dull to them both compared to the Moscow literati, and even went several times right across Moscow in a bumpy tram to visit the mentally disturbed Markonet aunt whose flat they had been allowed to occupy. Such journeys were much enlivened by Seryëzha, who talked loudly of the resurrection of the dead ('two cases just the other day, don't you know?') and the advance of Antichrist (with troops from Belgium, for some reason best known to himself). Blok shared his cousin's taste for baiting the philistines and informed his mother with delighted amusement that everybody had stared at them in great surprise, particularly when they took to conversing in ancient Greek. 'Seryëzha', he added with evident approval, 'is a real scamp.'

Bely introduced Blok not only to the Argonauts but to the whole world of decadent poetry and publishing. Together they visited Grif, with whose editor Sokolov Blok was already acquainted. Here, he concluded arrangements for the publication of his first collection of verse. At the Skorpion publishing house, he was introduced to the triumvirate Bryusov, Baltrushaytis, and Polyakov, enthroned beneath a portrait of Friedrich Nietzsche, and was told that *Vesy* would not publish his review of the Maeterlinck plays because they found it too critical. This was not the last time Blok's more Europe-oriented colleagues were to shy away from his cool assumption of equality with the West.

The poets forgathered at one another's homes, less formally than in St. Petersburg, and read their verses until late at night. Blok had the heady experience of being acclaimed as 'the first poet in Russia' by the Argonauts and, by Seryëzha's guardian, the effervescent Rachinsky, as 'superior even to Bryusov'; Bal'mont, the worse for drink, informed Blok that he had put him out of charity with his own verses and dedicated an off-the-cuff poem to Lyubov' Dmitriyevna.

Blok's manner of reciting—the same throughout his lifetime—astonished and at first disappointed Bely who, holding to the Symbolist doctrine of poetry as music, almost sang *his* verses. When Blok recited, his manner was austere; his voice, carrying but curiously level and hollow, seemed almost to march with the metre and the stress 'like heavy, armed feet', and he swallowed the endings of his lines. It was as though, hearkening to the voice of truth in his own poetry, he were affirming it, almost mediumistically: 'Yes, yes, yes ... this is how it is, is, is ... what is written, is written ... but what it is, I do not know.'[50] While reciting, he appeared to be invested with some absolute authority. If he liked and trusted his audience, however, he would look round questioningly when he had finished, almost as though asking them to enlighten him on what it all meant. Those who had once heard Blok read his own poetry, it was said, found it impossible to listen to it in any other interpretation. According to Bely, Bal'mont flung down his lines as a duellist his glove, whereas Bryusov presented his 'like a succession of excellently served-up dishes'.

Towards the end of one of these evenings, Bryusov, having tact-fully dismissed the ladies, read his 'Pale Horse' and the notorious 'Come along the path well-trodden'. The poem, an exercise in Bau-delairean necrophilia, tells of the violation of a corpse and, at the time, impressed Blok very much. He was, however, rather dis-appointed both in Bal'mont and in Bryusov as personalities (VIII. 88).

As an antidote to these heady, smoky evenings, Seryëzha and Bely walked the Bloks through wind and frosty sunshine round the Novo-Devichiy Monastery and the Kremlin, which delighted them with memories of pre-Petrine Rus'. On 16 January, they all devoted the morning to a service of commemoration for Olga and Mikhail Solov'ev and then, youth reasserting itself, dined at Seryëzha's expense in the restaurant Slavyanskiy Bazaar, a favourite haunt of the whole Solov'ev family. Here Blok and Bely drank *Bruderschaft* and Lyuba, too, acknowledged Seryëzha as *her* close relation by con-senting to address him with the familiar *ty*. To round off their stay in Moscow, they visited the comparatively new collection of Russian art in the Tretyakov Gallery and went to see Stanislavsky's produc-tion of *The Cherry Orchard*.

On 24 January, having taken regretful farewells of all their friends and relatives, they caught the night train from Moscow, leaving Seryëzha in bed with scarlet fever. On 25 January they arrived in Petersburg to hear that Russia was at war with Japan.

CHAPTER VII

The Denial

(January 1904–Autumn 1904)

I once knew something greater than art, not infinity, but the End, not worlds, but the World.... This I have lost, probably for ever; I have fallen, betrayed, and now I really am an 'artist' and live not from that which makes life full but from that which makes it black and terrible.

(VII. 163)

1

The stay in Moscow was the last fling of Blok's rosy youth and the consummation of his first success. The innocent companion-bride; the evenings of mystic talk and poetry; the ecstatic student friends; the sheltered security of family, a whole network of ardently approving 'aunts' and 'uncles' ready to put him up, give him dinner, applaud his eminently suitable marriage, and approve his literary success (if not his actual poetry); the flushed, snowy beauty of the ancient capital, so homely and so Russian with its solid two-storey houses—all this provided the perfect backdrop for the kind of poetry Blok had been writing for the past three years and it is curiously fitting that the publication of his first book, the *Verses about the Most Beautiful Lady*, should have been agreed on during this visit.

The return, also, was rich in symbolic nuances. In the gloom of early morning Lyuba and Blok stumbled out of their train straight 'into a sharp, hopeless wind with no snow in it, so that a fine powder was eddying aimlessly backwards and forwards along the pavements and it was as though the whole city had forgotten the number and direction of its streets' (VIII. 93). The return to Petersburg, the University, the Barracks, winter, and war plunged the poet into twentieth-century reality as into a deep, cold bath: one of those huge old-fashioned baths of chipped enamel with a line of rust under the tap and Svidrigaylov's spiders leering from the corners. An unpleasant experience—but invigorating.

Summing up the impressions of the six weeks that had elapsed since leaving Moscow, Blok wrote to Seryëzha on 8 March 1904:

I feel as though something important were approaching for me, and as though this is in some way a follow-on to our mystic meetings in Moscow. The nearest I can get to putting it into words (and that most cautiously) is to say that something in me is breaking off short and something new in a good sense is approaching, and that this is DESIRABLE for me as never before.... I am writing long poems,[a] often thoroughly indecent, which yet give me more pleasure than anything I have written up to now and seem more powerful. Don't scold me for the indecency, through it I am *still the same* inside as when I was writing the amorphous stuff which went before, only the outward form is now that of cries, madness, and—often—of painful dissonances.... (VIII. 93)

Cries, madness, and painful dissonances were in the air. Bryusov broke off his diary and almost dropped out of literature into a turgid romance with Nina Petrovskaya, and into experiments in hypnotism, drug-taking, and black magic which seem at the time to have done considerable harm to everybody but himself. Bely became Nina's confident, something in the nature of an amateur spiritual director, and the triangle led to volcanic disruptions of their literary alliance. The easy optimism of the turn of the century was ebbing fast and contemplative 'waiting for the End' was broken by the hideous reality of 'wars and rumours of wars'. Merezhkovsky and Rozanov, indeed, took the current struggle in the Far East to be the first of the many prophesied in the Book of Revelation. The Religious-Philosophical Meetings were forbidden.

At the University of St. Petersburg, the 'ancient legend' of Tsarism, of feudal devotion and service, rallied disaffected students to the banner of the autocracy. On 30 January they turned out to cheer the Tsar and Blok noted in his diary that this had been 'a good, lawful assembly' (Z.K. 60). His friend Leonid Semyënov was as happy as a child playing soldiers, and Blok himself was exhilarated by the war and felt it 'had woken people up' (VIII. 92). Typically, the gentle Zhenya Ivanov was the first to feel consciously and miser-

---

[a] 'Deceit' (II. 146).

ably guilty to be doing nothing while young men of his own age were setting off to die for their country. Ivanov felt that

... the long wait for that miracle which was to provide the impulse for the beginning of true dedication [*podvizhnichestva*] was fast becoming 'a supine lack of will' and this feeling was accompanied by an inexplicable 'starless despondency' which, I think, had to do with the mysterious workings of bloodshed; from this despondency beneath the weight of the sins of the world I ran for salvation to the Saviour, and He did indeed save from it.

Al. Blok, of course, could not but feel this weight of blood, and of the condition I mentioned before he spoke briefly and clearly in the verses of his Petersburg poem 'Day and night, devoid of will-power' [II. 144]. Before him, as before me at this time, the question jutting like a stumbling block out of the ground before our feet was:—What should we do to achieve being here on earth and not in some ethereal sphere only: what should we do on earth to justify the truth that we had wrested from some sphere beyond?

The decision could not be put off, depression spurred us on and the weight of blood.... The clouds lifted like a curtain to open up a strip of the dawn above the earth, a field with puddles of bog water and blood. We stood at the crossroads.[1]

How much Ivanov was influenced by Blok's poetry and how much his own thought at the time influenced Blok is impossible to determine. Obviously, they were extremely close. Zhenya's visits to the Bloks had become 'chronic'. Blok had met and liked his sister Maria, one of several deeply religious and spiritually distinguished women who were to love him with selfless, lifelong devotion, and the whole Ivanov household with its close-knit clannish atmosphere, its austere Old Believer icons, old-fashioned oil lamps, and homely Russian hospitality delighted the poet.

More than this: an unusual number of poems written over the first six months of 1904 were dedicated to Zhenya Ivanov and Blok wrote of him to Sergey Solov'ev and Andrey Bely as of a very dear friend, the most remarkable of all the Petersburg mystics, 'a fool-in-Christ, one of the poor in spirit'. Together with Ivanov, Blok explored the sinister, mystical, and the purely human, suffering aspects of St. Petersburg, the two faces of the city embodied in Pushkin's awesome poem, *The Bronze Horseman*. Ivanov and Semyénov fantasizing for a whole evening over Peter the Great infected Blok with the dark romanticism of the subject, and the hollow thud of the Bronze Horseman's hooves on the wooden streets of St. Petersburg sounds loudly throughout the poetry of 1904.

As to the 'weight of blood', the scandal of inaction, Blok must soon have come to feel this more keenly than any of them. Military realities were a part of life at the Kublitskys' flat. Visha Grek was posted to the Far East in the middle of March. The fate of the *Petropavlovsk* (a Russian battleship sunk by the Japanese on 31 March) riveted the poet's attention and touched off, for the first time, the theme of retribution. Trying to make sense of his impressions to Andrey Bely, he began by borrowing an image from the latter's poetry:

My throw was short, the hammer fell back, but the vault of heaven had already cracked *of itself*. And now I see how from one end an ant heap plunges down and goes crawling off in all directions *presumably* consisting of those squashed by the density of the air in the cabins, boiled alive below decks, caught up in a machine that could not be stopped ... and, at the other end of things, is our freedom, liberty, open spaces. And so it is everywhere: duality, a two-facedness which seems false even to oneself, for which, if I were a Titan, I would exact vengeance, but which, in the meantime, I can only *smooth over*. As you see, I write confusedly. I have finally lost the last grain of faith as to the possibility of arriving at any exact knowledge about the Last Things. I know nothing. But I often get clear glimpses of the rosy foam and the blue, gentle crest of the wave that is carrying me forward. That is why I know that it will bear me on through this, but what then—that I do not know. Sometimes, though, it just feels fine to be on the crest of the wave amidst the singing foam.

(VIII. 99)

At other times it felt far from fine:

9 March. Filthy mood [*Skverno*].
7 April. Depression [*Toska*]. Horror [*Uzhas*].
15 April. Little horrors [*Uzhasiki*].
16 April. Horrors.
17 April. Horror.

(Z.K. 61)

These entries in Blok's notebook foreshadow many such in the diaries of the 'terrible years' between the revolutions, where they are usually bound up with drink and debauchery, sometimes with family quarrels.

All that spring, Blok's poetry is splashed with red. It did indeed seem as though the 'workings of the blood' had seeped through to stain sky and water and reflect on metal surfaces, although in the poetry itself there is no word of war. Rather there are presentiments of spring and of anarchic rebellion. He wrote of

Sun like sequins, rushing water. Splashings and spring

(II. 146–7)

and of how

> ... in the summit of the belfry
> With hollow thud and brazen clang
> The freedom bell is leaping, yelling,
> And sticking out its blood-stained tongue.
>
> (II. 149)

He also wrote a last series of desperate 'prayers' to the Beautiful Lady
(I. 316–18). But already he was moving fast towards the final
renunciation of this 'impossible' theme.

In Holy Week his wife, mother, and aunt all kept a strict fast,
went to Confession on Ash Wednesday and took Communion on
Maundy Thursday, which happened to coincide with the Feast of
the Annunciation. Blok, who loved this feast, and whose first verses
in *Novyy Put'*, published just a year before, had been accompanied
by three pictures of the Annunciation, 'did NOT GO',[2] although
he did escort his family to Easter Matins on the night of 27–28
March.

It was on Good Friday that he wrote one of the last, and loveliest,
of the poems about the Most Beautiful Lady (I. 315). Again, as when
he introduced the 'cathedral' theme in the autumn of 1902, he used
the feminine first person singular, as if seeing himself through Lyubov's eyes. Later, he was to become suspicious of romantic aestheti-
ization of the lonely, apostate demon figure which was, perhaps,
his most constant double; but here, caught in the prism of maximum
intensity of feeling, it gave him a poem of piercing beauty. This took
the form of a girl's lament for the beloved from whom she has
become separated. With a prayerful compassion, she watches from
the 'far bank' as he rides sadly away across a flowering meadow. She
pictures herself as a pale, transparent convolvulus, wreathing about
the hooves of his weary, white-chested mount. He may 'trample her
immortality', but she will burn for him still, a quiet candle above
him, a fragile flower at his feet.

Outward circumstances—which Blok always dismissed as 'mere
facts' and which he considered supremely unimportant—intruded
little on the self-absorption of those months. There were the usual
family gatherings at Easter and at birthdays, notably Dmitriy Mendeleyev's seventieth which was celebrated with some pomp; the odd
visit to the opera and the theatre; one or two unsuccessful attempts
to adapt to Lyuba's previous social life—a dance to celebrate a girl-
friend's engagement and a visit to a fashionable shopping arcade
on the Nevsky Prospect in search of dress material. When this

uncongenial activity palled, Blok suddenly threw up his hands as if in extreme excitement and set off at a run between the colourful stalls with an agonized cry of 'Velvetee-een!', leaving his slow-moving beloved helpless with shamefaced laughter. After that, Aunt Maria recalls, Lyubov' vowed never to take Blok shopping with her again, which was very probably the object of the exercise.[3]

There were to be no examinations at the University that year, so the Bloks decided to leave early for Shakhmatovo, as soon as Lyubov' had sat her examinations at the Bestuzhev Courses. Meanwhile, Blok himself worked conscientiously as ever and, perhaps significantly, decided against writing his diploma study on 'The Miracle-Working Icons of the Mother of God' in favour of an obscure, thoroughly down-to-earth eighteenth-century author, A. T. Bolotov (1738–1833), editor of the first Russian agricultural newspaper and of Novikov's *Economic Gazette*.

The appearance of Blok's verses in *Almanakh Grif* and a second visit from its editor Sokolov made him regret that he was publishing his first book with Grif rather than Skorpion. During Sokolov's two-day stay in Petersburg the poet told him precisely what he thought of his publishing house,

... so that by the time he was due to leave (over dinner at our house) dear, kind Sergey Alekseyevich was all puffed up with grief and reminded everyone very strongly of Krabb.[b] Everything became quite revolting and, to add to it all, you couldn't help feeling sorry for him. He left for the station, aggrieved and offended. A few moments later I leapt from my seat and dashed after him. I caught up with him at his hotel, saw him off at the station, said I was sorry, asked his pardon, he was quite touched. In general the end went off better. But, in the last analysis ... Grif is an indubitable fake and a great sin against art with relation to people (the public): the public cannot distinguish good from bad and will curse everything, Grif and non-Grif, without distinction. And just lately fakes are beginning to be fabricated in indescribable quantities at art exhibitions (*all* the Academy of Arts) and by Grif itself. All this is most regrettable and makes one fear undesirable consequences....

(VIII. 95–6)

Many of Blok's early reviews are directed against such 'fakes', pretentious and superficial attempts to exploit a growing fashion for mysticism, which he demolished with quiet, astringent humour. Tolerant enough in life, he was, from the beginning, extremely severe in art and reacted like Shelley's sensitive plant to the least false

[b] Aleksandra Andreyevna's little dog.

note. In literature, as in his relations with those he really loved, he
practised a harsh candour which, as can be seen from the story of
Sokolov's visit to Petersburg, was as painful to him as to those on
the receiving end.

2

Although the ostensible reason for the Bloks' unprecedentedly early
departure for Shakhmatovo on 21 April that year was to get there
'in time for the violets', it is very probable that, after their brief taste
of emancipation in Moscow, the couple were longing to be alone
again. Blok was nervous and exhausted after the city winter. Shakhmatovo, as always, soothed him and there was much pleasure in
showing it all to Lyuba and planning improvements for the summer.
They installed themselves in the annexe (four tiny connecting rooms
grouped round a tiled stove). The agent, Martyn, was occupying
the house.

At last, Blok had brought Lyuba home to 'the places where he
had wandered lost in longing for her' and where now they were
to stroll together, absolutely at peace in a country on the verge of
upheaval and—though they were still reluctant to admit this even
to themselves—just a trifle bored (Z.K. 233).

To begin with, though, everything was excitement and emancipation:

Dear Mama,
   We had a very good journey and are living in the annexe. At the station
we were met by Martyn in the trap with completely *round* horses and Yakov
with the luggage cart. The drive to Shakhmatovo took about two hours
(the road was excellent almost everywhere) and as soon as we got here they
brought us sweet bread and sponge cake baked by Darya, milk, tea, ham
with a quite special taste (pale pink as the dawn with a bright streak of
flame, tender, not salty but lightly smoked) and so on. Having eaten we
walked—a lot.... In the house upstairs I've put in bookshelves right up
to the ceiling so that only people of sufficient stature to appreciate them
can get at the books. Anan'evna [one of the servants] is tidying the garden
which is still all transparent, the leaves unfolding more every day, tight
early buds on the lilac and bird cherry. The narcissi, irises, and lilies of the
valley are just beginning to come up. The house is very clean inside, for
the final spring-cleaning we'll get in a daily as Anan'evna has more than
enough to do in the garden and Darya has brought sixteen pink piglets
into the world which are now being nursed by two magnificent sows. The
third sow and the boar, with smugly clever and peaceful expressions on

their faces inhabit a separate *dortoir*. . . . Martyn suggests we *buy a mare*. Alto-gether he has spent (including his wage, the barn etc. etc.) about 250 roubles, and there is still rent to collect (from 22 houses). It seems to Lyubov' and me that this is not excessive. He promises insistently that Shakhmatovo can be made to pay for itself, praises it, suggests we sell the piece of land where Negin has already bought the wood from us to Fominsky. They offer 500–600 roubles, the buyer is an innkeeper, the land is quite separate from the rest of the estate. . . . For the moment our expenses will have to be covered principally by the PIGLETS (5 roubles apiece in the autumn), then, possibly, by selling wheat. . . . The piglets are excellent creatures.

Two calves have been left for stock.

I have written two enormous reviews for *Novyy Put'*. . . .

We very much want to live in the annexe because it's so convenient.

We've made a new wicket gate.

Why did you have the lawn near the house spoilt by that new flower bed?

There are birds singing everywhere.

This chronicle of events is intended for *Vesy*.

And so he goes on, delighting in old family jokes and words, talk-ing nonsense, giving news of each separate field and copse, of the state of the spring ploughing and the winter wheat, of the dogs and the new puppy 'about two inches high', of a ferocious turkey, and of the tenants who have already come to the house to welcome them (having distributed eight roubles to the first delegation from the home village Lyuba and he had ignominiously hid from two other parties of peasant women from further afield).

I have not yet written any poetry. I keep on thinking about the piglets, the geese, and the turkey.

The piglets don't have much bristle yet. . . .

Finally, after a few requests and a message from Lyuba, the letter ends:

Just wait until you see the piglets for yourself,

Your
SASHA[4c]

[c] This letter, undated but written before 28 April 1904 and first published in 1927, con-firmed Andrey Bely in his most hostile estimates of Blok's character: not a Fet but a Shen-shin, he insists in *Nachalo veka* (1933), more concerned with the price of piglets than with his own reviews for *Novyy Put'* and ready to describe a slice of ham in terms any self-respecting poet would have done better to reserve for his bride's pink dress. Bely turns all the radiant content of this first visit to Shakhmatovo to a chronicle of creature comforts, and Lyuba and Blok are transformed into a huge, bucolic couple of Rabelaisian appetites, incapable of reasoned thought, never mind speech, and quite unworthy of the intellectual efforts of himself, Petrovsky, and Solov'ev to 'clarify Blok's position' for him; too lazy, sensuous, and thoroughly down to earth even to *want* to clarify that position.[5] Bely of

The days passed idyllically, working in the garden, walking far afield in search of spring flowers, enjoying Darya's country cooking, entertaining Seryëzha Solov'ev who came storming out from Moscow between examinations, once arriving half-frozen at eleven o'clock at night and waking them up to drink tea until almost three in the morning, giggling comfortably together at the undisguised disgust of Martyn who considered Seryëzha's goings-on positively ungodly. Of course, Seryëzha was, if anything, excessively godly. The difficulty was to tell when he was in earnest. In his new theocracy, to establish which he was threatening to overthrow the autocracy and abolish the entire *status quo*, he had appointed Lyuba to the position of Female Pope (the representative of Hagia Sophia, the Eternal Feminine, on this earth), and he and Andrey Bely had had their photographs taken sitting stiffly one on either side of a small, round table on which were two framed pictures—one of Lyubov' Dmitriyevna, the other of Vladimir Solov'ev. In the transparent Shakhmatovo spring amidst the aggressive geese and the fourteen thriving piglets (there were only fourteen, after all), this seemed something between a schoolboy joke and a rather charming undergraduate tribute. Blok informed his mother without apparent misgiving that he and Lyuba were to be presented with a copy of the photograph.

Yet there was, as ever with Blok, another side to this idyll. In his notebook for the end of April he wrote:

We live far more quickly than those around us. We are plunging earlier than they into the violet cold of daylight. She is *to be felt* only in early youth and before death (Seryëzha says it was so with Vl. Solov'ev). Now what is needed is more intellect; to give up certain things; and, over this coming summer, to shake off certain memories, to get strong again, to *sober up*, to compare many things, to read and to think things through. *A truce with the positivists?* There are all kinds of possibilities. (Z.K. 63)

'I love her', he wrote of Lyuba. Yet they were still prisoners of their curious relationship. The beginning of May was a desert with no poetry: 'Lord! So long without poetry! How will it end? How dark my soul is. How desperately tired.'

He could no longer write on the old themes, even when he felt in the mood to do so. The expressions and images were all used up. His 'torch had gone out' but of that, too, he had written before.

---

course did not see them like this at the time, as his earlier memoirs make evident. Rather his genius for the grotesque ran away with him, taking that succulent piece of lightly smoked ham firmly between its teeth.

My soul is in the power of darkness
In the dark fields, in every grove
In every hollow strives my soul
To build new dwellings for my love.

In every dwelling lives a princess
They do not live—they flower and wait
There is no waking these princesses
From the evening ...

                                    Ach?!!!
                                    7 May ...!!?

On this there follows a frantic attempt to modernize, a flashback
to Bad Nauheim in which Blok rhymes '*povleklís*' with 'lawn tennis'
and '*prodavshchiká*'—with 'Kodak-á'....[6]

Here, the poet is reaching out towards a technique which he was
to make very much his own over the next year or two: he was bringing his dream—the Astarte aspect of his dream, 'the devilish alloy
of many worlds' which he called the 'Stranger'—down to earth and
surrounding her with all the vulgar elegance of Edwardian civiliza-
tion. Degas, Toulouse-Lautrec, and Renoir all have their part in the
pretty, shimmering, bitter world into which Blok later introduced
his infernal Lilith. Before he could bring her to life, however, he
had to set her in his own Petersburg, in the smoke and the squalls
of wet snow, amidst the cobbled streets and filthy taverns.

Even in the country, he persisted this summer in trying to write
of Petersburg. Bryusov now hindered him more than he helped.
Finding rhymes for words like 'asphalt', trying to express in verse
the rhythms of pistons and wheels and the blasts of factory sirens
was an intriguing exercise, but for Blok it *was* an exercise—no more.
Now, '*post Lucem*', the experience of the Beautiful Lady shone with
an abiding brightness which showed up the shadows and horror of
the world in a light Bryusov would never see. What Blok needed
was to find words and techniques to express the physical world in
all its mutability and transparency. Broken-off lines of poetry, trying
to convey this new content through the old images and vexatiously,
blasphemously reminiscent of yesterday's more imminent hopes,
limp through his notebook for spring 1904, combined with a new
awareness

That millions of twilit people
Have never looked into the eyes of joy.[d]

[d] Against these words in Andrey Bely's copy of this poem is a pencilled remark indicating
that Bely took this awareness as a 'turn towards socialism': certainly the thought is the
basis of Blok's acknowledgement of the justice of revolution and retribution.

The most curious event of that May was the visit of Anna Nikolayevna Shmidt, who spent the night of the 12th–13th at Shakhmatovo. This strange woman had first appeared to Vladimir Solov'ev
to inform him that she was the incarnation of his Muse, the earthly
embodiment of the Divine Wisdom. Since Solov'ev's death, she had
sought out other poets of the Eternal Feminine, visiting Georgiy
Chulkov, now the secretary of *Novyy Put'*, in exile in Nizhniy-Novgorod, and this May she had announced her intention of calling on
Blok. Seryëzha, who was acquainted with the lady, ratted on his
cousin, flatly refusing to come to help entertain her, and Aleksandra
Andreyevna for once remained deaf to her son's agonized SOS in
a letter of 4 May. So Blok and Lyuba had to receive the rival Incarnation as best they could.

Surprisingly, the visit went quite well. Anna Nikolayevna had
much to say about Solov'ev which Blok agreed with, although he
felt it all as belonging irrevocably to the yesterday of his poetry. It
must have come as a relief to find out that she had a purely practical
aim: to organize, in memory of Vladimir Solov'ev, a collection of
verses by his followers. She died later that year without having
achieved her object.[e]

Maria Beketova, preceded by her faithful personal maid
Annushka, was the first of the family to join Blok and Lyuba at
Shakhmatovo; then, 'in the full glory of the lilac and apple
blossom', came Aleksandra Andreyevna and Frants Feliksovich.

By the end of the month the weather had grown wintry again:

All through May the weather was appalling, about the 20th snow fell and
lay on the grass and the firs, sprinkling the apple and cherry trees.
Hopelessly heavy-hearted from everything, most of all for the same
reason as she is. *It will be better*. God grant . . .

(*Z.K.* 65)

So Blok wrote in his diary at a time when, according to Maria
Beketova, he and Lyuba, apparently oblivious of the snow, were joyfully rifling his grandmother's chest to decorate their annexe with
'bright paper fans, a new patchwork quilt and a rag-bag of bright
cottons', and running back and forth from house to annexe like nest-
ing birds, followed by the two small dogs, Pik and Krabb.[7]

---

[e] For more about Anne Shmidt see S. D. Cioran, 'The Affair of Anna N. Schmidt and
Vladimir Solov'ev, *Canadian Slavonic Papers* XVI, no. 1 (1974), 39–61.

3

Blok had hoped to fit in a visit from Andrey Bely before his 'positiv-ist' cousins, Andrey and Ferol, arrived with Aunt Sofia at the begin-ning of June. Bely, however, was never a considerate friend and, unlike Blok, was quite incapable of making plans in advance and sticking to them. Everything he did seems to have been decided on impulse, on the spur of the moment. When he finally came to Shakh-matovo it was not in late May but in July (by which time most of the inhabitants had given up expecting him), and not alone but accompanied by his friend A. S. Petrovsky whom nobody had in-vited at all.

When they arrived, Blok and Lyuba were out walking. Aleksan-dra Andreyevna and Aunt Maria, having had no warning to help them exorcise their natural Beketov resentment of visitors, quite failed to conceal their dismay at the unexpected arrival of two strange young men. The polished manners of Ferol and Andrey startled Bely almost as much as he startled them when, the following morning, he came dancing down to breakfast with a large Catholic cross gleaming through a totally transparent cambric shirt.

Only Blok and Lyuba, more than ever like a fairy-story prince and princess, at once put everybody at their ease and set about creat-ing an atmosphere in which, after all, it was possible to talk and to enjoy Shakhmatovo and one another's company.

Blok was a good host and Bely, as generous as he was inconsider-ate, was horrified to look back on his own selfishness in Moscow.

There was this very homely, warm, unobtrusive, affectionate care for every last detail of our comfort on the part of a host who wished to make his guest feel at home as it were in 'the innermost sanctum of his house', a host who would not invite just anyone, but who would fling wide his doors to those he *had* invited, would share all he had with them, including his very soul, but who yet remained, in spirit, alone, intact, incomprehensible.

Bely had arrived at Shakhmatovo thoroughly keyed up after an exhausting year during which he had taken his final examinations in natural sciences besides leading an extremely active literary life. In the spring his father, with whom he was just beginning to establish an adult relationship, had died, and his summer had been shadowed by the neurotic triangular relationship with Bryusov and Nina Petrovskaya. Blok saw his friend's exhaustion and set out to relax the tension, to slow down the tempo.

Bely shared a room in the main house with Petrovsky and they

Caricature by Blok of himself and Lyuba at Shakhmatovo, drawn between 1904 and 1906

seem to have spent much of their nights discussing their host and hostess. Their day began with breakfast with Aleksandra Andreyevna, who reminded Bely of Olga Solov'eva and with whom they had the kind of questing intellectual conversation which had been usual in the Solov'ev family. At eleven o'clock Lyuba and Blok would come strolling through the garden from their annexe, relaxed and friendly, and the mood would become lighter. From anxious speculation about religion, philosophy, and the end of the world the talk would turn to personalities, jokes, literature. Blok, who was beginning to emerge from his brief period of whole-hearted admiration of Bryusov, at once shocked and delighted Bely by dismissing the older poet as 'a mere mathematician'.ƒ

Till lunchtime they would sit and talk, then go for walks, sometimes all together, sometimes without Lyuba, sometimes Bely and Petrovsky on their own while the Bloks returned to their annexe. In the evenings they would talk again, or sit in companionable silence on the moonlit veranda. The beauty of midsummer, of the sunny, sweet-scented garden and—not least—of their host and hostess themselves, combined to make the days pass for the two visitors from Moscow 'like a cycle of verses to the Most Beautiful Lady'. 'I used to live there', said Lyubov', pointing towards Boblovo, and it seemed to Bely that the vivid, black-browed woman in the flowing pink dress was pointing into the evening sky.

'Who is he?' Blok asked his mother, nervously observing Bely's ecstatic mood but uncertain of his true spiritual condition. 'He neither eats nor drinks.' Blok admired Bely and accepted Petrovsky, but his friends' idealization of himself and Lyuba irked him. He felt a fraud.

One day, he took Bely by the arm after one of those long, desultory talks during which Bely read into the pauses and silences a golden communion 'in all that was most important', and led him out through the garden and into the fields beyond. They walked slowly, pausing often:

A.A. [Blok] began to speak of himself, of his character, of his non-mysticism, of what an important part inertia, blood, and heredity play in a man's life, of how he felt these hereditary forces at work in himself and how he was 'dark'. And I recall that this was the first time I had heard him strike

ƒ Only a month or two before Blok had wryly admitted Bryusov's influence over both himself and Bely, writing of a poem of Bely's that, if it was not 'by Valeriy Yakovlevich', then it was at least 'by Valeriy Nikolayevich Bugayev'. 'The same thing', he added, 'keeps happening to me, but even more so, so that nothing remains of my name but the tail-end: ok (V.Ya. Br.... ok!)' (VIII. 101).

the note which afterwards sounded so clearly in *Retribution*. I did not want to hear that note. I remember I was quite lost and looked helplessly up into the calm blue sky of July—and the sky seemed black.[8] The black sky appeared before my eyes for one moment, but A.A. told me that he saw no light at all for himself in the future, that he was in the dark, that maybe death would triumph?...

Bely did not want to understand. He did, however, pour out the story of this conversation to Petrovsky, who said quietly: 'Surely Aleksandr Aleksandrovich is not burnt out too?' 'By this he meant', wrote Bely, 'that the disenchantment which he himself was inwardly undergoing and I too (I had in many ways lost faith in the imminence of a new epoch; A.S. [Petrovsky] in his hopes of a renaissance within the Church) must also have touched upon A.A.'[8]

They were all of them lonely, Bely continued, and for that very reason desperate for companionship. Blok saw the loneliness, offered the companionship ... but in fighting and suppressing their own doubts they insisted on fighting and ignoring his. The Blok they needed was the author of *Verses about the Most Beautiful Lady*, and it was hard for them, especially when confronted with the idyll of Shakhmatovo, to accept that his face was already set away from the pastoral morning of his vocation.

Seryëzha's arrival did not help. Just as Bely and Petrovsky had decided to leave he turned up, to a merry jingle of harness bells, still in his school uniform but free from school at last, about to join Bely (who was starting University all over again) as a first-year student in the Philological Faculty at Moscow University. Seryëzha was in tearing spirits, had the whole household in fits of laughter with his talk of the French Professor Lapan who was to write the history of the 'Blokites' in the year 2200 and with his virtuoso solo performance of the quartet 'I am afraid' from Tchaikovsky's *Queen of Spades*. Bely speaks of 'the explosive merriment of those last days' but adds that it 'did not disturb the quiet state of recollection in which we all had our being'.

Aunt Maria, however, recalled that:

...the behaviour of the 'Blokites' was not always on a level with the serious significance they attributed to their cult. In their enthusiasm there was a good deal of affectation and in their talk much superfluous exaggeration.

[8] A striking example of how Blok and Bely sparked one another off is the way in which this 'black sky' got into Bely's novel *The Silver Dove* (*Serebryannyy Golub*) and Blok took it back from Bely in his article 'On the Present State of Russian Symbolism': 'In this way at the beginning of his *Silver Dove*, a novel of genius, Andrey Bely flings out the question: "And the sky? What of the pale air of it, pale at first but then, if you look hard enough.

They gave Lyubov' Dmitriyevna positively no peace, drawing mystic conclusions and generalizations from her every gesture, movement, the way
she happened to have done her hair. It was enough for her to put on
a bright ribbon, sometimes even to gesticulate with her hand, and the
'Blokites' would exchange significant glances and pronounce portentous
conclusions. It was impossible to be angry with them, but it was tiresome
somehow, and the atmosphere was rather strained. Seryëzha's jokes and
self-parody did make things easier but even in this there was a kind of disagreeable aftertaste. Aleksandr Aleksandrovich himself never joked on such
subjects, he took no part whatsoever in all this and, having quite a different
attitude to it all, preferred to escape into silence. . . . In all this joking there
was, however, a serious basis, which is clear from Andrey Bely's statement
in his memoirs that, on the evening they returned to Moscow, 'we all met
up at S. M. Solov'ev's new flat and burnt incense before the icon of the
Mother of God to honour the symbol of our dawns, hallowed by our days
at Shakhmatovo'.[9]

Bely's own later version[h] of the end of their stay in Shakhmatovo
omits the incense-burning episode, and shows Lyubov' Dmitriyevna
in a more sober light:

... I and A.A. were twenty-three years old; L.D. only twenty-one, A.
Petrovsky twenty-two, and Seryëzha eighteen.

Sometimes a stillness would come over us; especially towards evening.
Blok smiled, his blue eyes confused; the shy inclination of the large head
in the twilight has remained in my mind's eye; and L.D. glowed with the
faintest of flushes, like apple blossom; and became all white and trans-
lucent. . . . It was as though beneath the head scarf, she kept hidden a vast
potential of lawless energy, all wrapped up, just the tip of her nose and
the narrowed sapphire of her eyes smiling out at us from the scarf; she
spoke to me; not in so many words, but she encouraged me in my difficult
personal situation (the business of Bryusov and N.) and strengthened my
determination to hold firm; I had grown fond of her.

Sometimes it seemed that, for all the youth, beauty, and vivid personalities of L.D. and A.A., what one felt in their vicinity was not warmth but
a coolness, like a light breeze; and in this there was a sadness, and to shake
off the sadness Lyubov' Dmitriyevna, as if by an effort of her wide, rounded

---

absolutely BLACK air? . . . Hey there, don't be afraid, this is the air you are breathing . . ."
Yet it is precisely in this black air of hell that the artist who sees into other worlds does
indeed find himself' (v. 434).

[h] Andrey Bely wrote three accounts of his relationship with Blok, two 'synoptic' apo-
logias written in the early 1920s and published in *Zapiski Mechtateley* and *Epopeya* respec-
tively, and the last, written many years later in a spirit of resentment, engendered at least
in part by the posthumous publication of Blok's diaries and notebooks and by such
reminders of his own callow tactlessness as Maria Beketòva's version of the 1904 stay at
Shakhmatovo, in his memoirs *Na rubezhe dvukl stoletiy* and *Nachalo veka*, published in
Moscow in the 1930s.

shoulders, shrugged on her theatrical pose, as though to make up for the
simple meaning of human life by empty play-acting; all the more did I
appreciate her sparks of heart-warming friendliness.[10]

4

While all this was going on, the flames of Blok's inward rebellion—
rebellion against self-discipline, other-worldliness, accepted suffering, humility, and Christ—burned steadily higher. On 5 June he had
written to Bely:

*Christ was never there, and is not there now, He is walking somewhere very far
away.* Maybe in *those* countries. But that is none of my business, because
I live mostly in *these* countries, whereas from *those*—'I ran away with the
Queen'. *The country in which I am now living* is 'a pale-blue prison' and a
'green planet' (both are clearly to be seen in good weather) where I can
dig the earth and make fences.... I very much want to develop my muscles
as I do every year, making up for what was lost over the winter.... Do
you know, in the middle of a good quiet summer I have sometimes
managed to find a good kind of simplicity in myself and learnt not to spare
quite vivid colours. Here there is no sparing of colours. The trees and
bushes, the sky, the earth, the clay, the grey walls of the izbas and the orange
beaks of the geese....

                                                            (VIII. 103)

He had told Bely everything. He had no more part in Christ's
'country' because, having paused in wonder on the threshold, he had
thought to glimpse the World Soul incarnate in a woman and had
'run off with her', taking her to live with him in a green garden
where he could build her a little house with a fence round it. He
was trying hard to persuade himself that there was nothing more
he wanted of life.

To Ivanov he wrote in the same vein ten days later:

Rarely has anything in the contemporary world been so close to me in *means
of expression and perception* as your words, especially in your last letter.[i]

When you spoke it was somehow more *proud....* But then suddenly you
come running down from your mountain ... and we meet like two children
who have lost their toys (toys—in the best sense)....[j] You *in yours* are in
far greater pain than I, but I am also in pain in *mine*. We both complain

[i] Ivanov had written[11] declining Blok's invitation to come to Shakhmatovo to meet
Bely and Solov'ev because 'the talk will be of Christ' and he felt he had the truth but
was quite unworthy to unfold it to others.

[j] In the letter of 5 June to Bely, Blok had complained that Christ had never given him
any toys whereas he, being spoilt, had always 'insisted on toys'.

that our souls are arid. But not for anything, and I say this to you now finally, will I go to be healed of Christ. *I do not know Him* and *have never known Him*. There is no fire in this denial, only naked rejection, now full of spleen, now of indifference. . . . In this self-negation I feel myself healthy and wide-awake, as though I had thrown off a heavy weight.

He would not, he goes on, have found it easy to admit such a thing to the Merezhkovskys, whom he had long felt as hostile to Vladimir Solov'ev; but to Zhenya he had no hesitation in confessing that he had come to grips that summer with the philosopher's *Apology for Goodness* and had found *nothing* in it,

. . . except one or two witty formulae of medium profundity and in-communicable *boredom*. My reaction is a lively desire to go to the *opposite extreme* in all things out of sheer contrariness. There is Vladimir Solov'ev and his verses—a unique *revelation* in their own way—and there is 'The Collected Works of V. A. Solov'ev'—boredom and prose.

(VII. 104–7)

Ivanov did not care much for Solov'ev, but the denial of Christ shook him to the core—and he blamed himself:

Dear Aleksandr Aleksandrovich,

'But not for anything, and I say this to you now finally, will I go to be healed of Christ. I do not know Him and have never known Him.' Dear Aleksandr Aleksandrovich! What is this? How is this!? Tell me . . . Strange . . . strange.

It's *not* your words. It's me, I see now what I truly am. Your words have just delivered one of the last, perhaps the heaviest blow, straight to the heart, straight to my heart. No, it is not you who are guilty of this denial, the guilt lies on me.[12]

'It was not at Shakhmatovo that that denial was conceived', Zhenya later affirmed:

It was born in Shakhmatovo but it was conceived in the nocturnal city of Peter the Bronze Horseman.

True, it was not as simple and clear-cut as it may seem to many people. Not clear-cut for the simple reason that further on[k] he says: 'Some of it pleases me but it is just not good enough, when something just happens to please you or not as the case may be—without suffering'.[l] Nevertheless, it was still a denial—and apostasy entails consequences for the spirit, and subsequently for the life of soul and body as well. By words are we justified, by words condemned. . . . The letter containing the denial was written on 15 June and three days later, on 18 June, he wrote his superb vision—the poem: 'There they are—the steps down to the tomb'.[13]

---

[k] i.e. further on in the same letter.

[l] An extract from Blok's reply to Zhenya's agonized letter (VIII. 107–8).

There they are—the steps down to the tomb.
No one else. All alone. You and I.
Sleep then, tender companion of days
All submerged in that light from on high.

And your smile seems to beg: let me sleep.
In your white-covered coffin—at rest.
Golden curls clustering thick on your brow
And an icon of gold on your breast.

The last rites of immaculate death
Are performed—and the waxen hand kissed.
In the blue firmament all the rest
Lies deep-buried in fathomless mist.

Sleep—no one shall now break your rest.
There are paths unexplored at our feet.
But here, on the threshold, a light
Burns all night through the snow and the sleet.

18 June 1904   Shakhmatovo

(I. 323)

This poem is the last of the cycle *The Crossroads* and the concluding poem of *Verses about the Most Beautiful Lady* in all editions of Blok's poetry. It is a full stop, as seemingly clear-cut and definite as the denial. Yet neither is a declaration of disbelief. Blok was deliberately walking out of *that* world—the world of the spirit and religion—into *this* world—the world of soul in the sense of anima, of the body and of nature magic—because *this* was the world of art. In *that* world, however, or on its borders he had run into appalling temptation: the temptation of confusing ultimate good and ultimate evil. It became clear to him that he could not continue to serve two masters. The work[m] of religious contemplation and lyric poetry did not go together. He chose poetry and 'the hell of art'.

The last poem to the Most Beautiful Lady puts Her for ever beyond the reach of Blok's 'conjuring', of all those servile little demons 'who are at the beck and call of every artist'. Christ was not to be so banished. He was always in both worlds and always He haunted Blok, in dream and in waking, in work and in life, not pursuing like Francis Thompson's Hound of Heaven but present; albeit alien, somehow, to the man himself.

---

[m] The 'work' in the sense used by monastic contemplatives who seek, as Julian of Norwich puts it, to put 'a cloud of forgetting' between themselves and all things but the 'naked being' of God.

This rebellion brought excitement, beneath the surface of which yawned an abyss. Blok tried to reassure Ivanov:

It is not you that are the cause of my flight from Him. It is the *time*. . . . We are all in a bad way now—it is a hopeless time. We are growing in the shade and our stems, though full of sap, are still white. Surely the sun will penetrate our shade some day and we will grow green. . . . If I had met you a few years ago I would, perhaps, have taken the sacrament from your hands with warmth. But I am blind drunk, I can perceive only the sharp corners of madness. . . . You say that on one of the turnings of the way I shall meet the Galilean—maybe! Only, for God's sake—not now!

(VIII. 107–8)

The experience of emancipation—first in spirit and in literature, then in life—was extraordinarily vivid, ecstatic even. Plunging thus, 'without one Holy Name', into the hell of art, Blok had absolutely no wish to encounter any restraining force. The compulsion to make poetry rather than the pride of the flesh engendered that Augustinian 'not now!'. Christ might have persuaded him to give up his 'toys', might even have exorcised the demon which was his Muse. This he had no intention of allowing to happen.

5

After the final renunciation of the attempt to write about the Most Beautiful Lady, words and groups of words began to appear to Blok which were later incorporated into the poems of his next book:

> But in the church there is forgetfulness of God
> And in the cries of the marketplace—ecstasy . . .

> The slender, trembling tears of the marshes

> There He is, Christ—in chains and roses,
> Outside the windows of my gaol.

> The leaden sunset.

> The leaden sunset
> Flames through the scrub.

Then

> Through the scrub the leaden sunset burnt
> I lay in wait for my prey at the bridge
> The wind blew drops in my face and made the waves choppy.

And at last:

> Eternity poured out
> The leaden sunset over the town....
>
> The hems of the sky are ripped
> The side streets hum
> The factory windows tell stories
> of wild nights.
> The factory siren howls
> Lead is poured out into the sunset....
> The evening guest, the usual guest
> Has thrust his head in at the door.[14]

Blok thought of such given words as great fixed stars over which he flung the nebulae of his verse. Over the next year, he was to take these stars and make poetry of them.

On 25 August 1904, the poet and his wife returned to Petersburg (again in advance of the 'grown-ups'). Two months later, Blok made a brief journey to Moscow to collect copies of his first book. On his return, he sent one to his father with an accompanying letter:

29 October, Petersburg

Dear Papa,

Today at last I have received my first collection, which I am sending to you. For the moment I have no regrets at having published it, all the more so as Grif has lavished much care on it and, I think, good taste.

I was aiming at 'well-bred unpretentiousness' and so I did my best to avoid dedications to 'celebrities', not counting my teacher Val. Bryusov and my dear, close friend Andrey Bely. As to Vl. Solov'ev, he is, I fear, only too pertinent in the epigraph. It may be that I owe so much to his poetry that it would have been better to pass over 'the bright daughter of dark Chaos' in silence and not to quote him.... But it was made necessary by the chaos all about us and 'literary' stupidity. Sometime I shall meet Vladimir Solov'ev in person—but that will be in the spacious and light-filled window of the sky rather than in the gaslit window of a bookshop.

For now I write you only about this. My work at the University continues as usual and my long candidate's essay ('Bolotov and Novikov') is finished.

My wife and Mama send you their regards.

Your son
ALEKSANDR BLOK
(VIII. 111)

Sometime that autumn, as Lyubov' wrote 'with malice aforethought on my part, unpremeditatedly on his', she had become his wife indeed. She could not remain for ever, now that she no longer had that strange second being in Blok's poetry which had somehow made the marriage bearable, as a child-companion. It was a desperate bid for the fullness of love and it was unsuccessful. Lyubov' Dmitriyevna, tired of thirty-odd years' speculation about her marriage, stated brutally in her memoirs that their 'meetings', then and until the winter of 1906, 'when even that little ceased altogether', were occasional, brief, and unsatisfying. She had no experience: 'I considered my passivity inevitable.' Blok approached the whole business 'with masculine egotism'.[15]

Yet now and always, in his own way, Blok loved and needed Lyubov'. She, for her part, loved and hoped: hoped against hope for years to come. If Blok recorded his feelings at this time, he subsequently destroyed the records. There remain a few broken fragments of verse about a seductress in black silks who retains her 'chaste power' even in 'the fall'; a bitter, vaguely smutty Latin joke:

Nunc ego sum exclusissimus
Said he running out on to the public square, flung out by (1) his wife for debauchery and (2) his mistress for bankruptcy

and, with tragic regret: 'After this nothing is possible. All *that* is over, passed, "expended"' (*Z.K.* 66–7).

Blok always denied that the Beautiful Lady turned into the Stranger. In as far as Lyubov' Dmitriyevna, in some mysterious, limited way, did indeed embody the principle of the Eternal Feminine in his poetry, she could not embody also the principle of dark mysticism and passion. This awaited incarnation in another woman and, eventually, simply other women.

Andrey Bely and Sergey Solov'ev posing with pictures of Lyubov' Dmitriyevna, Vladimir
Solov'ev, and the Holy Bible on the table in front of them (1904).

Къ убійству самарскаго губернатора И. Л. Блока.

Прахъ И. Л. Блока въ гробу, окруженномъ вѣнками, и его портретъ.

Остатки разбитаго взрывомъ фаэтона.

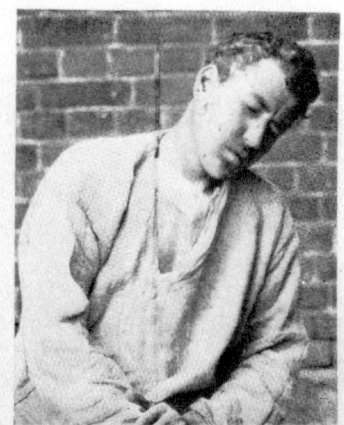

Убійца И. Л. Блока, назвавшійся Фроловымъ. (Лицо изуродовано осколками снаряда. Снятъ въ тюрьмѣ.)
Фот. А. Васильева.

The assassination of Blok's uncle Ivan, governor of Samara, in 1906 (*Iskry*, no. 32, 1906).

CHAPTER VIII

Revolution and the Old Gods

(Autumn 1904–Autumn 1905)

I have raised a revolution against myself. I prayed before
three icons of the Mother of God in the Kazan and St.
Isaac Cathedral: 'Grant neither happiness nor joy ...'
While I was in the Cathedral of St. Isaac, the doors on
to the square where the statue of Peter the Great stands
suddenly swung open (workmen were bringing in
planks) and so I went out to Peter— straight from what
always used to be the darkest and most homely corner—
out from the Mother of God.

(Letter of October 1905.)[1]

1

Blok's spiritual rebellion 'against himself' was already in full spate
before the dams which contained the pent-up energies of Imperial
Russia had begun to crumble and, by the time they broke, he too
had shaken off all restraint and made himself 'free in worlds of
magic'. The poetry to the Beautiful Lady is still and deep; the poetry
of rebellion, once the poet had found the words and rhythms he
needed to express an entirely new state of mind, has all the elemental
force of a mountain torrent. The revolution, he always maintained,
was but a symptom of events in 'other worlds' which 'we have witnessed in our own souls' (v. 431).

Nevertheless, outward events also played their part in this tremendous release of energy. After the death of her parents in the summer
of 1902, Maria Beketova, together with her maid Annushka and
Andrey Beketov's disagreeable little dog Pik, had taken a flat within
a few minutes' walk of her sister's and so was able to write of this
period very much from the point of view of one of the family.
Her account registers the simple fact that Blok's view of the 1905

revolution was profoundly coloured by the geographical situation
of his home and by his situation as the stepson of a serving officer:

The industrial part of the town where the Kublitskys and the Bloks were
living, as also the conditions of regimental life, afforded us all the opportunity to see things that many people in Petersburg had no chance of knowing. For a long time before 9 January [1905] the atmosphere was palpably
uneasy. Aleksandr Aleksandrovich was exhilarated by this and intently
observed all that was going on around us. When the strikes began at the
yards and in the factories, workers' delegates were to be seen on the streets
in the vicinity of the barracks. From the windows of the flat you could
watch how one man out of such a group of delegates would wave his hand
as he passed the blazing windows of a factory and how, at the wave of
that hand, all the lights in the workshop would immediately go out. This
spectacle produced a strong impression on Aleksandr Aleksandrovich. He
and his mother became very strung up, waiting for something to happen.[2]

Such periods of tense expectation were never productive. The
autumn and early winter of 1904 was a dull period in Blok's life and,
in his writing, was marked by his final struggle to cast off the outward
forms of 'decadent mysticism', which persisted in obtruding themselves in his poems. It was in December of this year, for instance,
that he produced the line: 'Uronila matovye kisty/V zerkala' (And
she plunged into the looking-glasses/Opaque wrists) (II. 158).[a]

To Bely, he wrote of his acute desire to cure himself of imagining
things that he had formerly experienced. Yet the thought of repen-
tance still seemed a possibility and the excitement of the first stirrings
of revolution persistently sought expression in the old forms. He was
trying to write a long poem to be called 'The Coming of the Most
Beautiful Lady', later published as a cycle of short lyrics under the
more ambiguous title Her Coming (II. 50–6). His rising impatience
with his own inability to escape from the old fairy-tale imagery
found expression in a letter written on 23 December 1904:

I have got to the place where She is supposed to appear. I know how it
should be ... but there is a golden thread here which I have neither the
desire nor the strength to break off nor—most probably—to spin out any
further. The thing is that She should be arriving on a ship. On the ship
is a barrel, that most ordinary-looking barrel stowed away amongst bales

___

[a] The word I have translated as 'wrists' can also mean 'paint-brushes' or 'sprigs', so that
in the Russian these lines are more recondite even than in translation. Blok, fortunately
for his critics, relieved us of the obligation of explaining them. When an indignant reader
actually made a public offer to pay for an interpretation, his only comment was that he
was not at all sure himself what they meant.

and sacks. In the barrel is a child.[b] That is only the background, but against this background the most real and idiotic thing has appeared: a good-natured, shaggy puppy with a lilac-coloured tummy with fleas crawling over it. If I am to retain my integrity I must exchange the child in the barrel for precisely such a puppy....

At this time, Blok was finding it less and less possible to take either himself or even his more reasonable aspirations for his country with any degree of seriousness:

I think 'how true, we do need a constitution!'—quite sincerely and often with a really serious feeling of anger against the government. But that is just when the 'child-me' comes running up and, pointing his finger at me, cries out all sparkling with laughter: 'He wants a constitution.' And I take this child up in my arms and kiss him and 'he and I are one' ... again— one.

(VIII. 114–15)

This child, at once the wise Socratic child and the innocent of the burial service secure in his 'true covenant',[c] was altogether to be trusted, for he knew something that was hidden from the clever, educated grown-ups who saw no further than the 'evil of the day': he knew not only that a constitution was no cure-all; he knew that it was too late for a constitution, at least for such a moderate constitutional monarchy as most people of Blok's milieu were thinking of in December 1904.

This dreadful knowledge, moreover, was common to many of the so-called 'decadents' and is the rational explanation of their passivity. Georgiy Chulkov, who was to play an increasingly important part in Blok's life over the next few years and who had the effrontery to claim that he taught Blok to 'listen to the music of revolution', says in his reminiscences of the poet and his time:

The frightening had superseded the boring. Neither the government nor our liberal intelligentsia were prepared for what was about to happen. Hardly anybody foresaw the future or understood the past. In one of the last articles he wrote N. K. Mikhailovsky[d] expressed sincerest astonishment as to how and why decadents had appeared in our midst. There in the West, he thought, the appearance of decadence was in the order of things; it was

---

[b] The child in the barrel is a time-honoured concept of fairy tale. Cf. for instance, Pushkin's 'Tsar Saltan', where the prince who grows up to be the hero of the story is washed ashore in a barrel.

[c] Blok's description of the 'true covenant' of resurrection granted 'in his first youth' (see epigraph to Chapter IV) is a reminiscence of the Orthodox funeral service for children who die in infancy.

[d] Mikhailovsky, the grand old man of Russian populism, died in 1904.

the fruit of an old, weary culture that had outlived its own usefulness. But here, at home, were we not just beginning to live? ... Yet still decadents *had* appeared and the very fact of their existence was in itself evidence that we were not newcomers to history. You could not think up decadents like that if you tried. They were real poets and they came as heralds of a great cultural crisis.

Chulkov, an explosive young man who had himself suffered a period of exile for revolutionary activities, went on to point out the curious affinity which, at that time, existed between the Marxists and the decadents. The populists—who still dominated the periodical press—tended to consider both as figures of fun, imitators of the West with no roots in Russia. And so, from diametrically opposed stand-points, mystics and materialists often clubbed together in an uneasy alliance, overlooking their differences on the strength of a mutual awareness that political and sociological compromise was no longer a feasible proposition. On occasion, the two tides of thought actually merged in individual minds, and Chulkov was himself to be in-strumental in effecting a group merger in the journal *Novyy Put'* that very autumn.

The Merezhkovskys, disoriented by the landslide towards revolu-tionary political action, felt the need of more politically experienced allies. It was Chulkov who persuaded them to invite the Marxists-turned-idealists, Bulgakov and Berdayev, to share and, in a very short time, to take over the direction of their journal.[e] The autumn of 1904 was a season of shadow-boxing, of theoretical experiment and of stock-taking rather than of creative achievement. 'In a word, Blok and I', wrote Chulkov,

met at a time when ... contact had been lost with roots and subsoil. The super-ficial opposition and free-thinking of the average intelligentsia could not satisfy either our future 'communists' or those who had been labelled 'decadents'.... The spirit of revolution was already wafting over the country. The soporific reign of Alexander III now seemed infinitely un-inspiring. If he had been succeeded by some great new Peter, it is possible that the monarchy might have found the strength and the will to live, but the throne was occupied by an unfortunate, stubborn, blind man, a typical 'last monarch'.[3]

Even as Blok's attempt to write of the coming of his country's salvation in the great ships was frustrated by 'the good-natured

---

[e] Under the new editors the journal changed its name from the first number of 1905 to *Voprosy Zhizni* (Questions of Life). With the exception of Vasiliy Rozanov, most of the contributors to *Novyy Put'*, including Blok and the Merezhkovskys themselves, con-tinued to publish in *Voprosy Zhizni*, which lasted for one year only.

puppy', so were most of the decadents' civic aspirations undermined by romantic irony, the by-product of catastrophic maximalism. Blok's sympathies for the extreme left, which arose in him, as in the majority of his fellow countrymen, as an angry reaction against the misconduct of the war, tended to dissolve in wild laughter.

The revolution caught him—and his poetry—fairly amidships. So it was that his attempts to express his reactions to the unrest that he witnessed that autumn in the streets about his home, though interesting thematically, were no more successful in form than was the heavily symbolical *Her Coming*. In describing such scenes, he lost the element of other dimensions altogether,*f* with results that were at once diffuse and pedestrian. There was as yet no fusion between observation and inspiration, yet the inner significance of this transitional period lies precisely in the poet's preparation to become a fitting instrument to express more objective themes, to echo the chaos in the world about him, and to catch, in the words of another poet, Vyacheslav Ivanov, the 'reflection of the immutable in the wake of fleeting phenomena'.[5]

Perhaps the most vivid poem of that autumn was Blok's 'Hymn' (II. 152), written almost immediately on his return from Shakhmatovo to St. Petersburg. Again it anticipated events and is probably the most violently and uncompromisingly revolutionary piece Blok ever wrote. Significantly, his mother found herself completely at one with the iconoclastic pathos of the concluding lines glorifying 'all that is scorched, swept away, and burnt to the ground'.

Later poems were more thoughtful. Blok wrote of the working people who had 'arisen from the murk of their basements' to march in ordered procession through the fashionable streets of St. Petersburg: 'our city', as he called it, meaning the city of the Russian Enlightenment, of the nobility and the intelligentsia. He recorded how the streets of the formal imperial capital were flooded, with the quiet inevitability of a rising tide, by the semi-peasant masses from the industrial islands. These grey crowds, whose very speech sounded like a foreign tongue, were quite alien to him. Yet

> We sought neither to know nor explain.
> Let the new people come and replace us.
> Like us, they are children of pain
> And raised at the breast with caresses.   (II. 153)

f One of the first critics to define Blok's ability to write on 'two planes, one of customary everyday "reality", the second plane supernatural, on which those spiritual events take place which alone have any importance for the poet', was V. Zhirmunsky.[4] He maintains that Blok did not acquire full mastery over this technique until the spring of 1906 when he wrote 'The Stranger'.

The image of the rising tide of grey people turned to an image of the waves of time[g] in which the poet already felt himself and his fellows to be drowning. The recurrent watery imagery is a part of the mythology of St. Petersburg. In Russian literature since Pushkin's *The Bronze Horseman*, the rising of the waters which periodically flood the city has remained the archetypal symbol for all the cataclysms it has since endured. For the poet himself, the death-wish was very strong and he was ready to drift gratefully on the flood of annihilation; the more so as he felt no resentment towards the 'new people' but only a wondering trustfulness. There could be no ultimate evil in a world where mothers were so kind—and expected so much good of their children. For Blok, the almost dead cliché that men are essentially good and equal because all are born of women was a living conviction, a happy existential experience which took on added reality at times of upheaval because *his* mother, herself a rebel against life as she found it, wholeheartedly shared his desire to see the world transformed and went trustfully forward to welcome change, prepared for any personal sacrifice. In this shared readiness for sacrifice, inspired at once by faith and despair, lay the whole pathos of their grown-up relationship, and in these days they became very close, closer than they had been since before Blok's marriage.

2

The strikes and disorders which, throughout the autumn of 1904, had demonstrated the mounting desperation of a hungry, defeated, misgoverned people culminated, on 9 January, in a peaceful demonstration led by a priest, Gapon, which proceeded from the islands to seek audience of the Tsar; it was met by armed troops and dispersed by gunfire. On this day, which went down in Russian history as 'Bloody Sunday', the Tsar himself destroyed his legendary patriarchal authority over the hearts of his people. Proletarian atti-

[g] Cf. also the poem 'The barque of life is stranded' (II. 161), which uses an image of Russia corresponding almost exactly to one suggested by Tyutchev in a letter written fifty years earlier as 'a vessel stranded on a sandbank which cannot be shifted by any effort of its crew, for only the rising tidal wave of the people's will will be able to raise her and set her afloat again'.[6] Whether or not Blok was acquainted with the letter I do not know, but the correspondence of ideas is remarkable, although Blok replaces Tyutchev's simile of the incoming tidal wave by the more voluntaristic concept of 'someone in a grey padded jacket' who is strong enough to push the stranded vessel into navigable waters. Entirely his own is the conclusion of the poem in which he pictures the barque sailing merrily away into the distance in the certainty that he and his like will be left behind.

tudes diverged sharply from peasant attitudes. The people as a whole began to listen more readily to Marxist and other extremist agitators. For many, it was a turning point. For Blok also.

Georgiy Chulkov tells us how the majority of writers passed the night of 9 January:

... we who were, to some extent, participants in that tragedy took what happened to heart with such agonized intensity that I doubt if it is now possible to find the right words to communicate the experience. How can one convey, for instance, the night from the 8th to the 9th of January in the editorial office of *Syny Otechestva* [Sons of the Fatherland]? All the Petersburg writers had forgathered here, aware of their responsibility for what was going to happen. The most different people were all milling about together in one room, acutely aware that they were all in the same boat. Everyone was here from Maksim Gorky to Merezhkovsky. All night long the writers were in communication with the government. Our deputies came and went. There, behind the stone wall of the ruling bureaucracy, they were all passing the buck. It was as though no one was actually responsible for the fact that soldiers were pouring out from all the barracks and that they were preparing to fire on unarmed workers. The volleys loosed into the bodies of those unfortunates 'who had trusted the Tsar' were a terrible augury.[7]

Blok's experience of this night was at once more domestic and more immediate. While the writers were debating whether or not to seize a printer's shop and run off a newspaper without previous censorship, Frants Feliksovich was woken by his batman and told that the 'regimental commander required the presence of the officers at a meeting'.

When Frants Feliksovich had gone [writes Maria Beketova], Aleksandra Andreyevna dressed and went out. On the road beside the Barracks the whole regiment was already assembled and she heard how the colonel in charge of supplies shouted at the senior medical officer, 'Aleksey Ivanovich, have you laid on transport for the wounded?'

Realizing that something serious was afoot, my sister returned home, knocked on her son's door and gave him a brief account of what was going on. He immediately got up and dressed. Mother and son went out together into the street. Along the embankment at the Sampsoniev Bridge and at all the other bridges across the Neva pickets of cavalry were posted, called in from the outskirts of Petersburg. The detachment of Grenadiers with whom Frants Feliksovich had gone was occupying a position near the chapel of Christ the Saviour. Here also was a posting of Uhlans who had dismounted, lighted bonfires, and were organizing dances round them, probably to keep warm. Near the bridge a worker was amicably trying to talk a mounted soldier into abandoning his post, explaining to him that 'all of us, workers and soldiers, are the same kind of people'. The unfortunate soldier made no reply to his harangue but he obviously felt miserable. Another worker, dressed as though for a feast day, left his home and stood for a long time crossing himself before the church, but the bridges were all in the hands of the enemy and you could see how he bustled back and forth looking vainly for a free way through, his best pink scarf showing up brightly in the distance. A volley of gunfire sounded from the Petrovsky Park, then another. My sister called round for me. We walked about the streets together for a long time. Aleksandr Aleksandrovich went home a little before we did. On returning to her flat, Aleksandra Andreyevna found Andrey Bely there. I shall not repeat all that he has already set down in his reminiscences.[8]

Andrey Bely, absorbed as usual in his own affairs, had chosen this day of all days to arrive in St. Petersburg. From the station, he had made his way direct to the Grenadier Barracks where he had been offered hospitality by an acquaintance in the Guards, an offer he had accepted in anticipation of being conveniently close to the Bloks.

Having located my friend's flat I was told by the batman that 'his honour' had left his apologies—he was otherwise engaged but there was a room prepared for me. The Barracks, as I soon found out, were empty. The regiment had been led off and posted all over St. Petersburg in small detachments. Having washed off the dirt of the journey I immediately went round to the Bloks and found them all (Aleksandra Andreyevna, A.A., and L.D.) in a state of considerable tension. I don't remember exactly how we met but A.A. took me into the dining room to breakfast and I got caught up in the chain of conversation about the Petersburg troubles which the Bloks were taking very emotionally. A.A. and Aleksandra Andreyevna were in a highly revolutionary state of mind. Aleksandra Andreyevna was anxious for her husband who was in duty-bound to defend some bridge but profoundly disgusted by repressive action of any sort. Aleksandra Andreyevna was very worried as to whether or not F.F. would have to repel the workers. A.A. was more upset at the idea of the troops opening fire and killing people and expressed his indignation and contempt for a government that had succeeded in turning a peaceful demonstration into an uprising. Vague rumours came to us of how vast crowds of working people were going to the Tsar and it was said there had already been confrontations. I did not stay long with the Bloks but went on to the Merezhkovskys where I found a whole assembly of people, all most distressed by events. Here, there was definite news of shootings, rumours that Gapon was dead. . . . D. S. Merezhkovsky, Z. N. Hippius, and I went to seek out D. V. Filosofov and from his place went on to the now-famous meeting of the Free Economic Society, where they were discussing the position of Petersburg as a whole. There were calls to take up arms, to start manufacturing bombs, and people saying that the movement in Petersburg was a matter for the revolutionaries, not for the priesthood. The principal impression from this meeting was one of bewilderment in the face of the unexpected scale on which things were happening. I remember that Merezhkovsky went off somewhere.[h] I stayed on alone.[9]

Bely goes on to record how he glimpsed Gapon himself, in disguise and without his priestly beard, hoarsely exhorting the meeting to open rebellion. Yet, in spite of all this seething activity, he was struck by the fact that 'in this society there was none of that immediate, elemental reaction to the facts that I had met with at the Bloks where, of course, there could be no debate, no action, but merely complete absorption, emotion, feeling ...'.[10]

Indeed, the only friend of Blok's whose experience of 9 January equalled his own in real immediacy was Leonid Semyënov, who, in full expectation that the Tsar would receive his people and do his best to help them, had actually marched with the demonstrators and witnessed the shootings. From that hour Semyënov turned to the Social Revolutionaries, conceiving a violent hatred of the Tsar and his family that even led him to contemplate assassination. Semyënov 'went to the people' and, like Aleksandr Dobrolyubov to whose heroic sister Maria he was engaged to be married, eventually disappeared from literature. He was killed in 1917. For Blok, such total commitment to revolution was the only valid alternative to his own reaction of total withdrawal into poetry.

The night of the 9th Blok spent with his womenfolk in the undefended Barracks which, they were warned by a nervous C.O., might at any moment be subjected to siege by the forces of revolution. To this threat Blok reacted with detached irony, describing the officer to Bely next morning as a scare-mongering coward. Bely, who had decamped to the Merezhkovskys' precisely to avoid an enforced sojourn on the wrong side of the barricades, was back visiting Blok on the morning of the 10th:

Aleksandra Andreyevna looked calmer. Her husband had not so far had to take part in any clashes between the troops and the workers; his detachment was well placed from this point of view. It was on this occasion that I met Aleksandra Andreyevna's husband for the first time: he was a thin, plain-looking soldier with most beautiful eyes. He appeared modestly at the table, sat down modestly, and listened in silence to our indignant talk. I remember that I tried to moderate my speech, feeling for the difficult and delicate position of Frants Feliksovich, but A.A. on the contrary expressed himself bluntly, ruthlessly, and to the point, making it clear that

[h] Bely adds in a footnote that Merezhkovsky 'had been delegated together with some barrister or other to close down the Mariynsky Theatre as a gesture of national mourning'.

he had no sympathy for anyone who supported the government even though constrained thereto by main force. I remember I felt sorry for poor Frants Feliksovich. In general I noticed a certain callousness in A.A.'s attitude to his difficult position at this time.[11]

Indeed, Frants Feliksovich's position *was* difficult. When confronted by a question of principle, old Andrey Beketov had had no hesitation in resigning his Rectorship and his family had supported him as a matter of course. Aleksandra Andreyevna and Blok naturally expected some similar action from Frants Feliksovich and could not understand, though they might accept the *fait accompli,* how he could continue to place himself in a position where he might have to do anything so repugnant as to open fire on unarmed civilians. Frants Feliksovich, for his part, was wedded to his career and probably never seriously entertained the drastic possibility of resigning his commission. For the first time, the friendly indifference between Colonel Kublitsky and his stepson became a definite coolness and Aleksandra Andreyevna began to extend some of her contempt for military society in general to her own husband. Frants Feliksovich continued to do all in his power to placate his high-principled family, helping Zhenya Ivanov to get out of military service the following autumn to oblige his wife and Blok and making no attempt, as is clear from Bely's account, to enforce conformity or even to defend his own position. Nevertheless, in spite of his wife's express plea that he resign in the autumn of 1905, he stuck to his job. Eventually the inevitable occurred, and Frants Feliksovich found himself in command of a political execution, though he did not actually have to be present. This 'fact', which occurred in October 1906, disturbed Blok less than the attitude which made it possible,[12] an attitude already struck in January 1905.[i]

[i] Three years after the event, in a letter to V. V. Rozanov containing a very plain statement of his own attitude to terrorism and repression, Blok wrote:

How can I condemn terrorism when I see clearly, as by the light of a vast tropical sun, that: (1) the revolutionaries who are worth speaking of (and there are dozens of them), kill like true heroes, with a halo of the truth of martyrdom about their faces ... without the least self-interest, without the least hope of escaping torture, forced labour, or execution; (2) that the government, with a senile yawn and an indifferent wave of its plump fingers, slobbering with the lips of an Azef, dispatches its unfortunate tools, little officers *who are completely innocent* and who faint like nervous girls ... at the Medical Institute at the sight of blood, white-faced soldiers and haemorrhoidal 'civil servants': 'to shoot', 'to hang', and 'to be present at the execution of the death sentence'.   (VIII. 276–7)

Zhenya Ivanov's diary for 24 October 1906 gives an account of two executions, the memory of which probably inspired this letter:

About Konoplyannikova. She walked along eating apples all the time. The Preobrazhentsy were on duty. She is pretty and looks young for her age. She walked up on

'Frants Feliksovich, Borya,' Blok told me with a kind of dry harshness, 'is not over-fond of me.'

But I saw much pliancy in the gentle colonel.

'Frantsik is hot-tempered,' Aleksandra Andreyevna said to me. 'He can make terrible scenes but he doesn't bear malice!'

L.D. and he were good friends; I thought it was a case of different up-bringing: son and grandson of professors and—a regular soldier, rather scared in his own home because he was not a 'poet', but only a 'colonel'; he always seemed to be quietly slipping out of the door, spurs jingling faintly, clicking his heels in their polished boots.[14]

On the morning of 9 January, Bely had noticed Blok gazing out of the window over the desolate, ice-bound expanse of the river. It had seemed to him then as though his friend was 'trying to work up some indomitable resolution'.[15] Yet, after 'Bloody Sunday', Blok merely retired into himself and sat at home, inseparable from his wife.[j] At first indifferent, if not conservative, in her attitude to events, Lyubov' now gradually came to absorb something of her husband's smouldering sympathy for the grey people of the islands, something of his contempt for the 'full bellies' whose only anxiety was to set to rights that 'trough' which had just been so nearly 'overturned'.[k]

A much-quoted letter to Sergey Solov'ev written in January 1905 speaks of Blok's new-found readiness to accept majority decisions at students' meetings. At the same time, the demon of romantic irony is very much in evidence:

I don't know what will come of it all. Reading Andreyev's 'Red Laughter' I felt like going round and asking him when we were all to have our throats cut. I was nearly out of my mind but, next morning (I read it at night), I drank tea. Sometimes I 'mutter on' about politics, but less and less. In the autumn I was more liberal-minded. Yet when people started talking

---

to the scaffold, took off her starched collar, undid the neck of her dress and put her head in the noose. (She asked them not to put a sack over her head.) She swung. The terrible thing about the face of someone who is hung is the way the tongue sticks out.

Two Preobrazhentsy privates fainted where they stood. The officer said he felt so ill it was all he could do not to be sick.

Then the ones who were executed under Frants Feliksovich's orders. It was a judge-ment on a group who had tried to cause an explosion in a naval vessel.

Five of them. Two young girl students, one eighteen, the other twenty-six. The young one was pretty and sang as she went to her death, all the time.

And always the same song! 'We fell as victims in the fateful fight.' They shot them! Someone wasn't hit the first time and there were shouts and cries. On the twentieth the Medical Courses went into mourning for them.[13]

[j] 'The best people', Blok wrote at this time, 'are retiring into themselves and shutting themselves up in their own souls' (v. 566).

[k] The expressions are Blok's own; cf. the poem 'The Satiated' (Sytye) (II. 180).

of 'reforms' I felt that I would take no active part in them. As to that,
though, I can't really stand the conservatives either.

(VIII. 117)

To the Merezhkovskys, involved as never before in eager discussion of revolution and reform, Blok's passivity seemed little short
of political idiocy, and throughout the following weeks they ener-
getically tried to prevent Andrey Bely's constant 'escapes' from their
home, where he was still staying, to visit the Bloks. They could not
understand what drew so brilliant and agile-minded a man to seek
out such withdrawn company and suspected some 'sectarian' mysticism. Bely, however, continued to 'run off' to the Bloks, where he
revelled in the quiet companionship and cosiness of their home, the
sense of being one of a family for which he was always so avidly
hungry. He was also drawn by the existential depths of Blok's attitude to all that was going on around them. Both men sensed that
the Merezhkovskys' preoccupation with political and literary theory
did not reach down to the root cause of the need for change. This
lay in something simpler and more real. Blok was becoming ever
more aware of a side to Russian life which the Merezhkovskys
seemed to have quite overlooked:

Sometimes he would glance across at me, get up, come over to where
I was sitting. 'Come on; I'll show you the back streets.' He would lead
me from the Barracks along a winding back street full of people making
their way wearily to and from the factories; occasionally we caught a
glimpse of an exhausted prostitute; bright lights shone from cheap eating
places; he took it all in. Later, I was to recognize this landscape of back
streets in the book *Nechayannaya Radost'* [*Joy Unhoped-for*].[1]
    Slender, his face flushed, in his fur coat and fur cap, he would look round
at the gleams of glass, the workers with heavy loads, the police vans; the
look was swift and all-embracing....
    Then he would halt me and take in the whole street at a glance:
    'It's a wretched life: very sad ... They, the Merezhkovskys, don't notice!'
    And in that February things were already beginning to look like ...
October.
    'Ah well, come on!'[16]

So they walked under the green and crimson of the frozen northern sky, noses flaming in the frost, nostrils pinched with cold, hands
in pockets. Then, returning home, they would smoke and talk about
things close to their hearts, such as the heaviness Blok felt after meet-

---

[1] *Nechayannaya Radost'* is the name of an icon of the Mother of God depicted with Her
Child in Her arms and turning in forgiveness towards the kneeling figure of a repentant
sinner.

ings with his father, or his uneasy admiration for the composer S. V. Panchenko, Aunt Maria's unrequited love and his mother's good friend, who insisted darkly that no one in Russia had a right to an aesthetic attitude to life because there was too much misery, too many people who were leading almost subhuman lives. Yet always, beneath this comfortable, intimate talk and the sudden, understanding laughter that came and went between them, there was an under-current of catastrophe, a half-acknowledged premonition of change that would sweep away not only the Tsar and his government, not only themselves and their gentlemanly, leisurely way of life, but the liberals, too, reformers like the Merezhkovskys together with their embryo reforms, even the revolutionaries themselves.

Such were the premonitions that brought Blok and Bely together in January 1905: so close together that Bely afterwards looked back on that month as the one time when they had felt themselves to be simply Borya and Sasha, not Bely and Blok; so close that Blok ever afterwards recognized Bely as 'a brother', a relationship to which he admitted no other man.

It was this mood, too, stronger in Blok than in Bely, which separated him from the Merezhkovskys, of whom he remained, in human terms, intensely appreciative, even fond. Zinaida Hippius and her husband, however, understood him no more now than they were to do in 1917. When Bely returned from his walks along the back streets they would pounce:

'What were you doing with Blok?'
'Went for a walk ...'
'Well?'
'Well what?'
'Just like that—didn't you talk about anything?'
'We looked—at the back streets, the fences; the way "the hem of the sky is ripped ..."'
'Inconceivably apolitical, the pair of you: here are we discussing what is to be done and there are you two going off for walks!'[17]

Bely tried to make Hippius understand that Blok, in spite of his stubborn refusal to be absorbed into their circle of 'religious action', still appreciated and loved her and her husband, but for the Merezh-kovskys at this time you had to be either 'for' or 'against' and Hip-pius, in a poem dedicated to Blok, flatly rejected the merely human affection he had to offer, concluding magnificently:

Then take your warmth elsewhere! My blazing frostiness
Burns best alone.[18]

Bely, who always suffered agonies if his friends did not agree among themselves, persuaded Lyubov' Dmitriyevna to join him and Blok on a visit to the Merezhkovskys, who were openly fascinated by the couple's enigmatic ordinariness. Inevitably, the visit was no great success. Blok, on his part, tried introducing Bely to Zhenya Ivanov, but Bely was irritated by Zhenya's clumsy buzzing about the room and somewhat jealous of the curious deference with which his 'brother' treated this awkward and obscure friend; Zhenya, for his part, found Bely 'very, very nice' but too ready to demonstrate his 'all-acceptance to the point of complete sobriety of heart or else of hysteria'. Used to the more reserved manner of Petersburg poets, he found Bely's sing-song technique of reciting acutely embarrassing, although, he added in a manful attempt to appreciate his friend's friend, 'you get used to it'.[19]

At the theatre, the winter season of 1904–5 was a memorable one. Revolutionary excitement was fed by a splendid performance of Wagner's *Siegfried* and the complete oversetting of the conventions achieved by Isadora Duncan's dancing. Bely attended both with the Bloks, and Isadora Duncan appeared to him and Lyubov' as 'a symbol of the new, youthful Russia that was to emerge beyond the revolution, a great, green meadow on which new songs and dances would come into bloom like flowers'.[20]

Blok did not share these idyllic fancies. On the very day he saw Bely off for Moscow (4 February 1905), the assassination of the Governor-General of the older capital, Prince Sergey Aleksandrovich, came as a shock which served to confirm his most profound forebodings. On hearing the news he rushed to Zhenya Ivanov, then to Sergey Gorodetsky, hoping to talk, but they were both out and so we have two brief letters, one to Bely and one to Blok's old friend Aleksandr Vasil'evich Hippius, letters eloquent of total disorientation and an intense sense of isolation (VIII. 118, 119).

Chulkov says that Blok accepted the revolution 'not in its positive hopes but in its destructive element, first and foremost out of hatred for the bourgeoisie'.[21] But even the poem 'The Satiated', which Chulkov quotes in support of this idea, is inspired less by hatred than by distaste: 'Let them live out their lives as they are used,' the poet says; 'we would be sorry to disturb their well-being. Only', he adds almost primly, 'it is unbecoming for pure children to imitate the dullness of their old ways' (II. 180).

True, the poet was increasingly repelled by the outwardly well-ordered lives of such people as his own Blok and Mendeleyev relatives. A letter to his father of March 1905 speaks expressly of how irksome he was finding 'all relatives except the very closest' (VIII. 122). Yet although he could, and did, withdraw from their society, he could not dissociate the unpretentious, cultivated comfort of his own life from the whole structure of privilege. There was more of the repentant nobleman in his attitude than of hatred, and his anger against bourgeois society was on behalf of others, only very occasionally of himself.

In a poem written that January and dedicated to Chulkov he described the impotent fury of a prostitute against a woman sheltering behind lace curtains in an upstairs window. There is anger in the poem, but if the poet himself has a part to play in the pathetic drama, it is surely that of the 'someone' who picks up the prostitute's crying child, strokes its wet hair, and goes quietly on his way, weeping (II. 163–4). This was the man who, in the daytime, walked the back streets with Andrey Bely and, more and more often, at night on his own:

> Street of the city, ah street ...
> Shadow-folk silently hurrying
> Bodies to sell,
> And oblivion to buy,
> Then to plunge themselves yet once again
> In the city's slow river, the cold of the winter ...
>
> Sleep then, forget the old words and their radiance.
>
> If only those windows were free,
> Of the lights' fitful glimmering!
> Curtains and little puce flowers!
> Faces, bent over miserable labours!
>
> All's quiet.
> The moon has come up
> And the rows of the feathery clouds
> Stretch away to the distance.
>
> (II. 162)

This was the Petersburg the revolution had taught Blok to see. He knew it already, of course. It was the Petersburg of the Vvedensky School for Boys, of unhappy, underpaid schoolmasters, of miserable prostitutes, brutalized soldiery, seedy officers and seedier brothels, a wintry city of ice and slush and bitter winds. Before, however, Blok had shut this world out of his poetry—perhaps afraid that it might engulf him. Now, more confident in his vocation, protected from the loneliness of the city by marriage and the beginnings of success, he was strong enough, and honest enough, to receive it again.

This was a gesture of real courage; quite enough to explain the set look Andrey Bely had noted on 9 January. For Blok must have been aware, indeed it is evident from his poetry that he *was* aware, that to acknowledge the existence of this 'terrible world' was to acknowledge the necessity of doing something about it. Never, after this, could he hope to find refuge and oblivion in the newly rediscovered security of love and home or the flowery stillness of Shakhmatovo.

More and more often, Blok began to identify the persona of his poetry with the poor, homeless, drunken, syphilitic dregs of the city. 'The wind calling from the north' (1. 265) had found its way into his heart and, with his apostasy, he had relinquished the shelter of other worlds. His resolution of 9 January was not, like his friend Semyёnov's, a conversion to political extremism, but a commitment to the old, alternative 'way to salvation' to seek 'complete $\pi\alpha\phi o\varsigma$ in earthly form'. 'My flag is struck', he wrote at this time. 'Only the pennon on the roof sings all night long of that which is to come.'[m]

Although Bely was at one with Blok in his expectation of a catastrophic 'explosion', he clung to his rosily hopeful view of life and history. His 'azure-golden, snowy-purple Roses of Eternity'[22] were a great deal too lush for Blok's present state of mind, and the Solov'evian influence began to wane as soon as Bely left for Moscow. The white walls and golden domes of the old capital faded from Blok's poetry, and it became more and more concerned with the wet darkness and sunless courtyards of Petersburg.

3

It was in the course of 1905 that Blok's intimacy with his closest Petersburg friend, Zhenya Ivanov, was at its most meaningful for his poetry. On 22 February they began to address one another by the familiar 'thou' and to call each other Zhenya and Sasha.[n]

Ivanov was the perfect flint to Blok's tinder. The intensity of their conversations was relieved by a humorous undercurrent of self-parody. Zhenya saw himself as a red-haired, blob-nosed circus clown and Blok as the classic, pale Pierrot, and it was while talking and clowning with him that Blok first hit upon the idea of the mystics of the puppet booth, for the two saw all mystical frauds (and some-

[m] The Russian word *gryadushcheye* means literally 'that which is to come'. It is not analogous to *budushcheye*, 'the future'.

[n] Blok's far more rapid arrival at this stage with Bely is explicable first by the less formal *mores* of Moscow and, secondly, by Bely's old-established connection with Blok's cousin Seryёzha and by the part he had played on the night of Olga and Mikhail Solov'ev's deaths.

times even themselves) as puppets without real, inward being:
clowns stuffed with sawdust and bleeding cranberry juice, empty
dummies, faceless above immaculate stiff collars. The spiritual prototype of these human puppets they called 'the Devil's doll', a term
which appears to have been common currency in their literary circle.
Like Dostoyevsky's Stavrogin, the Devil's doll was related to but the
obverse of Lermontov's lofty Demon, a Promethean figure of barren
power and lonely pride, redeemed by the eternal anguish of one who
has known and lost God. Having lost this anguish, the Devil's doll
has lost reality itself, and the only way to regain it is through ecstasy,
revolution, miracle.[23] Zhenya was, from an infinitely respectful distance, in love with the actress Vera Kommissarzhevskaya, and in the
autumn of 1904 he had seen her play Ibsen's demonic heroine Nora.
There is a moment when Nora dances and, in Kommissarzhevskaya's
interpretation, '... those frantic movements to the rhythm of the
dance, that face with half-crazy eyes staring vainly into space *in
expectation of a miracle,*[o] created the impression of an unforgettable
danse macabre.'[24]

Of course Zhenya told Blok about Nora's 'tarantella' which he
saw as a symbol of revolution, an ecstatic dance to the death. And
Blok wrote of the Russian people in the 1905 revolution: 'They
demanded a miracle[o] before the time was ripe and were reduced to ashes
by the lilac worlds of revolution' (v. 431). 'The grey-purple, the
silver stars, the mother of pearls and amethysts' (VII. 300) which Blok
always associated with revolution are the colours of Vrubel's Demon
'lying up alone in the mountains'. But Zhenya, with his profoundly
Russian respect for accepted suffering, found another symbolic correspondence in Vrubel's art which suggested real hope beyond the
Romantic nightmares of rebellion, isolation, and madness.

Just imagine if, in a purely human way, we should feel with all our being
for all suffering, ... if we were to draw all sorrows into ourselves as a sponge
absorbs water, imagine how our face would be altered by the sufferings
of the world, it would be as though it reflected the bloody flames of hell;
seared by these flames, would it not become the face of the Demon?

We have seen the face of Vrubel's Christ in the grave. The face of the
God-man who has been through hell, is it not somehow akin to the hell-
seared face of the demon?[p] Otherwise He would never be able to understand the Demon or to bring him forth from hell.[26]

---

[o] Italics mine. A.P.

[p] This whole line of thought not only runs right through Blok's poetry but is evident
in the way his contemporaries later saw him as the incarnation of this poetry. 'A burnt
face', a 'face that seemed to have been seared by the fires of hell', 'scorched'; such epithets
we meet with again and again in descriptions of Blok in his maturity.[25]

For Ivanov, however, Christ was immanent. He did protect, save, and dominate. For Blok, He was always somewhere 'beyond the windows of my prison' (II. 84); approaching on a distant boat (II. 263); disappearing into a flurry of snow as in *The Twelve* (III. 359); approaching with the angel host on the Last Day 'just as we read in books, bored and disbelieving', while the poet lies helpless in his grave (III. 134).

Blok, closer to the tragic concept of the Demon, persisted in his rejection of Christ, yet this Easter of 1905 he sent Zhenya a card with the age-old salutation:

Christ is risen, dear Zhenya. I kiss you—and love you very much. There is a great deal of strength and a sort of severity about you which takes the self-confidence out of me [*pered kotoroy ya robeyu*]. I often think about it but do not put a name to it. I am troubled by the question: where shall we meet *face to face*? Will you not finally unmask me—on the occasion of some glorious Resurrection?...[27]

On a more mundane level, the relationship between the Russian Orthodox Church and the Merezhkovskys' circle had come to a head that spring over the Church's ambivalent attitude to the events of 9 January. The demonstration had been led by a priest and the demonstrators had borne icons and church banners as at a religious festival. It was felt that the hierarchy should have come out with a strong condemnation of the official action and two of Andrey Bely's friends from Moscow, V. P. Sventsitsky and V. F. Ern,[q] actually came to St. Petersburg to petition the Synod to do so.

In fact, although a few ecclesiastical voices had been raised in shocked sympathy for the demonstrators in some of the more liberal theological journals and in letters in the press from bewildered provincial priests, the upper hierarchy elected to avoid the issue. Nevertheless, this hierarchy had, for the first time, been made painfully aware that it no longer governed a flourishing institution truly representative of the people it purported to serve and guide. The press was abusive and even schoolchildren were demanding the abolition of Scripture lessons and the closing of the churches. Against this background, the voices of the 'godless' intelligentsia, who had attended the Religious-Philosophical Meetings and written for *Novyy Put'*, began to seem friendly, even understanding.

[q] The two men later founded the Christian Brotherhood of Struggle, an attempt to wrestle with Christianity's historic role with which neither Blok nor Bely was altogether in sympathy.

In a passionate appeal published in *Voprosy Zhizni* and entitled 'Now or Never', Merezhkovsky exhorted the official representatives of Russian Orthodoxy to shake off their civic timidity and to assume the leadership of the revolutionary intelligentsia. Coming at such a time, this appeal had its effect, and Metropolitan Antonin and other clergy consented to a meeting in the editorial office of *Voprosy Zhizni*. It is significant that Blok and Zhenya Ivanov were the only two of the younger generation of laymen invited to attend this discussion, and that it was Blok who relayed the invitation to Ivanov and not the other way about.

The meeting itself, however, proved disappointing. The Church's enthusiasms were centred about a possible revival of the Patriarchate.' Many of the intelligentsia, including Merezhkovsky himself, were opposed to this idea which they looked upon as an anachronistic revival with overtones of papistry. Blok, though interested beforehand, obviously heard nothing that touched or excited him. That he continued to be interested in and impressed by the Merezhkovskys is, however, clear from a letter written to his father on 28 March 1905, in the same week this meeting took place:

Meetings with the most various people are becoming increasingly frequent. The Merezhkovsky circle has broadened out. Over the last few months many new people have joined it from Russia (as opposed to St. Petersburg). Still, my closest friends remain Sergey Solov'ev, Boris Nikolayevich Bugayev (Andrey Bely), and Evgeniy Pavlovich Ivanov (from *Novyy Put'*). The part of 'background' is still largely played by the Merezhkovskys who are heartily detested by almost everybody for one reason or another. True, it is often their own fault (especially Z. N. Hippius's), but I see no one to replace them and it will be a long time before we get any others capable of creating such a stir as they have done (in their own sphere of magnificent theories, often impractical and almost foolish, always talented, always calculated to rivet the attention of laity and clergy alike).

(VIII. 123)

4

Amongst the Merezhkovskys' widening circle of friends 'from Russia' was a poverty-striken couple who, like Georgiy Chulkov and his wife, had only recently been permitted to reside in the capital

---

' This would have implied 'equal power' with the state and emancipation from the much-resented Holy Synod, a governmental body introduced by Peter the Great to subject the Church to more stringent state control.

after years of political exile. Having found asylum with the ex-Marxists of *Voprosy Zhizni*, the writer Aleksey Remizov took up residence in the editorial flat in the capacity of a *domovoy*, or 'house-goblin'. With him was his wife Serafima Pavlovna, an ardently religious Social Revolutionary from an old Ukrainian family, and their baby daughter Natasha. Remizov, a shock-headed hunchback, was one of the first modern interpreters of the frightful sufferings, the superstitions, and the sly, ornate humour of the Russian people. Myopic to the point of blindness, he wrote, in an exquisite calligraphic hand, prose of a calibre that had almost faded from Russian literature with the redoubtable Admiral Shishkov,[s] a prose which sought lovingly to maintain the Russianness of Russian syntax and the sappy richness of Slavonic roots.

The world of his own imagination was absolutely real to Remizov and he would transform his dwelling into a kind of occult den with weird decorations: cut-out figures, fishbones dangling from threads, fir cones and odd-shaped stones or pebbles. He had the gift of encompassing everybody he met in a strange world of his own: a grotesque Vyacheslav Ivanov with 'snuff on his nose'; a hefty Berdayev tipping out of a child's swing and Andrey Bely 'so surprised he swallowed a date';[28] Lev Shestov leading parties of decadents visiting 'in flocks'; Merezhkovsky taking baby Natasha on his knees, obviously mindful that 'of such is the Kingdom of Heaven', but succumbing to blind panic and shrieking 'Zina! Zina! Take her away!' when the little girl showed signs of being about to make a mess; Rozanov, comparing notes with Remizov himself on the sizes and shapes of certain male attributes not normally discussed, let alone measured in polite society, or lamenting Shestov's supposed weakness for the bottle, which was in fact a carefully nurtured invention of Remizov's own.

Of Blok he spoke in a different tone:

Often, A. A. Blok, a student in pale blue uniform, would call in at the editor's office. If I had to go to attend to anything I did not call Hanna [the maid] but simply handed Natasha over to Blok. Carefully and tenderly he would take her in his arms and she, looking into his moonlight eyes, would show off all the tricks I had taught her or sit quietly, enchanted by the pale blue.[29]

At *Voprosy Zhizni* Remizov not only acted as caretaker for the editors but kept accounts. In his book about Blok, written in 1922

---

[s] Chief of a movement in Russian literature which, at the turn of the nineteenth century, had opposed the Europeanization of the language introduced by Karamzin ably supported by the society Arzamas.

in the unusual form of a kind of one-sided conversation with the dead poet, he wrote:

... all their book-keeping was stowed away, signed (by me) and sealed by my employer D. E. Zhukovsky, if you remember: 'persons in authority' took it as a personal insult when I signed business letters: 'Ye Stewarde Aleksiy'. Mar'ya Alekseyevna, the junior clerk, was convinced that my *Pond*[t] was a novel translated from the German and had her doubts as to the genuineness of your surname:
'Blok! A pseudonym?'
So when you turned up at the editor's office, still in your student's uniform with the blue collar, the very first thing I said to you was about your pseudonym.
And from that first meeting, and it was in a very special Petersburg springtime, something came into being, something odd and pleasant, which made it impossible for you to talk to me without smiling.[30]

Blok smiled, but it was a smile of appreciation and understanding. Unlike many of his contemporaries, he did not think Remizov affected. Having preserved the child in himself, he was quick to recognize and to respect the child in others: the tragic, estranged, mischievous child in Remizov who saw things that other people did not; the honest, devoted child in Zhenya Ivanov, sticking doggedly to the rules of his own game; the brilliant, frightened, elusive child in Bely who kept trying to hide behind the grown-up, only to come storming out again demanding to be loved; the loyal, imaginative, spiteful, show-off child in Zinaida Hippius ... People who had suppressed or lost the child in themselves Blok feared and usually came to dislike. As for Remizov, he applied to Blok a description he used for his own wife and no one else: 'a naked conscience'.

The meeting of these two very different people was to spark off a new cycle of verse. At first, however, their association (except for little Natasha) was really on a business footing. It was Remizov who paid out Blok's fees from *Voprosy Zhizni*.

Through the year 1905 and until the autumn of 1906, by which time he had finally established himself as a leading poet, Blok wrote more reviews than at any other time. He needed the money, and his letters to his father show the pleasure he took in his growing ability to earn his living in so congenial a field. The exercise, moreover, sharpened his awareness of the general climate of literary opinion. Later, he was always careful to the verge of pedantry about his own collections, for looking at careless publications by other poets made him conscious once and for all of the importance of

---

[t] Remizov's novel *The Pond* was serialized throughout 1905 in *Voprosy Zhizni*.

selection, arrangement, and artistic presentation. Between autumn 1904 and autumn 1906 Blok wrote some 47 reviews, of which one is an omnibus effort dealing with 15 young poets."

Apart from these brief reviews, Blok reacted in a full-length article, 'Colours and Words' (v. 7–18), to the appearance on the decadent scene of a new but fully mature luminary, the poet and theoretician of Symbolism Vyacheslav Ivanov. This spontaneous re-action to the influence of a new mind within the familiar area of decadent thought sheds considerable light on the poetry Blok himself was writing throughout that spring and summer: a cycle called *The Bubbles of the Earth*, one of the first poems of which is dedicated to Remizov.

Both Remizov, in his work and his whole personality, and Vya-cheslav Ivanov in his richly persuasive theoretical articles and irre-proachable, if academic, poetry epitomized, each in his own very different way, a tendency to wake old gods, to search out the roots of myth in nature and in man. In his article on Vyacheslav Ivanov, Blok described this search as 'the way of symbols, a way that lies along forgotten tracks on which we remember the youth of the world' (v. 10). Elsewhere he wrote of it as an attempt 'to penetrate that region of paganism re-experienced that is ruled by Spring and Death' (v. 589)." He himself connected this 'paganism re-experi-enced' with Dostoyevsky's *The Devils* and thus with revolution, quoting Dostoyevsky's anti-hero Verkhovensky: '"We shall un-leash fires ... we shall unleash legends.... There will be such a stir-up as the earth never saw before.... Russia will be wrapped in mist, the earth will yearn for the old gods ..."' (v. 590).

Blok had no need to strain his imagination to conjure up his 'Bubbles of the Earth': 'certain beings that inhabit the forests, fields,

---

" It says much for the young critic's perspicacity that, behind the pseudonym Nik-To (which, meaning 'no one', struck him as being in 'naïve bad taste'), he detected a true poet.[31] As it transpired, Nik-To was none other than Innokentiy Annensky, then an un-known schoolmaster from Tsarskoye Selo. Later, though he did not live to see the publica-tion of their first manifestos, Annensky became one of the most influential figures amongst the Acmeists. He was particularly revered by Akhmatova and Gumilev, who wrongly blamed the Symbolists for overlooking his anonymous début.

" Abroad this pagan revival was associated with the names of Nietzsche and Wagner. Knut Hamsun, much read in Russia, represented the same tendency and so, in the opinion of literary Petersburg and Moscow, did Isadora Duncan. Amongst the artists of the *Mir Iskusstva* group, Vasnetsov and Vrubel were fascinated by the ancient pre-Christian Sla-vonic world. In literature Remizov's folk tales and Vyacheslav Ivanov's call to return to myth-making found an echo in the writings of many contemporary poets, and the ten-dency reached its apotheosis in the epic poetry of Velimir Khlebnikov. In music and the dance, Stravinsky's *The Rite of Spring* and such Diaghilev ballets as *L'Après-midi d'un faune* all typified the same trend.

and marshes' (v. 23–4) which, though near akin to furry creatures and fronded plants, had long since been exorcised by the holy and denounced by the wise as childish fancies. These bubbles had been fizzing and popping on the brink of his poetry for some time. When he 'lost the golden sword' of mystic discipline, the anarchic little creatures came bounding in all about him. It was enough for him 'to look at the marshy wastelands with the seeing eyes of the artist', and there they were: *nêchist*, 'the impure', as Russian folklore calls them, imps of fen and forest who brought him childish delight rather than satanic horror but who were, nevertheless, precursors. That Blok recognized them as such is evident from the allusion to the witches in *Macbeth*.

To Remizov, Blok wrote of the sense of supernatural horror suggested by his novel *The Pond*: 'Terror rears its head as you read the novel. . . . "it is finding its way out", "writhing", "creeping". I'm frightened to read it at night' (VIII. 126). Yet, at first reading, there is nothing very frightening in Blok's 'Little Devils of the Marshes': they are just dispossessed fiends, 'simpletons,/Non-things of the slime' (II. 10). Sometimes the poet sees them as perfectly real glow-worms unable to bear the light of day,*ᵂ* sometimes as imps 'snapping and yapping', 'writhing and repenting', 'green and tough and very small' (II. 13), begging to be spared the holiness that has come into the world and happy with their own 'pastoral Christ', their own 'Burning Bush' (II. 20–1), their own little black priest who is glad

> of every creeping thing
> and every beast
> and every faith.   (II. 14)

How delightful they are, and how restful this 'eternity of the marshes' (II. 17). Only the old sorcerers and witches in the villages mutter as the poet rides by on the familiar white horse, saying that the marshes are having their joke with him, the forces of darkness drawing him.

> And when they say things like this,
> The old men make the sign of the Cross,
> The elderly—snigger,
> And—as for the young girls—you can see quite clearly
> The white wings behind their shoulders. . . .   (II. 19)

ᵂ This association of ancient folk memories and the lower life forms is not fortuitous. Andrey Bely was writing at this time of the evolutionary atavism of the age and Mandelstam was later, in such poems as 'Lamarck', to associate the revival of pagan attitudes with a reversal of the evolutionary process.

5

On 27 April 1905, Blok and Lyuba—once again free of examinations, the University system having broken down completely between conflicting pressures from above and below—left St. Petersburg for Shakhmatovo. The tense winter season in the capital had ended in a series of lively literary scandals, most of which they now heard of at second or third hand in letters from their Petersburg acquaintances. Among the most sensational of these was a police raid on the premises of *Voprosy Zhizni* followed by the detention of Chulkov. Another was the philosopher Minsky's attempt to organize a 'blood-sacrifice', aided and abetted by Vyacheslav Ivanov and his wife Zinov'eva-Annibal, clad, as Zhenya Ivanov informed them, in a red toga with rolled-up sleeves like an executioner. Both Blok and his wife recoiled from the idea of this weird ceremony, at which all those present drank from a communal cup of wine mixed with a drop of the victim's blood (obtained, of course, by a mere pinprick). Lyubov' remarked caustically that the participants could have achieved their vaunted sense of communion just as well through straightforward amateur theatricals.

At Shakhmatovo, what Blok called 'the orgasm of the trees' was an experience of greater mystic immediacy than any half-baked Petersburg ceremonies:

> ... the sap was literally humming—through field and forest. After a few days, the woods had already stopped filtering the silence and become full of sound. Now they are all happy and full of fun—it's very noticeable. The frogs and things are also having tremendous fun and I am wandering about shaken like a reed in the wind with the two Krabbs. ...
>
> (VIII. 125)

Thunder-showers and warm west winds brought the lilac into luxurious early flowering. Away to the south, a mist and a smoke hung over Moscow and there were rumours that the city was burning. These, credible as they seemed at the time, turned out to be false. More tricks, Blok thought, of the 'elementals', and again he quoted from *Macbeth*, informing Zhenya Ivanov that the smoke had vanished

> Into the air, and what seem'd corporal melted
> As breath into the wind.

In June, Bely and Sergey Solov'ev came to stay. The visit was disastrous. Ever since parting from the Bloks in Petersburg, Bely had bombarded them with short, almost daily letters like a man in love.

Blok, who was in need of 'silence and simplicity' and suffering from a strong reaction against all 'the shouting and sobbing and leaping flames' of the books he was called upon to review (v. 565), had found it difficult to respond to Bely's passionate, ill-considered concern in such letters as this, written in early March:

My dear,

Why is there such weariness in your letter?

Can it be that the grey bird with silken wings has curtained off all about you?

Perhaps it is possible to raise the veil of melancholy and tiredness? ... My dear, do not lose heart. Christ be with you. After all, there *is* such a person as Isadora Duncan.[32]

Blok's replies were wary, cautious, as few and as down-to-earth as was consonant with the obviously very genuine affection the whole family had come to feel for Borya. On 19 May, in a letter inviting Bely to Shakhmatovo, Blok had sent him a poem which he subsequently used as an 'introduction' to his *Second Volume*, but which here bore the title 'Prayer'. In it, he once again apostrophized the Most Beautiful Lady, beginning:

> Thou art gone into the fields beyond recall—
> And hallowed be Thy Name.

This poem should have sobered both Bely and Seryëzha. Mature, firm, and reverent, it made it quite clear that the subject of the Beautiful Lady would be both painful and barren—and that Blok knew what he was about.

The two friends, however, decided that their beloved poet must be saved from himself. Seryëzha was insensitive and militant. Bely was estranged and offended by the poem 'The Little Devils of the Marshes', convinced that it was a parody on himself and the Argonauts.[x]

He was, moreover, labouring under two agonizing difficulties: torn between his love for Seryëzha and his love for his hosts, and between his love for Blok and a growing passion for Lyubov' of whom, as it seemed to him now, Blok had shown himself hopelessly unworthy. Seryëzha, for his part, had begun to disapprove of his

---

[x] Vl. Orlov suggests Bely was right,[33] but there are several arguments against this. First, the poem does not bear the hallmarks of parody or allegory, but of something felt and experienced: it is about devils, not decadents. Secondly, the 'we' of the lines 'so that just we two/might listen to the silent void' is clearly a dual plural, not a collective one. Thirdly, the dedication shows that, if Blok was thinking of anyone else when he wrote these verses, it was of Remizov, and that because he would have understood them, not because he was 'in' them.

cousin, both as poet and thinker. The most important things in poetry, he now maintained, were classic lucidity and morality. The new poems Blok read to them on this visit confirmed them both in the thought 'that Blok was no longer Blok'.[34]

Aleksandra Andreyevna took her son's part and was short with Seryëzha, deploring various traits in his character which she maintained were typical of their common relatives, the Kovalenskys. When Seryëzha was there, all the delightful cosiness of Bely's weeks in Petersburg vanished and he found himself continually 'betraying' one friend to the other. To add to this, Lyubov' Dmitriyevna, who had hitherto played the part of a good elder sister, reconciling and uniting the three young men, now tended rather to set them tilting one against the other and to observe the battle of wits with a strange, eager interest.

Lyubov' was not happy. She resented her husband's tragic passivity, his growing alienation from the values of the society to which they both belonged. She ascribed it largely to the influence of his mother, with whom he was so profoundly at one in his 'rejection of the world', and there was an increasing sense of strain between them. Married to a man she loved, a man who had courted her over many years and placed his very salvation in her hands, she felt drawn to Bely and Solov'ev who were, in their own albeit clumsy way, putting up a fight against the rising tide of damnation and despair that was threatening to engulf her beloved Sasha. Seryëzha, however, with his doctrinaire views and his increasingly brusque, self-assured manner, was becoming intolerable. Bely, on the other hand, was dear and familiar from the happy month in Moscow of the year before. In many ways, she thought as he did. Blok himself had taught them to speak the same language: the language of Symbolism. Besides, Lyubov' could not have failed to notice that the game of worship, the laughing, poetic, chivalrous cult of last year, was turning into real devotion. Though at this stage she was far from contemplating any response, it must have been comforting to have so ardent (and distinguished) a *cavaliere servente*, for Bely's reputation in Symbolist circles stood at least as high as Blok's own at this time. As she felt her power wane in her husband's poetry it was reassuring to see it wax over the mind and heart of his friend.

Andrey Bely has left us a masterly evocation of the atmosphere at Shakhmatovo:

How viciously angry with one another we all were!

I remember us all at table: there is S.M. [Sergey Mikhailovich]—deeply tanned, everything about him gone black somehow, his brows raised and

his lips compressed under the dark, bushy moustache, trying to bark out
some wild statement in the most violent terms on purpose to shock Aleksandra Andreyevna, who looks seriously grey-faced and with whom he is at
daggers drawn; in the very way he holds his napkin and tries to straighten
those round shoulders there is concentration and challenge; and Aleksandra
Andreyevna, turning pale, lets her napkin drop and wards off his paradoxes
with a nervous smile, shaking her defiantly cropped head; and her brown
eyes scurry over the surface of everything, the napkins, the edge of the
table, the chests of the diners; she avoids our eyes like a cat ready to defend
the life of its kitten.

'I think, Seryëzha', she replies quietly—quietly, almost in a whisper, 'that
all that is neither here nor there: it is Bryusovshchina!'

'And why not?' roars Seryëzha. 'In my opinion, Bryusov is our leading
poet; Pushkin himself feared neither the abyss nor any horrors. . . .'

'There you go again! Pushkin indeed! What Pushkin says is something
quite different!'

Lyubov' Dmitriyevna in her flowing tea gown, a shawl over her broad
shoulders, her face lowered inimically over her soup, suddenly rears up her
head:

'You've all become "Bal'monts", the lot of you: all Spaniards; baring
your teeth and feeling for your swords!'

And I reply:

'All right then—let's be outlaws!'

Stonily, sarcastically through his nose, A.A. pronounces:

'And why not! Let's!'

In this 'Let's!' there is a note of challenge, a kind of 'Ha!', not without
insolence ('how's *that* for you?') as though by his whole outward appearance he were giving us to understand:

'I keep myself to myself, I say nothing but if . . .'

'But if' what is not clear; the cheeks are stony, greenish-yellow (not
rosy), the deep-etched line between his brows seems to forbid the very
thought of a smile; and at the same time he does smile—sarcastically, bating
us:

'There you are, all of you: if I wanted—I could spoil everything, destroy
everything, break it all up; better not touch me.'[35]

The drama was helped along by a deeply involved audience: Aunt
Maria, blinking rapidly in anxious disapproval from her end of the
table; Andrey, stone deaf, but all the more acutely aware that something was wrong; Aunt Sofia and Ferol, bored and embarrassed by
the 'mystical' hints and literary allusions of the Bloks and their
friends.

Blok himself was utterly vulnerable, for the transition from the
high metaphysics of the Most Beautiful Lady to that 'realism bordering on the fantastic' of which he had written his father as long ago

as 1902 was proving hard to achieve, so hard that, throughout this spring and early summer, he had begun to fear he had been altogether mistaken in his vocation. He would spend hours alone in the woods, sitting on tufts of dry grass in the marshes, disdainfully tossing off his *Bubbles of the Earth*, which he accounted more of a pastime than vocational work. One of the best poems, 'The Little Priest of the Marshes', is dedicated to a pet hedgehog, and the loss of confidence which marks the first half of 1905 perhaps indicated that Blok doubted it was worthy of any more distinguished reader. Sergey Solov'ev's attempts to recall him to a system of images from which he was struggling to break free were exasperating, and his friends' hostile reaction to his latest poems had genuinely shaken his self-con-fidence.

Then, one thundery evening, things came to a head. Bely was reading a new poem to the Bloks when Seryëzha who, having heard it before, had gone up to his room to work, was seen, coatless and hatless, plunging down from the veranda into the dusky garden. Bely read on for a long time, then they talked. When evening tea was served they suddenly realized that no one had heard Seryëzha return to the house. They called, searched the garden, sent men to shout for him in the nearer woods where there were known to be danger-ous patches of bog. When they looked in Seryëzha's room they found his baptismal cross:

... a terrible thought flashed through our minds, like lightning.
'No!'
'You think—not?' A.A. asked me.
'Never!'
'Sure?'
'Certain!'[36]

As dawn came they sat in Seryëzha's room and spoke of him with infinite tenderness. Aleksandra Andreyevna and Bely were sure he was dead. When it was light enough, Blok galloped off on Malchik to search the woods and men were sent to make enquiries in all the neighbouring villages. Bely went with them. By asking after Seryëzha at a local market, he learnt that his friend had spent the night at Lyubov' Dmitriyevna's old home of Boblovo and hastened back with the good news to Shakhmatovo. All were immensely relieved but Aleksandra Andreyevna was pardonably irritated, all the more so as Seryëzha did not send word or turn up himself until that evening, when he arrived in perfect comfort and excellent spirits in the Boblovo troika. Far from apologizing, he came out with an involved story, plagiarized in the most shameless fashion from Blok's Beautiful Lady verses, about having followed a star and met a girl in a pink dress who had invited him to stay the night in the hospitable Mendeleyev home. The walk had been undertaken with the 'mystic purpose' of saving 'the dawns' that had brought Blok, Bely, and himself into such elevated communion. Aleksandra Andreyevna was beside herself with relief and rage and there was a scene.

Bely's nerve broke. He decided to leave. Seryëzha insisted on staying on for a day or two longer. According to Blok they played cards all the time and the crazy incident found its way into a poem (II. 66), a fascinating example of the way odd details from real life (the market where Bely got news of Seryëzha; Seryëzha's deep tan and the song he always hummed as he played cards; the green of the countryside; the hysteria; the sense of fate and numbness) got all jumbled up together and emerged as quite a separate, independently valid image: a gypsy telling the cards at a country fair. The song ('Three Cards' from Tchaikovsky's opera *The Queen of Spades*) even found its way into an article on Lermontov Blok happened to be writing at the time, and his explanation of this to his editor Pertsov echoes the conversation at table recalled by Andrey Bely:

... it is the 'masquerade' point (Lermontov's *Masquerade*), that magic point where there is no longer 'Pushkin's' and 'Lermontov's' as 'two faces of the Petersburg period', but where 'Apollonian' Pushkin has gone sailing into the abyss, pushed over by Tchaikovsky, a *magician and a musician*, and Lermontov, who knew what it was like in the abyss, has taken up his stand on the edge and is shouting down at Pushkin: 'Enough, great builder!' ['*Dobro, stroitel!*'] That is when 'everything, whirling, disappears into darkness....'

(VIII. 149–50)

'Everything, whirling, disappears into darkness...'—all that Blok wrote this summer of 1905 suggests precisely this. The poetry began with a cycle of disenchantment, a series of dialogues between a little girl and a boy or grown man.[y] In one poem, a man explains to the little girl that there is no way through from 'this' world into 'that', that the Beautiful Lady will never come to them while they are upon *this* shore 'because She does not travel on a steamship'. Another poem took up Zhenya's theme of the puppet booth:

> Now the puppet booth is open
> For the children good and gay

[y] Originally written as a series to have been entitled '*Skazki*' (Fairy Stories) but eventually published as separate poems.

And a girl and a small boy have taken
Their places to look at the play.
There are ladies, kings, and a devil,
Introduced by a devilish tune,
Who seizes the babe to the wail of a fiddle
And the cranberry juice runs down....

BOY:

He'll be rescued, he will, from the darkness
By a wave of the pure white hand.
See, there! The little lights sparkle!
Don't you see the smoke? and the brands?
It must be the Queen herself has hearkened.

GIRL:

No, no. You're making it up.
That is the devil's following....
The Queen—she walks when the sun is up,
Rose-garlanded, long train billowing
And borne by knights with swords at their hips!
She has lovelorn knights in her following.

Suddenly, hanging over the ramp, head down,
The clown screams: 'Help! I am bleeding!
I am bleeding to death from cranberry juice!
All bandaged up in a twist of rag!
And on my head is a cardboard helm!
And in my hand—a wooden sword!'

The little girl and boy went crying away
And that was the end of the jolly puppet play.

(II. 67–8)

It was years, said Andrey Bely (who promptly identified with the unfortunate clown) before he could forgive Blok that 'cranberry juice'.

Indeed, Blok never took Bely's tragic infatuation for Lyuba altogether seriously, which must have been tiresome for them both. Bely declared himself on the day he left Shakhmatovo. The declaration was accepted almost as part and parcel of the old game of chivalrous devotion. Everybody at Shakhmatovo seems to have known about it (at least we are indebted for *our* knowledge to Aunt Maria's diary).[37] Blok chose to overlook it and to interpret his friend's abrupt departure as the result of a misunderstanding brought on by Seryëzha's tactless behaviour and the lack of sympathy between his family and his friends. In a letter of 23 June he warned Chulkov not to come and visit him and Lyuba that summer because they were cohabiting with people who 'as we saw from the visit of A. Bely and S. Solov'ev, find the kind of conversations we enjoy desperately wearisome, almost to the point of physical nausea' (VIII. 129).

Nevertheless, although prepared to defend his friends from the 'positivists' of the older generation, Blok was shaken and angered by the events of that fateful ten days. It took him over a month to force himself to reply to Bely, who had written twice and ended the second letter: 'I love you, Sasha, I wish to send you that snowy oblivion which is softly spreading all about me ... Amen.'[38]

When Blok did reply, it was affectionately enough, but with a certain blunt frankness and an ironic note of challenge not evident in his earlier letters:

19 July 1905
Shakhmatovo

Dear Borya,

I love you tenderly and often think of you and remember your words and think them over. Why I don't write to you—I do not know. Thanks for the snowy oblivion and for the news about *Iskusstvo*.[z] ... I had a dream in which you and I were together in a dewy, shady forest and the two of us had walked a long way and got separated from the rest of the party. Then I began to show that I was able to fly in various ways, both sitting and standing in the air. The feeling was pleasant and light and you were very much impressed and envious. This went on for a long time and I didn't want to interrupt it. The memory has remained—a pleasant one.

Your stay here with Seryëzha—the last—was possibly of more importance to me than all the others—tremendously exhilarating. For me there was much joy unhoped-for in it. Now, however, I am uneasy at heart about Seryëzha, it constantly seems to me as though there had been some misunderstanding here, as though one play had been replaced by another 'owing to the indisposition of the artiste and the horse'. The action of the play really does take place in the circus, so powerful is the critical moment and so tragic. I am reading Dostoyevsky and that is why I am writing such involved sentences—on purpose.—What is going to happen about Seryëzha? I embrace you and do not know whether things go ill with you, or well.

Your SASHA

P.S. The waltz in your poem[aa] was a revelation to me.[40]

---

[z] A short-lived decadent journal published at this time in Kiev. Sergey Solov'ev had become one of the editors and had asked Bely to invite Blok to contribute.

[aa] Evidently the lost poem 'Child of the Sun' which Bely had been reading the night Seryëzha disappeared.[39]

To Zhenya Ivanov, a day or two after Seryëzha had left, Blok had written in the same spirit of exhilaration:

For a long time I was upset and miserable and there were some absolutely black days. Now everything's fine. The other day Bugayev and Solov'ev, who had arrived together bringing with them the voice of events going on in the most important sphere of all, 'the Unsaid', left: first Bugayev, then Solov'ev.

Do you know what I want to be rid of? Meekness and readiness to back down. This is absolutely essential with respect to *certain* things and *certain* people. Do you know that loneliness, for as long as it remains a mere feeling, makes you fragile and tender and prevents you thinking and beckons you on. Yet there is a moment when it suddenly changes from a feeling to a *certainty*, and then it gives strength, brings you up to the bridle, makes you draw on YOURSELF again: 'Draw, draw, until the source runs dry, and if you live that long, you will be strong.' ... It is easier for me to write this than to say it; if we were talking I would go lazy again, grow discouraged, talk through my nose—you know the way I do go on most of the time. I can't write everything, either, but what I can say clearly all centres about one thing: I want action, I feel that *fire* is close again, that life does not wait (it hasn't time to wait—the whirlwind will come all unbidden). I want to hate many things, to be tougher. That's not quite it, though; if I come to discover more, I will write. The fire is approaching again, of what kind I do not know. The old is collapsing. Never will I accept Christ. Write whether there is anything within you that still responds to me now, don't hurry.... Perhaps it will all turn out for the best, there is much harmony about.

Your loving SASHA

I am sending this letter all as it is in its impressionistic, muddled state. Perhaps somewhere you will get a glimpse of what I feel I have not managed to say. What a momentous time we are living in! A great time! Joyful!

(VIII. 130–1)

Ivanov replied with his usual profound yet delicate concern for his friend's relationship to his Saviour, and it is typical of Blok's mood this summer that his answer—written after a gap of more than one month, in August 1905—should begin:

Dear Zhenya,
    I already think otherwise than how I wrote in my last letter.

In what this 'otherwise' consisted, Blok specified only in so far as to make clear that his mood was less rational. He insisted, however, that he was farther than he had ever been from *religion*. Still, it seemed to him that his way and Ivanov's were yet destined to cross:

Evgeniy Pavlovich Ivanov, 1910.
(From the collection of N. P. Il'in)

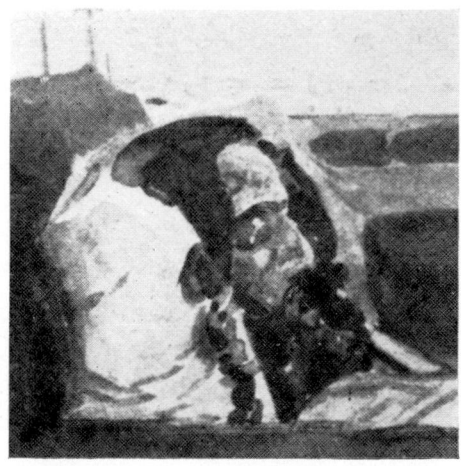

Mikhail Vrubel: Christ in the grave,
1903.

Mikhail Vrubel: Ceramic head of the
Demon, 1903.

The railway station at Ozerki, scene of 'The Stranger'.
(From a postcard in Blok's archive)

The lake at Shuvalovo, outside St. Petersburg near Ozerki and one of Blok's favourite
haunts. (From a postcard in Blok's archive)

You are one of those I love best in all the world. Something will happen between us in the future. To all the people in my life now, especially to those close to me, something will inevitably happen on some October day of thaw. . . .

(VIII. 132–3)

This curious, spine-chilling prophecy is accompanied by asseverations that not for ages has he felt so young and light-hearted.

The obverse of the poet's refusal of the passive, religious way in poetry, the desire to break the window and fling himself out into a younger and more immediate world,[bb] is expressed in a poem which, like the impressionistic verses touched off by the appalling three-day card game, was inspired by something that actually happened.

After the departure of his friends, Blok decided that the attic of his annexe needed a window, a semi-circular affair like the one above the veranda of the main house. Always a good workman, he set about the job himself, and it seemed to him as though, having sawed through the wooden wall of his own home, he would at last see beyond the quiet garden where the older people strolled up and down amidst the luxuriant green:

> I can sense the far view. Resin pearls
> Well from under the saw's strident sighing
> Through the sinewy pine of the walls . . .
> And the pungent gold sawdust is flying.
>
> Now a last whistling split, the saw's screech
> And the plank hurtles down past recalling.
> With a sharp scent of resin, the breech
> Opens up the whole country before me.

(II. 73)

This poem and one or two others, such as the exquisite 'Autumn Freedom' (II. 75–6) with its echoes of Lermontov and anticipations of Esenin, or the related 'Freedom, do not beckon me' (II. 77), breathe an elation which becomes an ecstatic presentiment of passion in 'There in the howling cold of night' (II. 81) and 'Now the wind of day is failing' (II. 82). The preponderant note in the poetry of the summer, however, continues to be one of sadness. The happy bride of his private myth is dead and buried and the church where they were wed has 'fallen into the weed-grown pond'; the old mother

---

[bb] The symbol of a leap through a broken window, always connected with an attempt to enter the 'real world', to achieve incarnation, a kind of kenosis, recurs constantly throughout Blok's poetry, particularly in the years 1905–6.

is left alone 'in a house that is weary of waiting for youth'; only the mice gnaw at the wainscot and dance over the cupboards and old armchairs," and the old woman sits and spins, and in the mirror:

> The threads are the same and the mice are the same
> And the same dark icon looks down from its frame.

'It is quiet', he wrote, 'and the quiet will surely grow' (II. 82).

6

With the shaking off of all mystical and rational restraint, Blok's genius had developed an entirely new range. Midas-like, he was beginning to turn everything he touched to gold.

Everything—with one exception. He still had not learnt to describe the real events of revolution: yet the revolution moved him ever more deeply. Soon after the family's return to Petersburg, the country was virtually paralysed by a general strike. Study was out of the question. The whole city was living precariously from day to day.

Yet Blok continued to react as it were at one remove. His reading of Dostoyevsky that summer had sharpened his awareness of the obverse of city life and of unsavoury incidents recorded in the newspapers. Such an incident, absorbed and retransformed to fit the poet's own hushed, expectant world, is the story of the murdered child in 'In the distant, pale-blue night nursery' (II. 83). 'The Meeting' (II. 172-4), his first attempt that autumn to return to the subject of the revolution, was also an 'occasional' poem. It is written from the point of view of a bystander, not of a protagonist. In a sense, the poem is an exercise in verse journalism (albeit of a superior type and incorporating a subtle moral), and Blok found it necessary to take a poetic model: Bal'mont's translation of Oscar Wilde's 'Ballad of Reading Gaol'.

The Imperial Manifesto of 19 October 1905, which sought to re-establish civic peace and order by guaranteeing certain basic liberties and granting a limited constitution, split the country anew and the impressions of that day furnished the poet with a more immediate stimulus. Conservatives were relieved; liberals elated; the Left, however, was still defiant and called for the continuation and intensifica-

---

" As usual, the images are suggested by reality. The church *was* reflected in the village pond and, in his usual report to his mother on the state of Shakhmatovo that spring, Blok had complained that 'the mice have eaten an awful lot'.[41]

tion of revolutionary activity. Blok's heart went out to those who rejected compromise, to the penurious and underprivileged who stood to gain little immediate benefit from the promised democratic freedoms and constitutional rights. As was natural for anyone living just over the river from the industrial powerhouse of Petersburg, the Vyborgskaya Storona, sympathy for the poor meant sympathy with the comparatively highly organized industrial workers.

The lesson the poet had learnt from the confrontations of the year 1905 was that the will to power in Russia was distributed between two camps: the old order, still backed by the might of the army, the police, and the civil service, and the formless, rebellious element of 'the people', a mighty population, capable of casting not only the Russian government but all that it stood for, good and bad, to the four winds. Factories plunged into darkness in obedience to the upraised arm of an anonymous workman and dark, lampless streets haunted his dreams from then on.

On the other hand, Blok had every reason to know the strength of the old order. His father's family were provincial governors, lawyers, administrators: proud, hard, capable, and ambitious, they worked through such efficient and dutiful servants as Frants Felikso-vich and were supported by the cultivated, polyglot energies of people like Aunt Sofia's husband, Adam Feliksovich, and his son, Blok's childhood playmate, Ferol. Blok was aware of the might of the state machine as few members of the intelligentsia were; to some extent, he judged its strength by his own. He had never sought power but, in his own way, he had it: power over words, power over women, power over the imaginations of others, even over his own strong, disciplined body. These were the gifts of heredity and up-bringing. Yet often—increasingly often as he grew older—depres-sion would overcome him and the world seem empty. At such moments he would have been glad to die. In the same way, the strength of the autocracy seemed to him to be largely the strength of inertia; certainly there was an element of senility about it. Yet one has only to look at newspaper photographs of the assassination of the poet's uncle, Ivan Blok, governor of Samara, blown to bits in 1906 by a Social Revolutionary terrorist, to see where the balance of power still lay and to understand why Blok—instinctively—knew from the beginning that civil strife in Russia would not cease with the granting of a constitution. What he saw was the fatal confronta-tion of two worlds: one senile, replete, and stuffy, yet with its own delicate, dry beauty, its own code of devotion to the 'ancient legend' of autocracy, and, above all, with long experience of power; the

other formless and young, unaware of its own strength, inexperienced and irresponsible yet full of the sap of life.

Blok was not without feeling for the 'ancient legend'. That
autumn he dreamt that he was watching one of the royal palaces
quietly burning down and in his dream he 'loved the Tsar' (*Z.K.*
71). Yet, if Russia were a Sleeping Beauty (Gogol's Pan Katerina or
Wagner's Brünhilde set about with a ring of flame), Blok would
not be on the side of Katerina's father, the old sorcerer who has slain
his daughter's lover and cast her into an enchanted slumber, nor
would he be *for* Wotan *against* Siegfried.[dd] Nevertheless, he understood the tragic grandeur of both protagonists, and his best poems
of the 1905 revolution are not descriptive pieces, but two symbolic
statements of the tragic fatality between the opposing forces, both
written on the day of the October Manifesto.

The first is about the Bronze Horseman:

> Pendant above the universal town
> Imprisoned in the dust of ages past
> The monarch sleeps on through the lyre-soft dawn
> Lulled by an autocratic dream of rest.
>
> Royal-cast in iron, looming above the mist,
> His mighty forebear's steed the serpent tramps,
> And still the mob's wild clamour, many-voiced,
> Is not yet master on the Neva's banks.
>
> Already on the houses flutter flags,
> And new-fledged birds prepare to fly the nest.
> Yet slowly flows the Neva's welling flood,
> And blind the windows of her palaces.
>
> Though now the face of Freedom be revealed
> Before that was revealed the serpent's face.
> And not one single, shining coil is crushed,
> And every armoured scale is yet in place.[ee]

(II. 175)

[dd] Wagner's opera was performed again that autumn in St. Petersburg and Yershov, the
singer who took the name part, gave the role powerful contemporary significance by
emphasizing the smith's apprentice in his powerful, 'shaggy' Siegfried.

As to Pan Katerina, Blok and Bely had spent much of their days at Shakhmatovo that
summer discussing the appositeness of this story to the situation of Russia. Bely got in
first with an article 'The Green Meadow' (*Lug zelyënyy*) before Blok had finished writing—
a typical example of Symbolist 'collective creation'.

[ee] D. E. Maksimov, in his brief analysis of this poem,[42] calls these last two lines 'the conclusion' to be drawn from two other lines from this and the next poem: i.e. from the
statements that the people are not yet master on the Neva's banks and that no one is sorry

And the same day he wrote:

> Still drained of hope—the far, grey distance.
> Still beautiful—the far, grey sky,
> Still to the beggar's starved insistence,
> They turn a blind eye, all turn a blind eye.
>
> And the voice of the mob is lost in the delta
> Dissolved and lost in the Neva's dream.
> And the despairing shouts: 'Dethrone, dethrone him!'
> Awake no pity in its sleeping stream.
>
> The Winter Palace of the Tsar is gleaming
> In the cold light of morning grey and wan.
> The warrior in black armour will not answer,^{ff}
> Until he himself is touched by the dawn.
>
> Then, flaming crimson over the deep waters,
> To ward off the wild mob, in useless strife
> He'll sink his sword more grimly, and, defending
> An ancient legend, will lay down his life.

(II. 176)

The dreamlike, tonic metre of the second poem and its haunting repetitions convey a muted sense of doom all the more effective when one remembers the day on which it was written: a day of rejoicing and self-congratulation for the liberal-minded and well-intentioned; of hasty reappraisal and replanning for extremists of both persuasions; of street meetings and shootings, panic, noise, and extreme activity.

On this particular day, Blok had chosen not to be an onlooker. Fired by sympathy for the workers from the islands, he had joined in one of their processions carrying a red flag. This was an act of some moral and even physical courage. Blok's aesthetic friends, though they might sympathize with the revolution, left it to professional agitators to wave red flags and march with the common herd. Moreover, the army was out in strength to keep order and

---

for the poor and the hungry. It seems to me that the symbol of the snake may be read differently; in the statue, it represents the *enemy* of the Bronze Horseman, who in this poem undoubtedly stands for autocracy and Empire. The conclusion is thus not so much that the revolution has failed to crush the autocracy as that the autocracy has failed to crush the forces which oppose it: that the final battle is only postponed. This, as will be seen, would correspond to the implications of the last verse of the next poem.

ff The warrior in black armour is one of the statues on the roof of the Winter Palace. On 16 October Blok had written to Zhenya Ivanov: 'Worthy of observation now on the roof of the Winter Palace is a sad man-at-arms with a lowered sword. His sharp profile is sad against the grey sky. Petersburg in these October days is the most intoxicating town in the world....'[43]

the soldiers were trigger-happy. Anything might have happened[gg] and Blok with his military bearing and fair colouring must have been a conspicuous figure amongst the grey lines of heavy-featured, underfed Slavonic workmen. Lyubov' was very proud of him. More sober people like Bryusov, however, looked on the gesture as an undergraduate prank rather unbecoming in a serious poet, whereas the Merezhkovskys, still convinced of Blok's political passivity, ventured the opinion that he had got mixed up in the procession through sheer absent-mindedness.

Yet Blok was by no means the only 'decadent' to feel sympathy for the extreme Left that autumn and there is nothing so very startling in his calling himself a 'Social Democrat', albeit lightheartedly and in inverted commas.[46] N. Minsky, an old associate of the Merezhkovskys whose book *The Religion of the Future* Blok was engaged in reviewing, became responsible editor of the first-ever legal Bolshevik newspaper to be published in Russia, *Novaya Zhizn'*, and found it possible to declare in his first editorial: 'Mysticism, bold and pure in its very essence, can ally itself in the sphere of freedom with an equally bold doctrine of equally unbounded horizons such as social democracy.'[47] Bal'mont contributed a revolutionary poem to the same paper; Vyacheslav Ivanov, in his poetry, was celebrating a new Russia that was to rise phoenix-like from the flames of revolution, sacred frenzy, and bloodshed; Chulkov was writing of the

[gg] Maria Beketova describes this procession as part of 'the general rejoicing' in honour of the constitution,[44] but D. E. Maksimov is right to point out the significance of the red flag and the fact that such processions were dispersed. Zhenya Ivanov records just such an incident in which he himself and a relative of the painter Ge were involved:

18 October: the constitution has been proclaimed, flags and manifestos with the four freedoms. The political strike continues. At twelve o'clock the sun came out and the University was chock-full of an unbudgable crowd. Red flags on the Duma, one of the revolutionaries tore down the city banner and hoisted a red flag.... I went to the Gostinyy Dvor, turned down Ivanovsk Street and saw just by the school a crowd running in panic.... The impression was that a volley was being fired into their rear. But you couldn't tell where from. I joined the stampede! That'll be something for you to remember, won't it? How did you conduct yourself? What part did you play in the revolution? I took an active part in the general panic! Oh, false pretender! N. P. Ge, on the other hand, happened to be at the corner of Zagorodnyy and Gorokhovoy at the critical moment and he told us what had happened. There was a group of people gathered round a flag and an orator was addressing them from a road block. Suddenly a horn sounded. Then a volley from the windows of the Semyënov Barracks. The orator fell, blood trickling from his mouth; everyone scattered, upsetting the flag and losing their galoshes. But he (N. P. Ge), smiling at himself—'really, after all, one can't behave like that'— waited awhile and then went and picked up the flag.... And I am a lukewarm bourgeois, happy to enjoy the freedoms at other people's expense.[45]

It may well have been to escape this last feeling that Blok yielded to the strange compulsion to join *his* procession.

'orgasm' of street fighting and the 'orgasm of the awakening soul'.[48] In Moscow, Andrey Bely and his friend Ellis had become ardent students of Marxism and Bely was preparing an article on Karl Kautsky.

Bryusov, though he was shocked at Lenin's concept of literature as 'a little wheel' or 'a little screw' in the machinery of social democracy,[49] had scornfully rejected the October Manifesto as a half-measure and stormed against the powers-that-be for losing the war: his hopes in the revolution centred round the possible emergence of a Russian Napoleon.[50] The Merezhkovskys, though opposed to the militant materialism of the Social Democrats, were extreme enough in their fashion, cultivating the company of 'illegal' revolutionaries and terrorists such as B. V. Savinkov, and claiming, for several years to come, to be more revolutionary than anybody else.

Blok's circle combined a heady self-identification with the revolutionary element with a claustrophobic sense of being under glass. The decadents were no longer imprisoned within their own personalities, as they had been during the Nineties, but they were imprisoned within their own small, isolated public. Blok, writing in *Voprosy Zhizni*, compared his own generation to the Alexandrian poets, burning with a subtle, secret flame while rebellion and palace revolution flared on every side and the ancient faiths were exhumed and re-examined 'at a time of secret rebellion which simply made more profound the stillness into which the Word was to be born'. It made no essential difference, he declared, either to the Alexandrians or to his generation, whether individual poets joined in the palace revolutions (which he saw as symptoms rather than causes) or 'withdrew to be alone with their white, languorous Muses' (v. 8).

It was Vyacheslav Ivanov who gave Blok this historical perspective on events, and whose article 'The Hellenic Religion of the Suffering God', published in *Novyy Put'* in January 1904, now served him as a guide to the way in which his own poetry should develop. The Alexandrians, Blok wrote, had been wrong to imitate Homer, although their nostalgia for the 'native element' of epic and folklore was understandable. The way back to a great, objective art did not lie in trying to put back the clock to early morning now that it was already late afternoon; it lay through the life-giving 'ascesis of prayer of the heart'. Blok's use of this monastic term, which describes an advanced spiritual exercise only to be undertaken under direction and by one leading a life of great austerity, is loose, even symbolic:

Such 'prayer of the heart' by which poets preserve their strength when they
have abandoned the native folk element is a state of questioning, of hearkening for a scarcely audible answer 'quite undistinguishable to others'. The
questioner must learn to master that unique word or incantation which
has not yet become a lie.

(V. 9–10)

Words, like all temporal things, grow old and die. They are strong
by virtue of their power of suggestion, of the chain of association
they set off in our imagination. In these last days, Blok wrote, words,
too, had grown old and tired and could no longer be used in their
primary meanings but only as 'pointers', 'hints', and 'symbols'. To
find such words was to find the way back into the creative darkness
of myth. Through the use of the 'true word', the symbol that is only
given in answer to the tense listening he described as 'prayer of the
heart', the poet becomes 'the unconscious transmitter of folk
memory' and so 'redeems his estrangement from the popular element'. Blok saw himself and Vyacheslav Ivanov as heirs to the traditions of Russian Romanticism: '... at one time Russian Romantics
defended folk poetry, studied it, made magnificent, inspired imitations of it. Its right to existence is established. Now a new dream is
being born: to drown once more in the soul of the people' (v. 18).

'To drown once more in the soul of the people' was not to 'go
to the people' as the *narodniki*, the populists of the preceding generation, had done. The time had passed when educated men and women
had thought it their duty to dress like the people and live alongside
them in order to teach the ways of enlightenment. Blok, convinced
of the tragic implications of the great gap of mutual incomprehen-
sion which existed between the poet and 'the mob' and which was
one of the data, the given premises from which he had to build his
life and work, sought rather to intensify his isolation and to seek common *roots* and *aims* in depths.

The march with the red flag was his last gesture of participation
and now, as the first revolution began to ebb away from the high-
tide mark of general strike and October Manifesto, he withdrew
from outward activity and stubbornly defended his hushed, listening
privacy. To his father, in his usual obligatory New Year epistle, he
wrote:

I have written a great deal of poetry but feel that it somehow lacks form,
the transitional process has been going on for several years now.... My
attitude to the 'liberation movement' found expression, alas, almost exclusively in liberal conversations and, at one moment, even in sympathy for
the Social Democrats. Now I am retiring even further into myself, having

absorbed everything I can (of the 'sociological') and cast off that which
the soul does not accept. And it accepts practically nothing of this sort—
so let that towards which it really strives reassume its proper place. Never
shall I become a revolutionary or a 'builder of life', and not because I see
no point in either the one or the other but simply by nature, by the quality
and theme of my spiritual experience.

(VIII. 144, 145)

7

Three poems Blok wrote in October 1905 are evidence of the way
in which he had been pulled this way and that at the height of revolution.

In one, he remembers Christ. Zhenya Ivanov, to whom this poem
is dedicated, had pictured Christ 'coming into ear' in the Russian
fields and, from the sanctity of the earth and of those who worked
it, re-entering the cities of the modern world with salvation and healing. He had succeeded in communicating the picture down to the
last details of 'cornflowers and moon daisies and small yellow-
breasted buntings' (VIII. 105). At the same time, the poet's austere
religious sense told him this rustic Second Coming could not happen
in any exterior manner, but only if each individual human being
were prepared to renounce all worldliness and become 'the way' for
the Saviour to pass through from the dimension of the ideal into
our phenomenal world which, in this poem, he calls 'a prison':

> There He is—Christ—in chains and roses
> Outside my prison window bars.
> There the meek Lamb in snow-white garments.
> Has come to gaze in through the bars.
>
> In the simple frame of the blue heaven
> His icon at the window shone.
> A simple craftsman made that heaven
> But the Face and the azure heaven were one.
>
> No other like Him, stern, a little saddened.
> Behind Him—a field where the ripe ears swell.
> On the rising ground—the cabbage beds and
> Birch trees and firs straggling down into the dell.
>
> It is all so near and yet so distant
> That, standing close by, you cannot pass,
> Cannot reach through to that blue-eyed distance
> Until you yourself become like a path.

Until, like Him, you are utterly poor and
Trampled in that lost dell you lie.
Till you know no more and you love no more and
Like grain you fall to the ground and die....[hh]

10 October 1905

(II. 84)

The call of Christ is followed by the call of revolution. On 31 October 1905 Blok wrote (II. 86)[ii] of a very different visitor outside his 'prison window bars': a wild girl on a great horse who comes to call him to cast off his chains and to follow her out on to the steppes, beckoning him, her fluttering sleeve 'aflame with a red shout', teasing, mocking, petting the foaming neck of her plunging charger. Receiving no answer, she gallops off contemptuously in a cloud of dust, leaving the poet to his philosophizing: it is not him she loves, but the gleam of plunder and bandits whistling round the midnight fire. This is the romantic call of the wild, the imperious summons of anarchy and rebellion. The poem is charged like a magnetic field with the spirit of Russian outlawry, from the legendary Solovey-Razboynik to the historical Razin and Pugachev. Shaggy, half-glimpsed presences, they lurk just outside the circle of the wayside fire at which the spirit of revolution shakes loose her unkempt, flowing hair. The poet knows that he is none of their company, that he will not yet break his bonds to follow her call. Yet neither will he dissociate himself from those who do. The beauty is too intoxicating, the excitement too intense.

It is to the voice of the third poem (II. 179) to which Blok—for the time being, at least—yielded himself most completely: a soft, plaintive voice which promised no immediate liberation. It is the quiet, sad singing of the captive soul, of fallen, disinherited humanity, of poverty. Like the pastoral Christ, like the outlaw girl, the voice is very Russian. The poem was suggested by a *chastushka*, an improvised quatrain sung with heart-rending peasant pathos to the cheerful wail of an accordion and the rhythmic clapping of hands, a woman's

[hh] Blok himself noted the influence of the Russian 'pre-Raphaelite', Nesterov, on the visual imagery of this poem. The 'face' of the Saviour, 'in chains and roses', must also have been suggested by the peasants' icons with paper flowers pinned round the heads of the figures and a *lampadka* swung from three chains suspended from the ceiling before the icons.

[ii] This poem has a dancing, galloping metre and full, uninhibited rhyme which gives it tremendous rhythmic *élan*. The metric scheme is

$$\prime\prime\,{\_}\,\prime\prime\prime\,{\_}\prime$$
$$\prime\prime\,{\_}\,\prime\prime\prime\,{\_}\prime$$
$$\prime\prime\,{\_}\,\prime\prime\prime\,{\_}$$
$$\prime\prime\,{\_}\,\prime\prime\prime\,{\_}$$

song of work and the deceitful ways of men (*Z.K.* 70). Blok had heard the song 'one raw September night' and, on his lonely walks, he must often have glimpsed the singer, as he described her in the poem, a white-faced girl at the small, secret double windows of a Petersburg back street, her head bent wearily over her sewing. From experience, he knew how hair-fine was the line that separated seamstresses like these from the bitterly cold streets, prostitution, and disease: 'And the silent girl behind the narrow windows weaves me my Ring of Suffering all through the night: her work awakes me to soft songs of despair, songs of Resignation' (II. 369).

CHAPTER IX

The Stranger
(Autumn 1905–Autumn 1906)

And so, it is done. My own magic world has become the arena of my personal actions, my 'anatomical theatre', a *puppet booth*, where I myself have a part together with my wonderful dolls (*ecce homo!*) ... Life has become art, I have made the invocation, and before me has arisen at last that which I (personally) call 'The Stranger'; the beautiful doll, the blue phantom, the earthly miracle.... She is far from being just a lady in a black dress with ostrich feathers in her hat. She is a devilish alloy of many worlds.... I stand before my own creation and do not know what I should do. In other words, what should I do with these worlds, what should I do with my own life that, from now on, has itself become art, for by my side *lives* my own creation, neither alive nor dead, the blue phantom.   (v. 429–31)

1

'I have slammed to the oven doors of my own soul. I hope that in the resulting hermetically sealed space it will prepare well for the future' (VIII. 136), Blok wrote to Andrey Bely on 2 October 1905.

From Bely's irritated reaction, he seems to have heard nothing in these words but the iron clang shutting him out from his friend's inner world:

You have 'slammed to the oven doors' of your own soul—but what for? To prepare election lists, or for some other purpose? As far as I have understood you, you set great store by the idea of transformation of personality, but can there be any such transformation without a clear awareness of the means of achieving those aims which you have set yourself (of the manner in which you intend to work out your own destiny)?[1]

Blok, with his country upbringing, had used the homely simile without thought of offence.[a] Having built up an intense spiritual

---

[a] The image is highly evocative to anyone who has ever handled a Russian stove. You begin by lighting a roaring fire in a large brick stove which has a square or fan-shaped

blaze (in which all the previous values of his art had gone up in flames) he had mixed a powerful brew of experience, study, and lyrical feeling and pushed it in amongst the glowing embers. Now it remained for him to close the oven doors and let all this 'cook', quietly. At this period in his life everything was still simmering and changing and it was a torment to him to explain the process. Instead of attempting to do so, he had simply sent Bely a selection of his recent poetry accompanied by a chaotic letter which he himself subsequently described as 'a verbal abomination' (VIII. 137). Bely replied with accusations of mystical confusion and apostasy, quite uninhibited by the awkward fact that he happened to be courting his friend's wife. Bely's critics, both at the time and ever since, have found it less easy to reconcile the roles of seducer and 'ghostly counsellor', but it is a part of the man's exasperating charm that he never even noticed the incongruity.

Bely was too sensitive an artist not to realize that the poems Blok had sent him were 'thrilling' and 'new'. He was ready to concede that Blok might become the interpreter 'of the elemental forces of the Russian countryside', but he wanted to know, or rather demanded to be told, how his friend intended to combine this passive mystical role with the active, theurgic duty of a 'knight' vowed to the service of the Most Beautiful Lady.

Point by point, he attacked the looseness of Blok's mystical terminology, 'being very attached to clear definition and precision if only in the field of symbolic experience, and also being an interested party in the development of your way (which is so important to me)'.

Particularly objectionable to Bely had been Blok's statement that he hoped to become a 'Burning Bush'. As a student at the Imperial University of St. Petersburg and a contributor to a serious religious-philosophical journal such as *Voprosy Zhizni*, Blok, he felt, had no excuse for not knowing that the 'Burning Bush' was a symbol for the Mother of God. 'Either I'm an idiot, or You[b] are playing at mysticism and this it does not permit, not to anyone. Mysticism is always

---

opening in one wall. When the blue flames have died down and all that remains of your fire is a red glow of hot wood ash, you close the flues, put in your cooking, and close the fan-like opening with a kind of iron screen, the *zaslonka* which I have translated as 'oven doors'. Your cooking is then coddled: soup comes out strong and aromatic; meat tender; milk a rich toffee brown with crisp caramel skin. It matters little how long you leave the food in the warm stove, so long as it is undisturbed during the critical period of actual cooking.

[b] See p. 92n. The use made by both Blok and Bely, when writing to one another, of a capital letter for the familiar 'thou' form—presumably as a token of profound mutual respect—was an affectation which later came to irk Blok considerably (VII. 217).

real, if it truly is.' Either Blok has been guilty of a great blasphemy, or all his talk of the Eternal Feminine has been 'nothing but agreeable relaxation over a nice cup of tea ... whereas I, always, since the very first poem of yours that I read, have assumed that You worked in the name of a duty owed to the Most Beautiful Lady'.

In a burst of self-pity, Bely described his own agonies and difficulties in search of 'the MEANS' to hold to his 'COURSE'. During his last disastrous visit to Shakhmatovo it had seemed to him that Blok had actually been sitting back and enjoying his and Seryëzha's intense sufferings. That summer, Bely continued, Blok had abdicated from his duty to the future and it would be better for him to admit now, once and for all, that he had become a creature of the past, an apostate to instinct, to nature magic and the lower forms of life, bestial and vegetable. Any confusion of such apostasy with higher mysticism would only produce what Bely called 'the Sphinx', the beast-God, or 'psychological mysticism'.

He ended:

There you are. Now I will speak of your verses. There is a mist of the unsaid above them, yet they are full of 'brackets'ᶜ and ambiguous evasions that sometimes purport to be mysteries.

Dear Sasha, forgive me these words addressed to You out of my love, but I speak to You as one responsible for the purity of a certain Mystery, which You are betraying or are about to betray.

I am warning you: where are you going? Recollect! Or else give up, forget the Mystery.

You cannot be for God and the Devil at the same time.

May the powers aid You. Forgive my plainness. But at this moment nothing will prevent my speaking, for I am

ONE IN AUTHORITY.[2]

Blok's family reacted indignantly to this letter. Lyubov' was incensed and, when Bely followed up his exhortation to her husband by an equally impassioned appeal to her 'to save him and Russia', she wrote him an angry letter, stating flatly that she would not accept any more letters from him until he altered his tone of condescending superiority towards Sasha: 'You have forgotten that I am with him; if he is lost, then I shall be lost, also; and if I am saved, it will be through him and *only* through him.'[3] 'Good girl', the loyally partisan Aunt Maria added in her private account of this incident, 'with her white neck and her golden waves of hair'.[4]

Blok, however, accepted Bely's admonitions in the spirit in which

---

ᶜ Bely had, earlier in the letter, begged Blok to 'open the brackets of his equation' to which he felt he had no key.

they were offered and replied at once and in detail, denying only the charge of having taken pleasure in watching his friends' suffering, which, he said, was so wide of the mark that it had not even hurt his feelings. The rest he admitted as all too true, even expressing surprise that Bely had not forced him into a more open discussion earlier. Only the Burning Bush he had not meant as a symbol—had just had a picture in his mind's eye of a bush, burning. In general, all the mystical talk in which they had indulged since the very beginning of their correspondence was getting them nowhere. He himself had persisted in it compulsively in his letters to Bely, yet always with revulsion, feeling how inadequate were set symbols as a means of expression or communication.

In general I have never (note, NEVER, even when I was writing all the verses about the Most Beautiful Lady) been able to express my experiences exactly and, indeed, I never had any experiences, the word means nothing to me. It was just that I was leading a beautiful and aimless life that I now lead no longer (and I would not if I could, it is not at all what is needed) and, having stopped, there is much that I do not understand. Why do you think that I am a mystic? I am not a mystic but, I think, have always been a hooligan. It may well be that my place is not with you, a seer who knows the way ahead, at all, but with M. Gorky who knows nothing, or with the decadents who know nothing either.

Why I write like this you know. Nevertheless, there is a difference between me and the decadents. For one thing, I find decadents increasingly repellent. For another, they do not know, and I 'know in all serenity' (I do, really, sometimes), but what I know is the 'what' and not the 'how'. I shall never be able to explain this and am even given to denying it in words when people try to force me to explain. If you are going looking for blasphemies in my words, you will find only too many of them and, perhaps, sufficiently grave to hit me over the head with and put an end to me. My brains are too elementary to withstand much weaker pressures than yours. Sometimes they understand a great deal, at others—nothing at all. There is no limit to my lack of discipline in all that touches the depths, nor to what you call my 'immobility'. But the absence of discipline is worse than the immobility.

This is all really what one *would* expect of a student at the Imp. SPb. University and a contributor to *Voprosy Zhizni*. But I do not want to play at mysticism. I play at words, very boringly and very badly. As to mysticism, I know that it is real and terrible, and that it will punish me.... But how can it punish me more than I am punished and what can it take from me when I am beggared?   (VIII. 137–41)

In conclusion, Blok acknowledged Bely's 'authority', pleading only his own inability to express himself in words and urging his friend to 'cross him out' if he felt him as a hindrance to his own spiritual progress.

Combined with Lyubov's ultimatum, this letter elicited an ardent apology, which Bely sent by his friend Ellis because the post was on strike. The following day, however, 31 October, unable to bear the thought that the Bloks might not have received the letter and might still be angry with him, he took the train for Petersburg and, on arrival next morning, sent round a note begging Blok to meet him at the Palkin restaurant at eight o'clock that evening, adding primly: 'If Lyubov' Dmitriyevna has nothing against me then it would also give me great pleasure to see her.'[5]

Touched, Sasha and Lyuba kept the appointment. Bely, vaguely conscious of throbbing Neapolitan melodies pouring forth from the bandstand, watched them coming:

The very slender student's figure, his head thrown back and his wide eyes looking before him, threading his way unhurriedly between the tables, the eyes searching for me; and before him L.D., thinner, in a black dress, walking as though uncertain of herself, head down. A.A. saw me and smiled affectionately, a smile I had not seen once during my last visit to him; a loving, brotherly smile; and L.D. blossomed to meet me with just such another smile, and in those smiles across the tables, to the throbbing singing of the Neapolitans, everything was explained away; the smiles said there was no need for an explanation; the fact of my coming and the letter were explanation enough.

Without Sergey Solov'ev, the atmosphere was more relaxed. Bely, in the first wave of relief, was able to sit back and bask in Blok's humorous, concerned affection and to accept the new basis for friendship suggested by him and Lyuba: no more 'theurgy', no more philosophy, no more mystic triumvirate with Sergey Solov'ev. The new friendship was to be something light, based on the artistic impulse of the moment. They would treat their life as a game, or a play, and accept the consequences of acting on inspiration. The mystery of the 'transformation of life' had become the mystery of the 'transformation of the moment'. 'This was the direct result of the awareness that She was "gone without return"; and all that remained, one supposed, was to take life by storm without Her.'

That, at least, was the way Bely saw it. The idea of life as a series of inspired improvisations he attributed to Lyubov' Dmitriyevna, whose passion for the stage was once more in the ascendant. It was, nevertheless, an idea inherent in Blok's poetry of this time and it is probably a mistake to seek one dominant spirit. Certainly all three were fascinated by *The Ring*: Wotan, Siegfried, and Brünhilde began to take shape in their own private drama as well as in Blok's thoughts about Russia and revolution. He had pictured Lyubov' often enough as unawakened, enchanted by a sleep. It must have been with helpless pain that he recognized how passionately she desired that kiss of life which he, in his present state of spiritual emptiness and confusion, felt less and less able to give. If Bely wished to play Siegfried to her Brünhilde, who was he to set her about with a ring of fire? Yet he felt intuitively that there was something wrong with the whole situation. Bely's love was not real. But was his? Everything had become boring and terrifying, at once stuffy and threatened. The only refuge, for him and Lyuba, was still—childhood:

... Once A.A. told me slyly that he now knew who I was, beyond any doubt.

'Who am I?'

At that L.D. burst out laughing, having decided that he'd never really say it; but A.A. gave a quiet little snort of laughter, dropped his eyes and said quietly:

'Don't take offence—it's just a game we play: Lyuba and I often play at animals.'

'Well, what sort of animal am I?'

'It's meant well, you know, you mustn't be offended: you're a fluffy white hare; they're one of our favourite animals. . . .'

Bely, whose nervousness, oddly slanting eyes (some said like a deer, others like a goat), and extraordinary lightness of movement really did make him very like a white winter hare, was not offended. He only hated Blok when he retreated from him or forgot his existence. There were times, however, when he felt a growing fear of him:

Sometimes this style of fairy-tale prattle deserted them: A.A. frowned; he exuded mists; I felt stifled; once he was particularly confiding; I was sitting in the dining room taking tea; he led me into his room saying that he needed to tell me something separately without Lyuba; sitting me down on the sofa he tried to find words for some very important inner discovery he had made; this discovery was bound up with his impressions of the colour dark lilac which, for him, had the same scent as the night violet:

'You know it has such a stifling smell: lilac and nocturnal somehow . . .'

At that time, Bely was working out a theory of colour symbolism and Blok wanted to know his opinion of the extraordinary domination this scented lilac colour was gaining over the landscape of his soul. According to Bely's theory,

It came out that the shade which so fascinated A.A. was the greatest imaginable seduction, leading away from the countenance of Christ; while A.A.

was quietly, excitedly telling me about his reaction to the dark lilac I felt physically unwell: as though a stove with fumes had been put in the room with us. I felt the fumes; the fumes of Lucifer; the 'maw of night' that had gaped open before me once before when I talked to A.A. out in the field, I saw again now for the second time; I saw A.A. walking away from me into the deep night; I knew I could not give him a true reaction because A.A. would not believe me, would be offended. I replied:

'Well, yes, that lilac shade is the acme of subtlety, but . . . the Countenance is not in it.'

'That doesn't matter . . . That's as it should be!'

And again I felt stifled.[6]

Evasions of this sort were damaging to the newly healed relationship. And worse was to come.

Blok proceeded to read Bely a new long poem, *The Night Violet* (II. 26–34), an almost exact description of a dream he had had on the night of 16–17 November and had promptly described in his notebook as 'the most important thing'[7] and, in a letter to Zhenya Ivanov written a fortnight or so later as 'something that has been the whole content of my life ever since. Such astonishing dreams come only once a year—once in two years' (VIII. 142).

The poem does indeed have the compelling a-logical quality of a dream although, as the most fleeting comparison of the rough drafts show, it was written with conscious art and marks a great advance in sustained music. Bely, on first hearing the poem, was shocked by the lines:

> Heaven, tired of cloaking over
> The acts and thoughts of my fellow citizens,
> Has fallen into the bog pool.

and later understandably hurt by the inexpressible relief with which, in the poem, the poet watches the departure of his unnamed friend:

> Most likely, some other desires
> Very soon overcame him,
> For he disappeared round a corner,
> Clapping his cap on his head
> And left me alone there
> (With which I was pleased beyond telling
> For what in the world is more pleasant
> Than the loss of one's dearest friends?)

Whether or not the 'friend' of the poem was merely another lascivious 'double', the trenchant aside quite obviously had a wider application.

The second part of the poem contains an apotheosis of the theme of the Eternal Return which had formed the dark centre of Blok's poetry all through the preceding summer. In a murky log house, lost deep in the marshes, sits 'She', older and no longer beautiful, and spins and spins while around her dream strange, stiff figures from a masquerade, slumping in all their finery at the rough wooden tables: the spur of one is caught under the bench; another has dropped his helmet; white grass, 'fated to live without spring', forces its way through the earth floor beside the helmet; a shield drops to the ground with a clatter and a merry mouse darts from beneath the long-forgotten helm. As for the hero, he has come without 'wedding garments':

> I was a beggarly tramp,
> A haunter of late-night cafés,
> Yet this was a gathering of kings;
> And I suddenly, clearly remembered
> That once I had been of their number.

And so he takes his place among them, to sit in the darkest corner, his eyes fixed dully on the queen whose silent distaff twirls as she spins.

Whether he sits for a few moments or for centuries he does not know; but gradually, above the sleepy, marshy breath of the night violet which pervades the dusty wooden house, the sound of the sea comes to him and a promise of 'joy unhoped-for' borne on great ships, driven before a brisk breeze from a happy land.

To Bely, the strange poem seemed like some infernal incantation. Again he was filled with an imperative desire to 'save' Blok, but thought better of it 'and A.A. noticed nothing'. More than before, however, he began to feel it his duty to 'save' Lyubov', and this thought persisted.

2

The social life of the capital was in full swing, and wit, beauty, and poetry flared all the brighter against the menacing backdrop of social and spiritual disruption. Blok introduced Bely to his Petersburg friends: the young poet Sergey Gorodetsky with his thick lips, fresh face, and fresh, uncomplicated talent; Vladimir Pyast (real name, Pestovsky), a typical hypersensitive Peterbourgeois for whom Aleksandr Blok was the very symbol and incarnation of their phantasmagoric, tragic city; Blok's old friend Aleksandr Hippius, now back from Siberia, married to a medical worker.[d]

[d] In Russian a *feldsher*: with a qualification between a doctor and a district nurse.

Bely, for his part, led the half-reluctant Blok back into the fold of the Merezhkovskys. This autumn, everybody was doing everybody else's portrait. Bakst 'did' Bely and Zinaida Hippius, and Blok soon found himself posing for Zinaida's sister Tata, whom he liked and whose album of drawings for children, *Kindisch*, had been one of the original inspirations for *The Bubbles of the Earth*.

It was Bely, too, who introduced Blok to Vyacheslav Ivanov's Wednesdays. These gatherings were soon to rival Rozanov's Sundays, Sologub's strictly poetic and gastronomic *jours-fixes*, and even the Merezhkovskys' ever-open house at the Dom Muruzi. Ivanov and his wife, Lidia Dmitriyevna, who together, according to Bely, represented 'a rare combination of wit, good nature, and eccentricity'[f] had taken up residence in a top-floor flat near the Tauride Palace, the drawing room of which formed one of those curious salients, beloved of late-nineteenth-century architects throughout Europe, which was to go down in literary history as 'the tower'.

Ivanov was of an older generation. A truly erudite man, he was a natural mentor and possessed the gift of bringing people together, of sparking off talent in others. Blok felt closer to Lidia Dmitriyevna, admiring her 'Dionysian' quality and, after her early death in 1907, his relationship with Ivanov dwindled to a mere literary acquaintanceship. For a time, however, he fell under Ivanov's spell. Bely recalls:

It was I who took V. Ivanov to the Bloks for the first time; and as I took my seat in the sleigh and looked thoughtfully at the figure he made, extremely round-shouldered, swathed in an enormous fur coat, his pince-nez trembling on the bridge of his nose, I thought: A.A. and L.D. will take fright; he's too 'professorial', and the conversation will dry up; but it did not dry up; V.I. wove an enchantment; L.D., I seem to remember, was particularly overcome by his words about the purple hues of clothing in the Dionysian mysteries and the little green Bacchantes; it was decided that we would try to found a 'collective'; V. Ivanov mentioned Chulkov as

---

[f] A connection of Lidia Dmitriyevna's, the late Olga Zinov'eva, once told me how, as a bride, she had been taken by her husband Lev Aleksandrovich Zinov'ev on a morning call to the Ivanovs'. The polite chatter between Zinov'ev, whose brother was at the time governor general of the province of Petersburg, and his distinguished female relative was interrupted by the sudden appearance of Vyacheslav Ivanov. Clad in dressing gown and bedroom slippers, his fleecy, flaxen hair rumpled round his curiously medieval face, Ivanov held a letter dramatically raised in one hand. Without pausing to greet the visitors, he addressed his wife: 'My dear, I *congratulate* you. Your reputation is made. Your novel has been banned as PORNOGRAPHY.' Lev Aleksandrovich removed his highly entertained young bride before they could bring further scandal on the family name by getting caught in the ensuing police raid.

a sensitive soul capable of understanding us; so Chulkov was included.... Chulkov began to talk of mystic anarchism, the exponents of which he originally considered to be A.A., Vyacheslav, and myself.... For the moment there was just the expression 'mystic anarchism'; the expression pleased us.

So it came about that Blok was present at the first of Ivanov's Wednesdays, which took the form of a kind of impromptu symposium on the subject of love.

The theoreticians spoke first: Ivanov, Berdayev, then Bely himself. Vasiliy Rozanov maintained a sceptical silence:

A.A. sat in a far corner, leaning his head against the wall, relaxed, listening very attentively, with a half-smile; when asked to contribute to the discussion he replied that he was no speaker, but that he would be happy to recite, and he recited '*Vlyublyënnost*';[f] he was in good form that evening; confidently, loudly, head thrown back, he flung the lines at us:

> *Vlyublyënnost*! You're sterner than Fate
> More compelling than forefathers' laws!
> More sweet than the bugle's 'to arms'![8]

Vyacheslav Ivanov, according to a sober witness from the world of politics, Ariadna Tyrkova-Williams,[g] 'loved not so much poetry as power over poets'.[9] For a time, he held Blok by the glamour of his learning and his gift for merging opposites. Himself pulled this way and that between poles of aspiration, in Ivanov's circle Blok felt at once excited and relaxed. Here, there were no decisions to be made as at the Merezhkovskys'. No one asked you whether you were 'for' or 'against'. Here, it was possible for Blok's own eminently respectable University professor, the classicist F. F. Zelinsky, to debate the meaning of Eros with Lenin's future Commissar of Education, Anatoliy Lunarcharsky, after which the whole company would sit down peaceably to drink wine and listen to poetry. The atmosphere tingled with the reflected excitement of revolution and the last Wednesday of the year 1905 was interrupted by the police, who searched hopefully until morning for evidence of subversive activity.[10] Yet in spite of the presence of people from many walks of life and of widely differing ideological persuasions, the predominant tone was set by the hosts and was 'mystical', 'Dionysian', and,

---

[f] An untranslatable word usually rendered as 'love' or 'infatuation', but meaning rather 'the state of being in love'.

[g] The Russian wife of the *Times* correspondent in Petersburg, Harold Williams, and head of the moderate Kadet party.

above all, impromptu. New terminology sprang up overnight: 'mystic anarchism', 'mystic realism', 'neo–Christianity', 'individual catholicism'.[h] Even the later term 'Acmeism' had its origin in Vyacheslav Ivanov's tower, and it was here that the 'decadents' finally discarded the abusive label they had borne for so long and began to call themselves, as a matter of course, 'Symbolists'.

All this suited Blok. Here, he could preserve his essential silence and yet confidently take his place as a young prince of literature simply by reciting his poetry. For the first time, his physical beauty and his distinctive method of reciting, his whole personality, in fact, began to help him to project his verse.

Even then, at the height of his by no means inconsiderable intellectual powers, he still, as Zinaida Hippius observed, often produced the impression

> ... most transparently evident to anyone he happened to be speaking with, that he understood nothing. He looks, he sees, but for him everything remains half-said, unfinished, dark. From Blok there looked out a child, thoughtful, stubborn, startled, aware that he was all alone in an unfamiliar place.[11]

At Vyacheslav Ivanov's no one tried to subject this child to cross-examination, but the milieu was indeed 'an unfamiliar place', a world of sophisticated vices and ambitions in which he was oddly defenceless. This winter Blok's sensuality, finding no satisfaction in the broken sacrament of his marriage, was drawing him back more and more often into the underworld of his city, while the demonic, romantic streak in his nature yearned towards some new, dramatic, emotional confrontation. That autumn he had been reading and translating Byron. The Russian translation of *Don Juan* is one of the most marked and underscored books in his library. Vyacheslav Ivanov had a refined, intense feeling for the Dostoyevskian 'underground': psychological and sociological, sexual and religious. He was one of the first to perceive this aspect of Blok's nature for, though the poet never attempted to hide it, he continued to produce an impression of limpid purity. Ivanov bestowed his blessing upon Blok's 'underground' in sonorous classic verse:

> I saw: Praxitelean marble
> By Bacchus' breath revived again,
> And fiery liquor run and kindle
> And course through bloodless, branching veins.

[h] Russian *sobornost*: catholicism in the sense of universality.

And that pale gaze awake to madness
Eyes that divine and empty shone:
A demon had the god persuaded
To step down from the sacred stone—

On to the paths of tramps and drunkards ...[12]

Very often we tend to see ourselves as others see us. Blok, said
Gorodetsky, acted up to Vyacheslav Ivanov's picture of a god in the
stews. Also the older poet's explicit cult of myth and Dionysian
ecstasy encouraged Blok to transform his preoccupation with eternal
realities into a sparkling, irresponsible game. As Berdayev later
recalled, mystical and religious themes were treated rather as cultural
subjects than as vital philosophies of life at the Wednesdays.

Nevertheless, before abandoning himself entirely to the 'mystic'
element, Blok did pause to consider in what way it differed from
the religious, and thereafter kept religion, as he understood it, in its
own place. Perhaps it was Bely who goaded him into doing this,
but the fact remains that Blok's distinction is very much clearer than
any made by his 'mystic' friends. In a passage headed 'Religion and
Mysticism' he wrote in his notebook for 18 January 1906:

They have nothing in common. Although mysticism *may become one of* the
ways to religion. Mysticism is the bohemian element of the soul, religion
is standing watch.

As to 'religious art': there is *no* such thing except as a transitional form.
True art does not coincide in its aims with religion. It is positive and mystic
(both spring from the same source). Art has its own Rule, it is a monastery
of historical formation, i.e. a monastery that has no room for religion. Religion is (or is about) that which is to be, mysticism is that which was and
is.

Mysticism in everyday life is a fine theme and a rich one.... At the same
time, this theme ... is frequently taken for a *religious* one. What falsity there
is in that and what a rich potential of shallowness!... Mysticism manifests
itself most of all ... in ecstasy (which we shall define as an alliance with
the world against people). Religion is alien to ecstasy (we should sleep, eat,
read, and walk religiously). It is an alliance with people against the world
as distortion.[i] ... The cornerstone of religion is God; of mysticism—mystery.... Mysticism requires ecstasy. Ecstasy is solitude. Ecstasy is not religious. Mystics love to be poets, artists. Religious people do not, they divide
themselves from their craft (art).

(Z.K. 73–5)

At this time, however, Blok craved solitude and ecstasy. With
relief, he abandoned the apparently insoluble problems raised by

---

[i] Blok uses the word *kosnost'*, from a root meaning 'bent' or 'crooked'.

religion and life to try his wings in a world of beauty and subtle excitement, a world of vivid platonic friendships, where everyone was half in love with everyone else and altogether in love with art.

3

The literary results of the new 'collective' outlasted the human relationships. Bely returned to Moscow on a positive wave of good will, having endeared himself anew to all members of the Blok family, including Aleksandra Andreyevna.[j] Chulkov, full of plans for his new brain-child, Fakely (Torches), the publishing venture which was to serve as the organ of the 'mystic anarchists', suggested to Blok that he might turn his poem 'The Puppet Booth' into a play, for Fakely was to have its own theatre, directed by a young man who had recently broken away from Stanislavsky's Studio at the Moscow Art: Vsevolod Meyerhold. Blok agreed and, before the end of the year, Lyubov' was writing to Bely to be sure to return to St. Petersburg for the première of *The Puppet Booth* which, she assured him, would be 'very, very good'.[13] On 3 January 1906 Blok himself told Bely about the play. His tone was irritated, trapped:

All this concoction of highly cultured people like Vyacheslav Ivanov and highly enterprising people like Chulkov and Meyerhold is beginning to get on my nerves.... Do write and tell me, *ought* I not to speak out before these people who take me for a rebel and a mystic? *You* know that is not so.

(VIII. 146)

Yet, on 23 January, he informed Chulkov that the play was ready[14] and asked when it would be convenient to hold a reading.

In fact, *The Puppet Booth* was first read on 25 February to a circle of Blok's own friends and contemporaries (headed by Pyast and Gorodetsky) who had gathered about him and Lyuba that winter and formed the habit of meeting now at one member's house, now at another's. Times were still such that, when they met at the Barracks, the organizers had to give Frants Feliksovich their word of honour that there would be no discussion of politics.[15]

---

[j] Bely's epistolatory exuberance, however, soon began to try Blok's patience. He had left for Moscow not earlier than 20 December 1905 and on the 30th Blok was already writing on a note of mild reproof: 'Dear Borya, Lyuba has received eight letters from you, Mama one, and I three; I think there must be something wrong with the post....' Nevertheless, the overall tone of their correspondence remains loving and enthusiastic. On 14 or 15 January, Blok sent him the poem, 'Dear brother! Dusk is closing in', in which he refers to Lyubov' as their 'sister' (II. 91–2).

The young men, enchanted by Blok's reading and by the play itself, worked off their emotions on the way home by indulging in a vigorous snowball fight. The world was their oyster still, and that day they had come upon a most exquisite pearl.

From the opening scene, where a gathering of 'mystics' await the coming of a mysterious feminine figure and a white-faced Pierrot looks forward to the arrival of his fiancée, Columbine, we enter a world of broken communication. It is the world of the *Verses about the Most Beautiful Lady*, but without the golden sword, the organizing, disciplinary principle. Everything is topsy-turvy. Even the author, who from time to time erupts on to the stage to disavow the whole action of the play, does not understand what is going on. The mystics pretend they do, and are exposed as 'empty dummies'. Poor Columbine, whom the mystics greet with reverence and Pierrot with simple tenderness, is equally at a loss. Suddenly, a jingling Harlequin appears on the scene and, seizing the bewildered Columbine by the hand, having floored Pierrot with a vigorous push, leads her away in triumph. Trustingly, she smiles up at him.

As in a dream, the scene changes to a masked ball. Pierrot, disconsolate in the foreground, sings how his beloved has gone riding in a horse-drawn sleigh with Harlequin and has tumbled out on to the road. Harlequin did not hurt her. She fell of herself. And Pierrot could not help laughing and went prancing off with Harlequin to dance among the snow-needles. Together, they wept for Columbine.

Sadly, Pierrot leaves the scene. Masked figures take over and play out a parody of Blok's love lyrics: the cathedral theme; the theme of passion (the robber girl or the Stranger, cruel and elusive, followed by a submissive lover shadowed by his own double); the theme of the knight keeping vigil before the dawn and the pink maiden who has no substance, being but an echo of his own thoughts.

A clown teases the knight and, bashed over the head by his clumsy wooden sword, hangs over the balustrade with the familiar cry: 'Help! I am bleeding to death with cranberry juice!'

Follows a torchlight procession, led by Harlequin who sings joyously of how, having got rid of the fool Pierrot, he will leap out of the window into the spring of the world. But the view of a far country in the spring glimpsed through the window turns out to be a *trompe-l'œil* and Harlequin dives through it head first like a circus rider through a paper hoop.

The dawn breaks and against the sky appears the very figure the mystics have been waiting for: Death in the form of a beautiful woman with a scythe. Terrified, the merry-makers who have just

балаганчикъ

Лирическія сцены Александра Блока

Title-page by M. Dobuzhinsky for *The Puppet Booth* as published in *Fakely*,
Spring 1906

been taking part in the procession flatten themselves against the walls, 'like dolls from the ethnographical museum'. As the light grows, Pierrot alone advances trustfully towards the figure of Death and gradually her face becomes the face of a living woman: 'the lovely girl, Columbine'.

At this moment, unable to contain his triumph, the author again bursts on to the stage declaring that at last the actors have got things right, that 'that person' has disappeared through the window, and now the hitherto star-crossed lovers will live happily ever after. As he moves forward to join their hands, the props whirl into the air, the characters run off in all directions, and the author is left bending dazedly over the prostrate Pierrot.

'Realizing where he is, he rushes from the stage', and Pierrot, left alone, rises slowly to his feet and sings again the story of Harlequin and his cardboard bride, of how she fell down in the snow and how he laughed at her as she lay. 'It makes me very sad,' he concludes; 'and you think it funny?' 'Pierrot thoughtfully takes his flute from his pocket and begins to play a tune about his own pale face, the sadness of life, and about Columbine, his betrothed' (IV. 21).

So, laconically and irreproachably, Blok told the story of himself, Lyubov', and Bely; of himself, Lyubov', and his doubles; of himself and his 'wonderful dolls'; of himself and Lyubov'.

The perfection of the piece was beginner's luck. Blok, when he wrote it, had no experience of writing for the stage. Neither did the form he found spring from discussions with Meyerhold and Vyacheslav Ivanov, who at that time were dreaming of a revival of the Dionysian mystery play with immediate audience participation.[k] Almost certainly, Blok did not think of himself as an innovator. He was writing, albeit at Chulkov's suggestion, a purely lyrical drama: exteriorizing the self-hatred, irony, and anger that had been building up 'in the archives of the police department' of his soul (VII. 13). The play was young and cool, laughing and elegant. Yet in some innocent fairyland of dancing snow and jingling bells, it foreshadowed the agonizing gutter drama of *The Twelve*, 'when Russia herself ... turned out to be our own soul'.

[k] 'As to Fakely', Blok wrote Valeriy Bryusov on 25 April 1906,

I agree with you.... I think that Fakely was born of talk. It is dreadful to think how many words were spoken about it. Then a great deal went stale before it could be put into practice and the spirit of the mystery was lost. *Mystic anarchism, too, will not produce mystery plays, at least I don't think it will: I feel neither lightness nor laughter in it. Yet the contemporary Mystery is essentially a little puppet-like: it is shot through with laughter and turns somersaults.*

(VIII. 152–3)

(Italics mine. A. P.)

Andrey Bely, however, who—evidently unable to keep away—
had returned to Petersburg earlier that month, took the play-reading
as a declaration of war:

And so—the first reading of *The Puppet Booth*. Gorodetsky was standing
in that same drawing room, Evgeniy Ivanov, Pyast, I—who else? Blok went
up first to one, then another, his hand stretched out, offering his cigarette
case; then, snapping it shut, sat down comfortably: not to read, oh no,
to bleed to death ... 'with cranberry juice'; and he bled languidly; through
his nose:

'What is this—a mockery?'

Traditions of *bon ton*: I do up my jacket and put on a smile as one draws
on a glove.

'Yes, yes—you know ...'

To Blok himself—not a word ...[16]

The Puppet Booth is, indeed, a cruel play: though perhaps it is most
cruel to the author.

Whether or not Lyubov' was offended by it we do not know,
for the good reason that she was large-minded enough to appreciate
the artistry and to keep her private feelings to herself. What we do
know is that, at about this time, what little 'normal' married life she
had had with Blok came to an end. He was working hard for his
final examinations at the University and had begun to look for relaxation entirely on his own: drinking, walking in the outskirts of
Petersburg, seeking chance encounters with easy women, pursuing
dark dreams through a labyrinthine alcoholic haze. This meant in-
creased spending, and he was taking on more and more literary
commissions. He worked long and regular hours and avoided all
friends except those with whom he was preparing for his examinations. Andrey Bely mocked him openly, taunting him for turning
into 'an old man in a dressing gown'.

Lyubov's sexuality had awakened very slowly but now, neglected
by her husband, surrounded by an atmosphere of subtle, all-pervad-
ing eroticism, she found to her genuine dismay that what Blok had
told her about the inconstancy of passion was perfectly true, and that
she was responding in a quite unforeseen way to Bely. If Bely had
had any scruples, he threw them to the winds after *The Puppet Booth*.
It was decided that he and Lyuba were to go away together to Italy.
Bely broke the news to Blok who sat hunched and crumpled on the
sofa, plucking at the upholstery, forcing a smile: 'What can I say?
I'm glad.'

Bely left for Moscow to raise money for the journey. His conscience, however, was far from easy, and he at once began subjecting

Lyubov', Aleksandra Andreyevna, and Blok to a hail of letters in
which he now declared his readiness to remain 'Lyuba's brother on
the way to heaven', now to 'switch at any moment to the purely
outward point of view', and, in general and preferably, to die:
whether at his own hands or at those of a righteously incensed husband he does not make clear.

Blok, for his part, somewhere beneath the weariness of work and
the dullness of debauch, was dimly conscious that he was not 'glad'
at all. Nevertheless, he felt in no position to judge. Nor was he prepared to act the undignified part of dog in the manger, to retain
Lyuba either by a show of authority or by playing on her emotions.[1]

Lyubov' herself, still angry more than thirty years after the event,
wrote that Blok 'wouldn't have opened his mouth' to stop her going,
'... or if he had it would only have been to taunt me, coldly and
cruelly as only he knew how, with devastating derision, unflattering
analyses of my actions, their motives, myself, and my Mendeleyev
relatives for good measure.'[18]

Nina Berberova, who with Khodasevich heard Bely's version of
the story many times, says that Bely's 'private myth' was the story
of Joseph and the wife of Potiphar. Lyubov' Dmitriyevna recounts
in her memoirs, a residue of lively indignation tempered by a
redeeming gleam of humour, that there was a moment when she
had actually gone so far as to let down her hair ('in that day and
age the inevitable prelude to every "fall"') in Bely's apartments,
when some clumsiness or awkwardness arose between them and the
moment passed, for ever. Khodasevich suggests that Bely 'had the
lunacy to pretend he had been misunderstood'—and regretted it for
the rest of his life.[19]

On 9 March 1906, Lyubov' wrote to Bely in Moscow, a bewildered letter saying that she loved him but did not know what
she should do. Two days later, at the request of Aleksandra
Andreyevna, Zhenya Ivanov called on the Bloks and found Lyubov'
alone at the piano:

She was glad to see me and said that she had needed me that week and
hoped we would meet, but we had not.

As I had said, so would she have done.

And she told me what she had wanted to consult me about.

[1] Orlov, in his account of the affair, quotes an unpublished entry in Blok's diary for
26 December 1911 which shows with what scepticism he later came to regard his own
superficially irreproachable self-effacement: '[Gorodetsky] by refusing to take any part in
his wife's attitude to me (as I in my time refused to take any part in my wife's relationship
with Bugayev), is shifting all the responsibility on to me (as I once did on to Bugayev,
my God!)...'[17]

Boris Nikolayevich Bugayev loves her and can't live without her. What should she do? I said that Sasha was in such a state just now that it would be wrong to leave him.... So it was decided: for the time being, that is how it will be.

When we said good-bye, Lyubov' Dmitriyevna said: 'Evgeniy Pavlovich, bless me.' I made the sign of the Cross over her three times and we kissed fraternally in Christ. I am horrified at my self-appointed, empty pseudo-holiness.

She looked at me and said: 'That's that, then. All forgotten,' and smiled. 'I love Borya and I love Sasha, what am I to do? If I go away with Boris Nikolayevich, what will Sasha do? It is his appointed way. Boris Nikolaye-vich needs me more. He may die without me. Boris Nikolayevich and I think the same way: our souls are two halves which could be fitted together. And it is so long now since Sasha and I have been able to walk in step'.

They don't like the same things, she does not understand him.

'I can't understand the poetry, I can't understand a great deal of what he says, it's alien to me. There was always a certain fear in my love for Sasha. It was the child in him I felt at home with, and we came together in everything that touched on childhood, but there was never the ultimate togetherness, understanding almost before the other has spoken, the halves of our souls did not match. I could never give him real serenity, peace. All that I could give him was everyday comfort—and perhaps that was harmful. Perhaps I am killing the artist in him. Perhaps we just don't need one another any more. The way of the cross is to remain with Sasha. If I do that I shall become numb again, and Borya will too. How does one approach faith, tell me, how? All that doesn't mean I don't love Sasha. I love him very much and especially now, just lately, however strange that may seem, but I love Borya too, I feel I am letting him down. Oh Lord, save us all. When we saw Borya off at the station in February it was all quite clear and my heart was quite light and Sasha cheered up. But the last few days, since the 8th, Sasha has been miserable and begun to think of what it will really mean if I do leave him for Borya.' ... She could not stop reasoning, even after making up her mind.

She put her elbows on the table and the table was all shaking. A terrible tension. She buried her head in her hands. I could still hear: 'I'm sorry for Borya, what will Borya do.' I said: 'It's very hard for everybody.' 'Poor Sasha, what will become of Sasha?' ... Sasha had noticed the way things were going and had described it all in *The Puppet Booth*.[20]

After her talk with Zhenya Ivanov, Lyubov' sat down and wrote Bely:

I was at home just now, all alone, and Evgeniy Pavlovich Ivanov came. I talked to him about everything, I had to tell somebody and I trust him, he is honest. He understood everything, of course; he says that I should be with Sasha just now; that is what Sasha needs—he knows. And I feel myself that it is both my duty and my wish to be with Sasha now.[21]

A day or two later, she was writing that her lot was to accept the tragedy of love for them both, but by 19 March her decision was firmer:

... on the evening of the 16th I remained at home.... I felt like poetry and I took Vl. Solov'ev and understood him and reread him as never before. I understood that I might not betray this, that it is mine. I shall not betray my first love. I felt then that Sasha alone is my love; I reread all his earlier poetry.[22]

Nevertheless, she continued to write to Bely almost daily. Perhaps aware how vulnerable he was, perhaps reluctant to relinquish him altogether, she wrote very tenderly, insisting that it was for Blok's sake he had to stay away.

On 9 April, Bely, by mistake, put a letter to Lyubov' into an envelope addressed to Blok's mother and received separate and severe scolds from all concerned. Blok, though obviously angry, remained considerate of Bely's feelings, as he had been to the best of his ability throughout that troublesome winter:

Borya,
I write you now in all sincerity, or so I think and believe. I love my mother very much and now I am finally convinced that you are offering her a gratuitous insult. It makes me very sad that you should have addressed letters to Lyuba through Mama. It is my considered opinion that this is very bad. You take Mama for something other than she is. You may not believe me, but do not write to Mama in this way and do not suspect her of something of which she is innocent. The fact that you did write shows not only lack of love, but downright unkindness to Mama.

SASHA[23]

Of course, Bely was desperately apologetic. So despairing did his letters become that Blok telegraphed him to return to Petersburg and talk things over, presenting the receipt for the telegram to Lyubov', who was confined to the house recovering from a feverish attack of bronchitis, as if to emphasize that she was free to decide as she wished. Poor Zhenya was so worried he even had nightmares in which Andrey Bely appeared 'with quite a different face. His moustache was all curled and he was blond, but something in his face seemed to say that he would get his own way.'

To make matters worse, Bely had confided in Zinaida Hippius's sisters Tata and Nata. Merezhkovsky was writing Bely from abroad in the hopes that Lyubov' Dmitriyevna would soon be 'theirs', and Zinaida Hippius entered into correspondence directly with Lyubov'.

On 13 April, Zhenya Ivanov spent the evening with Lyuba and

Blok. Lyuba was giving no promises: 'Everything will depend on the first impression. As I see him, so I shall decide.' Blok, who had sat quietly throughout the evening, suddenly flared up: 'Borya has worked himself up into this love for Lyuba, but it's not real.'[24]

It was mid-April when Blok's little circle was electrified by the news of Bely's return to Petersburg.

4

Bely stayed in Petersburg until the end of the month. Lyuba, 'terrifyingly beautiful'[25] according to Zhenya Ivanov, spent much time with him. Blok kept out of their way, but once at midnight, as they were sitting together at the end of all words, Bely remembered:

... he came: he came in his crumpled jacket, strangely gray, and sat down; sat like a stone against the wall; L.D.:
'Sasha—drunk?'
A.A. admits it:
'Yes, Lyuba—drunk ...'
He had returned that day from the islands:[m] in a restaurant he had written the poem 'The Stranger' which was later to have such a success.... The poem figures in my memory as an autograph; I remember the piece of paper with the rough draft; I bent down over the writing; I compared the shape of the letters to those in his first letters to me; yes, yes, the hand had changed; there the letters were larger, more upright, bolder, clearer; here—more tails and curves; and the letters ran into one another: hastily!

The appearance had changed as much as the handwriting: 'a student'— quite devoid of polish; a crumpled cap; and the voice was rougher (a certain huskiness); the eyes were swollen: where was the rosy aura that had so moved us? The wrinkle between the brows was deeper; the nose jutted out more distinctly, more sharply, casting a sort of shadow on the hollow cheeks: Unattractive and dark, as though he were walking away from the light into shadow.[26]

It was not to be expected that Bely would like Blok's most popular poem: 'the crown of the antithesis', the long-awaited incarnation of the 'dead doll with a face faintly reminiscent of that other one glimpsed among the heavenly roses' (v. 430, 429).

The aesthetic élite who frequented Vyacheslav Ivanov's Wednesdays, on the other hand, could not hear it often enough. Korney Chukovsky, at that time an up-and-coming young critic from

---

[m] Bely is mistaken. Blok had not been on the islands but at Ozerki, a suburban resort to the north of Petersburg on the railway line to Finland.

Odessa, recalls the first time Blok read his 'Stranger'—soon after it was written—on the roof of the 'tower':

From the tower there was a way out on to the sloping roof and in that white Petersburg night all we artists, poets, and actors, excited by verses and wine—and in those days we got drunk on verses as easily as on wine— came out under the pale sky and Blok, deliberate, outwardly impassive, young, tanned (he always began to get brown right at the beginning of spring), climbed up on to the large iron box which protected the junction of the telephone wires and, yielding to our clamorous insistence, for the third and fourth time recited his immortal ballad in his restrained, hollow, monotonous, passive, tragic voice. And we, drinking in the masterly sound-pictures, began to suffer in advance that, in a moment, the spell would be broken, and we wished it would go on for hours and hours and then, suddenly, just as he pronounced the last word, up from the Tauride Gardens which lay immediately below, some errant waft of air brought a wave of bird-song, a chorus of nightingales.

'At that time', Chukovsky adds, 'Blok's poetry affected us as the moon affects lunatics.'[27]

It was the first time Blok himself had felt the power of his poetry over a wider audience, the first absolute triumph of communication. What was the secret of 'The Stranger' and the hypnotic effect it had upon Blok's contemporaries?

The fascination of the poem, impossible to convey in translation,[n] is in its effortless combination of a hopeless reality, in which even Nature is unensouled and flat, with a mystical insight leading, through many shifting dimensions, to a suggestion of unfathomable depths. The magic is true magic; 'the creative power of rhythm' (v. 52) which is 'the essence of invocation':

The person pronouncing the invocation is unafraid, he fears no God for he himself is a god; 'I will take my stand and not bless myself, I will take my stand and not cross myself'—so he says in the moment of extreme concentration of will. He is free in his own dark, dual element, his soul comes into flower and his words ring out and awaken sleeping forces. The rhythmic invocation hypnotizes, suggests, compels....

(v. 53)[o]

[n] The best approximation I know is Hugh MacDiarmid's adaptation in *A Drunk Man Looks at the Thistle*, which begins with the haunting line:

At darknin' hings abune the howff ...

But this has more to do with MacDiarmid than with Aleksandr Blok, even to the not so irrelevant detail that the lyrical persona is drinking whisky instead of red wine.

[o] Blok is writing here with his studies at the University still fresh in his mind and the primary subject of the article is genuine folklore: 'The Poetry of Spells and Incantations', October 1906.

The rhythm of 'The Stranger' does all these things:

$$'\_'\_'\_'\_''$$
$$'\_'\_'\_ \ \_$$
$$'\_'\_'\_'\_''$$
$$'\_'\_'\_'\_$$

But rhythm, of course, is more than any such abstract scheme can begin to suggest. The deliberate pauses, the interplay of assonance and alliteration, the aspirated (*sh*, *kh*) and slurring, reluctant consonants (notably *v*'s and *m*'s), imbue this basic metre with a suggestion of syncopation, like a gusty wind now plucking at the sails, now carrying the whole vessel forward in a smooth, gliding run. The poet himself seems to be rocked and carried on waves of sound. It matters little whither he is taking us: to where the warm, sick air of spring hangs still as death over the dull suburban scene where the poem opens; to the lake where rowlocks creak and 'ladies' squeal and the moon, 'inured to everything', surveys it all with a meaningless grin; or further to the grubby station buffet, where the drunkards cry '*In vino veritas*'.

It is in this sleazy, unstable world that, at the same time every evening, a mysterious figure, 'caught up in silks', materializes at the window amidst the billows of smoke and steam and, threading her way amongst the sordid tables, sits down—always alone—at that same window: all hung about with mists and perfume, her black silks redolent of the beliefs and legends of an older world, soft black ostrich feathers nodding in her hat:

> And, spellbound by this strange proximity
> Into the shadowy veil I stare,
> And see a thither shore of ravishment
> And an enraptured distance there.

Four days after his final examination, Blok's particular devil prompted him to introduce 'The Stranger' to Zhenya Ivanov:

He had a sort of conspiratorial look about him. He'd thought something up and didn't like to speak out in front of Mama. His face was not quite as our family were used to seeing it, there was something they didn't quite like. He was always so lucent, and this time there was something dark in his face.

'Zhenya, I've come to take you to Ozerki. For a walk. Will you?'

... We took the steamer. Got off at Novaya Derevnya. Then we took the train to Ozerki.

It was splendid on the platform between the carriages. You could sit down. Marvellous air.

We arrived. Walked alongside the lake where the 'rowlocks squeaked' and the 'women squealed'. We walked as far as Shuvalovo. There's a café there. We had a cup of coffee in the café. Then Sasha, with a sort of tenderness to me reminiscent of Virgil's to Dante, pointed out the gilded 'Krendel' on the café sign. He did the honours of the place most lovingly. As though he'd wanted to put my feet on the very way he had trodden that evening when the Stranger first appeared. At last he led me to the station at Ozerki (on the Sestroretsk line). From the big French windows you can see the level-crossing poles and all the things he talks of in the poem. In the window you can see the railway, the main line to Finland. Through trains rush past frequently.... A patch of green evening sky is now revealed, now hidden.

The appearance of the Stranger in the window is somehow bound up with those rushing trains.

'Now let's have a drink, Zhenya.'

I said something about the drunks with rabbits' eyes.

'Listen!' he said and rapped the table with the handle of his knife. His face was serious, an arrogant mask. I wanted to laugh; he too, but he stuck to his part.

'Here, waiter, a bottle of red wine!' and he indicated the wine list.

I felt like an innocent maiden brought here to be seduced by a villain. We laughed.

We drank the wine. Not an expensive wine but 'rough' and, most important, with the 'lilac glow' of the night violet, that is the secret of it....

Sasha really did seem to be waiting for someone to come: for her, the Stranger.

Most probably there really is someone who does come.

Quite honestly, I feel a bit awkward, I don't know how to behave here, I try to look like an innocent victim.

'Another bottle.'

Immediately the waiter brings another bottle.

We drink that. A bottle each.

'Sasha. Enough. I won't—'

'You will? Another bottle.'

The object of the exercise is to make the floor heave a little.

'Zhenya, leave that. I'm paying.'

'Now we can go. See how the floor heaves a little, like the deck of a ship.'

It's quite true. As though my legs had gone slightly numb, and the floor rises and sinks again, like the deck of a steamboat in a slight swell.

The Stranger did not come; we went home by the same route. We came off the boat by the Summer Garden. I had felt very sick after the first bottle....

10 May: I don't know about anyone else, but for me there is no truth in wine, not yet anyway. Such a revolting state! I feel sick, and I am sick. . . .

11 May: Was at the Bloks'. . . . They leave[p] today at 3.30. . . . Lyubov' Dmitriyevna laughed at us for getting drunk. Sasha exclaimed at my complaints of feeling so ill after the wine. 'Zhenya, only two bottles of light red wine, and you say you were drunk?' Lyubov' Dmitriyevna drank wine and laughed and laughed.

Visha Grek came. Is this the last time I shall see them?

Exactly the same people as the first time.

The Bloks want to live in a flat of their own, to leave the Barracks.[28]

It was not the last time Zhenya Ivanov was to sit with his friends, but it was the last time at the Barracks, the last irresponsible student gathering.

5

Before they left for Shakhmatovo in that spring of 1906, Blok had heard he had passed his examinations—obtaining, to his own surprise and gratification, first-class results in all subjects,[29] and had put the finishing touches to his poem *The Night Violet*, and to his new collection *Nechayannaya Radost'* which Bryusov, delighted at the younger poet's sensational turn from the path of virtue and much impressed by the growth of his genius, was preparing for publication with Skorpion.

At Shakhmatovo, the familiar quiet and greenness closed around him and Lyuba. Blok, exhausted, busied himself as usual in the garden. He read a good deal (Sologub, Gorky, whom he had met for the first time at Vyacheslav Ivanov's that winter and who was taking on an increasing importance for him,[q] Knut Hamsun and Hauptmann), but wrote neither letters nor poetry for some time. On 30 May, he wrote a poem to Lyuba which must have brought her cold comfort indeed, for he speaks of her greying hair and of himself as an old man: the ashes of the years, the fabulous years gone by, are preserved 'in a tall urn,' and he and she are living in azure memories of the past (II. 101).

This summer, even Shakhmatovo was slow to work its healing. Body and mind recovered their strength but the very thought of

---

[p] For Shakhmatovo.

[q] Not reciprocated. Put off by Blok's arrogant appearance, Gorky described him to a friend as a cold-hearted, ambitious boy, adding for good measure that his soul was '*sansculotte*'.

writing poetry seemed curiously remote.[30] The notebooks make joy-less reading:

Green boredom, and the town is grey boredom.

In the first circle of Dante's hell there is no pain but only depression. And that is considered 'the mercy of heaven'. But we seek pain to escape depression. And Dante's depression is full of light, 'the air is quiet and silent'—what could be more terrible for us?

(Z.K. 75)

The depression was more than the natural reaction of a nervous temperament to the hard work, emotional stress, and inspiration of the spring. Blok was in a state of total indecision about his future and of conflict with his milieu. It was the concerted opinion of the Beketov and the Mendeleyev relatives that the poet ought to be thinking about a job. A strong feeling of responsibility for the estate, which was still mortgaged, combined with his scrupulous honesty in money matters to make representations of this kind hard to resist. His allowance from his father was at an end, he had a first-class degree, an abundance of influential relatives, a fine appearance, bear-ing, excellent manners. It was customary for the Russian nobility to 'serve', and there must have been many positions not incompatible with the calling of a poet. Tyutchev, the Kovalenskys' neighbour, had been a diplomat; Vladimir Solov'ev a professor; Denis Davy-dov, an earlier connection of the Beketov family, had been a pro-fessional soldier and combined poetry with books on partisan tactics. Both Blok's tradition and his position as sole heir to Shakhmatovo,' required that he should begin to support his family.

Yet, in his heart, Blok knew he was not destined to become 'a builder of life'. Why should he devote a lifetime to preserving Shakh-matovo, to supporting the social structure, to founding a family with a tainted heritage? The revolution, which still flared spasmodically in riots and acts of terrorism throughout this summer of 1906, had confirmed his premonitions that his house, his society, and his family were condemned to pass away. His place, as their last repre-sentative, was out in the cold, snow-swept squares of the cities, from which would come destruction and renewal. This was his 'way': to leave the lovely, sheltered world in which he had lived up till now, precisely because he loved it and while he yet retained a sane vision of human society, in order to understand and to record what was

' The more affluent Adam Kublitsky-Piottukh and his family were thinking of acquiring an estate of their own, which meant that Blok's mother and aunt had somehow to find the money to buy out Sofia's third share of the property.

going on in the greater world without. The break became inevitable from this summer, when he consciously turned his back on useful work and on family tradition. There was in all this a certain cruelty, an overreaction against his own kin and their way of life. He was doing violence to himself and that was impossible without hurting others.

Lyubov' helped. Nature had spared her the desire for children (she had actually been relieved when, at the beginning of their marriage, Blok had explained that he did not think he ought to become a father), and she believed him implicitly in all that concerned his vocation, following unhesitatingly even when she did not understand. She was indifferent to material security and by the end of the summer she and Blok were actually speaking of giving everything away to a circle of Social Democrats, but this idea, which seems to have been more of a theoretical student dream than a practical plan, was not carried out. At the same time, vital and impulsive as ever, she fought his depression as no one else could. She had told Zhenya that to stay with Blok was 'the way of the cross', and she shouldered that cross bravely.

Zhenya Ivanov, who came to stay at Shakhmatovo from the 18th to the 26th of July, could not help noticing Blok's irritation with Lyuba's family, who clearly intended to resume their former way of life as soon as the revolution was safely over. Neither was he on good terms with Aunt Sofia and her sons. Zhenya's visit was a relief. His arrival was typical and put everyone in a good mood. In his letter of invitation, Blok had promised to send horses to the station. Zhenya, however, excited by the disbanding of the First Duma, the highly revolutionary assembly elected according to the system of suffrage granted by the October Manifesto, and by various other important matters, forgot to warn anyone of his arrival and, after an interesting journey in a carriage full of revolutionaries, had to walk from the station, carrying his suitcase slung over his shoulders on an umbrella, more than 21 versts up hill and down dale. At last, emerging from a steep climb through a little wood, he saw a man standing bare-headed by a fence which obviously marked the border of some estate:

It was Sasha. It must be Sasha. Would he recognize me at that distance?

I saw him looking in my direction and beginning to guess. Then evidently he decided it was impossible. Then suddenly he came running to meet me. 'Zhenya! It *is* you!'

We kissed: 'How did you do it? On foot and with your things! Come on. This is splendid. Come on! Mama, Lyuba! Here's Zhenya!'

From the gates Aleksandra Andreyevna and Maria Andreyevna came quickly out to meet me. Oh Lord, how truly glad they were.

Aleksandra Andreyevna called 'Lyuba, Lyubochka, come and see who's come.' Lyuba came flying out, and threw up her hands: 'Good heavens! And on foot! Zhenya!'[31]

Zhenya, like all Blok's friends from the town, was profoundly impressed by his first glimpse of the author of the *Verses about the Most Beautiful Lady* in his native habitat. After he left, Blok wrote to him:

With 'strangers' one almost always becomes the opposite of what one really is, blows up one's misery into the lightness of despair and laughter; then afterwards one feels even worse. With you I weep when I feel like it and laugh when I feel like it. I expect you yourself are simple and unconstrained, only with many more people than I am. . . .

(VIII. 159)

When Zhenya had gone, Blok found he was able to write again, and began to rough out the prose draft for *The King in the Square*, which included the dialogue *About love, poetry, and the civil service*, a direct exteriorization of his dilemma that summer later published as a separate work.

He and Lyuba, however, had been forgetting Andrey Bely. Assuming, wrongly, that Borya had understood the finality of his quietus that spring, Lyubov' had continued to write to him: friendly, formal, yet surprisingly relaxed letters. Bely, who was staying only thirty miles or so away with Seryëzha Solov'ev at Dedovo, reading Gogol, observing the revolutionary mood of the peasants and absorbing impressions that were later to find expression in his novel *The Silver Dove*, argued and suffered. At one stage he sent a registered letter of over one *hundred* pages. When Lyubov' wrote him: 'I think you are the greatest temptation of my life, a temptation of genius'[32] he was, perhaps naturally, flattered rather than discouraged, though it is difficult to see how he could have misunderstood her letter of 22 July:

Do you remember I told you how my love for Sasha developed, how fated everything I did seemed to be, how I thought of us as 'puppets'? Can there be any doubt that this love is not by my will, but by the Will of Him who sent me, that it has helped me, that it is precious, that it is my destiny? And if all this is so—in the name of that love I shall bear anything, destroy anything that is not compatible with it.[33]

This letter ends with her own vision of her covenant with Blok, very touching in its stark simplicity. She pictures them climbing a hill together, a long, waterless climb, and when they reach the top there is a vision of her home, Boblovo, and above it a blue sky with cranes flying and calling. This, she wrote, was the ultimate truth about herself that she had to give.

The correspondence might serve as an object lesson that the only way to break off a passionate romance is to break it off—'rompre', as St. François de Sales most emphatically advised his penitents. On 8 August, the Bloks became worried by the hysterical tone of Bely's letters and they agreed to meet in Moscow. Blok had some other business that day with the new Symbolist periodical *Zolotoye Runo*, and obviously hoped for a quick solution. When he had thought of his tiresome rival that summer, it had been 'with boredom and hatred'. As to Bely's relationship with Lyubov', it was 'incomprehensible' to him and 'in part unimportant' (VIII. 160). Nothing could have been more hurtful to Bely than this hostile indifference, and their meeting in the Prague Café only led to Bely's hurtling down the ornamental marble staircase on a valedictory threat 'to see them in Petersburg':

'No, definitely: you mustn't come.'
'I shall.'
'No ...'
'Yes ...'
'No ...'
'Good-bye.'

Blok, quite disgusted, went home and wrote coldly that he *had* intended to dedicate *Nechayannaya Radost'* to Bely but would not now do so as he had ceased to understand him (VIII. 166). He had lost the thread of his work again, and the incident plunged him back into impotent depression. Bely, who had hoped for quite another outcome, returned to Seryëzha at Dedovo, full of thoughts of suicide. The revolutionary sympathies of the two young men (Seryëzha was rather dismally struggling to convince himself that it was his sacred duty to marry a servant girl, and Bely had narrowly escaped detention while on a brief visit to his own utterly neglected family estate for inciting the peasants to seize his own property!) led to a grandiose row with their hosts, the Kovalenskys, and their abrupt departure for Moscow. Here, alone in a dusty flat, Bely sat for several days in a half-mask, contemplating 'transgression' in the spirit of Dostoyevsky's *Crime and Punishment*: in particular, the rights and wrongs of assassination and suicide, a theme that was on everybody's mind owing to the current wave of terrorism and repressions.

In Bely's case, however, thoughts of political assassination became confused with his humiliations at the hands of the Bloks. His friend Ellis, who was at that time perilously involved with a band of expropriators, came to discuss his own revolutionary 'to be or not to be', in which he was so absorbed that he never even remarked on Bely's mask:

He intensified my mood; together we sat and discussed the decision to call A.A. out; I knew perfectly well: I couldn't kill him; from this it followed that it was a form of suicide; however, I concealed this from Ellis and sent him to A.A. as my second; he clapped his bowler on his head, and, twitching his left shoulder (it was a nervous tic he had), set out immediately in pouring rain and storm. . . .

Ellis arrived at Shakhmatovo—after a sobering journey from the station in an open vehicle under a steady light rain—to find Lyubov' and Blok out walking in the glistening garden. Lyubov' claims that she talked her husband out of accepting the challenge, though Ellis told Bely he managed to lead him aside and deliver it in conventional privacy. Either way, Blok declined:

'But why a duel, Lev L'vovich? What cause is there? There's no cause. . . . It's just that Borya's terribly tired.'
And A.A. asked tenderly [wrote Bely] after all the details of how I was living; well, of course I must come to see them in Petersburg. Who was to stop me? It was all a misunderstanding.[34]

Blok kept Bely's sopping, twitching emissary at Shakhmatovo until the next day and even sat with him late into the night listening to his views on life and his translations of Dante. By the time Ellis returned to Moscow the following afternoon, quite enchanted by Blok and determined—for once—to act as peacemaker, Bely's mother had come back from the country and persuaded her son to unmask. For a brief while, the world became a sweeter and a saner place. Bely seems to have been mollified mainly by Ellis's report that he and his welfare had been the chief subject of conversation at Shakhmatovo all the preceding day and much of the night. After all, they *did* care what became of him.

Blok had other troubles than those caused him by Bely. The only poems he had written throughout the summer were two lyrics to Lyubov'. Even in Russian, the second of these has the stiffness of occasional verse. Written on 17 August, the anniversary of their wedding, and entitled 'Guardian Angel', it was a fair statement of his sympathy for the 'strong and the free' who made the revolution, of his determination not to 'sell his day' to the Establishment. It was also a muted but firm reaffirmation of love:

> Together, with you I looked out on those dawns,
> With you I now gaze where the black abyss yawns,
>
> And dual the destiny each must fulfil:
> As sullen, dark slaves! As souls of free will!
>
> Submit! No, rebel! Leave me not! Go away!
> Before us: through fire or through darkness—which way?
>
> Who calls there? Who weeps? Where does our way lie?
> Together—for ever—just you now, and I.
> To rise at the last? Or to perish? Or die?

(II. 103)

This renewal of his vows to Lyubov' marked not only the reknotting of a tie almost broken: it marked the beginning—for both of them— of a new life of total uncertainty.

The question of whether or not to seek regular employment had still to be decided. To scrape along from day to day on free-lance literary earnings was a daunting prospect. Regular work, too, seemed to hold out some hope of escaping depression. Yet Blok's kind of poetry required absolute concentration of a kind impossible for an honest man receiving a regular salary for some other activity.

Moreover, the political ferment all around demanded that Blok make a *political* choice: declare himself for or against the revolution; for or against terrorism; for or against the Tsar. The State Duma even offered a choice of political parties, however ineffective.

It is revealing that, amongst all the revolutionary authors whose works had become available after the abolition of preliminary censorship, Blok was drawn first to Bakunin: anarchist, aristocrat, hero, romantic, and uninhibited sponger; and that Bakunin interested him because, in his life and work, the poet could distinguish 'the music of old Russian families, a music that has fallen silent now amongst our soft youngsters and loose-lipped degenerates' (v. 34). Yet Bakunin could not serve him as a model in his own life. Blok disapproved of the great anarchist's free-and-easy attitude to his friends' money, his egotism and his grotesque appearance. Bakunin, he considered, lacked 'harmony'. Yet he was profoundly struck by the famous affirmation of faith in 'that eternal spirit which only breaks and destroys because it is the inexhaustible and eternally creative source of all life. The passion of destruction is at the same time a creative passion!'[s]

With the clairvoyance which burdened him all his life (even the 'positivist' Aunt Maria remarks somewhere that students of Blok will have to accustom themselves to the fact that his works almost invariably *anticipate* events, both in his own private life and in the life of his country), Blok was already aware, throughout the revolutionary turmoil of that uneasy summer and autumn, of the imminent onset of reaction. Choice seemed pointless.

The Tsar, he was now convinced, was not a true living Tsar, but an idol who would topple from his throne at the first touch. The individual was doomed to be overwhelmed and destroyed by the masses and the world, he felt sure, would have to change completely before things would settle. To Chulkov he had written on the 7 July that same summer:

You write harshly and justly. The harshest thing you could say now is contained in those words: 'socialism, fortunately, has ceased to be day-dream'. This, just now, is the most poignant circumstance; in words like these at a time like ours there is *absolute truth* (and that is so rare in literature in general). What it all adds up to is this: the whole gypsy encampment is packing up and setting off along the road after a long stay in one place. Over the abandoned camp only crows dive and swoop. That is the harsh truth of socialism in its present phase. All this has no part in what has gone before ... so drastically is the continuity broken that religious people are even inclined to take it as a punishment for their sins and, in their own way, they may be quite right: they hoarded and hoarded—and, suddenly, they have to give it all away, right down to their fiancées' letters and the piece of nail used to nail Christ to the Cross.

(VIII. 158)

These were the thoughts that Blok was struggling to express in dramatic form in his play, *The King in the Square*. The prose draft written at Shakhmatovo offers no solution: just a broken admission that only 'the Father' can help the world (and the poet) through a terrifying new phase.[t] The second version, written in blank verse

[s] This passage is now so well known as to sound trite. It should be remembered that, to Blok, it was new. This first wave of long-suppressed books had an extraordinary impact. Leonid Semyënov, for instance, wrote to Blok of Chernyshevsky's *What Is to be Done?* that it would not only outlive Turgenev and Dostoyevsky but, in wisdom and conviction, was rivalled only by Socrates![35]

[t] The prose version of *The King in the Square* is in fact a more vivid work than the polished verse play we can read today in any collection of Blok's plays. Strangely, it is not included in the 8-volume Collected Works, but only in the earlier 12-volume Leningrad edition (vol. VI, 277–98).

and completed in Petersburg that October, offers the same conclusion in terms of a theological allegory: it is characteristic of Blok's
theology that the Son is mentioned, but not shown, whereas there
is an attempt—inevitably unsuccessful—to represent the Father and
the Holy Spirit as 'the Architect' and his 'Daughter'. Blok himself
was subsequently to describe the play as 'unconvincing'. It is the
questions it puts which remain valid:

What is love and individual feeling in the face of a collapsing
society? What is the role of the poet? To pay lip-service to either
autocracy or revolution, or to reveal the 'hidden thoughts' of his
people, even though to read their own secret thought may send that
same people demented? Would it not be better, after all, to opt for
a simpler vocation and to enter the civil service?

6

It was with all these vital problems still unsolved that Blok and Lyuba
left Shakhmatovo before the end of August to take up their new
abode in a modest three-room flat in a rather down-at-heel quarter
of the Petrogradskaya Storona, Lakhtinskaya Ulitsa 3, flat 44. Aunt
Maria tells us that 'they had few things, extremely slender means,
but the whole atmosphere of their rooms breathed the usual charming individuality'.[36] The windows of the flat looked down into a
desolate Petersburg back yard and Blok's neighbours were no longer
soldiers but artisans, clerks, and small shopkeepers.

One of their first callers was Andrey Bely. Blind and deaf to everything but his own overpowering need, he had disregarded their plea
for an emotional truce and was deeply hurt when Lyubov' received
him only after an agonizing wait of ten days, putting him off with
the formal excuse that they were not yet settled in the new flat. When
she did allow him to call, it was to deliver an ultimatum in Blok's
presence that he should return to Moscow. Within half an hour, poor
tormented Bely was rushing headlong down the dingy stairs from
the unfamiliar fourth-floor flat, out into the dismal street and back
to his lodgings. Here for nine sleepless hours he contemplated suicide.
The morning brought a loving note from the Bloks and at a last,
friendly talk they persuaded him to go abroad and rest.

Blok felt the removal from his mother's house as yet another ejec-
tion from Eden. There was a lightness beginning to grow in him
at this time and he was not above aestheticizing the position. Now
he pictured himself again as 'the heir', setting forth on a quest with

his mother's blessing and coming home at last to die (II. 108–9). Now
in a whole cycle of verses he and Lyuba are seen as a latter-day Adam
and Eve, passing through squalid places to an accursed existence of
toil and want (II. 191–200, 205–6). Now he even takes leave of Lyuba
and she, like his mother, blesses him bravely on his way; and he
promises to bring her back the spring on the point of his spear ...
(II. 115).

In this world of shifting values and threatened realities, the poet
had come to identify one material being that would not pass away:
his country, Russia, or as he still preferred to call her, using the old
name, Rus'.

Rus', girdled all about by rivers,
Ringed by great woods, a trembling haze,
Where skylark sings and peat bog quivers,
Held by the sorcerer's dim gaze,

Where tribes of varied countenances,
From far and wide, from high and low,
Are circling in nocturnal dances
Lit by their blazing homesteads' glow,

Where sorcerers and village wizards
Lay charms upon the standing corn,
And witches call down blinding blizzards
To dance through with the devil's spawn,

And where the driving snow soon buries
The fragile dwellings men have made,
And where, beneath the snow, unhurried,
The girl once wronged now whets her blade,

Where living riot of cranberry bushes
Spreads over all your paths and ways,
And harsh winds whistling through the rushes
Sing legends of the elder days ...

There, in my sleep, I came to know her,
My country, in her poverty,
And gathered up her rags to cover
And warm the naked soul of me.

(II. 106)

The more Blok retreated from all thought of active interference
in the course of events, the more he identified himself with Russia:

with her very helplessness, with her night soul of myth and legend."
In 'The Maiden of the Rosy Gate and the Ant King' (v. 83–94) he
tested his present overwhelming feeling for Russia against his pre-
1905 impressions of Bad Nauheim: 'Everything is real, there is no
room for dreams', he wrote, contrasting the folklore of his country
with German tales of knights and ladies. 'Here from horizon to horizon, there is nothing but thin scrub. You may perish here, yet you
love it with a mortal love; you go out into that scrub, stand somewhere in the midst of those bogs, and there is nothing more you
want. Gold, gold sings somewhere in the depths. . . .' (v. 91). To seek
this gold in the depths of Russia's poverty: this, surely, was a worthy
vocation for a poet.

That autumn, people excited him. The world of literature, the
world of the theatre were awaiting him with open arms. He was
writing again: writing with facility in prose and verse. Drunk with
his increasing power to imbue the everyday world with intensified
life from the 'other' worlds of art and historical recall, he wrote to
his mother at the beginning of October:

In these days I am very tense and I want this tension to increase; strangers
no longer tire me, on the contrary, they call forth in me a being whom
I genuinely love, more and more, and I am almost constantly in a state
of inner ecstasy. . . . I live constantly on one note, and the more it frees
itself and shakes off everything extraneous the louder and more solemnly
it sounds.

(VIII. 161, 162)

Arrogantly, he rejected polite society as he had known it hitherto:
the regiment and his own relatives, *en masse* and as such: 'I shall never
accept any of them. By the very fact that they are relatives they have
become as nothing to me, cast out for ever. . . . Not only can they
not, they have no right to know who I am' (VIII. 162). At the same
time, careful as ever of his mother's feelings, he excepts her ('I never,
for one minute, stop loving you in all reality') and, to a lesser degree,
'Frantsik' and 'Auntie'.

This break with the conventional world in which he had been
brought up; this plunge into 'the world of art', of illusion and aliena-

---

" The article on folklore ('Invocations and Spells', v. 36–65) which he wrote in October
1906 shows his continuing preoccupation with the themes he had first touched on in the
article on Vyacheslav Ivanov and in *The Bubbles of the Earth*. The lyrical article '*Bezvre-
meniye*' (v. 66–82), its title a peculiarly Russian word meaning something between 'timelessness' and 'stagnation', but applied specifically to periods of cultural and political reaction,
conjures up the same symbolic landscape of lonely marshland as *The Bubbles of the Earth*,
again perceived through the eyes of a wandering hero enchanted by stillness, blundering
through slipping time sequences.

tion, through which he and Lyuba had moved hitherto like gracious strangers, was painful and violent. To complete it some new passion was essential, and the poet had his eyes fixed on the approach of this passion when he wrote his third and last 'lyrical drama'—once more an elaboration of a short poem: *The Stranger*.

The play opens in a sleazy tavern which had a perfectly real existence 'on the corner of Geslorovsky Lane and Zeleninaya Street'. Even the regular customers (one—the image of Paul Verlaine; another of Gerhart Hauptmann) had their real prototypes. Even the wallpaper, with a design of ships with foam at their prows, was a symbol presented by life itself. The great ships which, in *Her Coming*, *The King in the Square*, and *The Night Violet* are harbingers of joy and transformation, have here closed in all about the poet's drunken head, going nowhere, endlessly repeated—whirling round and round in a drunken storm.

From the very first words this play carries a conviction that the more allegorical *King in the Square* totally lacks. With delicate irony, Blok lets loose his dreams in the most sordid, commonplace setting. Amidst trite dialogue, talk of bargains and prices, of food and drink, the dreams flutter from mind to mind as though possessed of a life of their own; and in their wake follows a scum of gross, cynical laughter, of ugly curses.

One character, called simply 'the poet', talks to the waiter:

To stroll the street. To pick up the tail-ends of unfamiliar words. Then— to come here and tell all your soul to whoever will listen ... To see many women's faces. Hundreds of eyes, great and deep blue, dark, light. Narrow, like the eyes of a lynx. Wide open, infantile. To love them. To desire them ... And through that blaze of eyes, through that whirlwind of gazes, there will suddenly arise, as though coming into flower under blue snow, the one face: the one truly beautiful countenance of The Stranger ... beneath a heavy, dark veil ...

(IV. 76–7)

The second scene, 'on the bridge', has also a real setting in St. Petersburg. Here stands the Astrologer and observes the falling of a star while the poet is hustled past him by the chuckers-out of the tavern and deposited ignominiously in a snowdrift offstage.

Meanwhile the star, alighting upon the bridge, has become a beautiful woman, and the poet returns, transformed, to speak with her. Both are touched with blue starlight, outlined by soft snow. It is the poet's longing, his invocations that have brought 'the Stranger' down to earth. Now, she wishes to hear 'earthly speeches', but the poet can speak only of mysteries. His 'blood is silent', but the Stranger demands passion and, even as she speaks, the blue figure fades into the snow and is immediately replaced by a gentleman in a top hat, a personification of libidinous vulgarity:

THE STRANGER

Do you wish to love me?

GENTLEMAN

Oh yes! No objection at all.

THE STRANGER

And can you embrace me?

GENTLEMAN

As to that, I should like to know why
I should not embrace you?

THE STRANGER

And as you touch my lips
Will you love and caress me?

GENTLEMAN

Come with me, my beauty!
'I will do all you command',
As good old Shakespeare once said.
There, you see, dear, I too
Know my way about poetry!

The Stranger meekly gives him her hand.

As he leads her away, the Astrologer reappears, weeping for his fallen star. The poet returns, no longer gleaming blue but as he was when hustled by at the beginning of the act, and asks the Astrologer if he has seen a woman in black. The ensuing dialogue is highly reminiscent of the epistolary dialogue between Blok and Bely and, like Pierrot and Harlequin in *The Puppet Booth*, the two end by weeping together for their lost love.

The last scene is a modish reception which begins (and continues) with echoes from the first. Like the frequenters of the tavern, the guests are occupied first and foremost with questions of money, food, sex, and drink; only their language is more elegant and some have foreign-sounding names like Zhorzh. Even the Stranger, Maria, the fallen star, is anglicized and becomes Mary.

The poet recites a parody of Blok's Beautiful Lady verses. The Astrologer enters, delighted at having turned the incident of the fallen star into a first-class lecture. In spite of a tormenting sense of *déjà vu*, the poet has forgotten everything. The Stranger, abandoned by her 'gentleman', forgotten by poet and Astrologer alike, stands lonely by the long curtains. One minute she is there for all to see and the next there is nothing but a bright star shining steadily in at the window.

CHAPTER X

The First Tarantella

(Autumn 1906–Autumn 1907)

> I often feel physically tired, more and more often. Probably
> it is the same thing as with pregnant women. The curse
> attached to bearing new life; for me, the curse of rebirth.
> It is impossible to call with impunity upon Dionysus....
> If I am not transformed, then I shall die of weariness.
>
> (*Z.K.* 84, entry for 21 December 1906)

1

On 21 December 1906, Blok wrote disgustedly in his diary:

> I have been dissatisfied with my poems since the spring. The last were 'The
> Stranger' and *The Night Violet*. Then began the depression of the summer,
> then the busy whirl of Petersburg and the two plays in which I said what
> I had to say, but the verses I just wrote for the sake of writing, half necessary.
> I strung them out. Threw myself into rhyming. But perhaps this new, fresh
> cycle will come soon and Aleksandr Blok—to Dionysus.
>
> (*Z.K.* 85–6)

This preoccupation with Dionysus was in part due to the influence
of Vyacheslav Ivanov, in part the reflection of a new interest in
Nietzsche[a] and of the poet's growing absorption with the theatre,
or rather with one particular theatre.

Chulkov's plans for a 'mystic-anarchist' theatre having come to
nothing, Meyerhold had accepted an invitation from Vera Kommissarzhevskaya to work with her re-formed company in a newly

---

[a] Blok breaks off a conspectus of Nietzsche's *The Birth of Tragedy* (which he was reading
in the autumn of 1906 in a Russian translation published in 1900) with the words: 'N.B.—
on myth and religion. I can't write it all out—too long. Anyway I would have to copy
it word for word—this book is such a revelation.' Among the excerpts he did copy were
the words addressed to Euripides: 'Because you have abandoned Dionysus, so has Apollo
abandoned you' (*Z.K.* 84, 120–1).

acquired theatre on the Offitserskaya Ulitsa.[b] The autumn of 1906
saw the first performances in this 'theatre of the free actor'. The company's artistic credo was that outward effect should spring from inner
understanding, from the actors' and producer's ability to identify
with the text. Their aim, however, was to achieve a lyrical rather
than a psychological understanding, for they were concerned with
communicating the finer shades of modernist drama. Theirs was to
be a new theatre of the spirit, designed to express the essence of con-
temporaneity. Meyerhold dreamt of achieving such expression
through stylization of décor and the introduction of distinct rhythmic patterns in dialogue and action. Kommissarzhevskaya, on the
other hand, placed more faith in cultivating the intelligence of her
actors and their sensitivity to the 'new art'.

It was to this end that, sometime before the opening of the season,
she began to organize Saturday receptions in the theatre club at
which her interpretive artists could meet those who provided their
raw materials: the musicians who wrote their incidental music; the
artists who designed costumes and décor: the playwrights and the
poets. Blok and Lyubov' were invited to the first Saturday and the
glamour of the theatre, which they had both loved so much in their
teens, reasserted itself.

The company, except for the actors, was much the same as at Vya-
cheslav Ivanov's or Fyëdor Sologub's. Sologub himself read his play
The Gift of the Wise Bees at the first Saturday. The artist N. N.
Sapunov and the poets Gorodetsky, Chulkov, S. A. Ausländer, and
M. A. Kuzmin soon became regular guests. Artists from the *Mir
Iskusstva* group—S. Yu. Sudeykin, L. S. Bakst, K. A. Somov, and
others—came and went. Nevertheless, literary St. Petersburg had
never seen anything quite like Kommissarzhevskaya's first reception.
The actresses had persuaded Nikolay Sapunov to do what he could
to improve the appearance of the awkward studio theatre of the Latvian Club where the reception was held. Pale blue open-work
material reminiscent of fishing nets or cobwebs was draped round
the walls, the ugly, cheap couch was covered with a rug, and on
the tables, covered with coarse cloth, stood tall candles. 'Vibrant and
solemn as before a first night performance' Vera Kommissarzhevskaya awaited her guests.

The evening was an unqualified success. After Sologub's reading
of his play, Blok and Gorodetsky recited their verses, Kommissarzhevskaya declaimed and sang, Kuzmin sang his 'Alexandrian

[b] Now the Ulitsa Dekabristov; in this street Blok himself was to live from 1912 until
his death in 1921.

Songs', to which he had composed both words and music, and the whole troupe gave a rendering of Vyacheslav Ivanov's 'Dithyramb':[c]

In the intervals between the recitals and the singing the company broke up into animated groups, chatting and getting to know one another. There were women's smiles, locks of hair, trailing scarves ... the whirlwind movements of Filippova, the smooth, sliding walk of Munt, Volokhova's burning eyes, the languid, enchanting grace of Ivanova, and, like a burning torch above them all: Kommissarzhevskaya herself. All these women listened eagerly, admired and admiring, moving lightly from one group of writers to another.

The end of the evening, Munt, Ivanova, Volokhova, and I spent in the company of Blok and Gorodetsky.[1]

So Valentina Petrovna Verigina, the liveliest and most readily amused of the young actresses, recalled that first evening.[d] Natal'ya Nikolayevna Volokhova,[e] she of the 'burning eyes', takes up the tale:

We young actresses were detailed to receive the guests, engage them in conversation and ply them with refreshments. Naturally, we accorded everyone a warm and hospitable welcome but made special efforts with those whom we happened to like.

Aleksandr Aleksandrovich was immediately surrounded by a large group of young people. He was bombarded with questions, beset with sandwiches, tea, cakes, and wine. He stood looking a little overcome at such an enthusiastic reception, smiling meekly and shifting from one foot to the

---

[c] The poem 'Dithyramb' had appeared that year in Chulkov's almanac *Fakely* and was considered a key work by the 'mystic anarchists'.

[d] A sweet-faced blonde whose parts were wicked or comic, Verigina, in her reminiscences, achieves the extraordinary feat of being constantly entertaining yet never saying an ill word about anyone. Devoted wife, mother, and hard-working grandmother, she remained an actress at heart to the end of her long life. It was my privilege to know her for more than ten years and, whenever I went to Leningrad, I would visit her in her crowded family flat. Her memory was extraordinary and she was an excellent *raconteuse*, eager to communicate her own abounding appreciation of her friends: 'Natasha' Volokhova, Blok, Lyubov' Dmitriyevna, Meyerhold, she defended not only against all outside criticism but even, in the case of Lyubov' Dmitriyevna whom she considered had been grossly unfair to herself in her memoirs, against themselves.

[e] N. N. Volokhova was a stage name. Born Anfytserova, Volokhova was the same age as Blok. She had graduated from the school of the Moscow Art Theatre in 1903 and had made the acquaintance of Vsevolod Meyerhold during two seasons in Tiflis. With him she had returned to Moscow in 1905 to work in the studio theatre attached to the Moscow Art, of which Meyerhold was chief producer. In 1906 she joined Kommissarzhevskaya's troupe and remained with her for three seasons, playing many parts including the title roles in Wilde's *Salome* and Hofmannsthal's *Elektra*. Except for a brief period after her marriage when she bore and lost a daughter, Volokhova continued as a professional tragedienne well on into the 1920s. It is perhaps significant that among her parts was Dostoyevsky's Nastasya Filippovna. She died in Moscow in the 1960s.

other. Aleksandr Aleksandrovich was dressed in a long black frock coat which I think he was wearing for the first time[f] and was obviously feeling very much the hero of the occasion: pleased, but a little embarrassed too. Of course, there were requests to recite. And that evening he recited 'In the distant, pale-blue night nursery ...' Aleksandr Aleksandrovich recited well, with a sense of music, in a rather hollow voice, with quiet dignity, even solemnity.

This solemnity was always characteristic of him when reciting poetry: solemnity, not pomposity: a kind of reverence for that which he bore in himself. This was a feeling that went through his whole life; poetry was not just writing but a kind of mission to which he was doomed. That is why he often could not, as he would say himself, change this or that in his verses, even when he did not fully understand them himself: he had to write it *like that*; to say it *like that*. When we asked whether the child [in the poem] were dead or asleep he answered sincerely and rather at a loss:

'I don't know, really I don't.'[2]

Verigina, less reserved and more persistent, elicited a more definite response.

I asked: was the child dead? and received the answer 'His mother smothered him.' I remember exclaiming without pause for thought: 'Impossible! There's no murder there!' Aleksandr Aleksandrovich smiled and said: 'Well, then he just died. You can take it like that.'

The actresses begged the poets to write them verses for recitation. Gorodetsky and Blok obliged.

On the following Saturday, Blok read *The King in the Square*, 'and he produced', Verigina remembered,

a still more irresistible impression on us. The poet sat at the table, between two red candles. He did not bend his face over the manuscript. Only the eyes were lowered. I think that the delight I felt at the essential harmony between the poet, his appearance, voice, way of reading, and the poetry itself, was shared by all those who were present.[3]

The play, in spite of its weaknesses, was enthusiastically received.[g] Meyerhold and Kommissarzhevskaya wanted to stage it but, like Blok's next play, *The Stranger*, it failed to pass the theatrical censor.[h]

---

[f] Volokhova was quite right. Blok had formerly worn a student's uniform throughout the winter season.

[g] It was disputed by three publishers: Bryusov for *Vesy*, Sokolov for *Grif*, and Ryabushinsky for the new Symbolist journal *Zolotoye Runo* (also, at that time, edited by Bryusov), to which it finally went.

[h] *The King in the Square* on political, *The Stranger* on religious grounds, the censor

Meyerhold had already, however, succeeded in interesting Kommissarzhevskaya in *The Puppet Booth*, and it was agreed that this should form part of the season's repertory.

From that evening on a smaller, more intimate group began to form about Blok and Lyubov', a group consisting of Meyerhold, the assistant producer Pronin, and four young actresses: Volokhova, Verigina, Munt (Meyerhold's sister-in-law), and Ivanova.[i] From the poets came Gorodetsky, Ausländer, and, occasionally, Georgiy Chulkov and Sologub. They had *carte blanche* to attend rehearsals and soon began to meet after work at the Bloks' or in Vera Ivanova's flat. Punch, tea and sandwiches were the order of the day as there was little money for spirits or luxury foods.

When the season opened, Blok began visiting backstage with Verigina, Volokhova, and Munt who shared a dressing room. He obviously felt happy and natural with the actresses and was a great favourite. Verigina touched off the clown in him and they would talk 'inspired nonsense' for hours on end.

Most of all, and especially at the beginning, Blok talked to me, and N.N. [Volokhova] even thought that he came behind the scenes principally for the sake of Verigina, but once, during the dress rehearsal of *Sister Beatrice*,[j] she learnt with astonishment the true reason for his frequent visits.

Blok called in on us in our dressing room as was now his habit. When the interval came to an end we saw him to the head of the stairs and Volokhova remained standing at the top to watch him go. Suddenly Aleksandr Aleksandrovich turned and took a few indecisive paces towards her, then stepped back again and finally, putting his foot on the first stair, said shyly and solemnly that he had just understood the meaning of his forebodings, his confusion of the last months. 'I have just seen it in your eyes, I have just this moment realized that it is they and they alone which bring me to this theatre.'

The fact that Blok was in love soon became obvious to everybody.

The scandal was all the more enjoyable because of the literary overtones. The poem 'The Stranger' had fascinated Blok's public. The play on the same theme intrigued them further. Now the incarnation of the Stranger was there for all to see: Blok was writing love lyrics to one of the most beautiful women in Petersburg, yet his heroine seemed more like a creature of his imagination, com-

---

maintaining that the latter contained improper though indefinable allusions to the Virgin Mary.

 [i] Later they were joined by one of the actors, A. A. Golubev.

 [j] Volokhova, who was very tall, played the abbess in this play and Kommissarzhevskaya herself the title role.

pounded from the 'living darkness' and 'aimless cold' of his poetry. When Blok had been writing his poems about the Most Beautiful Lady, he had brushed aside indelicate speculation and had drawn a reasonably firm line between his art and his private life. Now, his life had become art. In the spirit of the Dionysian Hellenism of Vyacheslav Ivanov, he appeared almost as a ritual victim of his own passion: 'There is no way out of the storms and to perish is merriment' (II. 250).

The very story of his declaration, as Verigina tells it, is like a scene from a play. And so it went on:

Of course the poet's infatuation could not remain a secret from his wife, but her attitude was unusual. She felt that in Volokhova he loved his Muse of the moment. The verses about 'The Stranger' had forewarned the 'Most Beautiful Lady' of the appearance of a rival but, in spite of that jealousy which, in the circumstances, was only natural, she paid full tribute to the beauty and significance of Volokhova, at the same time, perhaps, instinctively aware that she herself was not transient in his life.... When he spoke of her to us Aleksandr Aleksandrovich would often say: 'Lyuba is wise'.[4]

Lyubov' herself recalled the winter of 1906–7 as a time in which nothing was real: neither passion, nor jealousy, nor love: 'It was simply that all of us that winter were quite sincerely and naturally living not within the deep, fundamental strata of our natures but in a kind of light intoxication of the heart.'[5]

Volokhova, for her part, recalled how

... we were all very young, all aflame with the love of our art: poetry, the theatre, painting. And all of us were head over heels in love with life and art, with the force of life and the power of beauty and truth in art. It was this which made our meetings so vivid, light, and beautiful.[6]

2

Of course, not everybody saw it that way. The set which for two seasons centred around Blok and Lyubov' was exclusive, ironic, and sometimes arrogant, with all the devastating, unforgivable arrogance of youth and success. When a stranger (a poet who did not happen to be 'one of them') gate-crashed their table in a restaurant and suggested they should all recite, Blok, to the surprise of his companions, instantly agreed. 'But', he added seriously, '*I* shall recite some verses by Valentina Petrovna.' Verigina, like many schoolgirls of her generation, had composed a solemn ode on the occasion of the death of Alexander III the naïve pomposity of which had so appealed to Blok's sense of the ridiculous that he had learnt it by heart. This ode he now proceeded to deliver, perfectly straight-faced, while the unfortunate gate-crasher struggled to compose his features into a suitable expression—until the rest of the party rescued him with a burst of laughter.

The group of friends met most often at one another's homes and in the theatre, and their exclusiveness and freedom from convention, together with their habit of turning night into day, gave rise to whispers of orgies and scandal of all kinds. Even Blok's friends were nonplussed.

Zhenya Ivanov continued to visit the Bloks at Lakhtinskaya, but the theatre people understood neither his esoteric symbolist language nor his peculiar humour. He did not fit in and withdrew, anxious and palpably a little hurt. Blok tried to explain to him:

For me to come and visit you is a matter of choosing the right moment because often we should be simply *bored* together and have nothing to say to one another.... I have not lost the abyss for ever. Always I hear it on the brink of sound. Even when I am quite broken and completely dead.... I had no use for you while the human being in me was still in the process of being broken. Now it is broken, and I *respect you deeply and love you* (as the dead the living?).

(VIII. 166)

Andrey Bely, languishing in self-imposed exile in France and once more in Lyubov' Dmitriyevna's bad books for having published a story and poetry based on his relationship with her and Blok, was naturally disgusted to hear how his friends were treating that sacred tie to which he had so recently, as he undoubtedly believed, sacrificed his own hopes of earthly happiness. These hopes were still being sustained by the active sympathy of the Merezhkovskys, with whom he stayed for much of the time he spent in Paris. Zinaida Hippius kept him informed, if somewhat belatedly, of all that was going on in St. Petersburg, and the tone of her winter conversation can be judged by that of her spring letters:

Tata wrote me that Lyuba has gone to the country with her sister but that Blok has stayed on in town, is going to bed at five in the morning and getting up at three in the afternoon, and spending his life in the theatre. Vyacheslav Ivanov's Wednesdays have come to an end, having degenerated into something altogether indecent.[7]

And the following summer, after Bely had returned to Moscow:

I have already had occasion to write a little about the unfortunate Blok. Really, there is a kind of idiotism about him. I heard not long ago that he almost parted from Lyuba this winter, having fallen in love with some actress—but then it all passed off, because she herself is going to become an actress. . . . And in general everything goes on there in such a bad atmosphere that it is better not to raise the curtain. It's true, isn't it, Borya, that you have more or less regained your equilibrium as far as she is concerned?[8]

Hippius, of course, was known to have a waspish tongue and a curious predilection for mischief-making, but she was not alone in her estimate of the life Blok and Lyubov' Dmitriyevna were now leading.

The real course of Blok's passion was more subtle[k] and the bohemian element was very much on the surface. It was Lyubov' Dmitriyevna who first invited Volokhova and Verigina to drop in at their flat after the theatre, and this soon became a habit. They would sit comfortably talking theatrical shop and laughing together into the small hours. Verigina's impression of Blok at this time does not tally with the rumours of orgy and debauch:

Blok, in his essence as a poet, was stern and even dour, but he had a merry double, who wanted nothing to do with the stern poet and his lofty mission. They were quite separate. . . . I heard only the vibrant ringing of his merriment and, at that time, I saw only his snowy image. Everybody knows that Blok's life was far from sinless but, even so, his contacts with the base earth seemed to have made no impression on his essential personality. . . . N. N. Volokhova once said: 'Many dirty hands reached out towards Blok. For some reason many people seemed actually to want to pull him down into the mire, but everything just slid off him as if from ice and he remained transparent.' At the beginning of our acquaintance I flatly refused to believe in Blok's numerous inamoratae and once, when reading us 'The blizzards have blown in my door', he reached the words: 'And women and their poor embraces are so familiar, known so well', I burst out laughing: these words on Blok's lips seemed strange to me and quite inappropriate. And I said so straight out when, with a surprised smile, he asked me what I was laughing at. Aleksandr Aleksandrovich and Lyubov' Dmitriyevna, in their turn, began to laugh at me. She reproached me for thinking of Blok as

[k] Blok's diaries and notebooks shed little or no light on the nature of his romance. His letters to Volokhova are lost. Lyubov Dmitriyevna's reminiscences have still to be published. In fact, it was not until the appearance in 1961 of Verigina's and Volokhova's accounts of their relationship with Blok, modestly tucked away amongst the learned articles in Tartu University's *Papers on Russian and Slavonic Philology* (see Reference Notes, p. 335), that the tendency to see the poet's 'Dionysian' romance as a carnal bacchanalia began to die a natural death.

a schoolboy. Of course, I did not think of him as anything of the sort, it was just that he always seemed to me infinitely far from the earth.[l] And the fact that I was at Lakhtinskaya almost every day and saw him in homely circumstances did nothing to disturb that impression. In Blok's flat lived the Poet and his Beautiful Lady: the real thing, without a shadow of that decadent affectation that was characteristic of certain poets of the time and more particularly of their ladies. Naturalness, unpretentiousness, and extreme sincerity distinguished them both from the majority of their contemporaries.[10]

Though, as Verigina noted, neither Blok nor Lyuba was affected in any vulgar sense, they were both, at this time, consciously 'acting their lives', and so was Natal'ya Volokhova. 'Having been endowed by nature with a tragic style of beauty, I had far too good taste to cultivate a cheerful personality', was the way she summed it up herself many years after the event.[11] The element of pose and self-admiration in Blok himself was, however, redeemed by his ever-present, underlying sense of destiny and the pain of loss:

I am aware that I am ceasing to be a man of the abyss and am fast turning into a writer, I know that every day I am putting on an act, that I am ceasing to be a human being and becoming more and more a creature of affectation. . . . If you will accept me[m] as you have done all this autumn I shall know that there is some support. But I doubt that I shall ever become a real human being, and at the moment I do not want to. I'm *busy*.

(VIII. 165)

Blok was 'busy' with that mounting ecstasy that led to the lyrical climax of The Snow Mask, a poetry of 'shining darkness' and 'sultry snows', poetry through which 'the wind sings of betrayals, sings of silks'. He was busy, too, with his first real contact with the professional theatre, with the anguish and delight of watching The Puppet Booth, that fragile product of his solitary imagination, transformed into a public spectacle: transformed, moreover, by one of the great theatrical geniuses of the twentieth century.

Meyerhold's appreciation of Blok knew no bounds. He considered him a supremely theatrical writer and a master of the grotesque, which he defined as 'constant endeavour on the part of the artist to lead the audience off one plane to which they have just become accustomed on to another which they in no way expect', and as an art 'based on the struggle between form and content'.[12]

[l] Georgiy Chulkov objected to this picture of Blok: 'All Blok's jokes and puns owed their peculiar charm to the fact that they were dyed black in his profound lyrical melancholy. Blok was not the innocent, charming humorist seen by V. P. Verigina.'[9]

[m] The letter, of 15 November 1906, is again to Zhenya Ivanov.

In 1912, in the Foreword to his book *About the Theatre*, Meyerhold wrote: 'The first impetus to lend my art definite direction was given by the happy invention with which I planned A. Blok's wonderful *Puppet Booth*.'[13]

Blok never altogether reciprocated Meyerhold's unqualified admiration. Perhaps their relationship was best summed up by Meyerhold himself in the inscription on a photograph which he presented to the poet in 1908:

Aleksandr Aleksandrovich Blok I learnt to love before I met him. When I part from him I shall take with me a love that will last for ever. I love his verses, I love his eyes. But he does not know me ...

Vs. MEYERHOLD[14]

Verigina put her finger on one of the differences between them:

For Blok there were no words without profound meaning. When he used words they were born of a complete belief in their significance, for which reason he could be very angry with anyone who saw nothing but an outer form in words. When the poet was amusing himself and joking, he joked within those bounds where levity is permissible, in contrast to Meyerhold, who could make a joke of anything. Thus Meyerhold would sometimes develop an idea in the most fascinating way, appearing to be in love with it and, in no time at all, could turn and make fun of the object of his love. I knew that Aleksandr Aleksandrovich did not forgive this sort of thing. . . . Meyerhold once said to me, half joking: 'I always wear a mask', and it seems to me that, in those moments when he was wearing a mask which he had completely made his own, Blok accepted him, but when he was trying on a new mask and still felt uncertain in it Aleksandr Aleksandrovich recoiled from him. When I speak of Meyerhold's masks, I have no wish to imply a criticism; it was his nature—truly theatrical.[15]

In their work on *The Puppet Booth*, however, Blok and Meyerhold understood one another perfectly within that 'sphere of irony' in which the action of the play takes place, and Meyerhold's own performance as Pierrot had a quality of eerie solemnity which safeguarded the delicate lyricism of the play. He worked in close cooperation with Sapunov, whose set of a stage within a stage was as successful as Meyerhold's inspired interpretation of the mystics' transformation into the 'empty dummies'. They sat facing the audience behind cut-out cardboard costumes, and all the actors had to do to achieve the desired 'faceless' effect was to duck their heads behind the collars and allow their hands to dangle limply from the cuffs.

Of course, such effects were broadly theatrical and, at the rehearsal stage, Meyerhold was constantly concerned that Blok would suffer from the inevitable coarsening of his original." On 22 December, just before the dress rehearsal, Blok wrote him a reassuring letter:

Dear Vsevolod Emil'evich!

I will write briefly about my impressions of yesterday. The general tone, as I have already told you, pleased me so much that it opened new perspectives on *The Puppet Booth* even for me; it seems to me that it is not pure lyricism, that there is already the framework of a play in it; *in general* there is only one thing I want to say: every contemporary theatre, even yours where there is more of the aerial breath of youth than anywhere else, is yet doomed to carry the imprint of a certain weariness: like a giant that has overcome the most incredible obstacles in his struggle with inanimate matter.... In this struggle, whether we will or not, the ringing clarity of tone tends to get lost, voices grow deeper and rougher; in so far as this moment is present even in your theatre I may rebel against it, *but only in the name of the ringing lyricism* of my play; immediately, though, I say to myself and to you: in the first place, the 'heavy flesh' of decoration in your theatre is as light and transparent as it is possible to make it ... in the second (which is the most important) *any* puppet show, mine not excluded, has ambitions to be a *battering ram*, to smash a breach in dead matter: the puppet show runs into, goes to meet, and shows up the dreadful, lewd embraces of this matter, as though offering itself as a bait, so that stupid, dull matter is lured on, begins to gain confidence, starts to make advances in its turn; and THIS is when 'the hour of the mystery' should strike. Matter has been tricked and now she is weak and submissive; in this sense I do 'accept the world'—the world with its dullness and immobility and dead, dry colours, but only in order to trick the bony old hag and to make her young again: in the embraces of a jester and puppet-master, the old world grows prettier, younger, and its eyes become transparent, fathomless.

Blok did, however, admit to some qualms which he expressed in his usual choppy manner, alternating flights of lyricism with references to the 'backcloths, ropes, swearing of carpenters, and the full-bellied self-satisfaction' he saw as an inevitable part of the theatre and its public. But on the whole, he assured Meyerhold, far from merely 'putting up with' the work on his play it was *necessary* for him to enter into the world of the theatre, '*necessary* that you should

---

" That Blok did suffer in this way is clear from his reply to Z. N. Hippius, who, after watching a rehearsal of a play of her own with Blok in 1916, asked him about his feelings towards the staging of his *Puppet Booth*. Blok hesitated, then replied firmly: 'I found it offensive' (*mne eto bylo oskorbitel'no*). On the other hand, there is Blok's letter to Meyerhold (quoted above), and the fact that he never missed a performance and wrote elsewhere that Meyerhold's production was 'perfect'. Blok did not approve of the modern playwright's tendency to withdraw from the actual staging of his work.

stage *The Puppet Booth*; there is a moment of catharsis for me here; a way out of lyrical isolation' (VIII. 169–71).

To the dress rehearsal Blok brought his wife, mother, and aunt. The elder Beketov ladies were tolerantly amused at Sasha's enthusiasm and critical of the actors, although they, too, fell under the combined spell of Meyerhold's direction, Sapunov's setting, and Kuzmin's music.

Verigina, who played the Red Domino, recalled the first night:

Once we had put on our masks and the music had begun, enchanting us, leading us on into the 'magic circle', something happened which seemed to compel us all to renounce our own selves. The masks made everything strange and wonderful. Even in the wings before our entrance we spoke to each other differently. I remember the moment before the beginning of the action when during the first performance I was standing and waiting for my own leitmotiv in the music with a special thrill of trepidation. My partner Betsky and his 'double' were quietly pacing up and down at some distance, wrapped in their cloaks. I sensed that someone was standing at my shoulder and turned round. It was the white figure of Pierrot. I suddenly felt anxious and vexed: What if he should say something ordinary, something of his own, what if he should crack a joke and break the spell? But I immediately felt ashamed of this involuntary doubt: Pierrot looked out through his mask with *other* eyes. He was silent. We were all in the mysterious world of Blok's poetry.... When the curtain went down it was as if none of us could come back to earth straight away. A moment later there was a storm of applause from one side and of protest from the other, though the latter, indeed, was considerably weaker. They called out Blok and Meyerhold particularly. All those who had contributed to the performance answered the calls with them. Whenever the whistles started up the applause grew louder. We realized at once that this was an unusual, a quite exceptional performance.[16]

After the first night, Blok presented his three favourite actresses with roses: pink for Munt, red for Verigina, white for Volokhova. Back in his quiet flat at Lakhtinskaya, on the last day of the year 1906, he wrote exultantly in his diary: 'Yesterday, 30.XII, I came out on the stage four times. One concerted, piercing whistling and applause: I acknowledged both' (*Z.K.* 91).

3

After the first night, there was a celebration. The Bloks, the Meyerholds, Kuzmin, Sapunov, Ausländer, Gorodetsky, Chulkov, and others received intriguing invitations from some 'paper ladies' who had recently, so they said, landed by balloon from the moon and were to hold a ball on the Torgovaya Ulitsa. The address of the 'paper ladies' happened to coincide with the address of one of the actresses, Vera Ivanova. When the men arrived, they were given masks at the door which they were obliged to wear throughout the evening. The ladies had agreed in advance to dress up in fancy dress of crêpe paper.

N. N. Volokhova wore a long, pale lilac paper dress with a train. On her head was a diadem which Blok in his verses referred to as a 'triple-crowned tiara'. That evening Volokhova had a kind of transparent beauty, though indeed all the others now appear to me as wonderful phantoms. As if someone had dreamt them, 'the ladies who had flown down from the moon': Munt with her vivid mouth, all in yellow like some exotic flower, sliding soundlessly about the room; Vera Ivanova, all rosy, slender, with nervous, weary movements; and the others. I, too, in scarlet petals of crumpled paper, hardly recognized myself in the big mirror. The thought flashed through my mind: was it not the waving of Vera's great fan that had brought us all to life? She would shut up her fan, and suddenly we would all vanish....[17]

Kuzmin, Verigina goes on, described the ball in his story 'The House of Cards', although in fictionalized form, and she quotes with delight how

... the women ... were in costumes of the same style but different colours made of fine paper trimmed with matching ribbons, in half-masks, unfamiliar, new and young in the light of the coloured lanterns. They danced, circled, sat on the floor, sang, drank wine which gleamed red in long glasses, tenderly and quietly making merry in the half-dark room.[18]

This was true carnival, though refined and poeticized. It was the rule of the evening that all the guests should address one another with the familiar 'thou'. Verigina recalls with a characteristically irreverent giggle that the more elderly and conventional of the party, conducting their usual staid conversations at the beginning of the evening, sounded perfectly demented as they unsmilingly complied with this mischievous edict. 'It was easiest of all to say "thou" to Blok. In the half-light among the other masks and the dancing paper ladies, Blok seemed unreal, himself a symbol.'

But, even as Blok's 'merry double' flickered and sparkled in response to the Red Domino, the poet in him tremulously contemplated Volokhova, the 'snowy darkness' of the 'winged eyes' behind the mask, the narrow waist and narrow hands, the sweeping lilac train. Cool and unapproachable, she had yet paid him the

compliment of dressing in the very colour of his Muse, the colour
of the Night Violet. That evening, she was no longer Natal'ya
Volokhova, an intelligent young actress who had not yet fully recovered from an unhappy love affair with another man,° but the
Stranger herself, a mysterious paper lady with no identity beyond
that which the poet at her side chose to confer upon her: a 'living
fire of snow and wine': a fallen star; a snow maiden.

> I will tell you any stories
>   You command
> I will conjure masks and visions
>   At demand
> In the firelight I'll bring shadows
>   At your call,
> And I'll set strange pictures dancing
>   On the wall,
> And all shall pay you homage
>   As is meet
> And shall lay the *blaue Blume*
>   At your feet....
>
>   (II. 240–1)

In the dining room, the poets gathered round the table to recite
their verses. Volokhova sat next to Blok, rapt and solemn. On re-
entering the main room with the Japanese lanterns they came upon
Lyubov' Dmitriyevna sitting in the corner of the sofa with Chulkov:

... with an almost imperceptible movement of her beautiful hand she was
stroking the edge of the fringe. Her eyes were lowered. I was puzzled by
the expression on her face, it was not childish or playfully wise as usual.
It was an expression I could not fathom. When Volokhova and Blok came
in she sat up straight and perfectly still for several moments. Volokhova
sank down into an armchair not far from the sofa. Lyubov' Dmitriyevna
rose, took off her necklace, and clasped it about the neck of the lilac mask.[19]

And so Lyubov' Dmitriyevna, too, entered into the fantastic
game, acting out her part, according to the ever-vigilant Aunt Maria,
'beyond all praise'. Perhaps to preserve morale, perhaps because the
affair with Andrey Bely had indeed, as she wrote in her memoirs,
woken her up, she allowed Chulkov to become her lover. This was
the first of many infidelities for which Blok—rightly—blamed himself.[p] Yet she did not seriously contemplate leaving him. Chulkov

---

° Volokhova had been deeply in love with a married man, the famous Moscow Art
Theatre actor V. I. Kachalov (V. I. Shverubovich, 1875–1948).
[p] In her memoirs Lyubov' Dmitriyevna expressly states that, had Blok wished it, she

too was married, to Nadezhda Grigor'evna, companion of his first exile, an intelligent and high-principled woman with whom he remained for the rest of his life. As for Blok, he might appear to forget Lyuba's existence but, in his present state of 'dehumanization', there were moments when he still needed her—more than ever before. As she later wrote:

Always Sasha's 'normal' state was thoroughly abnormal from the point of view of any ordinary person, and in this there was already a kind of 'sickness'; his changes of mood—from childish, unclouded merriment to gloomy, oppressed pessimism—his non-resistance, never ever the least resistance to anything bad, the flare-ups of irritability when he would break furniture and plates. After these he used to take fright and begin to weep, holding his head, and exclaim: 'What is happening to me! You see!' At such moments, however he may have hurt me just before, he at once became a child for me, I felt horrified that I had just been speaking to him as if to a grown-up person, had expected and demanded of him things one only has a right to expect of grownups, my heart was torn in pieces and I rushed to take him in my arms and he, as swiftly and childishly as before, submitted to the soothing, protecting arms, caresses, words—and again we would be 'comrades'.[20]

True, Lyubov' did once go to Volokhova and ask her in all solemnity if she were prepared to take responsibility for Blok, for the man and for his high calling. Volokhova replied that she had no wish to do so, but neither was she prepared to relinquish him— so exquisite was her enjoyment of his company. Lyuba proudly took refuge in the world of make-believe, began to dream of asserting herself as an independent personality, not just the wife of the poet, and of making a name for herself on the stage. To her first lover she remained always grateful for helping her to get over this very heavy ground as lightly as might be, and it is to his credit that, in an age when almost all his colleagues made copy of their affairs (including Blok himself, whose 'friend' in The Song of Fate clearly, and none too charitably, derives from Chulkov), he preserved a gentlemanly silence, stating merely:

Apart from ideas, running parallel to theory, life itself was extraordinarily complex and muddled. A sense of catastrophe came over the poets.... Aleksandr Blok at that time was the very personification of catastrophe.... Even in those years he said 'yes' to nothing, affirmed nothing but the blind element, surrendering himself to it alone, and believed in nothing besides.

---

would have found strength to take upon herself the part of the faithful wife, awaiting in cloistered isolation the return of her 'first love'. Instead, she followed him on what she describes as his 'Faustian path'.

Aleksandr Blok in 1907.

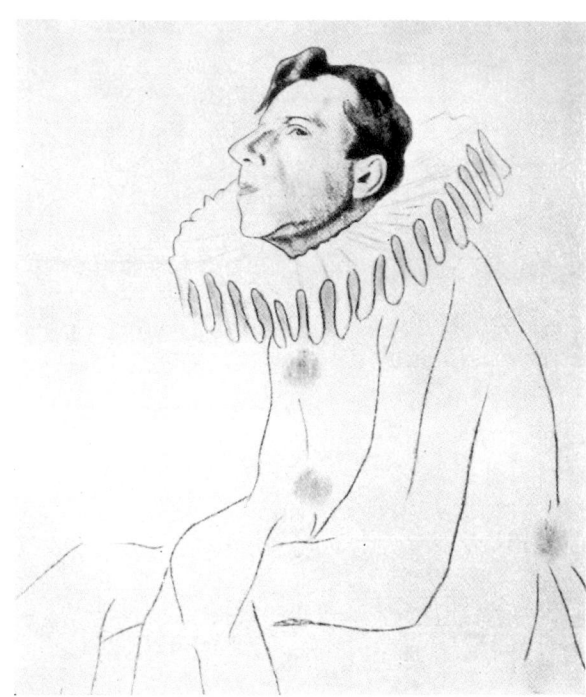

V. E. Meyerhold in the costume of Pierrot for Blok's play *The Puppet Booth*: a drawing by N. P. Ul'yanov, 1908.

Natal'ya Nikolayevna Volokhova.

Exceptionally punctual and neat, irreproachable in manners and life, proudly polite, enigmatically handsome, he was, for those who knew him closely, the most troubled, tormented and, in essence, already crazed man. Even at that time, Blok had burnt his boats. . . .

My relations with Blok were always uneasy. Sometimes we saw one another often (once it happened that we spent three whole days and nights together, wandering and sleeping in the outskirts of Petersburg), at other times we did not want to look one another in the face; it was difficult to pronounce a single word or to listen to what the other was saying. There were reasons for this.[21]

Yet the underlying sense of doom only served, that winter, to enhance the wild gaiety of the moment. During these magical 'twelve days of Christmas' and, indeed, throughout that mild and snowy season, the ethereal merriment continued. Blok and Volokhova, with or without their companions, moved in a world of their own:

Often, after the theatre, we went for long walks and Aleksandr Aleksandrovich introduced me to 'his town', as he called it. Passing the deserted Marsovo Pole, we would take the Troitskiy Bridge and gaze enthralled into the endless chains of street lamps, set like burning fires along the river and fading away at last into an infinity of darkness. We would walk further and stroll about the outskirts of the town, along the embankments, along the canals, crossing bridges. Aleksandr Aleksandrovich showed me all the places connected with his play, *The Stranger*: the bridge where the Astrologer had stood and met the Poet, the place where the Stranger had first appeared and the alley of street lamps into which she had vanished. We went into the little tavern which serves as the setting for the beginning of this play, a little tavern with painted walls.

Reality was so intermingled with the invention, the dreams of the poet, that I involuntarily lost the boundaries of the real and entered with awe and enchantment into this world of poetry that I had never known before. I had the feeling that I was receiving this extraordinary, legendary city as a gift at the hands of the poet.

Like Lyubov' Dmitriyevna before her, Volokhova was mesmerized by the suggestive power of Blok's imagination and, of course, by his poetry:

We did not content ourselves with loving and reading verses, we lived in them. Often we spoke in half-hints, half-words, yet we understood one another. Poetry was almost our everyday language. It was only natural that sometimes I yielded to the persuasive power of Blok's poetry and felt myself to be now Faina, now the Stranger.[22]

Maria Beketova maintains, though Verigina denies, that Volokhova did indeed owe a great part of her extraordinary charm to this
alchemy of poetry and autosuggestion:

I will say one thing. The poet did nc exaggerate the fascination of his 'Snow
Maiden'. Those who saw her at the time of his infatuation for her know
how spellbinding was her charm. A tall, slender figure, fine features, black
hair and eyes, truly 'winged' eyes, black, wide open 'the poppies of her
malicious eyes'. Striking, too, was her smile, glittering with the whiteness
of her teeth, a triumphant, victorious smile. Someone said at that time that
her eyes and her smile could flare through the darkness. Others said: 'a
sectarian madonna'. Yet, strange to say, all this radiance did not outlast
the poet's infatuation. He retired and she immediately faded. The mysterious glamour died away and left something not so very much out of the
ordinary—a pretty brunette.[23]

Be that as it may, Volokhova retained her own individuality sufficiently to turn Blok down—flat. For him, this was a new, stunning
experience. 'Nobody', he complained ruefully, 'has ever treated me
like this!' The poems of *The Snow Mask*, written in a bout of inspiration over two weeks, sometimes at a rate of as many as eight poems
in one day, celebrate the inspired play which masked the aerial
quality of the romance: the ball of the paper ladies; Volokhova,
laughingly making up the poet as if for the stage; the dark, snowy
walks; breath-taking sleigh rides with 'the blue wind playing over
sable furs'. Sometimes they seem to speak of more, but Volokhova
herself tells how Blok came to read her the poems he had written
and, coming to the lines about her kisses showered upon his upturned
face:

... he glanced up and, seeing the utter astonishment on my face, looked
somewhat disconcerted and, with a shamefaced smile, began to explain that,
in the realm of poetry, a little exaggeration is permissible. 'As the poets
say: "*sub specie aeternitatis*", which means literally,' he said with a smile,
'sauced up in eternity'.[24]

The Blok of this winter, the Blok who had set a whole theatre
dancing to the music of his verse, could not have been altogether
the hopeless, dark figure depicted by Chulkov. Yet one thing Chulkov said of him was perfectly true. It was indeed at this time that
he finally 'burnt his boats'.

> The great wings of a snowy bird
> Have made a blizzard of my mind

(II. 249)

he wrote, and the leitmotiv of the 'poems of this silver-snowy winter' (II. 213), this 'scorching winter' (II. 226), is perdition and death. The poet dedicated the *Snow Mask* cycle 'To the tall woman in black with the winged eyes, enamoured of the lights and darkness of my snowy city'. Acknowledging the dedication, Volokhova wrote in the poet's own copy,[q] 'Joyfully I accept this strange book, joyfully and with fear—in it there is so much beauty, poetry, death. I await the accomplishment of your task."

As the epigraph to *The Song of Fate* recalls, 'he who would save his soul must lose it'. Dazzled by the snowflakes, the street lamps, and the stars, deafened by the 'sultry moaning of the snow (II. 254), Blok was utterly lost:

> In the sky your dark eyes have blazed up
> So clearly:
> And I have forgotten the landmarks
> Of the beautiful country—
> In your blinding light, o comet!
> In your blinding light, o night of silver snow!
>
> (II. 218)

And to this aimless oblivion he clung: 'I want no ships out of the distance ...' (II. 224).

The 'winged trochees'[25] preponderant throughout this cycle were always, for Blok, the metre of death, and death is here his desire: to burn away amidst the snows of oblivion, to lie dead upon the snowy embankment and to forget those purposeful ships plunging on through the icy waters of the night:

> Snowy foam obscures the sunset.
> *You* rise behind me, far away;
> There, where the great ships lately vanished
> Into the unreturning spray.
>
> .   .   .   .   .
>
> From the white shore in the distance
> Calling of faint horns swells and grows ...
>
> (II. 214)

---

[q] Preserved in Pushkin House, Leningrad.

[r] In Moscow in 1960, I asked Natal'ya Volokhova what she had meant by 'the accomplishment of your task'. She thought for a moment, then queried with a little laugh in her voice: 'Didn't I say "miracle"? Blok and I often talked of a "miracle", of the possibility of his becoming a real, live human being. I suppose that is what I meant.... He avoided me after 1908 but of course I read his poetry—later on, after he died mostly. I think, in the *Third Volume*, he achieved his miracle.'

Out of the very heart of despair, Blok heard this far calling of horns, and, even as he cast off the last vestiges of his former self, he began, painfully and very slowly, to reach out towards a new, more limited incarnation. His dream of the Stranger had lulled him and led him on to transform life into art. The real woman, Natal'ya Volokhova, who 'knew beyond doubt that fairy tales were in books and that in life there was nothing but prose' (II. 245), refused to play the demonic part for which he had cast her. She would walk and drive and talk with Blok; she would sit withdrawn and melancholy at Vyacheslav Ivanov's bohemian gatherings in the tower, all incandescent with the reflected glory of his verse; but she would not love him—because he was not real.[5] The Snow Mask is the climactic cycle of Blok's demonic, self-destructive aesthetism. It contains only the faintest hint of the awakening to come: the far blowing of the horns, and the second stanza of the poem 'The Second Christening':

> The blizzards have blown my door in,
> The cold through my cottage flows,
> Baptised with a second christening I
> In a new-formed font of snows.
>
> On this new world's threshold pausing
> I see people, and deeds to be done....

Here, however, the 'new world' is immediately rejected:

> But the pride of this second christening
> Has turned my heart to ice:
> You tell me the spring will come again?
> You promise me yet more life?
>
> But see how the heart rejoices!
> The snows have blocked out the sky.
> There will be no spring. I don't want it:
> The third christening is—to die.

(II. 216).

And so, in the lightness of despair, Blok passed merrily through that winter: 'What I now call life', he wrote to his old friend A. V. Hippius on 20 January 1907,

... is something very like a nightmare, unrelentingly joyful or unrelentingly miserable—and all the rest is what I set down on paper sitting at my

---

[5] Aleksey Remizov speaks of Blok as a 'non-human', to whom, as compensation, a great gift was given: 'a different kind of ear; not our ear. Blok heard music.'[26] Through all the poetry of 1906–7, there is the sense of a Faustian pact with some demonic force, as though the poet had traded his humanity for poetry.

writing table and in that way give life to many things that are essential to me. I am writing a lot, in prose and verse, partly for money[f] and partly for myself, and I have no regular job. Thanks to all this our new flat which Lyubov' and I moved to (you don't know about that, do you? It's such an age since we saw one another) has taken on a bohemian character: the wind whistles, there are many visitors, much talk and many silences.... I actively do not want to take on a regular job and for the moment I manage to earn up to 150 roubles a month, which is enough for modest requirements. At a time when my requirements are becoming less modest (as, for instance, a taste for strong drink and such like) that is not always enough. As you see, all this is most strange and I sometimes rub my own forehead and wonder how it has all come about; nevertheless, it suits me better than any other way of life would because much is in a state of transition and burning itself out, and in that there is much joy—albeit 'unhoped-for'.

(VIII. 176–7)

The last event of the theatrical season which involved all Blok's set was Meyerhold's production of Leonid Andreyev's *A Man's Life*. This production, like *The Puppet Booth*, was a triumph. Blok went to almost every performance and watched from the wings, or rather from the darkness at the back of the stage. At this time, it seemed to him that Andreyev, with his rejection of all accepted values, and profound moral pessimism, was giving voice to all the anguish of his generation, though he did let fall the remark to Volokhova that the man was 'stupider than his own thoughts', and did not understand himself how great he could sometimes be!

Verigina thought even then that Andreyev's nihilism was overdone. She told Blok so after the first night and received a severe snub, such as the poet was past master at inflicting when the mood took him. Next day, 27 February 1907, he wrote her a most characteristic letter:

Much respected and dear Valentina Petrovna, please forgive me for what I said. I know very well that one should not speak so in front of other people. I want to say a few words of explanation but not of justification, for I feel I was in the wrong. I know that just now you do not feel Leonid Andreyev, perhaps because you are so tired[u] or perhaps because you do not know that last despair which bores into his soul. Every sentence of his is a hideous

[f] Blok was writing a commentary on Pushkin's verse for S. A. Vengerov, for whom he had already made several translations from Byron in the autumn of 1905 and, in 1906, a 'literary-historical compilation' (VIII. 144) on the early nineteenth-century playwright Griboyedov. The notes to Pushkin's early poems were published in vol. XI of the Brokganz-Efron Collected Works edited by Vengerov.

[u] It was the end of a strenuous season.

Title-page by L. Bakst for *The Earth in Snow*, 1907

screech, like a saw, when he is weak and a man, like a bestial roar when he is creative and an artist. These screeches and yells go right through me, I am frozen by them and become a part of them myself so that I no longer feel my living soul, become dull and hate everybody who is *not with us* (because in such moments I am with L. Andreyev—and we are both despairing and desperate). This last despair is too close to me and it produces a kind of last sincerity, and can be turned inside out. So there you are, please forgive me. I should like you to know how I feel towards you. Perhaps in you I scourge my own vices." I want to see as much truth as possible in all things. Please, give me a good scold and forgive me.

I kiss your hand

Your sincerely loving
ALEKSANDR BLOK
(VIII. 181)

When *A Man's Life* came to an end the troupe broke up and Volokhova left St. Petersburg to tour the provinces. She would not allow Blok to accompany her, feeling that it was not consonant either with the dignity of his vocation or with the fragile romanticism of their relationship. Before rejoining her friend on tour, Verigina went skiing with Meyerhold in Finland, then returned to stay for a few days with the Bloks.

Blok was sitting for his portrait, commissioned by the Moscow journal *Zolotoye Runo*, to the artist Konstantin Somov. Kuzmin, Chulkov, and Verigina took turns amusing the poet during the sittings. Aleksandra Andreyevna, already worried enough by the wild turn her son's life had taken, was horrified to note the Dorian Gray effect of Somov's picture, which shows, as Blok himself cheerfully inscribed it when he presented it to her:

> Myself, a venal, shameful figure
> With rings of blue beneath the eyes.

Volokhova considered the portrait deliberately malicious and declared in her memoirs that Somov took Blok out drinking the night before each session to obtain the seedy look he required. This look, she protested, was quite uncharacteristic of Blok who 'conveyed the impression of a balanced, sober person, well turned out and pedantic'.[27] Verigina, who had been present at several sittings and remembered Blok's face at the time as 'young', 'chiselled', and 'permeated with laughter', objected to the 'vampire lips'. The artist himself was not satisfied with his work. As for Aunt Maria: 'There was

---

" Here—irony and detachment.

almost no likeness—and that dreadful mouth, those bemused eyes. And instead of those golden, silky curls— where did that dull, woolly head of hair come from? ... one cannot but regret that the portrait gives quite a wrong impression of Blok.'[28]

The sitter himself was uncertain. There was something he admired in the work, but it irked him. Later he came to dislike it. Blok's own idea of his double was not the soft, self-indulgent sensualist of Somov's portrait. At about this time, seeing an old man in a shabby-genteel suit, arrogant head thrown back and eyes glassy with drink, he had noted in his diary—'*dvoynichok*' (an oddly affectionate diminutive of the word 'double'). Blok's evil double is usually older than himself: dry, brittle, eaten up by some devouring inner sickness. Somov would have done better to have sought out the poet's father, whom Blok so curiously resembled on his deathbed.

When Verigina too left Petersburg, she took with her the last echoes of their carefree winter laughter. Lyuba and Blok literally 'packed her off':

Lyubov' Dmitriyevna helped me to do my shopping. Aleksandr Aleksandrovich played the fool, going into ecstasies over every bit of nonsense. ... He took my new portmanteau and packed me into it, then he and Lyubov' Dmitriyevna solemnly carried me round the room, after which he pronounced with a sigh of relief: 'Yes, indeed, a thoroughly serviceable article!'[29]

4

The Bloks stored their furniture and let their flat. Lyuba, having bravely sought her mother-in-law's advice as to whether or not she and Blok should separate, went to Shakhmatovo without him. He moved back temporarily to the Barracks to be with Aleksandra Andreyevna who was preparing to follow Frants Feliksovich, now a colonel with his own regiment, to Revel.[w] From 16 to 20 April, Blok was in Moscow. There he saw Volokhova and arranged to write regular critical surveys for *Zolotoye Runo*. Then he returned to Petersburg to an entirely new situation.

Lyubov', alone among the Beketovs (with Aunt Maria, Sofia Andreyevna and her sons), practised for the theatre and possessed her soul in patience. Blok, alone in Petersburg, played with the idea of writing short stories (*Z.K.* 92), wrote insomniac, frightening

---

[w] The old Russian name for Tallin, the capital of Esthonia, at that time still a part of the Russian Empire.

poetry about the White Nights, and spent the warm afternoons wandering about the outskirts of the city, often in the company of Chulkov. It was doubtless at this time that they so assiduously sought 'truth at the bottom of a glass'.[30]

More than ever, Lyuba became identified in Blok's mind with Shakhmatovo. He wrote to her often. On 13 May: 'You are important to me and absolutely essential; just as much as N.N., though of course in a *completely* different way. Both of you are part of my fate. If that hurts you it can't be helped, it is as it should be.' On 21 May: 'My thoughts are darker and sometimes I feel a kind of terror, which doesn't happen when you are with me.' On 26 May: 'I am lonely without you. The sky is too high, the water is too deep.'[31]

Occasionally, he went down to see her. He made a poem of one of these visits in which his 'Tsarevna' greets him calmly and cheerfully, shows him where the white roses they had planted together were coming into bloom and where the convolvulus trained to overrun the porch had lately faded. When, overcome by restlessness, he again feels the call of life and poetry (or, in the language of fairy tale into which he still lapsed when writing of Lyuba and Shakhmatovo, of 'battle' and 'distant lands'), she bids him farewell, bravely and serenely as she had bidden him welcome, 'And once more the harness-bells ring out across the meadow' (III. 247).

He could not yet settle with Lyuba in Shakhmatovo, although it pleased him that she was there, in the sanctuary of his home. Once more, he was *busy*. He was writing a new cycle of longish poems inspired by his homeless wandering about Petersburg, dedicated to Chulkov and entitled *Free Thoughts*.

There is no sharper contrast in all Blok's poetry than that between *Free Thoughts* and *The Snow Mask*. It is as if, having turned his slow but powerful concentration away from the contemplation of nature and eternity, Blok had at first perceived his early twentieth-century city through a shimmering haze, and had only now, for the first time, achieved sobriety and sharp focus.

The free verse and blank iambs of the new cycle are in complete contrast to the dancing mixed metres and abundant internal rhyme and assonance of *The Snow Mask*. White, Apollonian clarity succeeds the Dionysian storms and music, even as the northern sun ruthlessly illumines the race course, the pleasure parks, the river-bound 'islands' and the shallow, sandy coast of the Gulf of Finland which formed the objects of Blok's contemplation on his idle summer jauntings about the capital.

Yet there is one link between the poetry of *The Snow Mask* and that of the ensuing summer: 'the shortest rhyme of all', 'the winged yet muffled rhyme of death' (II. 128). The first poem is actually entitled 'On Death' and begins:

> More often than before I stroll the town
> More often I see death—and then I smile
> A slow and thoughtful smile. And so, what of it?
> It's as I wish. It is my nature to be thus aware
> That, in her own good time, she'll come for me.
>
> (II. 295)

With the curious, analytical detachment of a True Thomas who has already spent his apprenticeship in the Land of Faerie, Blok contemplates human death. With a few masterly strokes he draws a picture of a drowned man, sighted among the floating logs by the shore. The crowd runs to pull him out,

> ... the water pouring
> From his long, outstretched corpse.

Indifferent, yet curious, they surround the body:

> ... And I listened
> While a pontifical but well-primed workman
> Laid down the law about the daily damage
> That people do themselves by drink ...
>
> I'll go and roam some more. While the sun shines,
> While the heat lasts, and while my head
> Is dull, my thoughts still slow ...
>   Heart!
> Be my guide. And with a smile observe
> This thing called death more closely. You will tire,
> You'll never stand so gay a life
> As that which I am leading. Such hatred
> And such love as those that I bear in me
> Are quite beyond endurance.
>   Yet I want
> Always to look into the eyes of people
> And to drink wine, and to kiss women.
> To fill the evening with untame desires,
> When heat prevents me dreaming dreams.
> And to sing songs! And listen to the wind.
>
> (II. 298)

This was the mood of Blok's summer. He wandered through the suburbs, recording all he saw with Olympian detachment:

> I stand on a steep bank. Above me
> A granite gravestone. And below me runs
> A path, white in the dusk.
> And anyone who looks up from below
> Might well take fright, so still I stand
> In my broad hat, amongst the graves of night,
> Arms folded, slender, in love with all the world.

(II. 299–300)

Like some adolescent poltergeist, he throws fir cones and sand at courting couples, like a satyr he pursues a girl across the dunes (II. 306–7). The lyrical persona is totally 'in ecstasy', 'in alliance with nature against people'.

It is hard to tell how much Blok's summer adventures, as recounted in *Free Thoughts*, were indeed 'sauced up in eternity'. It seems to have mattered little to him whether or not he was alone. Even when he appeared the life and soul of a merry company, he was essentially withdrawn, listening to the pulsing life of the world about him or to the slow, cool promptings of his own mind.

Korney Chukovsky, for instance, writes:

Reading his five-footed iambs on 'The North Sea' which in their precise, classical imagery are the only lines of this type in our poetry that can stand comparison with Pushkin's, I remembered the seaside resort at Sestroretsk with the big restaurant right on the edge of the shore and the tubby, pre-historic motor boat that was hired out by a half-naked, tattooed Greek and into which, after a perilous walk out along the wooden jetty, climbed Georgiy Chulkov, if I remember rightly, and Zinoviy Grzhebin (the artist and later the editor of Shipovnik),[x] and the unwithstandably, unbelievably handsome Blok—slender and tanned, in a wide-brimmed artist's hat.

That evening he seemed (to the superficial eye, at least) so victoriously happy, so supremely in harmony with all his surroundings, that I am still astonished at those wrathful lines which he wrote under the impression of this expedition:

> What have these dandies done to the seashore,
> These summer crowds, these fashionable wenches?
> They set up little tables and puff smoke,
> Chew food and sip their lemonade. Then stroll
> Along the foreshore, laughing mirthlessly
> And poisoning the salty air with gossip.[32]

[x] A Moscow publishing firm which brought out almanacs of new writing from 1907 to 1917.

There is no evidence to show that Blok was *deliberately* trying to improve his technique, to objectivize his hitherto strictly subjective Muse. As a poet, he never forced himself; indeed, he was constitutionally incapable of doing so:

> 'What needs must be—it needs must be,'
> So from my mother's knee
> I heard the organ-grinder sing
> And—took to poetry.
>
> And love bloomed in the tendriled hair
> The early-saddened eyes
> And I was caught in rosy snares
> By women, many times.
>
> As *needs must be*, it came to pass:
> The longing, love, and verse,
> All swept away and carried past
> With the calm river's course.
>
> As night is blind, so I was blind
> And thought no sight to need ...
> But once they set the dark door wide
> And said to me: *God speed!*
>
> That night the river rose in spate.
> The white ice cracked and split
> 'The river runs again', I thought,
> And rose, and followed it ...

12 April 1907
(II. 130–1)

With a rapt sense of purpose which brooked no interruption, yet with no clear idea why or whither, like a sleepwalker or an automaton, Blok was walking out of his earthbound, aristocratic nineteenth-century domestic idyll into the inimical industrial, gravity-defying world of the twentieth century. He persuaded himself that he was going to seek out Volokhova; that she was the wild, untamed spirit of Russia:

Only Natal'ya Nikolayevna is Russian, with her Russian 'by chance', not knowing from whence she comes, proud, beautiful, and free. With a few minor, slavish habits and an enormous freedom ...

(Z.K. 94)

He dreamt of meeting her again in Petersburg next season. The play, *The Song of Fate*, was already in his head; Nekrasov's *Koro-*

beyniki which, in the play, is a kind of theme song of Russia, was 'on his brain':

Korobeyniki is sung with a kind of secret sadness.... The voice loses itself tearfully in the rainy distances. In that voice are the great spaces of Russia, and the red rowan and the girls' coloured sleeves and all ruined youth. Autumn drunkenness. Rain and sunshine to come.

That is where *her* [Volokhova's] secret will lie, and mine. That is how I must write the play—*this autumn*.

(Z.K. 94–5, entry for 9 June 1907)

To Lyuba he wrote in a letter headed '24 May. Night':

Dear friend,

I am writing you from the station at Sestroretsk. I am sitting drinking. The play is getting along.... A large part of the first act is about you.

In the letter he folded a leaf from a wood where they had once walked together, and ended:

Write to me and help.

SASHA
(VIII. 185–6)

Together with the leaf, he enclosed a poem which was later to figure as the first lyric of the cycle *The Motherland*:

> You went away. Across the desert
> Of burning sands I stumble on.
> No word of pride, from this day onwards,
> Will form itself upon my tongue.
>
> For what is past—I'll not regret it,
> Your stature now is clear to me.
> For me—a Christ unresurrected—
> You are my native Galilee.
>
> What though another may caress you,
> What though wild rumour grow and spread:
> The Son of Man, in all this desert,
> Does not know where to lay his head.

30 May 1907
(III. 246)

5

In July, Blok joined Lyubov' at Shakhmatovo and, for a few weeks, they seem to have taken great comfort in one another's company.

In *The Song of Fate* German, the hero (a scarcely disguised self-portrait), sets off in search of the mysterious Faina (Volokhova in her romantic incarnation as the spirit of Russia, a sectarian madonna turned gypsy singer). Before he goes, he prays:

'O Lord, I cannot go on like this. I am too well off in my quiet white house. Give me strength to take leave of it and to see what life in the world is like. Only preserve the ardour of my young soul and my living conscience. I ask nothing more of You.'

(IV. 110–11)

Such prayers are granted. There was a place in Blok's soul where he could still sometimes dwell at peace with Lyubov', when she was sufficiently at peace to join him there.

Even these few weeks of respite, however, were disturbed by a new drama from an almost forgotten source. Andrey Bely had reappeared on Blok's horizon that spring with a review of *Nechayannaya Radost'*, published in *Pereval*. On 24 March, Blok had written him through his Moscow publishers, and thanked him for this review, which contained some sharp but percipient criticism. In his letter, he defended his 'present road', which, he felt, was 'appointed' for him and which it was his 'duty' to follow (VIII. 184).

A few weeks after this, however, Andrey Bely, Ellis, and Zinaida Hippius had launched a positive fusillade against the 'mystic anarchists' in *Vesy*. Several articles, particularly those of Hippius writing under the pen name of 'Comrade Germann', were not free of personal abuse and insinuations of an extra-literary character. The particular object of their execration was Chulkov. Bely, having heard rumours of the editor of *Fakely*'s success where he had failed, was beside himself with jealousy and moral indignation, a fact which became only too apparent in his polemical writings.

The crisis came, however, with Bely's reaction to a completely new departure in Blok's critical prose: his survey in *Zolotoye Runo* of the work of the realists grouped about the publishing house of Znaniye. This had been a part of the poet's springtime meditation on life and Russia, the literary equivalent of the symbolic *Korobeyniki*. It seemed to him at this time that a *rapprochement* with the best contemporary writers of the 'other' camp would be a natural and legitimate development for Russia Symbolism: 'The Symbolists are moving towards realism because they are fed up with the close air of their cells; they want fresh air, action on a wide scale, healthy work. In this movement there is something reminiscent of the Russian intelligentsia's going to the people....' (V. 206.)

In saying this, Blok had only given expression to a general tendency, even among the most refined exponents of Symbolism, to tackle more real, contemporary themes and to make peace with their foes of yesterday: the populists, the realists, Maksim Gorky and Leonid Andreyev.[y] Merezhkovsky, however, out of touch with the Russian scene, had chosen this moment to take philosophical issue with Gorky. In a book entitled *Le Mufle-Roi*,[z] he had launched a fierce attack against Gorky's Nietzschean hero, the 'tramp' who is without ties or faith and who despises the masses of hard-working, God-fearing people who live in houses, till the soil, and make things with their hands.

It was Gorky, first and foremost, whom Blok set out to defend in his survey. He reminded Merezhkovsky that he himself had once been an ardent defender of the Nietzschean-type hero, and continued:

I would even go so far as to affirm that, if there is a reality behind the concept of 'Russia', or, better, of 'Rus'', something quite distinct from territory, government, established Church and social hierarchy, etc.; if this great, spacious, sorrowful and promised land which stretches out beyond the bounds of our vision really does exist—then, to a very great extent, we have to acknowledge that it is Gorky who is its representative.... by blood, by the nobility of his aims, by the 'infinity of his ideal' (the words are V. V. Rozanov's) and by the sheer scale of his soul's agony, Gorky is a true Russian writer.

(v. 103)

For Blok, brought up in the Beketov reverence for literature, the words a 'true Russian writer' were the ultimate accolade.

It was only natural that, having broken out of his home, Blok should now break out of his literary circle and cast a friendly eye over that vast, sprawling plain of Russian literature which stretched out and away—at first sight unimpressive in its grey sameness—beyond the closed gardens and turreted, mock-medieval battlements of such Symbolist strongholds as Ory, Grif, *Zolotoye Runo*, *Pereval*, and Skorpion. His assessment of the realists' literary merits was conservative enough:

Taxes, the people, the proletariat, the police, officers, red flags, comrades, bayonets, barricades, pogroms, spies—all these overflow from one volume

---

[y] Filosofov and A. Gornfel'd had both written on this subject in the newspaper *Tovarishch*, and Shipovnik was already publishing Symbolist works side by side with realist contributions.

[z] Published in Paris; the Russian title was *Gryadushchyy Kham*.

to another—dull, yet so grandiose in sheer quantity that it achieves a kind of solemnity. There are absolutely no limits, no sense of measure, the instability of literary form is beyond all calculation, there is no telling the difference between a story, a feuilleton, an article, or a proclamation, or even between the old and the young.

(V. 112)

Such words could scarcely be understood as flattery and Bely himself would undoubtedly have subscribed to Blok's enthusiastic assessment of both Leonid Andreyev and of Sologub, the only two realist authors besides Gorky to merit his unqualified approval.[aa] He could not, however, forgive Blok his championship of Gorky against Merezhkovsky: neither could he forgive him for writing of the 'airless cells' of Symbolism. Above all, however, he could not forgive him for writing in *Zolotoye Runo*.

This was not for ideological reasons. The proprietor, N. Ryabushinsky, a rich merchant with a desire to patronize the decadents and a will of his own, had fallen foul of the original staff of the journal: first of Bryusov, whose aim it had been that the new Symbolists' organ should not get out of hand and impinge upon the importance of *Vesy* and *Skorpion*; and then of Bely. Bely had left the journal in a huff, intending to take with him Kuzmin and the Merezhkovskys, and now what must Blok do but pick up the post of staff critic which he had let drop, accepting conditions which he had found 'unacceptable'. Probably Bely had not realized that Blok, unacquainted with the situation in Moscow, had come to an agreement with Ryabushinsky in March, *before* he had determined his own course of action, and before all the correspondence, discussion, and 'gangings-up' had got fairly under way.[bb] Be that as it may, he saw

---

[aa] The appearance of the arch-decadent Sologub in a survey of realist literature may now seem surprising, but *Melkiy Bes* (The Little Demon), Sologub's short novel of provincial life first published in *Voprosy Zhizni* in 1905, had been widely acclaimed as a 'realist' work. In fact, it is a brilliant example of a peculiarly Russian form of grotesque deriving from Gogol, Saltykov-Shchedrin, and Sukhovo-Kobylin. Blok mentioned it in connection with the problems of sex, which he found the realists, with their heavy naturalism, had signally failed to resolve.

[bb] Valeriy Bryusov, for instance, did not write to Sologub of what was going on till 21 June 1907: 'As you will see from *Vesy*, there are all kinds of schisms among the "decadents". ... We have multiplied too fast and it remains only for us to devour one another, it's a question of the struggle for existence. You read our attack on the "Petersburg Authors" ("The stamped galosh"); that was a sortie against Ory and particularly against A. Blok. This Blok is now answering us back in *Zolotoye Runo*, which is only too glad to have its revenge on us. Of course, *Pereval* will not pass over "Trikhina" [a particularly scurrilous attack on Chulkov and Blok by Z. Hippius. A.P.] either. In a word—fighting all along the line.'[33] Z. Hippius was writing to Bely of her intention to leave *Zolotoye Runo* 'with you and Bryusov but *not* with Kuzmin' as late as August 1907.[34]

Blok's publication of his article 'On the Realists' in *Zolotoye Runo* as the action not only of a 'traitor', but of a 'strike-breaker'.

As at the beginning of their correspondence, Blok and Bely sat down to write to one another almost on the same day and, once again, their letters crossed. On 6 August, from the calm of Shakhmatovo, Blok wrote Bely a firm but, on the whole, conciliatory letter. Troubled by the tone of the polemics in *Vesy*—and still more by the fact that the secretary of *Zolotoye Runo* had refused to repeat so much as the gist of what Bely had been *saying* about him"—Blok began by reminding his 'brother' of their unique relationship in the past and of the fact that they were both of them 'in the service of Russian literature': 'The situation between us has become completely abnormal. It is not only that I feel a genuine emotional need to write you this letter, but I also consider it my duty to do so.' Patiently, and not without humour ('You say I am worse than Chekhov—a perfectly true statement, but curious!'), Blok pointed out the contradictions in all that Bely had written about him over the past few months and, above all, the mistake he was making in lumping together all the 'Petersburg' poets (Blok himself, Vyacheslav Ivanov, Chulkov, and Gorodetsky) as a 'group'.

He then went on to state his own position: he had, he wrote, nothing in common with 'mystical anarchism' or any of the other isms thought up in Vyacheslav Ivanov's tower; his poetry was 'Romantic' and 'Symbolist'—nothing more. While prepared to learn from constructive criticism he objected to criticism founded on ill-natured gossip; of the personalities involved he was prepared to defend Chulkov as a person; Vyacheslav Ivanov he thought 'a profound and educated writer and a splendid poet', but understood his *Weltanschauung* as something purely lyrical; Sergey Gorodetsky he considered an excellent poet. Finally, he valued Bely very highly and agreed with a number of his principles.

'I consider that I am firmly on course', he wrote, 'and that all I have written is an organic continuation of the original *Verses about*

" Just how damaging this was can be judged by the account of N. V. Valentinov (Vol'sky),[35] a straightforward, somewhat puritanical Menshevik who had spent many years as an illegal revolutionary, sharing Lenin's exile in Geneva in 1904. Vol'sky, who made no allowances for Bely's creative hyperbole and never met Blok, was so shocked by all Bely told him of Blok's cupidity and vice that, five years later, in 1912, he threatened to resign from his post as secretary of the Moscow newspaper *Russkoye Slovo* rather than yield to pressure from Petersburg to appoint Blok a regular contributor; and, years after the Second World War, he braved public opinion to revive the old polemics of 1907–8, seeking to show by quotations from Blok's diaries (read in the light of Bely's accusations) that Blok had been a positive monster of luxurious cruelty, degeneracy, and cold-hearted hypocrisy.

the Most Beautiful Lady. In view of this, I do not understand your attitude to my literary activity, in so far as you see my works as bearing no relationship to what went before.' The letter concludes with a request that Bely should indicate the basic points on which, in his opinion, they still differed, since their attitude to 'all these dock-tailed new theories' was in fact fundamentally the same (VIII. 188–91).

This was nothing less than the truth. Before writing his letter, Blok had noted his agreement with Andrey Bely and his disagreement with Vyacheslav Ivanov in his diary (*Z.K.* 96). Bely's contention was that Symbolism was faced with real problems which required to be examined in context by all its practitioners. Instead of this, the movement was apparently degenerating into a multiplicity of sects, and Bely, a passionate believer in community whose commitment to Symbolism was total and vocational, saw this as the disintegration of a sacred fellowship. Bryusov, who in fact never considered Symbolism as *more* than a literary movement but whose attitude towards it was thoroughly proprietary, encouraged Bely for reasons of his own. With his fanatical energy and effortless rhetoric, the younger man was a splendid sheep dog, and Bryusov, controlling Bely's almost demented activity by the occasional almost imperceptible signal, was happy to stand back and watch his attempts to round up the scattered flock.

Blok, perfectly well aware of this, had no intention of allowing Bryusov and Bely to pen him up exclusively for their publications (*Vesy*, *Pereval*, and *Skorpion*); yet, at the same time, he did not want to stage a break-away in the company of Vyacheslav Ivanov and Chulkov, or to be artificially separated from Bely with whom, in spite of all misunderstandings, he still felt he had more in common than with any other writer.

Nevertheless, the letter he received from Bely by the same post as he had sent off his painstaking exposition of his own position, tried his patience beyond endurance. Beginning with the insultingly formal address '*Milostivyy gosudar*' Aleksandr Aleksandrovich', Bely continued:

I hasten to inform you of a piece of news that should give pleasure to us both. Our relations are broken off for ever. It was difficult for me finally to renounce [my idea of] your inner image, for it is my custom to take seriously inward ties with people who call themselves my friends. For this reason I was extremely unhappy, tried to exhort you to answer for many of your actions (this was unpleasant for me as well as for you). I continued to observe you from afar. Finally, when your application to, *pardon*,[dd] article

[dd] In French in the original.

about the realists appeared in *Runo*, an article in which you shamelessly wrote things that you do not believe, everything became clear to me. Any further attempt to talk things out with you was clearly superfluous. Now I am at ease and calm. I hasten to tell you that, should we be fated to meet (which God forbid) at some future time and were you to offer me your hand first, I should return the courtesy. If, on the other hand, you try to pretend that we are not acquainted or if you simply avoid meeting me, I shall be the more relieved.

Accept etc.
Boris Bugayev[36]

Blok, fresh from his effort to achieve a better understanding, was really angry. He replied with an ultimatum. Either Bely was to apologize for his insinuations, or to send his second. Blok's letter was dated 8 August and he gave Bely ten days: 'If by 18 August you have done neither the one nor the other I shall be obliged to take the requisite measures myself' (VIII. 192).

On the following day, he wrote to Zhenya Ivanov, asking him to be his second, if necessary, and generally to take on the role of intermediary, since he was the only person conversant with the whole background story of the troubles between himself and Bely:

It is clear to me now that, unless he is mad, there is no way out other than a duel, the situation obviously calls for decisive action: either he is mad, in which case I am infinitely sorry for him and ready to do more than make peace with him, or not—and it is essential to put a stop to his conduct, and the only way to do that now is by a duel.

(VIII. 193)

None of them, however, really knew how a duel was conducted. Blok thought, though he was none too sure, that the principals should bear all expenses, and hastened to put the impecunious Zhenya's mind at rest in this score, assuring him that he was unusually flush and would pay his train fare to Moscow and any other overheads. Zhenya, however, had no taste for vicarious drama. In his imagination, he was already burying Bely darkly at dead of night and smuggling Blok out of the country:

Sasha, dear, what is to be done now? You have already switched the points like the linesman at Pavlovsk and the collision is inevitable ... but I implore you, do you understand, I implore you not to do it. ... It seems to me quite certain that you will shoot him and the thought turns me cold because it is not in our spirit: know ye not of what Spirit ye are? Of course he won't go into explanations and it's quite obvious he'll just agree to the duel as your letter challenges him to do: and that hint at his not being well in the head will hurt his feelings terribly.

Why did you go and pay attention to a lot of stupid rumours about your-self and let your faith in your own way be shaken? After all, you are older than A. Bely,[ee] and healthier, and wiser ... and you are an aristocrat by nature, so what does it matter to you what nonsense the *hoi polloi* may choose to talk, you have a care to yourself and be firm and patient, *that* is in our spirit.... Of course you will have realized by now that I shall refuse to be a second as I have no qualifications for the part. I have no idea what one is supposed to do, or how. How to get hold of weapons, how to conduct explanations. And various other minor details which are enough to make the blood freeze in your veins: where one takes the corpses after-wards, for instance, and what one does with them. As to talking to Bely, I suppose I ought to, only no good will come of it, because he's almost off his head and because whatever I say to him is only going to annoy him all the more, because he doesn't like me and, as he wrote himself, he sees me as an instrument of the devil.[ff] Nothing good is likely to come of our meeting and I shan't go just to make things worse. Anyway, I feel guilty towards Bely, though I don't really know why and I'm afraid he might take my personal apologies as coming from you and that might com-promise you.

After having said again, in no uncertain terms, that all Bely's wild accusations stemmed from unrequited love and that Blok would have done better to sympathize than to have challenged him to a duel, Zhenya called his friend to account for failing to live up to his own precepts:

You said yourself that it is better people should think worse of us than we deserve and now that the gossip has become really nasty you've let it get you down, but damn it all it is *only* gossip and you know perfectly well that no one will *seriously* believe in it, if only because, if you really must know, there are certain people to whom outrageous gossip simply does not stick and people don't believe the gossip about them, although of course this does not stop them repeating it.[37]

It was not Zhenya, however, but Bely himself who saved the situa-tion. As always, his fury had been fed by Blok's apparent indifference so, on receiving his beloved enemy's first letter, he had sat down at once to write a detailed and closely reasoned answer—quite forget-ting that he himself had just broken off their relations 'for ever'. While he was still warming to his theme in an almost 3,000-word reply, he received Blok's challenge. This, also, merited a lengthy answer. Sensibly, he kept them separate. Having expressed his

[ee] In fact, Bely, born on 16 October 1880, was a few weeks older than Blok.
[ff] The previous autumn Bely, while waiting for Lyubov' to summon him to the Lakhtins-kaya flat, had been acutely and jealously aware that Zhenya was already welcome there, and that, when he had visited Bely's rooms, it had been with a mandate from the Bloks to talk him out of insisting on an interview.

'extreme amazement' at Blok's violent reaction to his own letter, Bely, who had presumably kept a copy, took another look at it himself, found it genuinely rather unjust, and unhesitatingly withdrew the allegation to which Blok had most vigorously objected: i.e. that his article about the realists was motivated by a desire to publish his own work with Znaniye. Blok's first letter, Bely wrote, now opened the way for him to explain his *own* point of view in a less offensive manner. His 'older and wiser' friend, feeling more than a little ridiculous, accepted the apology with relief and apologized in his turn. To Zhenya he could now write reassuringly:

My dear friend Zhenya,
    Everything is all right. Andrey Bely has 'taken back his words'. He and I are now deep in a tremendously extensive correspondence. I no longer think that he is mad, his letters are intelligent. I won't write more now, but for your letter I hug you hard and kiss you.[38]

6

Bely, in both his letters—still couched in offensively formal language—proceeded to make the point that, however much Blok might disassociate himself from mystic anarchism in private, he not only constantly appeared in print together with Vyacheslav Ivanov and Chulkov,[gg] but he had made no move towards a *public* statement of his independent position even when their supposed alliance had been 'broadcast all over Europe' in an article in the *Mercure de France*.[hh] Blok was forcibly struck by the justice of this statement. Suddenly he realized that not only was Bely basically in the right, but that, behind all the hysteria, there were real and deep wounds for which he himself was partly responsible. He took the train to Moscow in the hope of meeting Bely and talking things out. Bely, however, was not at home when Blok's messenger (again from the Prague restaurant) called at his flat, and Blok returned to Shakhmatovo to compose a long letter which prepared the way for yet another reconciliation. Dated 15–17 August, the letter is an absorbing exercise in self-analysis; a painstaking attempt to define his relationship with Bely;

[gg] With Fakely, Ory, *Zolotoye Runo*, and the eclectic Shipovnik.
[hh] The author E. P. Semyënov (S. M. Kogan) had quoted Georgiy Chulkov as having told him that Russian Symbolism was subdivided into four schools: the Parnassians (Bryusov, Max Voloshin, and Sergey Solov'ev); the 'pure decadents' (Bal'mont, Sologub, and Kuzmin); romantic neo-Christians (Merezhkovsky, Hippius, Filosofov, Berdayev—rather surprisingly included among the poets—and Andrey Bely); and, lastly, the mystic anarchists (Chulkov himself, Blok, Gorodetsky, and Vyacheslav Ivanov).

and a literary document fundamental to the troubled history of Russian Symbolism.

Blok wrote of their temperamental differences; of his own see-sawing between 'extreme mystical tension' and 'mental lethargy, weariness, oblivion'. He preferred, he wrote, 'people to ideas'; having once accepted someone, he took him on trust. He asked Bely to do the same:

You wanted and still want to know my 'moral, philosophical, religious physiognomy'. I am not able to, I really can't reveal all this to you outside the context of the happenings and emotional experiences of my life; some of these happenings and emotions are not known to ANYONE ON EARTH and I did not and do not wish to tell them to you either. This has never been any barrier to my relationship with you, nor is it so now. You can call it 'secretiveness' if you like, but that is the way I was and am. What I *am* prepared to tell you now in writing and orally is this: the moral side of my soul does not accept the divagations of modern eroticism[ii] and I do not want the *stuffy atmosphere* created by eroticism, I want fresh air and space; as to a 'philosophical creed', I have none, for I am not a trained philosopher; in God I do not believe and do not dare to believe, for is to believe in God to have yearning, lyrical, sparse thoughts about Him? Yet *I assure you* that all these pronouncements add nothing to my physiognomy. I am prepared rather to say, to give you a better idea of what I *am* like, that I believe *very much* in myself, that I feel a kind of *healthy wholeness* in myself and the ability to be a *man*: free, independent, and honest. But even this will not give you my image and I am afraid that you will never really know me. You do understand, that, in saying all this, I am neither boasting nor humbling myself. ... *All these things I have experienced and they are a part of me*—I bear my own psychological characteristics like a cross.

Struggling on, he wrote helplessly, 'but I feel that with every word I write I become more and more alien to you. Yet I was *always* like that, and so why did you love me before.'

Suddenly, he found the right words, words to which Bely reacted immediately because they led back into the sphere of poetry where the two had originally met and where they were at home with one another:

The drama (I have not grown up to tragedy yet) of my *Lebensanschauung* consists in the fact that I am a lyric poet. To be a poet is fearful and merry. And behind the fear and the merriment gapes a hidden abyss, which it is always possible to fall into—and there'll be nothing left. Merriment and

---

[ii] Bely had complained particularly of Zinov'eva-Annibal and Kuzmin, who wrote on homosexual themes, but the word used by Blok, '*uklony*', means divagations rather than perversions.

fear are a veil of sleep. If my eyes were not shrouded by this veil of sleep, if I were not lured on by the Unknown Terror from which I am preserved by MY SOUL ONLY—I would not have written one of those poems to which you have attributed any significance.

Returning a little further on to this idea of the guardian soul, Blok answered Bely's repeated accusations of blasphemy with the words:

If I do blaspheme, then my blaspheming is *more than redeemed by standing watch*. So it was, is, and shall be. My soul is a sentry unrelieved, it stands watch over its own and will never desert its post. At night, though, doubts and fears may descend even upon a sentry.

He pleaded almost with Bely to reserve judgement, to *trust* him, in spite of his unpredictable, 'lyrical' waywardness:

I admit that our ways should part, i.e. that they should not continue to run together as they have done up till now, but I think that, even in separation, we should preserve that knowledge about one another which has been given by experience and life. I *preserve* it through all the gossip, doubts, misunderstandings, bitter vexations, and moments of forgetfulness. I always take you into account.

As far as their purely literary affairs were concerned, Blok made it clear that he was not prepared to 'gang up' against Chulkov or anybody else, but that, in view of the unfortunate article in *Mercure de France*, he *would* write an open letter to *Vesy* disclaiming mystic anarchism. This he promised to do as soon as he had seen the French text:

My letter to the editor will have for me the significance of freeing my hands and of a final breach with those trends which wish to put forward my instability (mystic anarchism really means adogmatism, irrationalism, etc.), whereas I myself should wish to put in the first place my unalterable soul: 'faithful through all infidelity'.

(VIII. 194–203)

Mystic anarchism, he added, was at best a mood, and could not claim to be theory, a principle, or a method.

To this letter, also, Bely responded immediately, dropping the formal '*milostivyy gosudar'* ' though not yet sure enough of the situation to return to the intimate 'thou'. So nervous was he that his warm response to Blok's letter and impulsive journey to Moscow might be lost in the post that he sent a second letter (registered) on the heels of the first. In a third letter, written two days later, he enclosed the text of the offending notice in *Mercure de France*, interspersed with his own sarcastic comments.[39]

On 24 August Blok came to Moscow, this time by arrangement. Bely's state of mind is shown most vividly in his own account of how he thought he had glimpsed Blok, pale and arrogant in a white suit and panama hat as he had once seen him in St. Petersburg at the end of the previous summer, riding past him in a cab on the afternoon of the day he was to come and see him. At seven o'clock sharp, Blok, who had not been in the Arbat at the time Bely 'saw' him, turned up at the Bugayev flat dressed in a dark suit and hat, his face tanned and ruddy.

In spite of this eerie beginning, the meeting was an unqualified success. The two poets talked seriously until nearly midnight, when Bely's mother joined them for 'tea'. After this, they chatted and laughed away the rest of the night, reverting inadvertently to 'Borya' and 'Sasha' and the friendly 'thou'. Blok's train left for Shakhmatovo at seven o'clock the next morning and Bely saw him off and returned through the waking town, beaming happily at nothing in particular.

Blok kept his promise and wrote his open letter to *Vesy*, very correctly warning Chulkov of his intentions. He did not, however, pay any heed to Chulkov's plea to publish his letter in some other journal less personally hostile, on the grounds that he was lastingly attached to *Vesy*, which, in spite of certain disagreements, he still considered the best and most 'spirited' Symbolist journal.[jj] Chulkov, inevitably, was hurt,[40] although Blok did make it a condition that 'the name of poor Chulkov whom everyone is persecuting' should not be mentioned. His formal renunciation of mystic anarchism, sent to *Vesy* via Andrey Bely on 26 August 1907, concluded with the words:

In the number of *Mercure de France* for 16 July of this year, [E.P.] Semyënov puts forward a tendentious schema in which contemporary Russian poets and Symbolists are put into various cages labelled 'decadents', 'neo-Christian mystics', and 'mystic anarchists'.... I consider it my duty to declare that, while I highly appreciate the work of Vyacheslav Ivanov and Sergey Gorodetsky, with whom I find myself in the same cage, I never have had, nor do I now have, anything in common with 'mystic anarchism', to which my verses and prose bear witness.

(v. 675–6)[41]

It was typical of Blok that he should have chosen to make this announcement in the midst of the 'enemy camp'. He was aware that Bely had been, albeit quite unconsciously, acting as a catspaw for

---

[jj] Cf. also Blok's letter to Bryusov of 20 October 1907: '*Vesy* is very, very dear and close to me, at the moment it is the only place where I feel myself not "a visitor"—and in this sense it is, for me, a continuation of *Novyy Put'*, my literary birthplace' (VIII. 217).

Bryusov. Yet, since he admired Bryusov and was convinced that he himself was doing the right thing, this worried him not in the least. Perhaps, however, it was as well he did not see Hippius's condescending comment in a postcard to Bely from Paris: 'Bryusov wrote to me that you had received a letter from Blok renouncing mystic anarchism. Well, yes, it was all rather beyond him....'[42]

CHAPTER XI

A Cold Winter

(Autumn 1907–Spring 1908)

The hardest thing of all is to cross the threshold.

(IV. 114)

1

At the end of August, Blok and Lyuba returned to Petersburg. Dmitriy Mendeleyev had died the previous January, leaving his daughter a legacy which permitted them to install themselves in rather more comfort in a four-roomed flat nearer the Kommissarzhevsky theatre in Galernaya Ulitsa, No. 41, flat 4, and to buy, albeit at second hand, a mahogany dining room suite. The flat was on the first floor and its windows looked out over a pleasant courtyard on to a small church. Many of their friends remembered the Galernaya flat as a happy, cosy place, but the Bloks' first winter there was not a happy one.

The introductory chord was struck by the cycle of three poems that Blok wrote shortly after their return to the town and called 'Autumn Love' (II. 263–5). The cycle is like a triptych; not a visual representation, as one might expect from a Parnassian poet, but a threefold evocation of mood; or, more precisely, of three spiritual states.

On the one hand is the poet, crucified together with his country yet utterly alone; and Christ, who is with Russia but not yet with the poet:

> When in the wet and rusty foliage
> Red rowan berries cluster, and
> The soldier with his bony forearm
> Has knocked the last nail through my hand.

And when above the leaden river,
Against the wet and sullen sky,
Before the face of my stern homeland
I'm raised upon the Cross on high.

Then out across the distant spaces
Through mortal tears and bloody sweat,
I look: and see on the wide river
Christ coming in a little boat.

And in His eyes—the hopes I treasure,
The same rough shirt upon Him—and,
Most pitiful beneath his tatters,
A glimpse of that nail-pierced hand.

Ah Christ! How sad our native spaces!
My strength is ebbing here on high.
But your boat—will it put ashore here
By this tall Cross where I must die?

(II. 263)

In the centre, the place of honour, is the high and poignant memory of first love, of the unattainable and inexpressible: joy and glory and a sun that had once shone; the still-beating, 'foolish heart' of 'a laughing boy'. On the other side is the demonic, romantic summons to rebellion that was Volokhova: cold shoulders in wind and darkness, a dark heaven, a dark, billowing cloak and the cold kiss of mortality.

Blok was still in love with Natal'ya Volokhova and, as the winter deepened, she was to reassert her melancholy enchantment and bring his poetry again into the 'circle of the moon', the 'country' of the Stranger. Over the warm summer months, however, a distance had sprung up between them and it was several weeks before the romance regained its desperate impetus. In a letter to his mother in Revel, Blok said that he was not seeing Volokhova often and even remarked that, were it not for the reviews he was writing for *Zolotoye Runo*, he would have been tempted to take Lyuba home to Shakhmatovo and enjoy the autumn in the country.

Soon, however, the gay company of the preceding season gathered once more about the poet and his wife, so homely in their bohemian 'homelessness', so devoted in their infidelity. For Verigina, delighted to be back with her friends, the winter was only shadowed by the departure of Vera Ivanova to seek a cure for tuberculosis abroad, and by the more frequent appearance in their circle of Fyëdor

Sologub, whose profound pessimism managed to cast a gloom even over her ebullient spirits.

Volokhova, on the other hand, remembered this second season as very different from that of 1906–7:   •

We had all of us 'grown older' by no more than a year yet it seemed as though we were much older, more serious somehow, more aware, more exacting in our attitude to ourselves, to life, to everything about us. We met less frequently, there was little fun, and there were many complications in the theatre[a] which affected us all profoundly. And the winter itself was bitter; very cold and very little snow. The temperature fell to −26° and −28° with absolutely no snow. Dry, frozen needles danced in the air and, on the eyes of passers-by in the street, you could see tears frozen to the lower lashes.

On the corners of the larger streets and squares bonfires were lighted and there would be a solid ring of poorly dressed people standing around each of them, warming themselves and trying to take just a little warmth away with them. Often it happened that the hems of these poor frozen wretches' coats would catch fire and they would not even notice this until the smell of burning reached their nostrils or some slightly less frozen by-stander raised the alarm.[1]

Blok, observing all this, feeling the cold in his own heart, seeing how it was creeping out to numb the world of art and literature, became aware of a whole chain of 'correspondences' and set out his impressions of the autumn—subjectively, symbolically, yet, for the first time, profoundly and coherently sociologically—in *Zolotoye Runo*:

The period of reaction which it has fallen to our lot to live through has hidden from us, perhaps for many years to come, the face of a life that was just beginning to stir and awaken. Under our very eyes we see several generations shorn of their dearest hopes. Only very seldom can you meet a man, even among the youngest, who is not mortally bored and unhappy or who does not hide his face beneath a now sickeningly familiar mask of refinement, soft living and exclusive self-admiration.... I am speaking of writers in particular; of aesthetes weary before their career is begun, and particularly of aesthetes of the very youngest generation, of those who simply do not want to know that their lives should be a constant torment— private and public—that they should tear their hands on all the thorns on the stem of beauty.

Talent, he maintained, entailed responsibility, but neither poets, prose writers, playwrights, nor actors showed any real anxiety for their public, any real care for what was going on in the country at

[a] Meyerhold was falling out with Kommissarzhevskaya and her brother.

large. That year, the Religious-Philosophical Society had started up
again without the Merezhkovskys, who thought it wiser to abide the
initial period of post-revolutionary reprisals in Paris.[b] It seemed to
Blok that those who professed religion and philosophy ought to

... torment themselves more than all the others put together: because, for
several years now, they have been enunciating certain proud truths from
the platforms of their religious-philosophical get-togethers, have preached
with the utmost self-satisfaction, have indulged in arrogant irony, have
entered into self-indulgent polemics with thick-headed priests, and because
this year they have again renewed their chatter (and nothing but *chatter*)
knowing that the poor in spirit are waiting at their gates and that these
poor are in need of deeds. Yet here are highly cultivated and maliciously
witty intellectuals who have gone grey in arguments over Christ and Antichrist, ladies, spouses, 'in-laws' in respectable jackets, deep-thinking philosophers, priests all shining with self-satisfied fat, all this stirred together in
an unimaginable, disgraceful brew, an idiotic shimmer of words.... While
outside the wind is blowing, prostitutes are freezing, people are hungry,
people are being hung and reaction rules the land, and life in Russia is hard,
cold, foul....

(V. 209–11)

Coming from Blok, the darling of Meyerhold's theatre and Vyacheslav Ivanov's tower, this diatribe caused considerable shock. Yet
it was a natural enough development and a direct result of the poet's
growing 'professionalism', of his sense of obligation to Russian literature. Since leaving the University, the knowledge that his only contribution to society was through his writing had made Blok increasingly aware of a responsibility, not only to literature and art, but
to ethical, civic, and spiritual values.

Since the early nineteenth century, if not before, Russian literature
had carried more than its fair share of responsibility for such matters.
Whereas more liberal states would spread the burden over the
preacher, the historian, the philosopher, the politician, and a host
of others who could speak plainly of matters nearest their hearts and
uppermost in their minds, such public discussion as there was in
Russia took place almost exclusively between the covers of the 'thick'
journals.[c] In a country where even sermons were frequently submitted to a preliminary censorship, the Aesopian language of art

---

[b] Merezhkovsky's part in closing down the Mariynsky Theatre on the night of 9 January
1905 had been a conspicuous one and throughout that year the couple had cultivated the
friendship of professional illegal revolutionaries and made no secret of their opposition
to the idea of autocracy.

[c] *Tolstye zhurnaly*: a specifically Russian term for compendious literary/socio-economic
monthlies intended to provide solid reading on a wide variety of subjects.

inevitably became the common currency of communication. The effect of this on Russian literature had been twofold. On the one hand, it had contributed much to that confusion of form of which Blok had complained in his article 'On the Realists'. Russian modernism had originated in a reaction against this confusion, as a series of vigorous and witty protests against the use of art as a vehicle for political half-truths. Art, the new critics had maintained, though concerned with truth, was in itself a method of cognition. A work of art could not with integrity set out to illustrate a truth already discovered: it was itself an act of discovery. In this, Blok still concurred.

On the other hand, the burden which Russian literature had borne for so long had given it an heroic strength, and, in its best manifestations, had invested it with a special dignity. Dostoyevsky and Tolstoy had thought in terms of the fate of Russia and the salvation of mankind. Nor had they lost sight of the individual: there is no more Russian declaration in literature than Ivan Karamazov's pronouncement that, if he were offered the entrée to paradise at the expense of the suffering of one small child, he would respectfully return his ticket. Such was the *scale* of Russian thought: a man's own soul could counterbalance the whole of history, the world, the universe. At the same time, the individual soul was not isolated, but always considered in relation to these immensities. Not the pursuit of happiness is the theme of Russian literature, but the pursuit of salvation. 'Happy ends' are unknown for the simple reason that it is in the nature of happiness to be transient and the only *end* is death. In literature, as in life, joy and suffering are interwoven, and explicitly irrational.

It was this weight of truth and of responsibility for the whole of man, for the whole of life, that Blok was now preparing to shoulder. The modernists, he did not doubt for one moment, had been right in their rebellion against utilitarian aims, in their insistence on individual truth and specifically *artistic* integrity. Now, however, it was becoming apparent that the pendulum had swung too far the other way. As reaction set in, politics and sociology were proving difficult, laborious, and dangerous. Society, scared by revolution, frustrated by unreasonable control of reasonable democratic initiative, was beginning to seek escape. Discussion of mysticism, sex, or aesthetics was, as Sasha Chërnyy ironically remarked: '*Polezno i pryatno/ Nauchno i zanyatno*' ('both useful and agreeable/both scholarly and entertaining'). There was a growing market for erotic and mystical literature. The 'decadents', who had advocated a return to 'eternal questions' in all seriousness, found themselves popular—and beset by a host of cheap imitators. It was this 'decadence of decadence' that Blok took it upon himself to castigate in the periodical press.

Now that the revolution of 1905 had burnt itself out, the government was once again tightening its hold upon the country. The constitution was under review, suffrage had been limited to ensure the return of a 'loyal' parliament, and even this far from radical assembly was to have little enough say in the running of the country. As so often in Russian history, there were 'reforms from the top'. Stolypin's attempt to create a solid class of yeomen farmers, his encouragement of industry and of limited local initiative on health and education by the *Zemstvos* were, in the long run, to prove beneficient. Yet to radical opinion, even to moderate Kadet[d] opinion within the country, all this appeared to be too little and too late; Stolypin figured as an oppressor. The censor was becoming active again and the police were hard at work. Arrests, prison, exile, Siberia were once again the order of the day. There had been hangings. There would be more.

In this atmosphere of partial emancipation, of the gradual withdrawal of concessions grudgingly granted and of sudden, frightening flashes of brutality, it seemed a mockery to renew those talks between the intelligentsia and the Church which, on the eve of 1905, had appeared to offer some hope of real action and real agreement and had, indeed, been forbidden for precisely this reason. To Blok, it showed a loss of all sense of shame and reality that responsible people should, at such a moment in history, gather together to 'gossip about God ... about whom one should only weep alone or speak of in whispers to one other person' (V. 211).

He frankly preferred the company of his actresses over a glass of champagne in the nearest *café-chantant* and did not hesitate to say so in print, which naturally rather detracted from the force of his protest and made it all too easy for V. V. Rozanov, for instance, to make him look ridiculous in an answering feuilleton.[e2]

It was not only the Religious-Philosophical Society, however, that roused the poet's ire that autumn. Kommissarzhevskaya's theatre opened its Petersburg season with Wedekind, Blok's *bête noire* at the

[d] The Kadets were the more liberal of the two non-socialist parties in the State Duma. They wanted to see a strong, united Russia, democratically governed and intelligently developed economically.

[e] The excuse which Rozanov offered Blok for his scurrilously personal attack was that the latter had had a relative of his wife's in mind when he wrote about 'the in-laws in respectable jackets'. Blok was so taken aback by this that he quite failed to carry out his intention of refusing to shake hands with Rozanov.

time. Even the vogue for Maeterlinck, who had, Blok said, 'stolen away the concept of the hero from Western drama and reduced the human voice to a hoarse whisper', now seemed a 'golden dream' compared to 'these vexatious, wearisome, flat days when *Wedekind* has become fashionable in Russia' (v. 195). However, Meyerhold's modernistic production of Maeterlinck's *Pelléas et Mélisande* pleased Blok no more than the Wedekind. His own *Puppet Booth* seemed somewhat the worse for wear and, in Andreyev's *A Man's Life* which had so impressed him at the end of the previous season, 'the general standard of acting' was 'not so good as last year' and reflected 'the general mood of all actresses—heavy-hearted, oppressed, and transitional' (VIII. 207–8). The reappearance of Isadora Duncan in Moscow also disillusioned Blok. He referred scathingly to the 'Polish hysterics' of her interpretation of Chopin, and his main care on this occasion seems to have been to avoid meeting the lady personally.

In the field of creative writing, everybody appeared to be writing *about* literature or composing stylizations (such as Aleksey Remizov's 'mystery play' *Besovskoye Deistviye*), or translations. Blok himself in the course of that winter translated a French mystery play (*Le Miracle de Théophile* by Rutebeuf), which was staged that December at the Starinyy Theatre; Grillparzer's romantic verse tragedy, *Die Ahnfrau*, for Kommissarzhevskaya's theatre; and, paradoxically, considering how critical he had now become of his plays, verses and several 'Little Tragedies' by Maeterlinck.

In general he complained that

... everyone has gone off the rails, we're all creeping about like autumn flies, we are work-shy and yet bored by doing nothing. As a result all these discussions with priests are only one aspect of our self-indulgence and not the most blasphemous. And indeed what can Russian *intelligenty* say at this time to Stolypin or the Synod? Their mouth is shut ... and, to give credit where credit is due, by a good firm cork which will hold for the next ten years or so. Indeed, it is humiliating to watch a man who is still making totally untalented efforts to protest (only in words, anyway) and who is constantly having his mouth shut for him. It is demeaning for the man himself. It is better to keep quiet.

(v. 213)

Blok, however, did not keep noticeably quiet. That summer, he had heard that the editor of the journal which had published his 'Guardian Angel' had been charged with publishing a poem that contained incitement to political assassination. Two out of his three plays had been forbidden the stage. Of his own immediate circle, Leonid

K. Somov's portrait of Aleksandr Blok in the spring of 1907.

Elizaveta Yur'evna Pilenko, the future
Mother Maria, to whom Blok addressed
the poem 'When you stand in my way'.
(From the collection of Igor Aleksandrovich Krivosheyn)

A group photograph taken after a champagne breakfast in the spring of 1908. From
left to right: Georgiy Chulkov, Konstantin Syunnenberg (pseudonym Erberg), Blok,
Fyëdor Sologub.

Semyёnov was known to have been arrested and beaten up by the police the previous year, and it was Semyёnov's account of the treatment of political prisoners that was to be instrumental in triggering off Tolstoy's 'I Cannot Keep Silent'; Semyёnov's fiancée, Maria Dobrolyubova, a patriot who had worked as a volunteer nurse in the Japanese war, had also suffered imprisonment, her health had broken and she was now dead—surrounded for ever by the romantic aura of youth and courage. N. Minsky was a political émigré.

At such times of reaction, people of every shade of political opinion tended to unite on the simple basis of opposition to the police state. Yet it was presumably to the advantage of the police themselves to infiltrate society rather than to indulge in indiscriminate punitive measures. Certainly, Blok suffered no infringement of his personal liberty and articles such as the one quoted above[f] continued to appear in print. Throughout this autumn, moreover, Blok supported every conceivable charitable gathering in aid of political prisoners, underground parties, or any other worthy revolutionary cause, yet never suffered so much as the inconvenience of a police search. Maria Beketova, looking fondly back at her nephew's early political enthusiasms, remarks drily that there were a great many unscrupulous people about arranging 'charitable evenings' for their own ends and that Blok, totally inexperienced in this field of activity, was 'had more than once'.[83]

In public and in private, at poetry readings in aid of political prisoners or in Vyacheslav Ivanov's tower, Blok remained himself. There was an aura of dedicated simplicity about him which contrasted compellingly with the esoteric sophistication of his verse. A chance visitor to one of these autumn readings, an unhappy fourteen-year-old schoolgirl in search of a cause, recorded some thirty years later how she was taken by an elder cousin, a medical student with Social Democratic sympathies, to hear 'the decadents' at 'a tumble-down technical school somewhere out near the Izmaylovskiye Barracks'.

[f] Originally published in *Zolotoye Runo*, then, under the title 'Religious Quests and the People', republished during Blok's lifetime in the collection *Rossiya i Intelligentsia* (1918). Cf. also the eight-volume Collected Works where it appears as 'Literaturnye itogi 1907 goda' (v. 209–32).

[g] Amongst the poet's revolutionary acquaintances at this time were two 'illegal' agitators: a certain 'Comrade Andrey' and a 'clever, convinced revolutionary girl' whom Aunt Maria recalled with approval. It was at this time, too, that Blok entered into a correspondence with the peasant poet Nikolay Kluyev, a correspondence which, though not concerned with party politics, did much to confirm his feelings of guilt towards the people and his premonitions of the inevitability of social confrontation.

There were quite a lot of them. One tall, chinless man with an enormous nose and straight locks of long hair in a long-tailed coat read his verse with a merry lisp—they said he was called Gorodetsky. Then there was Dmitriy Tsenzor. I don't recollect his face. And others I do not remember, and one more. Very erect, with a touch of arrogance, a slow voice, weary, metallic. Dark, copper hair, not a modern face, the face of an effigy from a medieval tomb, carved in stone, beautiful and immobile. He read verses, I supposed new ones: 'Above the restaurants at evening'; 'The Stranger' and other things. . . . In my soul there is a huge attention. This man with such a distant, indifferent, beautiful face is something quite unlike the others. Before me was something I had never encountered before, head and shoulders above anything I had ever known, something marked of fate. . . . I asked my cousin: 'Look in the programme: who is that?'

She replied: 'Aleksandr Blok.'[4]

2

Blok was in a curious mood all that autumn. He was at the zenith of his physical beauty and beset by admirers: society ladies, students, young poets who had begun turning to him for advice—even would-be publishers. For the first time, he and Lyuba were reasonably well off: she had her legacy from Mendeleyev; he was writing regularly for *Zolotoye Runo* and his books were now selling comparatively well. He had three published collections of verse, a volume of plays on the way with Shipovnik, was reviewing for various newspapers and periodicals and translating for the theatre—all of which brought in money. He was busy not only with writing but also with serious reading: contemporary literature for his 'surveys' and anything he could lay hands on about the history of the theatre. He also had plans to study the Russian schismatics, though his diaries contain less evidence of these having been put into effect.

Indeed, the beginning of the season seems to have been marked by a considerable increase in energy and self-confidence. Lyuba was with him to grace his home—an essential factor to his well-being[h]— and he was in demand at the theatre, at the Religious-Philosophical Society (in spite of his critical attitude), and to recite his own poetry or to lecture. On such occasions he often appeared together with Volokhova and she even read the name part to his rendering of the

---

[h] 'Svetlaya (my light one) is always with me', he had scribbled in his diary that August. 'She will come back to me again. I am not young any more. There is much "cold white day" in the heart. But the beauty of evening is not far off' (*Z.K.* 96, entry for 1 August 1907).

transformed poet ('Goluboy', the man in pale blue) in a concert performance of *The Stranger*.

Nor was this season totally devoid of fun. Verigina has left us a
riotous description of an 'improvisation' in honour of Ekaterina
Mikhaylovna Munt, who had invited her friends to celebrate her
name day:

The best part was composing the scenario.

Aleksandr Aleksandrovich took the chair at the end of the table and we
sat round it. Meyerhold, pacing up and down the room, made funny
suggestions. Sologub—facetious ones. Here he was definitely in the way.
Blok, as always on such occasions, had a mischievous sparkle in his eyes
and a boyish mouth. With a great air of self-importance, he set down the
outline of the play which, he said, was to arise naturally from the various
talents of the performers.

The characters of the melodrama were as follows:

Someone in black	Al. Blok
Jealous husband (always clutching at the frames of doors)	Golubev
Innocent wife (knits a stocking and walks on her points)	Munt
A low sort of person in red	Verigina
Silent lover in a black mask	Meyerhold
Natasha (a character from another play). . .	Volokhova
Prologue	Vera Verigina

Meyerhold had a silent part at his own request. . . . The plot developed
between the jealous husband, the innocent wife, and the low sort of person
in red.[j] This villainous creature, in love with the jealous husband, was to
offer the innocent wife poisoned milk and speak a soliloquy to 'the pock-
marked moon'. Natasha had to speak lines out of another play bearing no
relation whatsoever to the melodrama, leaving the other actors to get themselves out of the situation thus created as best they could. The function of
the silent lover in the mask was to throw the other actors out by his indiscriminate embraces, and the Prologue was to help them by explaining
to the audience that the actress playing 'Natasha' should not have been in
the theatre at all that day, that it was a matter of pure absent-mindedness,
and in general to save the situation when the performers became too confused. There was not one rehearsal. Blok said that otherwise it would not
be a proper improvisation.[5]

[i] Valentina Petrovna's younger sister.

[j] The only costume available for this character was bright yellow, but Blok insisted this
would enhance the effect.

Thanks to Blok's solemn, shadowy work as compère and to Meyerhold's Silent Lover who moved about the stage like an automaton, mechanically opening his arms to enfold men and women alike, the improvisation was a great success, and the actors, unwilling to cast off their self-created characters, kept on their costumes for the rest of the evening. Something of the light-hearted creative energy of *The Snow Mask* crackled once more about the heads of the participants.

Yet in spite of this superficial glitter, Blok was not happy and, on 28 September, he complained to his mother:

I have not written for some time and write little now because of a great many worries—large and small. The large ones are to do with life—Lyuba, Natal'ya Nikolayevna, and Borya. Borya will come here to me soon. He is closer to me than anyone else and terribly unhappy.[k]

(VII. 210)

Lyubov', of course, knew all about the reconciliation with Bely and, when Blok received an invitation from him to give a joint reading in Kiev, she approved his plan to bring Borya back to Petersburg, although her own relations with him had not been formally resumed since the preceding autumn.

On 2 October Blok set off for Kiev where he joined Andrey Bely, Nina Petrovskaya, and Sergey Alekseyevich Sokolov, the hapless proprietor of Grif whose lot it was to serve as a perpetual butt for the sharper wits of his fellow decadents Bryusov, Ellis, and Bely. Blok was chronically sorry for Sokolov. This time, however, the tables were turned and Sokolov was the hero of the occasion. Bely had lost his voice and both he and Blok were somewhat overwhelmed by the welcome accorded them by their southern brethren, by the exuberant advertising campaign that had preceded what Bely had looked upon as a serious academic occasion, and by the fact that they were expected to appear before a vast audience on the stage of the Opera House. Bely was outraged and frightened; Blok amused and apprehensive. Only Solokov, who had a fine bass voice and the constitution to enjoy Kievan hospitality, really rose to the occasion.

---

[k] From Bely's irritated reaction to his first sight of *The Puppet Booth* on the stage (the Kommissarzhevskaya theatre had had a short season in Moscow before returning to Petersburg that winter), it was clear that, left to himself and his Moscow acquaintance, he would soon lose his newly acquired faith in Blok. Blok, who was deeply impressed by the similarity of his and Bely's reactions to Leonid Andreyev's *A Man's Life* and by his friend's impressions of the work of the theatre which had come to mean so much in his own life, was, on the contrary, more convinced than ever that he and Bely should be allies, not enemies.

This was the first time—except for his schoolboy excursion to Nizhniy Novgorod on the Volga—that Blok had travelled in his own country south of Moscow:

The best thing about Kiev is the Dnieper: Gogolesque, enormous, shallow, foreign and infested with cholera (while we were staying in Kiev a hundred people a day were going down with it—a feast in time of plague!). But Malorossiya is alien. Sand and steppe, yellow leaves whirling past the train window, pyramid-shaped poplars already losing their leaves, although the weather feels almost like summer.

(VIII. 214)

On the night of 5–6 October Bely was seized with an attack of nerves which he took for the onset of cholera. Shivering uncontrollably, he made his way along the hotel corridor to Blok's room. Blok, though to judge from his own account of the incident in a letter to his mother he was none too sure, told Bely firmly that it was all nerves. He would not let him go back to bed, but dressed himself and sat up with him all night: chatting, chafing his hands, soothing, and just sitting (Bely recalled) in companionable silence:

There was no fussiness, no outward attention from him, there was inward attention; and warmth seemed to flow into me from A.A.; and the fit passed; exhausted, I sank on to a chair; and looked at him sitting there in front of me as unruffled and calm as a nanny: all through the night. I have always remembered that sitting with Blok, remembered the still, relaxed pose; he had already changed, changed most strikingly, altogether, not in face but rather in manner (in the course of the year that we had not seen one another); he had become simpler, more thoughtful; he was more obviously manly; there was a new, tired sternness; the soulfulness [dushevnost'] was gone; it had burnt out; what had previously shone out from him as an invisible aura, as an atmosphere, had burnt out and turned to ashes, shadowing the face; ... I understood that the A.A. Blok of the period of shadows, of all the imps and spirits of Joy Unhoped-for, was over and done with; in the dark of the night there are no shadows; there is a quiet, even darkness, set with stars.

In the morning, Blok did what he had set out to do: he persuaded his 'brother' to return with him to Petersburg. He also called a doctor and offered to read Bely's lecture for him that evening. The doctor diagnosed mild bronchitis and nervous exhaustion. A change of scene, he said, would do the patient good. It was decided they should take the night train together immediately after the lecture. Bely, warmed through and through by the happy realization that not only had Blok come to Kiev expressly for his sake but that Lyuba, too, had given her approval to their returning together to Petersburg, recovered sufficiently to read his own lecture with the utmost success. Exhausted after their sleepless night, the two friends boarded the train and slept until twelve o'clock the following morning. Then they made their way to the restaurant car and spent a friendly, lazy day in absorbing conversation over several bottles of Rhine wine.

The *rapprochement* did not last long. Bely, happy beyond measure while he was the centre of Blok's attention, loving him perhaps more than ever before, was bewildered and alienated by his busy Petersburg *train-de-vie*. Neither Blok nor Lyuba was ever alone. Lyuba, too, had changed:

Whereas before she had been quiet, limpid, silent, profound, with a gift for pursuing a subject right down to its deepest roots, now it was as though, on the contrary, she had flung a veil of frivolity over all her words; it seemed to me that she had grown thinner and grown up; she talked a great deal, superficially, in *exalté* tones; and she was full of all kinds of fuss and day-to-day cares; it would have been perfectly possible to have had an 'explanation'[1] with the Lyubov' Dmitriyevna of 1906, but an 'explanation' with the Lyubov' Dmitriyevna of 1907 would, it seemed to me, have been nothing but an 'explanation' with a sophisticated lady full of her own concerns, cares and pleasures (as if she had time for 'explanations'!). So I, seeking to explain myself, never really did explain myself properly; and there arose between L.D. and me a light, half-jesting style—not of friendship, even, but rather of *causerie*.

Both Blok and Lyuba did their best to include Bely in their circle. But he, who had so loved their quiet family life in the winter of 1905, now felt only a piercing sense of loss at the way in which Blok had 'opened his doors to the blizzard':

A.A. was caught up in some kind of element; he was all dynamic, stormy, I would say *in love* with something, with someone; and in him himself I could clearly detect something of the rhythms of *The Snow Mask*; he was very handsome and very well-dressed in his elegant jacket with a white rose in his buttonhole, with that fine head thrown back, with an assured half-smile, with a rich scarf blowing out behind him ... he was like a blizzard; and I often felt the breath of the blizzard touch me, emanating from him; we were hardly ever alone together.... A.A. and L.D. surrounded themselves with a whirlwind of fun; but soon I noticed that they did not know themselves whither this whirlwind was carrying them; that they were in its power, and the whirlwind was not whirling them together; L.D. was flying into the whirlwind away out of A.A.'s life; and A.A. was flying away from her; I noticed they were always flying apart even when

[1] *Ob'yasneniye*, lit. 'explanation', but used in Russian to mean a heart-to-heart talk.

they came together over a cup of tea, over a meal; only to fly apart again.
... this gaiety was the gaiety of tragedy; of flying above the abyss; I saw
the coming crash because the fun they had abandoned themselves to was
nothing but a game, a kind of *commedia dell'arte*, no more.

From Blok's poetry of that time there was one rhyme that haunted
Bely when he came to write about this winter: *molodo/kholoda*
(young/cold).

L.D. and A.A. were both young; they flamed with beauty, strength, health;
but instead of warmth in their life I could hear the whirlwind of cold that
had caught them up and was rushing them along the road of 'play-acting';
this was the word that defines what so dominated their lives at this time:
'play-acting', theatricality....[6]

If Blok had wished Bely to see for himself that his life in Petersburg
was not as degraded as it appeared from a distance to the fastidious
imagination of a Zinaida Hippius or to the cynical mind of a Bryusov, he was successful. As Maria Beketova wrote:

The Bloks' life was lived in full view of everyone. They lived quite openly
and not only did they not hide anything but even tended to flaunt things
that it is common practice to keep quiet about. The most monstrous
rumours were at that time a positive fashion in the literary and artistic circles
of St. Petersburg. The improbable legends about the lives the Bloks were
leading far exceeded the reality. But they both, all their lives long, had
the gift of ignoring all kinds of gossip and, indeed, one could only wonder
at the extent of their indifference.[7]

Bely saw no orgies, recorded no excesses. He sensed, too, the
suffering behind the gay front:

I understood that while I had been away abroad something important had
occurred in the life of L.D. and A.A. which had changed their whole style
of existence; once, when I came early to see the Bloks, I found them still
in bed; I was waiting for them in the room between their bedrooms; then
the bell rang; it was Maria Andreyevna; it was our first meeting:[m] she kept
asking about my life abroad; then she went on to the Bloks and their life;
and she began to nod her head with a kind of long-sighted sorrow.
    'Yes, yes: it's not what it was, not what it was.... The bloom has gone....
You've noticed, I dare say?'
    'What?'
    'Their life is different: the flowers have lost their petals, got crushed....'
    It seemed to me that Maria Andreyevna really was speaking from a kind
of second sight: one of the Parcæ, perhaps: I glanced across at her with
resentment. At that moment, from behind the wall, came the sound of

    [m] i.e., since Bely's return from abroad.

Blok's painful, hoarse coughing; I felt suddenly, profoundly perturbed; that cough was nothing; yet there was a note of such suffering in it.

Bely was quite alien to life 'behind the scenes' and the element of creative play in the Bloks' relationships with Meyerhold and his actresses was beyond his understanding. He liked Verigina, and took it upon himself to initiate her into the mysteries of Marxism (Verigina considered herself one up on Blok at this time since she had actually read the first volume of *Das Kapital*, whereas Blok had *not*).
Volokhova Bely found more difficult to accept:

... very slender, pale and tall with black, wild and agonizing eyes with blue shadows beneath them, with narrow, thin hands, with very compressed, thin lips, a wasp waist, black-haired and dressed all in black—she seemed *réservée*. Aleksandr Aleksandrovich was obviously afraid of her; he treated her with the utmost respect; I remember how she stood up, flicking her gloves, and said something to him in a commanding voice, while he, also on his feet, bowed his head and listened. ... there was something distinctly lilac about her; I don't remember whether or not she wore a little lilac veil; perhaps it was her *lilac, dark aura* that suggested the idea of a veil; my impression of Volokhova: the word 'dark' suited her very well; there was something about her that really was—'dark'.
I did not like her.
Nevertheless the evenings we spent together" were cosy and amusing. ...

Volokhova, of course, could no more escape the dark, demonic image conferred upon her by Blok's poetry (and Bely's assessment of her is preceded by liberal quotations from *Faina*) than Lyubov' had been able to dissociate herself from the radiant majesty of the Beautiful Lady.

People said of A.A. at that time that he was in love.
On this visit to Petersburg, I loved A.A. very much. But I spoke to him little; I was—so sad; I felt: the life he was cultivating was not real life; it was a light intoxication to cover up a new drama in his experience of life that was already creeping up on him; he knew what I was thinking: it was as if he were begging me:
'Don't disillusion me: try the life I am leading here, try it for yourself.'
And L.D. said more than once:
'Come, it will be fun.'
But it wasn't fun, not for me: on the contrary, I was sad.[8]

So Bely, in spite of all his revived affection for Blok, felt himself drawn back by the familiar, more academic atmosphere of Moscow and, since polemics were still raging fiercely and since he had still

" Bely, the two Bloks, Verigina, and Volokhova.

not understood the sober concern for Russian culture behind Blok's new critical prose, into the Moscow literary camp. He divided the winter between the two cities. He could not, however, resist forcing an 'explanation' on the elusive Lyubov' Dmitriyevna, and this led to yet another quarrel, yet another breaking off of relations.

As to Blok, he had done all he could for his 'brother'. He was seeing Volokhova every day, 'at her place, in restaurants, on the islands, etc.' (VIII. 218) and, by the end of November, she had completely reasserted her baleful dominion.

3

At the same time, Blok was concerned for Aleksandra Andreyevna, who, as radical and outspoken as he was himself, was finding the part of 'colonel's lady' in occupied Revel very little to her taste. Having fallen foul of her husband's first C.O. who, before he himself was transferred to another command, had been about to demand her removal from the city as a bad influence on regimental morale, she had established a good personal relationship with his successor; but the necessity of constantly being on her guard and minding her tongue for the sake of Frants's career, combined with the unaccustomed separation from her son, had brought on a recurrence of depression and apathy.

On 9 December, unable to find comfort for her or for himself, Blok wrote her:

Life gets more and more difficult—it is very cold. Senseless spending of large sums of money and total emptiness all around: as though everybody had lost their love and deserted me, though most probably they just never did have any real love for me. I found myself on one of the islands in the midst of a cold, empty sea (and there is almost −20° of frost now with virtually no snow and a piercing wind).... On all the island there were only us three° with our peculiar relationships to one another—and yet we wanted for space. I think that if you were in this town you would only add your own fourth misery to these three miseries. We are each miserable in our own way. I know that I ought to and am fitted to find a profession and hope in creative work, and that it is time I took the hammer in my hands. But I have not the strength—it is so cold. And these two, these women with seeking souls, so different, yet in some ways so very alike— are frightened and cold as well. The weather in our souls is just like the weather in the outside world.

(VIII. 220–1)

° Lyubov' Dmitriyevna, Blok himself, and Natal'ya Volokhova.

Natal'ya Nikolayevna had returned to Petersburg sad, anxious, and disillusioned, and the poetry of this winter makes it clear that this was precisely what Blok found irresistible: her sorrow, her indifference, her 'otherness':

> She came from some barbaric distance
> Daughter of night and times gone by.
> No one to welcome her, no kinsmen,
> No greeting from the shining sky.
>
> Only the Sphinx's time-worn visage
> Above the Neva's mighty flow
> With a soft cry of recognition
> She greeted one wild night of snow.
>
> Sometimes the snow storm would bejewel
> With stars her shoulders and her breast—
> Still she would see her native Egypt
> Beyond our turgid, northern mists.
>
> And yet she took my iron-grey city,
> The wind, the glimmer, gloom, and rain,
> On trust, as though it were a kingdom
> She had accepted for her own
>
> (II. 267)

Volokhova tried to dissociate herself from this romantic image:

I often quarrelled with Aleksandr Aleksandrovich. As a poet he constantly tore me away from the 'earthly plane'.... This embarrassed and inhibited me very much because I knew perfectly well that offstage I was not endowed with this kind of elemental destructive power. But he insisted that these forces did live in me without my being aware of them and that I was always trying to suppress them by my culture and intellect. Hence the duality of my psyche, the tragic features of my face and character, the constant sense of loneliness and alienation.[9]

It was almost as though he were trying to force her to take up some vocation he himself had laid on her.

A 'mad year', a 'joyless passion', wind, darkness, and a slow, anguished awakening from a kind of frozen numbness, that lyrical sleep, at once fearful and merry, of which he had written to Bely. Volokhova was not gentle with Blok's ego. In his verses, in her incarnation as Faina, she carries a whip. It writhes and whistles through the poetry of this winter and, in the play *The Song of Fate*, Faina strikes the hero across the face. Elsewhere, Blok saw Fate as a circus rider who slashes the clown's 'white pancake of a face' as she gallops past him:

In the soul of the clown there is a conflagration of laughter, despair, and passion. From beneath the red, three-cornered brows the blood is pouring—which is why he cannot see his way. He gropes on, staggering and, fooling—but don't put out your hand to help and don't try to save him.

(II. 373)

By her steadfast refusal to take him seriously as a 'real person', by her melancholy, impatient question: 'Why *aren't* you the sort of man I could have loved?' Volokhova not only hurt Blok in his self-esteem, she woke him from the awful somnolence which had always threatened him in moments of 'mystical' exhaustion. She brought him to life, bewildered still and lost, but angry and determined to prove himself. For this reason he treasured the pain; for this reason, like the blinded clown, he would brook no helping hand. For this reason, the central cycle of that winter, entitled 'Invocation by Fire and Darkness' (II. 272), is written in an unexpectedly major key and bears an epigraph from Lermontov:

> For all things, all, to thee my thanks I render
> For all my passion's secret agonies—
> For bitter tears, and poisoned kisses tender;
> Vengeance of foes, and good friends' calumnies;
> Ardour of soul, poured out in desert places.

The cycle opens with the stirring 'O, spring without end, without limit', a defiant greeting to life. This poem contains the lines which Volokhova, in her memoirs, says best describe her relationship with Blok, for it is *her* demonic gorgon-image with a wild wind blowing through the serpent locks and the 'unguessed name of God' on her cold, compressed lips that the poet meets on the threshold of 'life in the world':

> In this meeting, hostility smoulders.
> I'll not lower the shield from my eyes ...
> You'll not let the cloak fall from your shoulders,
> But above—dreams run riot in the skies.

The second poem runs from acceptance and riches unutterable into the heart of a furnace of terror and splendour: a baptism by fire. In the cool darkness of the third poem, 'Only night and freedom', the pursuit of the impossible begins again through fire and darkness, a pursuit in which the poet becomes ever more uncertain, forgetful of everything, losing his way even in his own lines and verses, dancing out 'like a light bird of oblivion' in a crazy dance of death. The tarantella motif sounds again and passes into the whistling of the blizzard, into the leaping rhythms of the Russian *plyasovaya*: but the words themselves tell not of gaiety and dancing but of the waters of Lethe, the call of self-destruction. Then the poet, tearing himself from the hypnosis of eternal calm, rushes out 'into the fields, the snow, the night', where freedom and pain will revive him and force him to take up again the burden of life. At last, the snow begins to fall again in a strange, halting, dreamlike rhythm. Russian folk rhythms reassert themselves, the accordion thrums and 'She', 'Faina', 'Russia' is circling out alone, arms raised above her head in the smooth sweep of the peasant woman's classic dance, but even as the singer celebrates her wild beauty, she is swept away from him by a crowd of other dancers.

In the last, eleventh poem, there is a complete change of mood. Defeated, abandoned, like Pierrot at the end of *The Puppet Booth*, the poet takes refuge in the old songs and the old manner: the draw-ing-room romance that he permitted himself now but sparingly, sensing the danger of anachronism:

> Again I'm silent at her feet
> The feet of one long loved in vain,
> The snow storm at our door may beat
> The white-winged blizzard come again ...
>
> But to repeat your subtle name
> To me is sweetest suffering
> And to my lips I raise your train
> As the white blizzards sing, and sing ...

(II. 282)

This system of writing in cycles, of grouping loosely connected short lyrics under a single title and arranging them to convey a sequence of mood, a spiritual pattern, or even, elusively and sym-bolically, to suggest a narrative, had, with *The Snow Mask*, *Faina*, and 'Autumn Love', become an established form. It conveyed, as no other form could have done, the disintegration of the lyrical world of Blok's poetry.

Life, however, goaded the poet on. Volokhova, unhappy herself, blew hot and cold upon his passion. Now we find a note in his diary: 'She left our party without saying good-bye.' In January, she left Petersburg altogether for a week or so. It was almost as if Blok wel-comed this coldness, as though he was driven to make a waste land of his private life in order to write.

I was particularly depressed before the New Year and over Christmas. Such cold loneliness: wandering from tavern to tavern, drinking. True, I only drink occasionally, all the rest of the time I am cold sober, full of malice and ready to snarl at all comers: in print and orally.

The colder and angrier this unsuccessful 'private life' (but where will you find a 'successful' private life these days?) the deeper and wider are my plans in the field of ideas and intentions. . . . The most important thing is the play. I have already roughed out three acts.

(VII. 224)

So he wrote to his mother on 8 January 1908.

This idea of fuelling his work from his private life, to the point of self-destruction, sounds strongly in a poem he wrote a few days later when he saw Volokhova off on her departure from Petersburg:

> It's fun to live! it's fun to know
> There's nothing new beneath the moon,
> That life luxuriantly grows
> From dead men's words—a curious boon ...   (II. 287)

While she was away, on a brief tour of the Baltic capitals with Kommissarzhevskaya, Blok used the time to renew his acquaintance

... with various writers with whom I still maintain some smouldering remains of a relationship. Why, I don't know, mostly it is just business and a diplomatic act of courtesy. But I live in my own world and my friends no longer poke their shiny noses into it.

(VIII. 225)

If this was Blok's mood, it is scarcely surprising that one of these 'diplomatic acts of courtesy' sowed the seeds of yet another quarrel with Bely, who was quite incapable of loving anyone and not 'poking his nose' into their world. That autumn, in Moscow and Kiev, Blok had been the one to make advances and allowances. By Christmas, however, he was tired and had refused rather sharply to come to Moscow for a charitable evening which Bely was planning for 20 January. Mainly for Blok's sake, Bely had come to Petersburg, as it happened just when Volokhova happened to be away, to give, on 15 January, a lecture arranged by Verigina in aid of the Social Democrats. Blok did not attend the lecture. He did, however, meet Bely in a restaurant and the two had a reasonably satisfactory talk during which they decided that they should remain 'friends' in their private lives but 'enemies' in literature: a position patently untenable for two lyric poets.

Volokhova's return to Petersburg was no happier than her departure. What she had given Blok was invaluable, but the poetry he had written that winter was in itself proof that this curious, cold passion was wearing itself out. There were longueurs and repetitions. Sometimes, it was as though the poet had lost control over the fluctuating music of his verse, himself passive amongst the tempestuous rhythms. Perhaps it was in part as a corrective that, on 6 February, Blok produced two sober free verse poems: 'When you stand in my path' and 'She came in from the frost'.

The first poem was addressed to the young girl, Liza Pilenko, who had been so struck by his personality earlier that season. Disoriented and very unhappy, having lost a dearly loved father the year before and been removed from her home on the sunny borders of the Caucasus to the 'rusty mists' and bitter cold of St. Petersburg, she had 'found out the secret of the grown-ups, that there is no God and that there is sorrow in the world, and evil and injustice'. At the poetry reading, Blok had struck her as one grown-up who had faced up to this secret and in whom there was no pretence. She read all his verse, found out his address, and called three times at his flat. Twice he was out. The third time, a bitterly cold day even for that bitter winter, she plucked up courage to ask the maid to allow her to await his arrival. Alone in the small dining room with its large, solid furniture she stared up wonderingly at the huge portrait of Mendeleyev. Could her poet be a chemist? she wondered. And why was everything so *tidy*?

At last Blok appeared, wearing the black smock with the large white collar that Zhenya Ivanov called his Shakespeare shirt. It must have been something of a surprise to find awaiting him a rather plump, untidy schoolgirl whose short-sighted eyes beamed at him shyly from behind a pair of serviceable spectacles.

He was very quiet, very shy.

I didn't know how to begin. He waited and didn't ask why I had come. I was desperately ashamed, most of all because after all I was still only a young girl and he might not take me seriously. I would soon be fifteen years old and he was grown up—he must be at least twenty-five.

Finally, I plucked up courage and poured out everything all in one breath: I don't like Petersburg, I hate the rusty mist, I can't live through this autumn,[p] I know that there is unhappiness in the world, I wander about the islands for hours on end and I know almost for certain that there is no God. It all came out at once. He asked why I had come to him, of all people. I spoke of his verses, how they had simply got into my blood and how I thought he held the key to the mystery, and I asked him to help.

[p] In fact the meeting took place in early February. It was in the autumn that she first heard Blok read.

He was attentive, respectful, serious. He understood everything, did not try to tell me what I should or should not do, and, it seemed, did not even notice that I was not grown up.

We talked for a long time. It grew dark outside the window and windows in the other flats began to light up. He did not switch on the light. I was at ease, I felt at home, although there was much I could not understand. I feel that the man beside me is a great man, that his pain is greater than my own, that he is even more unhappy than I and that the pointlessness of everything has not been overcome or destroyed. I am astonished by his extraordinary attentiveness, a kind of careful tenderness. I feel dreadfully sorry for this great man. I begin, cautiously, to comfort him, comforting myself in the process.

It was a strange feeling. As I left Galernaya, I knew I had left a part of my soul there. It was not one of those half-childish passions. The feeling in my heart was more like a mother's anxiety and care: and at the same time there was a feeling of ease and joy. How good it was that there was so great a longing in the world, a great life, a great attention, a great, undefended, seeing soul.

A week later, Blok paid a brief visit to his mother in Revel and from Revel Liza Pilenko received a long blue envelope. It contained a poem and a letter.

The letter said something about their all being dying people and how it seemed to him that I was not yet one of them, that I would still be able to find a way out in nature, in contact with the people. 'If it is not too late, turn away from us, who are dying....' I don't know why, but I was indignant. I should run, should I? Very well, then. And I tore up the letter and tore up the blue envelope.... You go on and die, then, and I shall go on fighting death and evil,[q] and I shall fight for you, because I am sorry for you, because you have entered into my heart and will never leave it, never.[11]

The poem that accompanied the offending letter was Blok's first experiment in free verse for the shorter, lyric forms:

> When you stand in my path,
> So alive, so beautiful,
> Yet so unhappy,
> And speak of nothing but sorrow,

[q] This was precisely what Liza did go on to do. She was married twice, had three children, was mayor of her native town in the south during the revolution and saved it from sack by Bolshevik sailors. In the emigration, she eventually took the veil and, under the name of Mother Maria, cared for hungry and homeless Russians, was arrested during the German occupation for harbouring Jews and finally, voluntarily, took the place of a younger woman called out for the gas chambers at Ravensbruck during the last days of the Second World War.[10]

Think of death,
Do not love anyone
And despise your own beauty—
When then? Surely I'll not take advantage of you?

Oh no! I am not a violent man
Not a deceiver and not proud,
Although I know a great deal,
Have thought too much since childhood
And am altogether too introspective.

You see—I am a writer,
A man who calls everything by its own name,
Who can steal the scent from the living flower.

However much you may speak of sorrow,
However much you may think of ends and of beginnings,
Nevertheless, I dare to suppose,
That you are no more than fifteen years old.
And for that reason I should wish
That you might fall in love with an ordinary man
Who loves earth and heaven
More than rhymed or unrhymed speeches
About earth and about heaven.

Indeed, I would be glad for you,
Because it is only people in love
Who have the right to call themselves human beings.

(II. 288–9)

The second poem in free verse, which bears the same date as that
addressed to Liza Pilenko, is about Volokhova, but, perhaps for the
first time, one feels that it was touched off not by the fateful Snow
Maiden but by the woman herself, bursting in unexpectedly on the
poet at a quietly studious moment, a vivid stranger in the ordered
world of his domesticity:

She came in from the frost,
All flushed and bright,
Filled the room
With the tang of fresh air and her own perfume,
And with her clear voice
And a torrent of chatter
Quite without proper respect to my studies.
Almost immediately, she let fall on the floor
The thick volume of an art review
And at once it began to seem
That there was very little space
In my large study.

All this was rather annoying
And ridiculous, somehow.
However, she promptly demanded
That I should read aloud to her
From *Macbeth*.
Hardly had I got to *the bubbles of the earth*,
Of which I cannot speak without excitement,
Than I noticed that she, too, was excited
And looking anxiously out of the window.

It transpired that a large tortoise-shell cat
Was slinking carefully along the edge of the gutter
To ambush a couple of kissing pigeons.
I was annoyed most of all
Because it was the pigeons, not we, who were kissing,
And because the times of Paolo and Francesca were gone for ever.

(II. 290–1)

Volokhova, recollecting the incident, again grants us an insight
into the way Blok juggled with reality to make, in his best lyrics,
something 'yet more real':

Once Lyubov' Dmitriyevna and I went off together to some place quite
a long way off and were so frozen on the way home that tears sprang to
our eyes and froze on our cheeks. The Bloks' flat was nearer than mine
and so Lyubov' Dmitriyevna invited me in. She immediately began preparing something hot to warm us up and took me into Aleksandr Aleksandrovich's study. He was sitting at his writing table, working. I felt that I had
appeared at a rather awkward moment. But he said very gently yet firmly
that first I must get warm and so he would light the fire and that I should
sit with my legs up on the sofa and put a rug over my knees. I did as I
was told. Soon the fire was blazing and Aleksandr Aleksandrovich began
to read me some passages from *Macbeth* (one of his favourite tragedies).
Under the influence of the agreeable warmth and the sound of his melodious voice I began to doze off. This happened at the very moment when
Aleksandr Aleksandrovich was reading about the 'bubbles of the earth',
of which he could not 'speak without excitement'.[12]

Lyubov' Dmitriyevna's great friend was Verigina, but she was also
on surprisingly good terms with Volokhova herself and all that
winter they had attended classes of dancing and movement together.
When Kommissarzhevskaya and Meyerhold agreed to part, both
Volokhova and Verigina decided to follow Meyerhold on a tour
of the provinces and Lyubov' went with them to play Columbine,
walk-on parts, and Clytemnestra. The role of rejected, neglected
wife—however much beloved, however greatly needed—had

become more than her very considerable pride could bear. If Blok
had irrevocably left his 'quiet, white house', as he had written in the
first act of his new play that spring, the one of which he had told
Lyubov' that it was 'all about her' and which he was now reworking
with total absorption, then she was not going to sit at home and
wait for him to return. Last winter, when she had suggested that they
might go abroad together, to Italy, she had received the cruel reply:
'With you? That would be dull!' Now *she* would be the one to leave,
and she would prove herself on the stage.

The very thought made Blok miserable. He knew it was his fault;
he strongly suspected that Lyuba was no great actress; yet, once
again, he did not raise a finger to stop her. He was besotted by Volokhova; perhaps because she still held out against him. He pursued her
grimly and hopelessly, almost with hatred.

With deliberate harshness, Volokhova forbade him to prolong the
agony of the winter by following her and Lyuba on tour. This gave
rise to their first serious quarrel. Lyubov' left with Meyerhold on
15 February 1908. Volokhova stayed on in Petersburg until 4 March,
after which she and Blok did not meet again until 9 June when, at
a rendezvous in Moscow, a final long, heart-breaking talk took place
between them. The last two poems' to Volokhova were sparked off
by the quarrel before she left and by their last meeting. Written in
November 1908, the last poem of all reads as the celebration of a
belated and unhappy attempt to consummate the long romance, to
immolate the personal element in the slow furnace of indifferent lust.
Angry and embittered, it implies that later 'the daughter of humiliation' fell 'immeasurably lower' and that the poet had now 'forgotten'
her. Possibly it suited his poetic imagination to endow his heroine
with all the gypsy promiscuity of Faina, ready to bestow her favours
on the 'old and grey' or anyone else who 'will give most clinking
coins'' (IV. 129). Verigina ascribed these last poems to anger at her
friend's steadfast rejection. Certainly, after the revolution Blok left
a Moscow theatre before the interval to avoid meeting Volokhova,
by then a much subdued married woman who had recently lost her
first child, and these were the only poems which he did not show

---

' 'I recall the long-drawn torments' (4 March 1908) and 'With bitter tears the spring
wept with us' (20 November 1908) (II. 292, 293–4).

' Blok's imagination may have been sparked off by the fact that, the following autumn,
he saw Volokhova dance the dance of the seven veils at the dress rehearsal of Wilde's *Salome*,
a production so heavily erotic that it was banned before the first night. Also, Natal'ya
Nikolayevna's name had been linked with Count Sergey Witte's, who is most probably
the prototype of her 'old companion' in *The Song of Fate*, but there is no evidence that
the elder statesman was more than just another admiring slave to the actress's beauty.

her at the time of writing them. When she did see them, much later, she was deeply hurt: 'Involuntarily, I again remembered: *"Sub specie aeternitatis"*, but this time I did not smile.'[13]

4

In spite of everything, Volokhova had helped Blok. She had weaned him from the cosy but unreal domesticity of his youth and, finally and irrevocably, 'brought him to life'.

Now, with Aleksandra Andreyevna in Revel and Lyubov' and Volokhova both away touring with Meyerhold, the poet was left alone to come to terms with himself and his vocation. It was a painful business and, in the course of adjustment, Blok succeeded once again in alienating Andrey Bely.

The trouble arose over Bely's insistence that Blok should send him a considered opinion of his 'Fourth Symphony: The Cup of Blizzards', which, he wrote eagerly, was 'the most sincere of the four' and 'the key' to his 'soul'.[14] Blok, irritated by Bely's attacks, both in print and in private letters, on his friends in literary Petersburg, was thoroughly out of sympathy with him. He had, moreover, actively disliked the new 'Symphony' and had already decided not to do more than acknowledge receipt when Bely sent him a second letter on the subject. Now, something in the tone of this letter and, immediately thereafter, in the hectoring, patronizing manner of Sergey Solov'ev's polemical article, 'Gospodin Blok on agricultural workers, long-bearded Arians, beer froth, me and much else besides',[15'] had brought back all the bitterness of their clumsy attempt to 'save' him and 'rescue' Lyuba in the summer of 1905. Blok went round for several days 'spitting as though a bed-bug had got into my mouth' (VIII. 237), and then sat down to write to Bely—as usual, without taking the least trouble to 'sugar the pill':

24 April 1908

Dear Borya,

For a long time I did not reply to your letter because I could not. It is still difficult for me to do so. I read 'The Cup of Blizzards' and found it not only alien but profoundly hostile to me in spirit. From my point of view there is much blasphemy there, but as you found blasphemy in my *Joy*

[']The article was supposedly an answer to Blok's critique of S. Solov'ev's poetry in his survey 'On Lyric Poetry', in *Zolotoye Runo* no. 6, 1907. As in the old days at Shakhmatovo, Seryëzha adopted a tone of insufferable superiority, attempting to instruct his cousin in his own profession of writing lyric verse.

Unhoped-for and in the plays, I am at a loss and ready to admit that we have finally and irrevocably lost the ability to judge one another. You write that this symphony is the most sincere of them all; in that case I understand nothing about you and never will, and nor will anyone else. Even from the outward point of view (the literary) I find absolutely nothing to my liking in this symphony with the exception of a few places, if only because I don't understand the half of it (but nobody else understands it either). To this is added the dreadfully unpleasant impression from your reviews in *Vesy* of Sologub, Hippius, the 'camp-followers'." I cannot help believing that our relationship with one another is based on something greater than ourselves, for this has been attested from the beginning and still is attested by mystical facts. But more complex internal relations I have never had with anybody. All my life has been and is a single 'unshakeable truth' of a mystical nature, and from the point of view of that truth I am bound to pronounce your symphony essentially hostile.

(VIII. 238)

Bely replied in a letter postmarked 3 May 1908:

Dear Sasha,

Thank you very much for your truthful opinion of me. It shows how alien we are to one another. You maintain that nevertheless there are mystical facts that bind us; *I maintain that there are not and never were* (what you call 'mysticism' is evidently not the same thing as I understand by the term). In view of the 'complexity' of our relations *I liquidate* that complexity by breaking off relations with you (except for chance meetings, greetings in the street, etc.)

Don't answer.

All the best.
BORIS BUGAYEV[16]

This time, the break lasted for more than two years.

Like Blok himself, Bely and Solov'ev considered themselves primarily writers and artists." Yet, unlike Blok, they were not prepared to sacrifice life to art, fearing 'to lose their souls'. Like drowning men, each was seeking an ark in religion. Later, each was to find his own refuge: Solov'ev in Orthodoxy; Bely in anthroposophy. This idea of using religion as a personal lifebelt was alien to Blok. If God was real, He would manage very well without Aleksandr Blok, all of whose efforts were at that time directed to kicking away every last

---

" The 'camp-followers' was Bely's name for the epigones and hangers-on of Symbolism. Bely himself admitted in his memoirs that, in the spring of 1908, he had been writing such abusive criticism that he had become completely isolated and had scarcely a friend left in literary circles.

" Although Blok disliked the 'Fourth Symphony', the novel on which Bely was engaged at the time of this quarrel, *The Silver Dove*, he considered a work of genius and almost frighteningly close to his own feelings for Russia.

support, rejecting every ark life offered: religion; society; marriage; literary success. He was irritated beyond measure at the lifebelts and spars thrust at him by his floundering friends." All the outward forms about him were crumbling, yet he believed in the greater reality behind these illusory realities, and he also believed very much 'in himself' and wanted no help—from friends, or from Christ, or from angels.

None of this could really be explained: only suggested in his poetry. He knew only that his demon, his Muse, to use the well-tried classical expression he used himself, could brook no rival; that to write as he wished to write he must die to all security, to all ready-made values. He had so much to give up: and the sunny life that might have been, the life of 'Sasha Beketov', young and strong, heir to Shakhmatovo and husband to Lyubov', was to go on hurting till he died like an amputated limb. Now, dizzy still with the euphoric narcosis of his *commedia dell'arte*, fresh from the surgeon's knife, he was not to be touched, not to be preached at, and not to be comforted.

He ran from his father—in Petersburg for the Easter vacation with his favourite pupil Spektorsky—most uncharacteristically telling a downright lie about having been 'called out' unexpectedly 'to discuss the foundation of a new publishing house', and, having escaped, spent 'a remarkable night with a very beautiful women'—a chance pick-up in a strange hotel.

He ran, too, from his God. Lyuba came to see him in the last week in Lent—theatres throughout the country being closed—and, on Easter night, having seen her off to rejoin her troupe, he roamed the town alone, like Lermontov's Demon, glowering darkly at the merrymakers and the flaming torches round St. Isaac's Cathedral: 'There is something in these great Christian holidays—Christmas and Easter—which I am beginning to feel is really hostile to me and somehow humiliates me' (VIII. 236), he wrote to his mother.

It was little wonder he ran also from his 'best friends and "patrons" (with Andrey Bely in the lead)' (Z.K. 108).

'Loneliness is not to be overcome by comparing mystical experiences', he wrote that spring to a young man who had wanted to talk to him about dreams.

With the people with whom I had most talks (mystical talks, I mean), such as A. Bely and S. Solov'ev and others—I have now broken; our relationships have become hopelessly confused and I strongly suspect it is because

---

" Compare the rejected scene at the railway station in *The Song of Fate* (IV. 436–44).

of the systematic 'falsehood of spoken thoughts'. . . . It may be that loneliness can only be overcome by the rhythms of real life, by passion and hard work ... But surely you do not think that I deny the validity of your dreams? That would be to deny my own 'anamnesis'. It's just that I don't want to talk—or better, I am *not able* to talk about that.

(VIII. 241)

Both passions and hard work, however, continued to elude him. At Easter, the broken ice from Lake Ladoga had passed down the Neva and the great river had resumed its purposeful flow towards the sea. 'My life rolls on in heavy waves like a river', Blok told his mother; but like the river he still had no conscious goal.

Chulkov and Sologub lured him out under the dimly blue, rain-washed skies of April to a champagne breakfast with oysters. Women sent him flowers, love letters, invitations. After sleepless nights he would wander out into the Maytime fields, gazing drowsily at the fluffy yellow dandelions, poring with delight over Kuzmin's delicately sensuous verse. 'And why not get drunk sometimes, since life has turned out the way it has: there are moments when something terrible and tragic comes quite close and a keen wind blows through the soul; and others when "life is so light, so very light"' (VIII. 239).

THE BEKETOV FAMILY

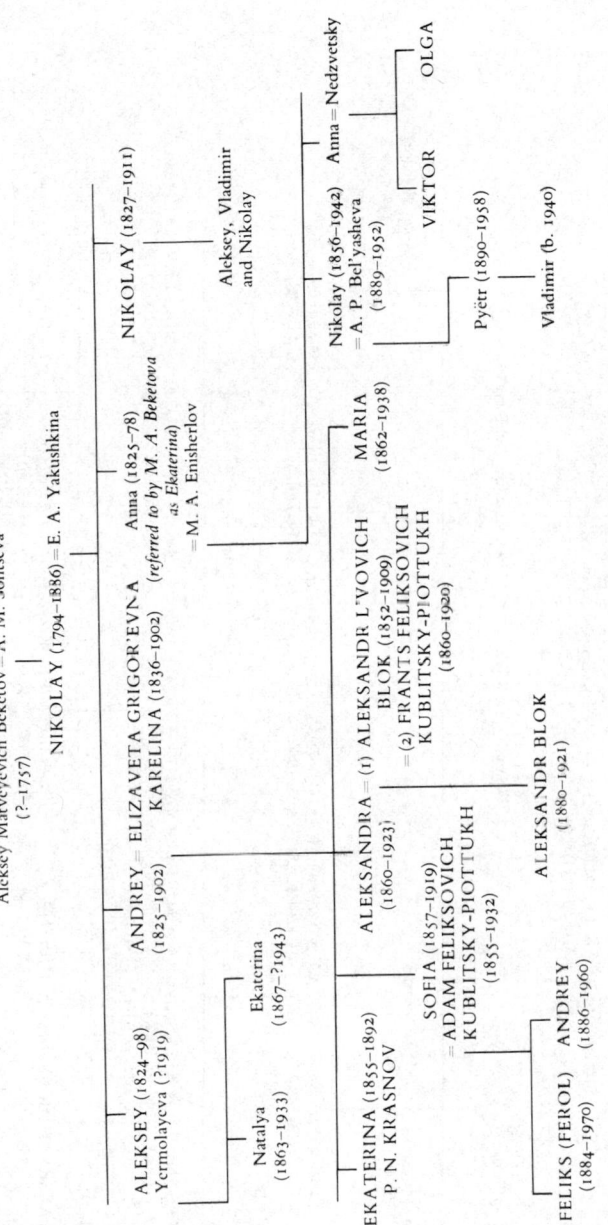

Aleksey Matveyevich Beketov = A. M. Sontseva
(?–1757)

NIKOLAY (1794–1886) = E. A. Yakushkina

ALEKSEY (1824–98)
Yermolayeva (?1919)

ANDREY = ELIZAVETA GRIGOR'EVNA
(1825–1902)   KARELINA (1836–1902)

Anna (1825–78)
(referred to by M. A. Beketova
as Ekaterina)
= M. A. Enisherlov

NIKOLAY (1827–1911)

Aleksey, Vladimir
and Nikolay

Natalya
(1863–1933)

Ekaterina
(1867–?1943)

EKATERINA (1855–1892)
P. N. KRASNOV

ALEKSANDRA = (1) ALEKSANDR L'VOVICH
(1860–1923?)   BLOK (1852–1909)
= (2) FRANTS FELIKSOVICH
KUBLITSKY-PIOTTUKH
(1860–1920)

MARIA
(1862–1938)

Nikolay (1856–1942)
= A. P. Bel'yasheva
(1889–1952)

Anna = Nedzvetsky

VIKTOR   OLGA

Pyëtr (1890–1958)

Vladimir (b. 1940)

SOFIA (1857–1919)
= ADAM FELIKSOVICH
KUBLITSKY-PIOTTUKH
(1855–1932)

ALEKSANDR BLOK
(1880–1921)

FELIKS (FEROL)
(1884–1970)

ANDREY
(1886–1960)

THE BLOK FAMILY

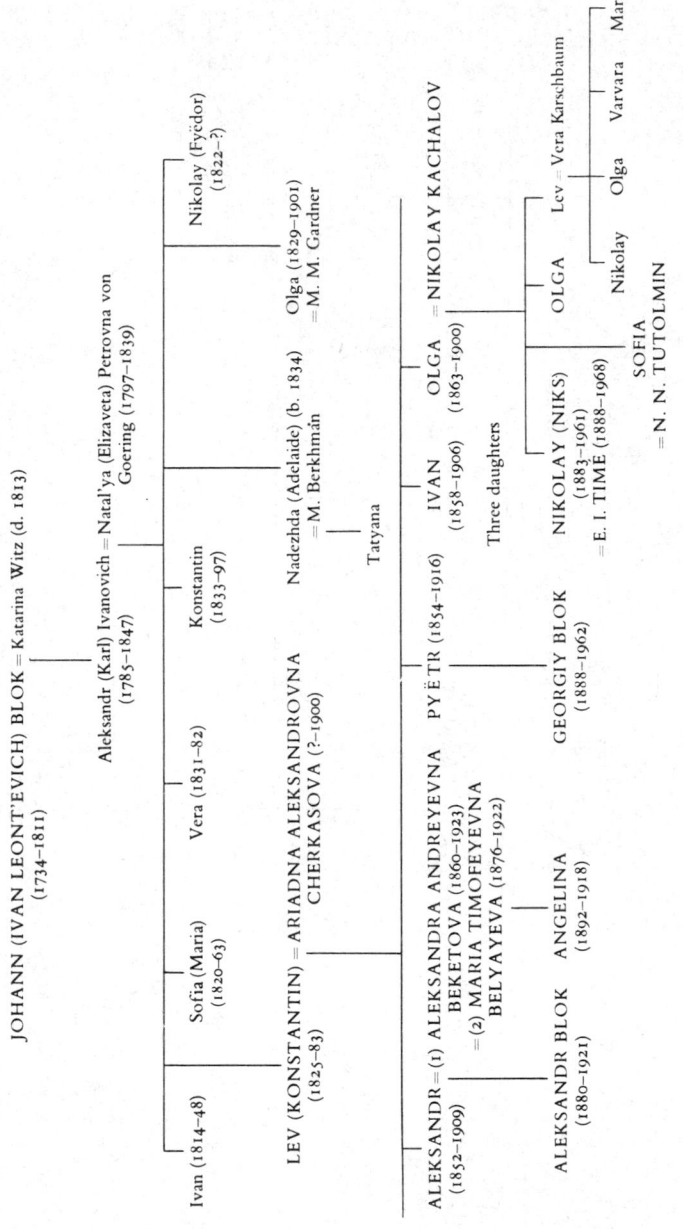

THE KARELIN FAMILY

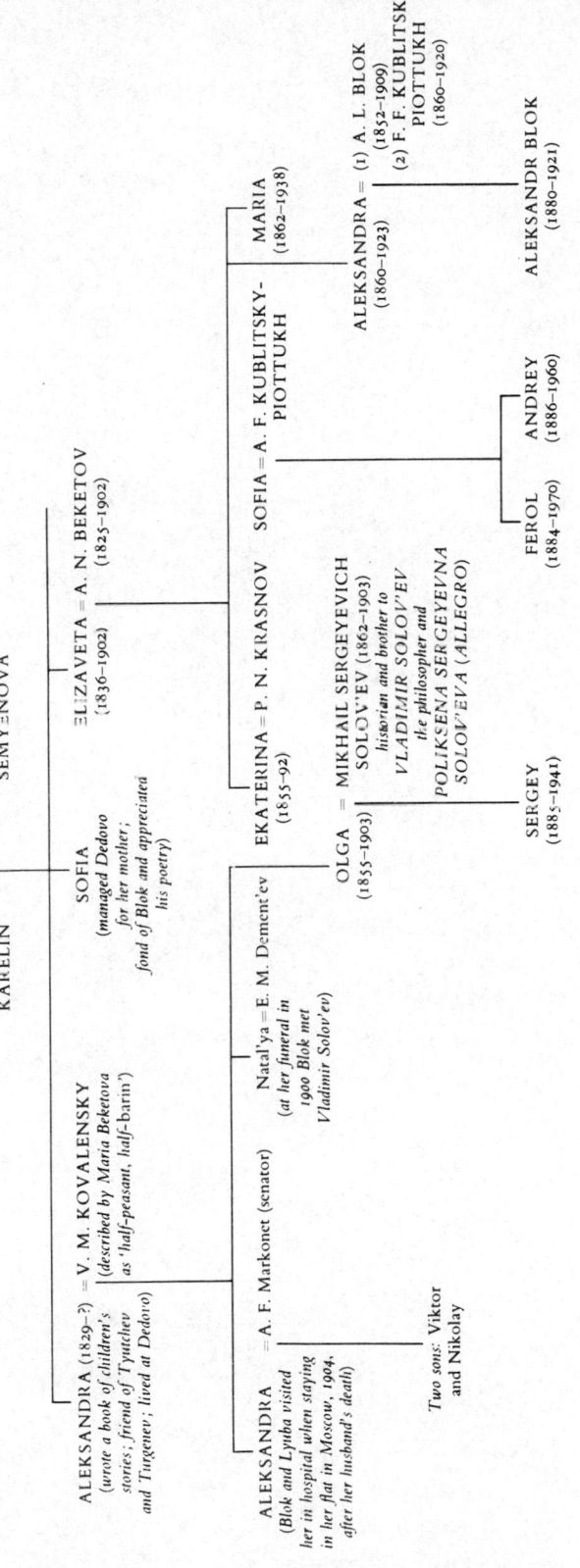

PRINCIPAL SOURCES FOR VOLUME I

This list comprises the principal sources, published and unpublished, for Volume One, with the shortened forms by which those sources cited frequently are referred to in the Reference Notes which follow. Other sources less frequently drawn on are cited in full in the notes. A detailed bibliography of Blok's published writings is given at the end of Volume Two.

The two major repositories of unpublished Blok material in the Soviet Union are the Tsentral'nyy Gosudarstvenyy Arkhiv Literatury i Iskusstva (Central State Archive of Literature and Art), Moscow (cited as TsGALI), and the Institut Russ-koy Literatury (Institute of Russian Literature) (Pushkin House), Leningrad (cited as IRLI).

<table>
<tr><td>I BY ALEKSANDR BLOK</td><td>Cited as</td></tr>
</table>

PUBLISHED

Sobraniye Sochineniy v vos'mi tomakh, ed. V. N. Orlov, A. A. Surkov, K. I. Chukovsky (Moscow-Leningrad, 1960–3)	S.S.
Zapisnye Knizhki, ed. V. N. Orlov, A. A. Surkov, K. I. Chukovsky (Moscow, 1965)	Z.K.
Pis'ma Aleksandra Bloka, with introductory articles by S. M. Solov'ev, G. I. Chulkov, A. D. Skaldin and V. N. Knyazhnin (Leningrad, 1925)	*Pis'ma A. Bloka*
Pis'ma Aleksandra Bloka k rodnym, ed. M. A. Beketova (Leningrad): vol. I (1927); vol. II (1932)	*Pis'ma k rod-nym*
Pis'ma Al. Bloka k E. P. Ivanovu, S prilozheniyem piscm Al. Bloka k M. P. Ivanovoy i 'Petersburgskoy poemy' Bloka, ed. Ts. Vol'pe, preparation of text and commentary A. Kosman (Moscow-Leningrad, 1936)	*Pis'ma E. P. Ivanovu*

UNPUBLISHED

Letters to his wife Lyubov' Dmitriyevna Blok *née* Mendeley-eva, 29 Nov. 1901–20 July 1917. Arkhiv A. A. Bloka, TsGALI. F.55, Op. no. 1, ed. kh. nos. 97–105

3 letters to Lyubov' Dmitriyevna Blok, 1902, 1903. Arkhiv A. A. Bloka, IRLI. F. 654, Op. no. 1, ed. kh. no. 405

7 letters to L. Ya. Gurevich, 1907–16. Arkhiv L.Ya. Gurevich, IRLI. 19.814 (XXXV b 3)

Letters to A. V. Hippius, 1900–15 (copies). Arkhiv A. A. Bloka, IRLI. F.654, Op. no. 1, ed. kh. no. 419

Letters to E. P. Ivanov and M. P. Ivanova. Arkhiv E. P. Ivanova, IRLI. F. 662, nos. 71, 86

Letter to S. R. L'vovich, 13 Jan. 1901. Arkhiv A. A. Bloka, TsGALI. F. 55, Op. no. 1, ed. kh. no. 113

4 letters to A. M. Remizov, 1913–18. Arkhiv A. M. Remizova,   *Cited as*
IRLI. F. 256, Op. no. 1, ed. kh. no. 33

Letters to Anna Akhmatova; Fyëdor Sologub; El'tsina Rozalia Sëmënovna (copies). Arkhiv A. A. Bloka, IRLI. F. 654, Op. no. 1, ed. kh. no. 422

Zapisnye Knizhki 1–49 (nos. 13, 15, 19, 34–8 and 40–3 missing). Arkhiv A. A. Bloka, IRLI. F. 654, Op. no. 1, ed. kh. nos. 321–60

Vestnik. Exercise books of family journal and *Kolos*, a collection of works by A. Blok and F. A. Kublitsky-Piottukh. Arkhiv A. A. Bloka, IRLI. F. 654, Op. no. 1, ed. kh. no. 164

25 drawings. Arkhiv A. A. Bloka, IRLI. F. 654, Op. no. 1, ed. kh. nos. 167–8

Album with photographs of ancient Egyptian, Greek and Roman art and Western art 1909–11, and an album of reproductions of western European painting. Arkhiv A. A. Bloka, IRLI. F. 654, Op. no. 1, ed. kh. nos. 401, 402

2 albums of postcards: (1) Italy, Berlin, Antwerp, Ghent (Flemish pictures), Bruges, Heyst-sur-mer, Revel, Bad Nauheim, and 3 postcards of Vrubel's 'Demon'; (2) Brittany, Paris, Bad Nauheim, Shuvalovo, Ozerki; circus posters (1912). Arkhiv A. A. Bloka, IRLI. F. 654, Op. no. 1, ed. kh. nos. 403, 404

II OTHER SOURCES

PUBLISHED

M. A. Beketova, *Aleksandr Blok. Biograficheskiy ocherk* (Petersburg, 1922)   M. A. Beketova, 1922

——*Aleksandr Blok i ego mat'* (Leningrad-Moscow, 1925)   M. A. Beketova, 1925

Andrey Bely, 'Vospominaniya o Bloke', *Epopeya* (Moscow-Berlin), nos. 1, 2, 3, 1922   A. Bely, *Epopeya*

——*Vospominaniya ob Aleksandre Aleksandroviche Bloke*, with an introduction by Georgette Donchin (Letchworth: Bradda Books, 1964). Reprinted from *Zapiski Mechtateley* (Petersburg, 1922)   A. Bely, *Vospominaniya*

Aleksandr Blok i Andrey Bely, Perepiska, ed. V. N. Orlov (Moscow, 1940)   *Perepiska*

Blokovskiy Sbornik (Tartu): I, ed. V. Adams, B. Egorov, Yu. M. Lotman (responsible editor), D. E. Maksimov (1964); II, ed. Z. G. Mints (responsible editor), V. I. Bezzubov, Yu. M. Lotman, D. E. Maksimov (1972)   *B.S.*

Uchenye Zapiski Tartuskogo Gosudarstvennogo Universiteta. Trudy po russkoy i slavyanskoy filologii (Tartu): vol. IV (1961); vol. XI (1968)   *Trudy*

UNPUBLISHED   *Cited as*

M. A. Beketova, 'Shakhmatovo. Semeynaya Khronika' (unpublished reminiscences), 1930. Arkhiv M. A. Beketovoy,
IRLI. F. 462, no. 4
——'Dnevnik.' Arkhiv M. A. Beketovoy, IRLI. F. 462, no. 1
L. D. Blok, Letters and telegrams to Blok, 22 Nov. 1901–18
July 1917. Arkhiv A. A. Bloka, TsGALI. F. 55, Op. no. 1,
ed. kh. nos. 159, 163, 164, 166, 167
—— 65 letters and 1 telegram to A. Bely. Arkhiv A. Belogo,
Manuscript Room, Lenin Library (Moscow). Bel. 9.18
—— 26 letters to Blok's mother, A. A. Kublitskaya-Piottukh,
1907–10. Arkhiv A. A. Bloka, IRLI. F. 654, Op. no. 7, ed.
kh. no. 24
—— 'I byli i nebylitsy o Bloke i o sebe' (unpublished memoirs).   L. D. Blok,
Arkhiv A. A. Bloka, TsGALI. F. 55, Op. no. 1, ed. kh. no.   memoirs
520. (Copy in the possession of the author)
G. I. Chulkov, 7 letters to A. Bely and 1 postcard, 1905–7, 1917,
1925. Arkhiv A. Belogo, Manuscript Room, Lenin Library.
Bel. 25.12
N. Chulkova, 'Vospominaniya o Bloke'. In Chulkova's posses-
sion, Moscow, 1964, and (Moscow, 1974) in the collection
of N. P. Il'in
Ellis (L. L. Kobylinsky), Letters to A. Bely, 1907–11. Arkhiv
A. Belogo, Manuscript Room, Lenin Library. Bel. 25.31
S. M. Gorodetsky, 3 letters to Blok's mother, 7 March 1906–
23 Aug. 1921. Arkhiv M. A. Beketovoy, IRLI. F. 462, no.
166.
Z. N. Hippius, Letters to A. Bely, 1902–10, 1917–18 (some un-
dated), Arkhiv A. Belogo, Manuscript Room, Lenin
Library. Bel. 14.6
——Letter to L. D. Blok, 25 Dec. 1906. Arkhiv A. A. Bloka,
TsGALI. F. 55, Op. no. 3, ed. kh. no. 82
E. P. Ivanov, Letters to Blok, 8 Apr. 1904–17 July 1920. Arkhiv
E. P. Ivanova, IRLI. F. 662, no. 42.
—— 'Mat' i syn' (unfinished study). In the collection of N. P.
Il'in
A. V. Kartashev, Letters to A. Bely, 26 Nov. 1905–5 Feb. 1917.
Arkhiv A. Belogo, Manuscript Room, Lenin Library. Bel.
17.8
A. A. Kublitskaya-Piottukh, 20 letters to A. Bely. Arkhiv A.
Belogo, Manuscript Room, Lenin Library. Bel. 18.5
——Letters to E. P. Ivanov, June 1906 et seq. Arkhiv E. P.
Ivanova, IRLI. F. 662, no. 60–2
——Letters to M. P. Ivanova, 20 Sept. 1907–1922. Arkhiv A.
A. Bloka, TsGALI. F. 55, Op. no. 1, ed. kh. 534–44
D. S. Merezhkovsky, 24 letters to A. Bely, 1904–9. Arkhiv A.
Belogo, Manuscript Room, Lenin Library. Bel. 19.9
Minsky (N. M. Vilenkin), 7 letters to A. Bely, 1906–7. Arkhiv
A. Belogo, Manuscript Room, Lenin Library. Bel. 19.16

Pyast (V. A. Pestovsky), 3 letters to A. Bely, 13 Apr. 1908 and
2 undated. Arkhiv A. Belogo, Manuscript Room, Lenin
Library. Bel. 21.36

A. M. Remizov, Letters to A. Bely, 1905–12. Arkhiv A.
Belogo, Manuscript Room, Lenin Library. Bel. 22.5

V. V. Rozanov, Letter to Blok, 19 Feb. 1909 (copy in Blok's
hand) (published *B.S.* II). Arkhiv A. A. Bloka, TsGALI. F.
55, Op. no. 3, ed. kh. no. 55

O. M. Solov'eva (*née* Kovalenskaya), Letters to Blok's mother,
11 Jan. 1896–31 Dec. 1902. Arkhiv A. A. Bloka, TsGALI.
F. 55, Op. no. 1, ed. kh. no. 551

S. M. Solov'ev, Letters to A. Bely, 1898–1901, 1905, 1906,
1908–9, 1910. Arkhiv A. Belogo, Manuscript Room, Lenin
Library. Bel. 26.1–5, 6, 8, 9

REFERENCE NOTES

All works cited are by Blok unless otherwise attributed

CHAPTER I

[1] D. V. Grigorovich, 'Iz Literaturnykh Vospominaniy', in *F. M. Dostoyevsky v vospominaniyakh sovremennikov*, I (Moscow, 1964), 135–6.

[2] F. M. Dostoyevsky, letter of 26 Nov. 1846, *Pis'ma v chetyrëkh tomax* I (Moscow, 1959), 103.

[3] F. M. Dostoyevsky, *Novoye Vremya*, no. 1721, 14 Dec. (Sunday) 1880, quoted in *Neizdanniy Dostoyevsky. Literaturnoye Nasledstvo. Zapisnye Knizhki i Tetradi 1860–1881* (Moscow, 1971), 678–9, 703.

[4] A. I. Mendeleyeva, 'A. A. Blok', chapter 12 of her reminiscences, *Mendeleyev v zhizni* (Moscow, 1928), 132.

[5] M. A. Beketova, 1922, 22.

[6] M. A. Beketova, 'Shakhmatovo. Semeynaya Khronika', 1930. Arkhiv M. A. Beketovoy, IRLI.

[7] M. A. Beketova, 1925, 9.

[8] M. A. Beketova, 1922, 26–7. Cf. also M. A. Beketova, 1925, 110.

[9] Details of the Blok family from an unpublished letter of 23 June 1930 from the state archivist of Mecklenburg, written in response to enquiries from Pushkin House. Original in IRLI; copy in the collection of N. P. Il'in. Cf. also *S.S.* VII, 462, note 3.

[10] E. S. Spektorsky, *Aleksandr Blok. Gosudarstvoved i Filosof* (Warsaw, 1911).

[11] A. L. Blok, *Gosudarstvennaya vlast' v evropeyskom obshchestve. Vzglyad na politicheskuyu teoriyu L. Shteyna i na frantsuzskiye politicheskiye poryadki* (St. Petersburg, 1880).

[12] M. A. Beketova, 1925, 14.

[13] A. I. Mendeleyeva, op. cit., 130–1.

[14] E. A. Beketova, letter to her sister Sofia of 9 June 1882, in the collection of N. P. Il'in. It is largely unpublished.

[15] M. A. Beketova, 1925, 124–5.

[16] E. A. Beketova, letter to E. G. Beketova of 13 June 1884, in the collection of N. P. Il'in.

[17] F. A. Kublitsky-Piottukh, partially published by V. P. Enisherlov as 'Chastitsa ego lyubvi k Rossii', with a foreword by S. Lesnevsky, in *Smena* (Moscow). The rather fuller manuscript is in the collection of N. P. Il'in.

[18] Cf. A. N. Beketov, unpublished letter to Sofia Kublitskaya-Piottukh of 13 Aug. 1894, in the collection of N. P. Il'in.

[19] A. N. Beketov, *Iz zhizni prirody i lyudey* (St. Petersburg, 1870).

[20] M. A. Beketova, 1922, 40.

[21] M. A. Beketova, 1925, 19.

[22] Ibid., 28.

[23] These first childhood 'works' have been fully published with an excellent introduction and commentary by Z. G. Mints in *B.S.* II, 292–308.

[24] M. A. Beketova, 1925, 31, 33.

[25] M. A. Beketova, 1922, 43.

[26] A. A. Kublitskaya-Piottukh, unpublished letter to E. P. Ivanov of 29 June 1911. Arkhiv E. P. Ivanova, IRLI.

[27] Letter to E. G. Beketova of 27 Dec. 1893, *Pis'ma k rodnym* I, 18.

[28] Letter to E. G. Beketova of 2 Sept. 1894, ibid., 24.

[29] M. A. Beketova, 1925, 99.

[30] Letter to his mother, before 22 June 1892, *Pis'ma k rodnym* I, 12–13.

CHAPTER II

[1] M. A. Beketova, 1922, 47.

[2] V. N. Knyazhnin, *Aleksandr Aleksandrovich Blok*, in the series Bibliografiches-kaya Biblioteka (Petersburg, 1922), 28–9.

[3] A. A. Kublitskaya-Piottukh, letter to her parents of 9 May 1895, published by Z. G. Mints with notes by M. E. Koop in *B.S.* II, 435.

[4] Id., letter of 12 May 1895, ibid., 436.

[5] Id., letter of 7 May 1898, ibid., 439.

[6] Id., letter of 16 May 1898, ibid., 439.

[7] Id., letter of 21 May 1898, ibid., 440.

[8] Letter to his mother of 20 Aug. 1897, *Pis'ma k rodnym* I, 36.

[9] F. A. Kublitsky-Piottukh, partially published by V. P. Enisherlov as 'Chastitsa ego lyubvi k Rossi', in *Smena* (Moscow), but quoted here from the full version of the reminiscences in the collection of N. P. Il'in.

[10] M. A. Beketova, 1922, 42.

[11] F. A. Kublitsky-Piottukh, op. cit.

[12] M. A. Beketova, 'Shakhmatovo. Semeynaya Khronika', 1930. Arkhiv M. A. Beketovoy, IRLI.

[13] F. A. Kublitsky-Piottukh, op. cit.

[14] Ibid.

[15] S. M. Solov'ev, 'Vospominaniya ob Aleksandre Bloke', in *Pis'ma A. Bloka*, 10.

[16] Letter to E. G. Beketova, of 16 Jan. 1894, *Pis'ma k rodnym* I, 22.

[17] M. A. Beketova, 1922, 55.

CHAPTER III

[1] M. A. Beketova, 1925, 135.

[2] Ibid., 133.

[3] Ibid., 129–30.

[4] Ibid., 131.

[5] Ibid., 134.

[6] See L. V. Zhavarina's introduction to Blok's letters to K. M. Sadovskaya, 'Pis'ma A. A. Bloka K. M. Sadovskoy', in *B.S.* II, 310, in which there are extensive quotes from M. A. Beketova, 'Razroznennye materialy eyë o zhizni i tvorchestve a Bloka. Chernoviki', Arkhiv M. Beketovoy, IRLI.

[7] M. A. Beketova, 1922, 56.

[8] Quoted by L. V. Zhavarina from M. A. Beketova, 'Razroznennye materialy', *B.S.* II, 310.

[9] A. A. Kublitskaya-Piottukh, unpublished letters to her parents of 30 and 22

July 1897, quoted by A. Turkov, *Aleksandr Blok*, in the series Zhizn' zamechatel'-nykh lyudey (Moscow, 1969), 22.

[10] Letter to K. M. Sadovskaya of 13 Aug. 1901, *B.S.* II, 323.

[11] M. A. Beketova, 1925, 71–2.

[12] O. E. Ozarevskaya, *D. I. Mendeleyev* (Moscow, 1929), 147.

[13] Maria Gribovskaya, 'Vospominaniya ob Aleksandre Bloke', *Rizhskiy Kur'ër* (Riga), no. 208 (evening edition), 7 Sept. 1921. Listed incorrectly as *Rizhsky Vestnik* by Nikolay Ashukin, *Aleksandr Blok sinkhronisticheskiye tablitsy zhizni i tvorchestva 1880–1921. Bibliografia 1903–1923* (Moscow, 1923). I am indebted for this correction to Boris Plyukhanov of Tallin, Esthonia, a connection of the Blok family and editor of the publication 'Pis'ma A. Bloka k E. F. Knauf (Manguskovskoy)', *B.S.* II, 407–10.

[14] L. D. Blok, memoirs.

[15] M. A. Beketova, 1922, 62.

[16] Cf. M. A. Rybnikova, *A. Blok, Hamlet* (Moscow, 1923), 13.

[17] L. D. Blok, memoirs.

[18] Ibid.

[19] A useful discussion of the influence of the images and relationships of *Hamlet* on Blok's poetry and life is to be found in T. Rodina, *A. Blok i russkiy teatr nachala XX veka* (Moscow, 1972), 103.

[20] Cf. V. Rozanov, *V mire neyasnogo i nereshennogo* (St. Petersburg, 1901), 246–7. Rozanov quotes the letter of a Father I. Petropavlovsky to the editors of the periodical *Grazhdanin*.

[21] Letter to K. M. Sadovskaya of between 5 and 12 Apr. 1898, *B.S.* II, 318.

[22] A. A. Kublitskaya-Piottukh, unpublished letter to M. P. Ivanova of 24 March 1913. Arkhiv A. A. Bloka, TsGALI.

[23] M. A. Beketova, 1925, 138.

[24] Ibid.

[25] Ibid., 136.

[26] G. Blok, 'Geroy Vozmezdiya', *Russkiy Sovremennik* (Moscow-Leningrad), no. 3, 1924, 172–83.

[27] S. M. Solov'ev, 'Vospominaniya ob Aleksandre Bloke', in *Pis'ma A. Bloka*, 11–12.

[28] G. Blok, op. cit.

[29] Ibid.

CHAPTER IV

[1] For more detailed studies of Blok and Vladimir Solov'ev see A. Slonimsky, 'Blok i Vl. Solov'ev', *Ob Aleksandre Bloke* (Petersburg, 1921), 265–84; D. E. Maksimov, 'Materialy iz biblioteki Al. Bloka', *Uchenye Zapiski Leningradskogo Gosudarstvennogo Pedagogicheskogo Instituta* CLXXXIV (1958), Vypusk 6, 351–86; Z. G. Mints, 'K genezisu komicheskogo u A. Bloka (Vl. Solov'ev i A. Blok)', *Trudy* XVIII (1971), 129–94; in English, S. D. Cioran, *Vladimir Solov'ev and the Knighthood of the Divine Sophia* (Waterloo, Ont.: Winifred Laurier Univ. Press, 1977); and, in German, Armin Knigge, *Die Lyrik Vl. Solov'evs und ihre Nachwirkung bei A. Belyj und A. Blok* (Amsterdam, 1973).

[2] O. M. Solov'eva, unpublished letter to A. A. Kublitskaya-Piottukh of 25 March 1897. Arkhiv A. A. Bloka, TsGALI.

[3] Id., unpublished letter to A. A. Kublitskaya-Piottukh, undated. Arkhiv A. A. Bloka, TsGALI.

[4] Letter to his mother of 7 Aug. 1898, *Pis'ma k rodnym* I, 42.

[5] Letter to his mother, dated (by M. A. Beketova) 4 July 1898, *Pis'ma k rodnym* I, 41.

[6] O. M. Solov'eva, unpublished letter to A. A. Kublitskaya-Piottukh, undated. Arkhiv A. A. Bloka. TsGALI.

[7] Id., unpublished letter to A. A. Kublitskaya-Piottukh of 19 Oct. 1898. Arkhiv A. A. Bloka, TsGALI.

[8] Id., unpublished letter to A. A. Kublitskaya-Piottukh of 22 Aug. 1900. Arkhiv A. A. Bloka, TsGALI.

[9] Id., unpublished letter to A. A. Kublitskaya-Piottukh of 3 Sept. 1900. Arkhiv A. A. Bloka, TsGALI.

[10] Unpublished letter to A. V. Hippius of 30 March 1901. Arkhiv A. A. Bloka, IRLI.

[11] L. D. Blok, memoirs.

[12] Cf. also *S.S.* VII, 51; III, 24; V, 192, for other references to Solov'ev's poem, 'My soshlis' s toboyu ne darom'.

[13] Vl. Pyast, 'O pervom tome Bloka', in *Ob Aleksandre Bloke* (Petersburg, 1921), 213.

[14] N. A. Pavlovich, 'O doblestyakh, o podvigakh, o slave', *Dumy i vospominaniya* (Moscow, 1966), 23–4.

CHAPTER V

[1] B. V. Nikol'sky, diary entry for 10 Feb. 1902, quoted by V. I. Bezzubov and S. G. Isakov in 'Blok—uchastnik studencheskogo sbornika', *B.S.* II, 329.

[2] Id., diary entry for 17 Feb. 1902, ibid., 330.

[3] These and all future references to Lyubov' Mendeleyeva's religious beliefs are, unless otherwise stated, based entirely on her own unpublished memoirs.

[4] *Anatoliy Lunacharsky on Literature and Art* (Moscow, 1965), 182.

[5] L. D. Blok, unsent letter to Blok of the end of January 1902, published by D. E. Maksimov, *Uchenye Zapiski Leningradskogo Gosudarstvennogo Pedagogicheskogo Instituta* XVIII (1956), Vypusk 5, 249–50.

[6] These letters (29 Jan. 1902, 5 Feb. 1902, and one undated) have been preserved in the Arkhiv A. A. Bloka, TsGALI. Another unsent letter torn out of a notebook and glued into Blok's diary is published in *S.S.* VII, 38–9.

[7] V. Bryusov, 'Svyashchennaya zhertva', *Vesy* (Moscow), no. 1, January 1905, 26–7.

[8] Cf. for instance, Z. N. Hippius, 'Neobkhodimoye o stikhakh', *Sobraniye Stikhov 1889–1903* I (Moscow, 1904), ii, and D. S. Merezhkovsky, 'Khristos i Antikhrist v russkoy literature', *Mir Iskusstva* (St. Petersburg), no. 4, 1901, 152–3.

[9] A. Bely, letter to Blok of 4 Jan. 1903, *Perepiska*, 7.

[10] Vl. Khodasevich, *Literaturnye stat'i i vospominaniya* (New York, 1954), 158.

[11] A. Bely, *Nachalo veka* (Moscow-Leningrad, 1933), 13.

[12] V. Bryusov, *Dnevniki 1891–1910* (Moscow, 1927), 98.

[13] A. Bely, *Nachalo veka*, 13.

[14] Z. N. Hippius, 'Moy lunniy drug', in *Zhivye litsa* (Prague, 1925), 11, 12.

[15] Ibid., 14.

[16] V. Bryusov, letter to A. Bely of 12 Aug. 1904, in *Valeriy Bryusov Literaturnoye Nasledstvo*, no. 85 (Moscow, 1976), 379.

[17] Iz literaturnogo nasledstva Aleksandra Bloka', ed. V. N. Orlov, Yunosheskiy Dvevnik, *Literaturnoye Nasledstvo*, nos. 27–8 (Moscow, 1937), 370, note 195.

The text of this letter with its word-for-word quotation from the Creed was given to Orlov by Lyubov' Dmitriyevna herself. It is omitted from the notes to the republished diary (*S.S.* VII, 473, note 165). Neither is it included amongst the poet's letters in *S.S.* VIII. It has, however, already been saved from the obscurity of a footnote by K. Mochulsky, who quotes it in full on p. 65 of his remarkable *Aleksandr Blok* (Paris: YMCA Press, 1948).

CHAPTER VI

[1] Where not otherwise indicated, the account of Blok's relations with Lyubov' Dmitriyevna is based on her memoirs.

[2] Letter to L. D. Mendeleyeva of 20 Nov. 1902. Arkhiv A. A. Bloka, TsGALI.

[3] L. D. Mendeleyeva, letter to Blok of 23 Nov. 1902. Arkhiv A. A. Bloka, TsGALI.

[4] Letter to L. D. Mendeleyeva of 24 Dec. 1902. Arkhiv A. A. Bloka, TsGALI.

[5] Letter to L. D. Mendeleyeva of 30 Nov. 1902. Arkhiv A. A. Bloka, TsGALI.

[6] Letter to L. D. Mendeleyeva of 15 May 1903. Arkhiv A. A. Bloka, TsGALI.

[7] Letter to A. V. Hippius of 23 Jan. 1903. Arkhiv A. A. Bloka, IRLI (copy).

[8] Letter to L. D. Mendeleyeva of 15 Dec. 1902. Arkhiv A. A. Bloka, TsGALI.

[9] D. E. Maksimov, 'Materialy iz biblioteki Al. Blok', *Uchenye Zapiski Leningradskogo Gosudarstvennogo Pedagogicheskogo Instituta* CLXXXIV (1958), Vypusk 6, 367.

[10] Letter to L. D. Mendeleyeva of 25 Dec. 1902. Arkhiv A. A. Bloka, TsGALI.

[11] For Blok's use of metre see Z. Zhirmunsky, 'Poeziya Aleksandra Bloka', in *Ob Aleksandre Bloke* (Petersburg, 1921), and Robin Kemball, *Alexander Blok: A Study in Rhythm and Metre* (The Hague, 1965), particularly, for this poem, 276.

[12] Letter to L. D. Mendeleyeva of 27 Dec. 1902. Arkhiv A. A. Bloka, TsGALI.

[13] Letter to L. D. Mendeleyeva of 23 Feb. 1903. Arkhiv A. A. Bloka, TsGALI.

[14] Letter to L. D. Mendeleyeva of 18 Nov. 1902. Arkhiv A. A. Bloka, TsGALI.

[15] O. M. Solov'eva, unpublished letter to A. A. Kublitskaya-Piottukh of 30 Oct. 1902. Arkhiv A. A. Bloka, TsGALI.

[16] Id., letter to A. A. Kublitskaya-Piottukh of 11 Dec. 1902. Arkhiv A. A. Bloka, TsGALI.

[17] Id., letter to A. A. Kublitskaya-Piottukh of 31 Dec. 1902. Arkhiv A. A. Bloka, TsGALI.

[18] The correspondence between Blok and Bely has been published in full, with an introduction and commentary by Vl. Orlov, under the title *Aleksandr Blok i Andrey Bely. Perepiska*, in the series Letopisi gosudarstvennogo literaturnogo Muzeya, Kniga 7 (Moscow, 1940). This is the source for all Bely's letters. For those letters of Blok which have been republished in *S.S.* (1960–3) I have given the more recent reference, since the Blok–Bely correspondence, though recently reissued, is a rare book.

[19] A. Bely, *Nachalo veka* (Moscow-Leningrad, 1933), 200–3.

[20] A. Bely, letter to Blok of 15 Jan. 1903, *Perepiska*, 14.

[21] Letter to A. Bely of January 1902, *Perepiska*, 15.

[22] A. Bely, letter to Blok of January 1902, *Perepiska*, 15.

[23] E. P. Ivanov, 'Vospominaniya i Zapisi Evgeniya Ivanova ob Aleksandre Bloke', ed. E. P. Gomberg and D. E. Maksimov, *B.S.* I, 370.

[24] D. E. Maksimov, 'Aleksandr Blok i Evgeniy Ivanov', *B.S.* I, 344–61. For further information about Ivanov see *Pis'ma E. P. Ivanovu*; also A. Ugryumov, 'A. A. Blok i sem'ya Ivanovykh', *Russkaya Mysl'* (Paris), nos. 887 (17 Apr.), 888 (19 Apr.), 890 (24 Apr.), 1956.

[25] E. P. Ivanov, op. cit., 362–3.

[26] Ibid., 364.

[27] Ibid., 382, note 9.

[28] Letter to A. Bely of 26 Nov. 1903, *Perepiska*, 66–8.

[29] Unpublished letter to L. D. Mendeleyeva of 21 Apr. 1903. Arkhiv A. A. Bloka, TsGALI.

[30] Letter to A. L. Blok of 25 June/7 July 1903 from Bad Nauheim, *Pis'ma k rodnym* I, 87.

[31] Letter to A. Bely of 18 June/1 July 1903, *Perepiska*, 34–7.

[32] M. A. Beketova, 1922, 81–2.

[33] S. M. Solov'ev, 'Vospominaniya ob Aleksandre Bloka', in *Pis'ma A. Bloka*, 19.

[34] M. A. Beketova, 1922, 82–3.

[35] Ibid., 84–5.

[36] Ibid., 85.

[37] L. D. Blok, memoirs.

[38] Letter to S. M. Solov'ev of 20 Dec. 1903, *Pis'ma A. Bloka*, 63.

[39] Notebook no. 6, Arkhiv A. A. Bloka, IRLI. Partially published in the supplementary volume (*Z.K.*) of the eight-volume *S.S.* Cf. entry for October, 55.

[40] E. P. Ivanov, op. cit., 365.

[41] Ibid., 366.

[42] Letter to A. Bely of 1 Aug. 1903, *Perepiska*, 43–6.

[43] Letter to A. Bely of 14 or 15 Oct. 1905, *Perepiska*, 158.

[44] Quoted from A. Bely, *Vospominaniya*, 63–5.

[45] S. M. Solov'ev, op. cit., 23.

[46] A. Bely, *Vospominaniya*, 80.

[47] S. M. Solov'ev, op. cit., 23.

[48] A. Bely, *Vospominaniya*, 81.

[49] Ibid., 107.

[50] Ibid., 96.

CHAPTER VII

[1] E. P. Ivanov, 'Vospominaniya i Zapisi Evgeniya Ivanova ob Aleksandre Bloke', ed. E. P. Gomberg and D. E. Maksimov, *B.S.* I, 375–6.

[2] Entry in Notebook no. 7 for 24–25 March, unpublished. Arkhiv A. A. Bloka, IRLI.

[3] M. A. Beketova, 'Vesyëlost' i yumor Bloka', in *O Bloke* (Moscow, 1929), 14.

[4] Letter to his mother, undated, *Pis'ma k rodnym* I, 113–17.

[5] Cf. A. Bely, *Nachalo veka* (Moscow-Leningrad, 1933), 331–47.

[6] Notebook no. 8 for April–May 1904. Arkhiv A. A. Bloka, IRLI. This notebook is partially published by V. N. Orlov in *Z.K.* and rather more fully by P. N. Medvedev in *Zapisnye Knizhki Al. Bloka* (Leningrad, 1930).

[7] M. A. Beketova, 1922, 86–7.

[8] A. Bely, *Vospominaniya*, 129.

[9] M. A. Beketova, 1922, 90.

[10] A. Bely, *Nachalo veka*, 346–7.

[11] E. P. Ivanov, letter to Blok of 3–4 June 1904. Arkhiv E. P. Ivanova, IRLI.

[12] Id., letter to Blok of 21 June 1904. Arkhiv E. P. Ivanova, IRLI.

[13] E. P. Ivanov, 'Vospominaniya ob Aleksandre Bloke', *B.S.* 1, 378–9.
[14] Notebook no. 8, *Zapisnye knizhki Al. Bloka*, ed. P. N. Medvedev, 36–7.
[15] L. D. Blok, memoirs.

CHAPTER VIII

[1] Letter to E. P. Ivanov of 16 Oct. 1905, *Pis'ma E. P. Ivanovu*, 43.
[2] M. A. Beketova, 1922, 92.
[3] G. Chulkov, 'Aleksandr Blok I ego vremya', *Pis'ma A. Bloka*, 97–8, 99.
[4] V. Zhirmunsky, 'Poeziya Aleksandra Bloka', *Ob Aleksandre Bloke* (Petersburg, 1921), 77. Translated by Victor Ehrlich in *Twentieth-Century Russian Literary Criticism* (New Haven and London: Yale Univ. Press, 1975).
[5] V. Ivanov, 'Razskazy taynovidtsa', *Vesy* (Moscow), no. 8, August 1904, 47–50.
[6] F. Tyutchev, *Sochineniya. Stikhotvoreniya i Politicheskiye stat'i* (Petersburg, 1886). The letter was originally written in French but the first Russian translation appeared in *Russkiy Arkhiv*, Bk. I, Carnet 4, in 1873. For locating the Tyutchev quotation I am indebted to Dr. Ronald Lane of Durham University.
[7] G. Chulkov, op. cit., 107–8.
[8] M. A. Beketova, 1922, 92–3.
[9] A. Bely, *Vospominaniya*, 154–5.
[10] A. Bely, *Epopeya*, no. 2, 167.
[11] A. Bely, *Vospominaniya*, 157.
[12] Cf. Yu. K. Gerasimov, 'Ob okruzhenii Aleksandra Bloka vo vremya pervoy russkoy revolyutsii', *B.S.* 1, 539–44; also E. P. Ivanov, 'Zapisi ob Aleksandre Bloke', *B.S.* 1, 399.
[13] E. P. Ivanov, op. cit., 413. Cf. also Yu. K. Gerasimov, op. cit.
[14] A. Bely, *Nachalo veka* (Moscow-Leningrad, 1933), 456.
[15] A. Bely, *Epopeya*, no. 2, 165.
[16] A. Bely, *Nachalo veka*, 458.
[17] A. Bely, *Epopeya*, no. 2, 209.
[18] Z. N. Hippius, 'Vodoskat' (written 1905 and dedicated to Blok), *Sobraniye Stikhov* II (Moscow, 1910), 81.
[19] E. P. Ivanov, op. cit., 389.
[20] A. Bely, *Vospominaniya*, 170.
[21] G. Chulkov, op. cit., 108.
[22] A. Bely, letter to Blok of 8 Feb. 1905, *Perepiska*, 123.
[23] Cf. E. P. Ivanov, op. cit., 390–3.
[24] D. Tal'milov, 'Kommissarzhevskaya', *Iskusstvo* (Moscow-Leningrad), 1939, 277; quoted in the notes to E. P. Ivanov's reminiscences of Blok, compiled by E. P. Gomberg and A. M. Bikhter, *B.S.* 1, 418.
[25] Cf. A. Bely, *Vospominaniya*, 170; V. Engel'gardt, 'V puti pogibshiy', *Ob Aleksandre Bloke* (Petersburg, 1921), 34; B. Eykhenbaum, '*Sud'ba Bloka*', ibid., 46; B. A. Zorgenfrey, 'Aleksandr Aleksandrovich Blok (Po pamyati 15 let', 1906–21)', *Zapiski Mechtateley* (Petersburg, 1922), 148; G. Blok, 'Geroy vozmezdiya', *Russkiy Sovremennik* (Moscow-Leningrad), 1924, 172–86; et al.
[26] E. P. Ivanov, op. cit., 392.
[27] Easter card to E. P. Ivanov, undated 1905, *Pis'ma E. P. Ivanovu*, 35.
[28] A. Remizov, *Kukkha*.
[29] A. Remizov, *V rozovom bleske* (New York, 1952), 300.

[30] A. Remizov, *Akhru—Povest' petersburgskaya* (Berlin-Petersburg-Moscow, 1922), 18–19.

[31] Letter to G. Chulkov of 19 June 1905 (*S.S.* VIII, 132) and the review itself (*S.S.* V, 619–21).

[32] A. Bely, letter to Blok of early March 1905 from Moscow, *Perepiska*, 127.

[33] V. N. Orlov, 'Istoriya odnoy "druzhby-vrazhdy" ' in *Puti i sud'by. Literaturnye ocherki* (Moscow-Leningrad, 1963), 485.

[34] A. Bely, *Vospominaniya*, 138.

[35] A. Bely, *Epopeya*, no. 2, 253.

[36] Ibid., 256.

[37] Cf. V. N. Orlov, 'Istoriya odnoy lyubvi', in *Puti i sud'by*, 624, note 1.

[38] A. Bely, letter to Blok of 25 June 1905 from Dedovo, *Perepiska*, 136.

[39] Cf. A. Bely, *Epopeya*, no. 2, 240.

[40] Letter to A. Bely of 19 July 1905 from Shakhmatovo, *Perepiska*, 136.

[41] Letter to his mother of 30 April 1905, *Pis'ma k rodnym* I, 137.

[42] D. E. Maksimov, 'Blok i revolyutsiya 1905 goda', *Revolyutsiya 1905 goda v russkoy literature* (Moscow-Leningrad, 1956), 263–4.

[43] Letter to E. P. Ivanov of 16 Oct. 1905, *Pis'ma E. P. Ivanovu*, 43.

[44] M. A. Beketova, 1922, 97.

[45] E. P. Ivanov, op. cit., 397–8.

[46] Cf. letters to A. V. Hippius of 9 Nov. 1905 (*S.S.* VIII, 141) and to A. L. Blok of 30 Dec. 1905 (*S.S.* VIII, 144).

[47] N. Minsky, 'Pro doma sua', *Novaya Zhizn'* (St. Petersburg), no. 3 (29 Oct.), 1905.

[48] G. I. Chulkov, 'Kriticheskiye Zametki', *Voprosy Zhizni* (St. Petersburg), August 1905, 207.

[49] V. I. Lenin, 'Partiynaya organizatsiya i partiynaya literatura', *Novaya Zhizn'*, no. 12 (13 Nov.), 1905, and V. Ya. Bryusov (Avreliy), 'Vekhi', *Vesy*, no. 11, November 1905, 61–5.

[50] V. Bryusov, letter of 13 Jan. 1905 published in 'Pis'ma k P. P. Pertsovu', *Russkiy Sovremennik*, no. 4, 1924, 234.

CHAPTER IX

[1] A. Bely, letter to Blok of 13 Oct. 1905, *Perepiska*, 155.

[2] Ibid.

[3] L. D. Blok, unpublished letter to A. Bely of 27 Oct. 1905. Arkhiv A. Belogo, Lenin Library.

[4] M. A. Beketova, unpublished diary, entry for 28 Oct. 1905. Cf. V. N. Orlov, 'Istoriya odnoy lyubvi', *Puti i sud'by* (Moscow–Leningrad, 1963), 624–5.

[5] A. Bely, letter to Blok of 1 Nov. 1905, *Perepiska*, 161.

[6] A. Bely, *Epopeya*, no. 2, 268, 274, 278–9.

[7] *Zapisnye knizhki Al. Bloka*, ed. P. N. Medvedev (Leningrad, 1930), entry for 18 Nov. (which also includes the first rough draft of a part of the poem), 50.

[8] A. Bely, *Epopeya*, no. 2, 286, 291–2, 293.

[9] Ariadna Tyrkova-Williams, 'Beglye vstrechi', *Rul'*, no. 256, 1921, reprinted *Novaya Russkaya Kniga* (Berlin), nos. 5–6, 1923; here quoted from *Sud'ba Bloka*, ed. O. Nemerovskaya and Ts. Vol'pe (Leningrad, 1930), 93.

[10] Cf. *Zolotoye Runo* (Moscow), no. 1, 1906, 133.

[11] Z. N. Hippius, 'Moy lunniy drug', *Zhivye Litsa* (Prague, 1923), 22.

[12] V. Ivanov, 'The God in the Lupanar' (*Bog v lupanare*), dedicated to Aleksandr Blok, *Sobraniye Sochineniy* II, ed. D. V. Ivanov and O. Deshart (Brussels, 1974), 327. Cf. also note on Blok and V. Ivanov, 728–32.

[13] L. D. Blok, undated unpublished letter to A. Bely. Arkhiv A. Belogo, Lenin Library.

[14] *Pis'ma A. Bloka*, 132.

[15] Vl. Pyast, *Vospominaniya o Bloke* (Petersburg, 1923), 34.

[16] A. Bely, *Mezhdu dvukh revolyutsiy* (Leningrad, 1934), 176.

[17] Cf. V. N. Orlov, op. cit., 627.

[18] L. D. Blok, memoirs.

[19] V. Khodasevich, *Nekropol'* (Paris, 1976), 72–3.

[20] E. P. Ivanov, 'Zapisi ob Aleksandre Bloke', *B.S.* I, 400–1.

[21] L. D. Blok, undated letter to A. Bely (written between 11 and 13 March 1906). Arkhiv A. Belogo, Lenin Library.

[22] Id., letter to A. Bely of 19 March 1906. Arkhiv A. Belogo, Lenin Library.

[23] Letter to A. Bely of 9 Apr. 1906, *Perepiska*, 175–6.

[24] E. P. Ivanov, op. cit., 402, 464.

[25] Ibid., 403.

[26] A. Bely, *Epopeya*, no. 3, 176.

[27] K. I. Chukovsky, 'Aleksandr Blok', *Lyudi i knigi*, Vtoroye dopolnennoye izdaniye (Moscow, 1960), 516, 517.

[28] E. P. Ivanov, op. cit., 405–7.

[29] Cf. letters to his father of 5 May 1906 and to Vl. Pyast of 7 May 1906, *S.S.* VIII, 154.

[30] Letter to E. P. Ivanov of 25 June 1906, *S.S.* VIII, 156.

[31] E. P. Ivanov, op. cit., 409.

[32] L. D. Blok, letter to A. Bely of 23 July 1906. Arkhiv A. Belogo, Lenin Library.

[33] Id., letter to A. Bely of 22 July 1906. Arkhiv A. Belogo, Lenin Library.

[34] A. Bely, *Epopeya*, no. 3, 185, 188, 189.

[35] Yu. K. Gerasimov, 'Ob okruzhenii Aleksandra Bloka vo vremya pervoy russkoy revolyutsii,' *B.S.* I, 541.

[36] M. A. Beketova, 1922, 102.

CHAPTER X

[1] V. P. Verigina, 'Vospominaniya ob Aleksandre Bloke', *Trudy* IV, 311, 312.

[2] N. N. Volokhova, 'Zemlya v snegu', ibid., 372.

[3] V. P. Verigina, op. cit., 312–13.

[4] Ibid., 315.

[5] L. D. Blok, memoirs, quoted by D. E. Maksimov in his introduction to the memoirs of Volokhova and Verigina, 'Teatral'nye vospominaniya o Bloke V. P. Veriginoy i N. N. Volokhovoy', *Trudy* IV, 307.

[6] N. N. Volokhova, op. cit., 373.

[7] Z. N. Hippius, letter to A. Bely of 14 March 1907. Arkhiv A. Belogo, Lenin Library.

[8] Id., letter to A. Bely of August 1907. Arkhiv A. Belogo, Lenin Library.

[9] G. Chulkov, 'V. P. Verigina. Teatral'nye vospominaniya ob Aleksandre Bloke'. Otzyv ne opublikovan. TsGALI 10246/204, quoted by D. E. Maksimov, *Trudy* IV, 305, note 2.

[10] V. P. Verigina, op. cit., 316–17.

[11] N. N. Volokhova, in conversation with the author, Moscow, 1960.

[12] Vs. E. Meyerhold, 'Balagan' (1912) in the book *Stat'i, pis'ma, rechi, besedy* (Moscow, 1968), 208, 227, 229.

[13] Vs. E. Meyerhold, Foreword to the book *O Teatre* (1913), reprinted in ibid., 103.

[14] Quoted by D. E. Maksimov, *Trudy* IV, 309, note 14.

[15] V. P. Verigina, op. cit., 319, 322–3.

[16] Ibid., 323. For a more detailed and technical account of the play (and particularly of Meyerhold's performance as Pierrot) see Verigina's highly professional 'Po dorogam iskaniy', *Vstrechi s Meyerkhol'dom. Sbornik Vospominaniy* (Moscow, 1967), 39–42.

[17] V. P. Verigina, 'Vospominaniya', *Trudy* IV, 324.

[18] M. Kuzmin, 'Kartochnyy Domik', first printed in *Belye nochi. Petersburgskiy al'manach* (St. Petersburg, 1907), 142.

[19] V. P. Verigina, 'Vospominaniya', op. cit., 325, 326.

[20] L. D. Blok, memoirs.

[21] G. Chulkov, 'Aleksandr Blok i ego vremya', in *Pis'ma A. Bloka*, 111–12.

[22] N. N. Volokhova, op. cit., 373, 376.

[23] M. A. Beketova, 1922, 106.

[24] N. N. Volokhova, op. cit., 375.

[25] A. Bely, *Epopeya*, no. 3, 22.

[26] A. M. Remizov, *Akhru—Povest' petersburgskaya* (Berlin-Petersburg-Moscow, 1922). 24.

[27] N. N. Volokhova, op. cit., 373.

[28] M. A. Beketova, 1922, 107–8.

[29] V. P. Verigina, 'Vospominaniya', op. cit., 337.

[30] G. Chulkov, 'Aleksandr Blok i ego vremya', op. cit., 117.

[31] Unpublished letters to L. D. Blok of 13, 21, 26 May 1907. Arkhiv A. A. Bloka, TsGALI.

[32] K. I. Chukovsky, 'Aleksandr Blok', *Lyudi i knigi*, vtoroye dopolnennoye izdaniye (Moscow, 1960), 514–15.

[33] *Literaturnoye Nasledstvo*, no. 15 (Moscow, 1934), 214.

[34] Z. N. Hippius, unpublished letter to A. Bely of August 1907. Arkhiv A. Belogo, Lenin Library.

[35] Cf. N. V. Valentinov (Vol'sky), 'Aleksandr Blok i Andrey Bely', *Dva goda sredi simvolistov*, ed. and introduced by Gleb Struve (Stanford, Calif.: Stanford Univ. Press, 1969), esp. 69, 228–35.

[36] A. Bely, letter to Blok of 5 or 6 Aug. 1907, *Perepiska*, 192.

[37] E. P. Ivanov, unpublished letter to Blok of 11–12 Aug. 1907. Arkhiv E. P. Ivanova, TsGALI.

[38] Letter to E. P. Ivanov of August 1907, *Pis'ma E. P. Ivanovu*, 61.

[39] A. Bely, letter to Blok of 21 Aug. 1907, *Perepiska*, 212.

[40] Cf. G. Chulkov, 'Aleksandr Blok i ego vremya', op. cit., 112.

[41] First published in *Vesy*, no. 8, 1907.

[42] Z. N. Hippius, unpublished postcard to A. Bely of Sept. 1907. Arkhiv A. Belogo, Lenin Library. The last sentence reads in Russian, 'Nu, da, ot neponimaniya eto.'

CHAPTER XI

[1] N. N. Volokhova, 'Zemlya v snegu', *Trudy* IV, 375.

[2] V. V. Rozanov, 'Avtor "Balaganchika" o Petersburgskikh religiozno-filo-sofskikh sobraniyakh', *Russkoye Slovo* (Moscow), 25 Jan. 1908. See also V. P. Verigina, 'Vospominaniya ob Aleksandre Bloke', *Trudy* IV, 338, and Blok's letter to E. P. Ivanov of 31 Jan. 1908, *S.S.* VIII, 228.

[3] M. A. Beketova, 1922, 111.

[4] E. Yu. Kuzmina-Karavayeva, 'Vstrechi s Blokom', first published in *Sovremennye Zapiski* (Paris), no. 62, 1936, as the recollections of Mon(akhinya) Maria; then, with an introductory article by D. E. Maksimov, in *Trudy* XI, Vypusk 209, 265.

[5] V. P. Verigina, op. cit., 340–1.

[6] A. Bely, *Epopeya*, no. 3, 290–1.

[7] M. A. Beketova, 1922, 111–12.

[8] A. Bely, *Epopeya*, no. 3, 296, 305–6, 302.

[9] N. N. Volokhova, op. cit., 376.

[10] E. Yu. Kuzmina-Karavayeva, *Trudy* XI, Vypusk 209, 265.

[11] For more detailed information see D. E. Maksimov's introduction to Kuzmina-Karaveyeva's memoir of Blok (cf. note 4), reprinted in the same author's *Poeziya i proza Bloka* (Leningrad, 1976), 498–517, and Sergey Hackel, *One of Great Price* (London, 1965). A fuller version in Russian is shortly (1977) to be published by the YMCA Press, Paris.

[12] N. N. Volokhova, op. cit., 375.

[13] Ibid., 377.

[14] A. Bely, letter to Blok of 6 Apr. 1908, *Perepiska*, 229–30.

[15] S. M. Solov'ev, *Crucifragium* (Moscow, 1908).

[16] A. Bely, letter to Blok of 3 May 1908, *Perepiska*, 232.

Index

B = Blok